REVIEW OF RESEARCH IN EDUCATION

Review of Research in Education is published on behalf of the American Educational Research Association by SAGE Publications, Thousand Oaks, CA 91320. Copyright © 2007 by the American Educational Research Association. All rights reserved. No portion of the contents may be reproduced in any form without written permission from the publisher. Periodicals postage paid at Thousand Oaks, California, and at additional mailing offices.

Member Information: American Educational Research Association (AERA) member inquiries, member renewal requests, changes of address, and membership subscription inquiries should be addressed to the AERA Membership Department, 1230 17th St., NW, Washington, DC 20036-3078; fax 202-775-1824. AERA annual membership dues are $120 (Regular and Affiliate Members), $100 (International Affiliates), and $35 (Graduate and Undergraduate Student Affiliates). **Claims:** Claims for undelivered copies must be made no later than six months following month of publication. Beyond six months and at the request of the American Educational Research Association, the publisher will supply missing copies when losses have been sustained in transit and when the reserve stock permits.

Subscription Information: All non-member subscription inquiries, orders, back-issue requests, claims, and renewals should be addressed to Sage Publications, 2455 Teller Road, Thousand Oaks, CA 91320; telephone (800) 818-SAGE (7243) and (805) 499-9774; fax (805) 499-0871; e-mail journals@sagepub.com; http://www.sagepublications.com. **Subscription Price:** Institutions $134; Individuals $49. All customers outside the Americas and Asia should visit http://www.sagepublications.com/journalscs/ for ordering instructions. **Claims:** Claims for undelivered copies must be made no later than six months following month of publication. The publisher will supply missing copies when losses have been sustained in transit and when the reserve stock will permit.

Abstracting and Indexing: This journal is abstracted or indexed in Current Contents: Social & Behavioral Sciences, ERIC (Education Resources Information Center), Scopus, and Social Sciences Citation Index (Web of Science).

Copyright Permission: Permission requests to photocopy or otherwise reproduce copyrighted material owned by the American Educational Research Association should be submitted by accessing the Copyright Clearance Center's Rightslink® service through the journal's website at http://rre.aera.net. Permission may also be requested by contacting the Copyright Clearance Center via its website at http://www.copyright.com, or via e-mail at info@copyright.com.

Advertising and Reprints: Current advertising rates and specifications may be obtained by contacting the advertising coordinator in the Thousand Oaks office at (805) 410-7763 or by sending an e-mail to advertising@sagepub.com. To order reprints, please e-mail reprint@sagepub.com.

Change of Address: Six weeks' advance notice must be given when notifying of change of address. Please send old address label along with the new address to ensure proper identification. Please specify name of journal. POSTMASTER: Send address changes to AERA Membership Department, 1230 17th St., NW, Washington, DC 20036-3078.

International Standard Serial Number ISSN 0091-732X
International Standard Book Number ISBN 978-1-4129-5795-3 (Vol. 31, 2007, paper)
Manufactured in the United States of America. First printing, March 2007.
Copyright © 2007 by the American Educational Research Association. All rights reserved.

REVIEW OF RESEARCH IN EDUCATION

Difference, Diversity, and Distinctiveness in Education and Learning

Volume 31, 2007

Laurence Parker, Editor
University of Illinois at Urbana-Champaign

 **American Educational Research Association**

 **SAGE Publications**
Los Angeles • London • New Delhi • Singapore

Review of Research in Education
Difference, Diversity, and Distinctiveness in Education and Learning
Volume 31

EDITOR

LAURENCE PARKER
University of Illinois at Urbana-Champaign

CONTRIBUTORS

BRYAN MCKINLEY JONES BRAYBOY
The University of Utah

ANGELINA E. CASTAGNO
Northern Arizona University

MICHAEL DUNSON
Stanford University

JULIE M. KITTLESON
The University of Georgia

SHARON S. LEE
University of Illinois at Urbana-Champaign

EMMA MAUGHAN
The University of Utah

CRIS MAYO
University of Illinois at Urbana-Champaign

ELIZABETH BIRR MOJE
University of Michigan

JENNIFER C. NG
University of Kansas

MOSES OKETCH
Institute of Education, University of London

YOON K. PAK
University of Illinois at Urbana-Champaign

LORI RHODES
Stanford University

CAINE ROLLESTON
Institute of Education, University of London

LEIGH K. SMITH
Brigham Young University

SHERRY A. SOUTHERLAND
Florida State University

SCOTT P. SOWELL
Cleveland State University

JOY ANN WILLIAMSON
Stanford University

EDITORIAL BOARD

AMERICAN EDUCATIONAL RESEARCH ASSOCIATION
TEL: 202-223-9485 FAX: 202-775-1824
http://www.aera.net/pubs

FELICE J. LEVINE
Executive Director

MELISSA JUNIOR
Director of Publications

BARBARA LEITHAM
Publications Coordinator

Contents

Introduction
Difference, Diversity, and Distinctiveness in Education and Learning

LAURENCE PARKER
University of Illinois at Urbana-Champaign

The introduction to this issue of the *Review of Research in Education* was prompted by exploring reviews of research perspectives that speak to our societal need to figure out how best to interact with youth who require our care regarding their education and social needs. The chapters in this volume speak to reviews of research that emphasize diversity and academic achievement in different education settings both here in the United States and other regions of the world such as sub-Saharan Africa. Educational research and social science perspectives that call for broad public policy changes in the socioeconomic and racial equity arenas, as well as a focus on high expectations, student-centered learning, use of test scores to inform instruction critically, and culturally relevant teaching, all could work in tandem toward reinforcing a more humanistic approach to accountability (Neckerman, 2004; Scheurich, 1998; Young, 2004). In this way, meaningful interactions and relationships among students, teachers, schools, and local communities can be fostered that hold all parties personally responsible for academic success (Conchas, 2006). Educational policy and programs designed to increase the level of academic success of low-income and minority students must go beyond the rhetoric of leaving no child behind. Indeed, there must be a culture of caring created in a school that is firmly grounded in the belief that students of diverse backgrounds can learn and that educational institutions should be enhancers and enablers of this learning.

The chapters in this volume call our attention to the salient research that has been undertaken regarding learning contexts within critical literacy, scientific literacy, and teacher education. This edition also contains reviews of studies related to the cumulative academic consequences of racism and homophobia for students, in both the higher education and K–12 settings. Chapter authors also address the effects of education policy decisions on equity in sub-Saharan Africa and the historical research implications of the definition of social justice in education.

Some of the authors in this volume explore the concept of social justice in education. Despite the controversy surrounding this term and its usage, some of the

Review of Research in Education
March 2007, Vol. 31, pp. xi–xv
DOI: 10.3102/0091732X07300546
© 2007 AERA. http://rre.aera.net

chapters seek out research studies and informed perspectives regarding how social justice should be defined and linked to curriculum and instruction. For example, Moje's chapter attempts to explain the term by discussing the ways social justice in subject matter instruction has been articulated in the education research literature. She examines how social justice has been described as access to expert subject matter knowledge, as the foregrounding of everyday knowledge, as access to usable disciplinary knowledge and ways of knowing, and as access to knowledge as a means for youth to produce and take ownership of knowledge. She then explores the connection between social justice subject matter instruction to disciplinary literary theory and research and the importance of language, cognition, and culture. Moje's review of the research offers a blended perspective of an emphasis on cognitive processes in disciplinary literacy across subject matter areas and how this process can connect to socially just instruction. Her chapter serves as an important fusion of social justice pedagogy perspectives with research-based outcomes that demonstrate student acquisition of discursive skills that also build on critical literacy knowledge to enhance student learning outcomes.

Southerland, Smith, Sowell, and Kittleson's chapter provides an overview of the research related to the question of how science should be taught in the current climate of accountability. The authors walk us through the reform efforts of the mid-1980s, which called for more emphasis on second-order science learning and emphasized exposure to higher order thinking skills, scientific literacy, and the incorporation of student contextual knowledge to peak and enhance student interest in science. The authors then highlight the current debate on science education through the pressure of the No Child Left Behind Act (NCLB) on schools to make science teaching more efficient through "drill and skill" testing and reducing the role of the science teacher as expert in order to present rudimentary science knowledge. Southerland et al. review this debate in science education pedagogy and categorize it as a "failure to communicate" between science educators, scientists, and education policymakers at the federal and state levels. The authors of this chapter review the limited reaction of the science education research community to the requirements outlined by NCLB and argue that some parts of the research community have resisted unlearning what we know to be important about science teaching and learning. Finally, they posit that it is irresponsible to engage within the current climate through the work with teachers by simply ignoring government policy. Instead, science educators must take a more active role in helping states, districts, and policymakers understand the importance of more fundamental changes to bring about true scientific literacy.

The next three chapters examine diversity in educational settings, both in the United States and abroad. To that end, Cris Mayo's chapter explores the general trends and shifts that have taken place in lesbian, gay, bisexual, and transgendered (LBGT) youth in education research. Her chapter also reviews the strengths and weaknesses of linking LBGT youth research in education to queer theory. For example, one caution Mayo notes in this review is that from a social justice perspective, the past research focused on demands for recognition, respect, and rights of LBGT youth. Now, however, there has been a shift in the research to explore issues related to discourse, psychoanalytic theory, poststructural theory, and new materialist theorization of bodies. Still, she reviews studies that stress findings related to LBGT youth as seeking normalcy in their same-sex relations and where they do not want to identify as gay. These findings illustrate some of the tension between queer theory and research on LBGT youth in which they feel the pressure to conform as the norm that creates difficulty as they attempt to live their lives.

The chapter by Ng, Lee, and Pak looks at the research and perspectives related to Asian Americans in education. This chapter draws on work done in Asian American studies and other fields to center the Asian American experience in education, not as the "model minority myth" but as a racial group that has varied and unique experiences regarding their ethnic diversity. Furthermore, Ng et al.'s review of the historical and current research in this area illustrates how Asian Americans have been viewed as immigrant foreigners who were feared and discriminated against, but also at times have been seen as "honorary whites" who can be used as allies or regarded as threats in educational policy campaigns against affirmative action (Takagi, 1993). Their chapter calls for more research that examines Asian Americans as a racialized group but that also captures the intersections and conflicts with social class, sexuality, gender, and so forth.

Oketch and Rolleston's chapter looks at issues of inclusion and exclusion within the context of sub-Saharan Africa. Focusing on a review of research done on the countries of Kenya, Uganda, and Tanzania, Oketch and Rolleston trace the evolution of free primary education policy and universal schooling, as well as the colonial and postcolonial periods, and explore the history behind the political and economic justification for universal primary education. This chapter highlights descriptive data on rates of education acquisition and the link between education and economic development in this region. Yet they also point out that the goal of universal education is still not a reality for the vast majority of students in the lowest socioeconomic stratum. Building on the work of Vavrus (2005) and Maclure (2006), Oketch and Rolleston conclude with a call for research-based policies that focus more on the local context and locally initiated policies in education. The themes of this chapter are useful for readers to compare and contrast the United States with other countries, as one of the fallout issues of globalization is the persistent inequity related to access and quality of schooling.

Finally, Brayboy, Castagro, and Maughan's chapter and Williamson, Rhodes, and Dunson's chapter focus on race, education, and social justice issues in different but complementary ways. Brayboy et al. look at race as a social construction within the current context of the schooling experience for students of color in the United States. The authors find gaps in the equitable treatment of students of color based on race and social class, and they attribute part of this discrimination to the historical and current struggles between the assimilation of racial minorities to conform to a White European American standard of learning versus the fight for group self-determination. This struggle is particularly important when examining the research on American Indian students (Deyhle & Swisher, 1997). Brayboy et al.'s review of the literature speaks to the importance of social justice as an expansion of opportunity to maximize the chances of educational success for students of color in terms of both academics and cultural affirmation.

Williamson et al.'s chapter concludes with an exploration of the term "social justice" and the controversies that have been debated about it in recent education policy circles. The authors then ask this question: What insights can we gain from historical struggles over social justice issues in education? By looking at how different racial groups have pushed for social justice in various ways, the authors call for both sides of the debate to explore the historical evidence to get a clearer sense of how the past struggle for social justice in education influences present-day debates about remedies and still-persistent effects of past discriminatory policies. It is also important to note that from this chapter, we can see that the call for social justice in education, particularly in the form of communities of color demanding excellence and quality schooling for their children, has a longer history than the current debate about NCLB. Thus, we as researchers may want to look at these historical calls for excellence to see how we could reexamine issues related to accountability and standards.

Overall, the chapters in this volume turn the question of "what works" in education on its head and answer that it depends on the context and specifics in relation to what is taught, how, why, and who is involved and engaged in a meaningful way (E. Moje, personal communication, January 4, 2007). Social justice's connection to discipline-based literacy, and how science is taught, is important for understanding the role of curriculum and instructional research in enhancing student learning and teacher pedagogy. The chapters in this volume also highlight the importance of utilizing current research to explore how education institutions (both K–12 and higher education) can structure positive learning environments that can connect teachers and students to each other with the common goal of fostering cooperation and academic excellence without resorting to cultural assimilation (Carter, 2005; Moses, 2001). Most of all, the themes of these chapters indicate that future reviews of research should explore the details of how diverse students learn in different and distinctive environments in order to enhance education and learning and develop more nuanced answers to the questions raised by what works in education.

REFERENCES

Carter, P. L. (2005). *Keepin' it real: School success beyond black and white.* New York: Oxford University Press.

Conchas, G. Q. (2006). *The color of success: Race and high-achieving urban youth.* New York: Teachers College Press.

Deyhle, D., & Swisher, K. (1997). Research in American Indian and Alaska Native education: From assimilation to self-determination. In M. Apple (Ed.), *Review of research in education* (pp. 113–194). Washington, DC: American Educational Research Association.

Maclure, R. (2006). No longer overlooked and undervalued? The evolving dynamics of endogenous educational research in sub-Saharan Africa. *Harvard Educational Review, 76,* 80–109.

Moses, M. (2001). Affirmative action and the creation of more favorable contexts of choice. *American Educational Research Journal, 38*, 3–36.

Neckerman, K. (Ed.). (2004). *Social inequality.* New York: Russell Sage Foundation.

Scheurich, J. J. (1998). Highly successful and loving, public elementary schools populated mainly by low-SES children of color: Core beliefs and cultural characteristics. *Urban Education, 33*, 451–491.

Takagi, D. Y. (1993). Asian Americans and racial politics: A postmodern paradox. *Social Justice, 20*, 115–128.

Vavrus, F. (2005). Adjusting inequality: Education and structural adjustment policies in Tanzania. *Harvard Educational Review, 75*, 174–201.

Young, A. A., Jr. (2004). *The minds of marginalized Black men: Making sense of mobility, opportunity, and future life chances.* Princeton, NJ: Princeton University Press.

Chapter 1

Developing Socially Just Subject-Matter Instruction: A Review of the Literature on Disciplinary Literacy Teaching

ELIZABETH BIRR MOJE
University of Michigan

In a 1996 *American Educational Research Journal* (*AERJ*) article, Deborah Ball and Suzanne Wilson (Ball & Wilson, 1996) made an argument for "integrity in teaching," in which they framed integrity as the commitment to "fusing" the moral aspects of teaching with the intellectual. The central question they explored was how to deal with conflicts between the intellectual work of teaching content concepts and the moral work of teaching those content concepts to human beings, that is, to people with varying perspectives on the value of the content, varying skill sets and ways of knowing that they brought to their learning, and rich and full lives that might or might not intersect with the content under study. Ball and Wilson argued that these tensions produced constant dilemmas for teachers who must negotiate a desire to meet content learning objectives with their respect for students' backgrounds and beliefs, which sometimes contradict or dismiss targeted content. Ten years later, I would like to draw from and spin that argument by suggesting that a corollary of Ball and Wilson's teaching with integrity is the concept of teaching with and for social justice. Teaching in socially just ways and in ways that produce social justice requires the recognition that learners need access to the knowledge deemed valuable by the content domains, even as the knowledge they bring to their learning must not only be recognized but valued. In this review, I revisit that notion of teaching as the fusion of the intellectual and the moral and ask a slightly different question: What does current research tell us about attempts to fuse the moral and intellectual in a way that produces socially just subject-matter instruction at the secondary and postsecondary levels? Furthermore, what would it look like to fuse the moral and intellectual to produce a subject-matter instruction that is not only socially just but also produces social justice?

Review of Research in Education
March 2007, Vol. 31, pp. 1–44
DOI: 10.3102/0091732X07300046
© 2007 AERA. http://rre.aera.net

The review takes this path: I briefly define what I mean by socially just pedagogy, contrasting it with the idea of pedagogy for social justice. I then lay out the range of thinking on socially just subject-matter instruction, including some perspectives that claim to focus on literacy within the disciplines. I distinguish these perspectives from each other, focusing on perspectives that revolve around language and texts within disciplinary instruction (i.e., what I am labeling disciplinary literacy theory) because these language and text-based disciplinary perspectives offer potential for developing socially just subject-matter instruction. What's more, these perspectives offer potential for subject-matter instruction that produces social justice, a distinction I clarify in a latter section of the chapter.

Within the area of disciplinary literacy, however, one also finds a range of perspectives, highlighting the different disciplinary traditions, theoretical stances, and research foci that undergird current work on disciplinary literacy pedagogy. I present both theory and research related to four types of disciplinary literacy pedagogy. For each type, I offer a broad scan of the disciplinary traditions and theoretical stances of those who write about disciplinary literacy from that particular framework and present a brief synopsis of findings in relation to any empirical research conducted from that particular approach to disciplinary literacy teaching. In addition, I provide details of two to three studies for each area that serve as exemplars of the work currently being done in that area. I then raise questions about what those stances might mean for the development of socially just subject-matter pedagogy. I do not advance one set of approaches over another but rather seek to uncover what it would take to produce disciplinary literacy pedagogy that produces socially just subject-matter pedagogy for a wide range of youth.

Given the scope of the review, I am not able to do justice to specifics of all studies available for review. Keyword searches on ERIC alone using the search terms *disciplinary literacy*, *mathematical literacy*, *scientific literacy*, and *historical/social science literacy* yielded 31 disciplinary literacy articles, 648 science and scientific literacy articles, 180 historical literacy articles, and 75 and 103 articles for mathematical literacy and math literacy, respectively. Many of the pieces uncovered in such a search were not relevant for this review, but the numbers give a snapshot of the scope of possibility for review using these identifiers. I also incorporated books and edited volumes as well as pieces that I deemed a form of disciplinary literacy, even when the authors did not identify their research as such, thus providing a massive corpus of potential studies. My interest here, however, is less on providing details of particular studies and more on showing how different perspectives on disciplinary literacy contribute to our understanding of how to develop socially just subject-matter instruction, particularly in secondary school settings.

As a result, I have chosen to highlight studies that are part of extended programs of research and/or single studies that have made a particular impact on the field in this area. Moreover, even within any one research program, I may only highlight one or two aspects of a larger body of work. This review, then, should be seen as a springboard for further study and conversation rather than as a definitive representation of the state of the field.

Furthermore, as might be suggested by my repeated use of the word *youth*, the review focuses primarily on subject-matter approaches for secondary and postsecondary educational settings. My rationale for delimiting in this way is in part pragmatic (this is the age group I know best) and in part substantive. In terms of substance, it is the case that sharp divisions among the subject-matter areas are most obvious when children leave elementary school settings and enter secondary (middle, high school, college, and university) settings. Although some scholars have demonstrated that the discursive practices of the subject matters begin to slip implicitly into the texts and teacher talk of elementary school at early ages (see Ciechanowski, 2006; McKeown & Beck, 1994), the slicing up of the secondary school day into neatly bounded subject-matter bites dramatically heightens disciplinary divisions. The disciplinary slices of middle school, high school, and university both underscore differences that exist in disciplinary practices and reify differences that are not as normative as the divisions may suggest. Ironically, these divisions also may hide the fact that much of what happens in subject-matter areas is an artifact of disciplinary thinking and cultural practices engaged in the service of knowledge production in those disciplines. Because students move from class to class and subject matter to subject matter, the practices of each area may appear to be artifacts of particular teachers, classroom spaces, or groups of students rather than artifacts of disciplinary thinking or cultural practice. For all of these reasons, the bulk of the review will examine studies of secondary and postsecondary settings, youth, and teachers, although I may refer to studies conducted among elementary-age youth when findings or perspectives warrant attention.

DEFINITIONS AND DELIMITERS
Socially Just Pedagogy or Social Justice Pedagogy?

The concept of socially just pedagogy covers a vast territory to which I am not able to do justice in this review. However, I do wish to set out the parameters for my thinking about subject-matter instruction and, particularly, disciplinary literacy pedagogy as a form of socially just/social justice pedagogy. In this regard, at least three aspects of social justice teaching seem relevant. One lies in the controversial distinction between the phrases socially just pedagogy and social justice pedagogy. These subtle differences in wording signal important differences in epistemological and practical orientations. The call for socially just pedagogy is a call to ensure that all youth have equitable opportunities to learn. In many cases, this view seeks to provide equal resources for learning, although the socially just pedagogue cannot always control access to material resources. It also can refer to ensuring that all youth learn conventional or academic literacy practices. Some would argue that this stance, although it equalizes skill and provides opportunities for all to achieve social and economic success (Moses & Cobb, 2001), risks reproducing the status quo in terms of cultural dominance. That is, it risks assimilating all people into a dominant, White mainstream rather than opening spaces for many different cultural practices to coexist and even nurture one another. By contrast, social justice pedagogy, or teaching to produce social justice, involves more than providing equitable learning opportunities implied in the phrase "socially just pedagogy," although such opportunities are necessary ingredients of social justice pedagogy. From a social justice perspective, opportunities to learn must not only provide access to mainstream knowledge and practices but also provide opportunities to question, challenge, and reconstruct knowledge (Ladson-Billings & Tate, 1995). Social justice pedagogy should, in other words, offer possibilities for transformation, not only of the learner but also of the social and political contexts in which learning and other social action take place (Saunders, 2006). Social justice pedagogy offers these transformative opportunities for all youth, even those who are privileged under current epistemological, social, and political structures. In other words, social justice pedagogy is not restricted to schools populated by youth of color or youth from low-income communities.

In relation to disciplinary teaching, then, both socially just and social justice pedagogies require that teachers provide all students with equitable opportunities to engage currently valued forms of disciplinary knowledge (Moses & Cobb, 2001). Social justice pedagogy takes an additional step and demands that youth learn to question and perhaps even offer changes to established knowledge. In more straightforward terms, this requires that educators teach students not only knowledge but also how to critique knowledge. It is important to note, however, that teaching the skill of critique without providing access to information and/or skills for accessing information (e.g., conventional literacy practices) is no more an example of teaching for social justice than is the act of teaching discrete bits of information to be memorized as taken-for-granted truths (C. D. Lee, 1993, 2005; Morrell & Duncan-Andrade, 2003; Moses & Cobb, 2001). For example, some forms of critical literacy teaching start with critique, and in so doing overlook the need to be able to communicate with proficiency across multiple audiences or to read and take information from multiple types of texts (see Wade & Moje, 2000, for more detailed analysis). Other critical literacy practices suggest that teachers should work only with the knowledge and practices youth already value, arguing that requiring youth to learn mainstream knowledge devalues their own knowledge and practices. As Delpit (1988) argued, such pedagogy is not necessarily socially just in the sense that it reproduces differential access to the culture of power that produces and labels knowledge as mainstream or marginal by not providing access to that culture (see also Ladson-Billings, 1999).

A second principle is that what counts as equitable opportunity is not straightforward. Equity is not a stable function whose parameters can be decided a priori but is rather a function of what people bring to an activity and the kinds of resources the activity can provide. Thus, prescription for either socially just pedagogy or social justice pedagogy cannot be offered, although broad principles of practice can guide pedagogy. Some students, for example, might need teaching that is explicit about taken-for-granted conventions (here again, see Delpit, 1988), whereas others might require pedagogy that encourages inductive reasoning and construction of knowledge over time. Some students might require a (temporary) focus on basic skill development, whereas others may need to learn how to hone and communicate critique to multiple audiences. Moreover, the same student may require different pedagogical practices at different points in development or, apropos of secondary school settings, in different subject-matter areas, depending on students' backgrounds, skills, and interests. In other words, there are not particular practices that are more socially just or that teach social justice better than others; those practices must be generated in response to actual learners, a point that links social justice/socially just pedagogy to the concept of culturally responsive pedagogy.

Culturally Responsive Pedagogy

In briefly defining the construct of culturally responsive pedagogy, I draw heavily from a chapter I previously coauthored with Kathleen Hinchman (Moje & Hinchman, 2004). In that chapter, we argued that all educational practice needs to be culturally responsive to be best practice. As cultural beings, young people deserve to experience pedagogy and curricula that respond to and extend their cultural experiences. Thus, culturally responsive practice attends to the funds of knowledge (Moll, Veléz-Ibañéz, & Greenberg, 1989) and discourses (Gee, 1996) of the youths' home; ethnic, racial, or geographic communities; youth culture; and popular culture, school culture, classroom culture, or discipline-specific culture (Ladson-Billings, 1994; C. D. Lee, 2001; C. D. Lee & Majors, 2003). These ways of knowing and "ways with words" (Heath, 1983) are present in school and also influence how people teach and learn in school. Such teaching also recognizes that needs and interests are always mediated by memberships in many different groups of people and by activities engaged in many different times, spaces, and relationships. However, the cultural knowledge and practices of some students—most often, students of color, English language learners and recent arrivals to the United States, or students from low-income homes and communities— are often unrecognized or dismissed in teaching practice, especially at the secondary level (Gonzalez, Moll, & Amanti, 2005; Heath, 1983; Ladson-Billings, 1994; C. D. Lee & Majors, 2003; Moll & Gonzalez, 1994; Nieto, 1994; Valdes, 1998; Valenzuela, 1999). As part of our review, Hinchman and I suggested that culturally responsive, or socially just/social justice, subject-matter pedagogy could be thought of in three—not mutually exclusive—ways (Moje & Hinchman, 2004, p. 323): (a) as a bridge from everyday knowledge and practice to conventional content learning (Gutiérrez, Baquedano-López, Alvarez, & Chiu, 1999), (b) as a way to teach skills for navigating cultural and discursive communities (Moje, Ciechanowski, et al., 2004), and (c) as a way to teach students how to challenge and reshape the academic content knowledge of the curriculum (Collatos, Morrell, Nuno, & Lara, 2004; Gutiérrez, Baquedano-Lopez, & Alvarez, 2001).

Subject-Matter Instruction

By subject-matter instruction, I refer primarily to the practices typically engaged for the purpose of teaching knowledge associated with different disciplines. Although subject-matter instruction can cover disciplines from English literature to physics, visual arts to mathematics, and social studies to music, in this review I confine my discussion to what are commonly considered the four academic subject areas: English language arts, mathematics, the social sciences, and the natural sciences. These domains represent the four subject areas for which most U.S. school districts prescribe core requirements and that largely define life (for both students and teachers) in modern U.S. middle and high school settings. In addition, these domains encompass many disciplines (e.g., the social sciences draw from the disciplines of history, political science, psychology, anthropology, sociology, philosophy, and economics).

The question of what counts as socially just subject-matter pedagogy—and thus socially just pedagogical content knowledge and disciplinary literacy pedagogy—is answered in different ways by different subject-matter specialists. Although any perspective on socially just/social justice pedagogy involves providing students access, one of the most important differences revolves around the question of access to what. That is, to what does a socially just/social justice perspective provide access? Is access to knowledge the key, or is access to skills and strategies more central to socially just pedagogy? These questions are answered in different ways across perspectives, depending in large part on whether the goal is to provide equitable instruction for all or to provide instruction that might enable youth to change society. I uncovered at least four distinct perspectives that frame socially just subject-matter pedagogy as providing students access to (a) expert subject-matter knowledge; (b) disciplinary knowledge they care about, generated in response to their own everyday concerns and interests; (c) disciplinary knowledge and ways of knowing that are useable in everyday life; and (d) disciplinary ways of producing knowledge via oral and written texts. I detail each of these perspectives in what follows and then zoom in on the final perspective, that of ways of producing knowledge, which I refer to as disciplinary literacy.

Social Justice as Access to Expert Subject-Matter Knowledge

This perspective suggests that the goal of subject-matter instruction should be to produce youth who are equipped with the content knowledge assumed necessary to work in disciplinary professions (i.e., training all students to be historians), regardless of whether they plan to do so. This perspective, well represented in college preparatory curricula, has largely fallen by the wayside in most education research, although lingering tenets of this perspective may remain. In general, however, this stance is typically considered unrealistic and even elitist; in fact, the only representation of this stance that I could locate in published research or theory was in the move of education researchers to dismiss it as valid (see, e.g., Duschl, 2005; Leinhardt, 1994). Indeed, in practice, few secondary schools attempt to prepare all students with elite knowledge. Most schools focus on educating some students to work in the disciplines or to prepare for college, whereas other students learn cursory applications of disciplinary knowledge (e.g., honors courses designed to foster the beginnings of disciplinary expertise compared to general courses designed to fulfill state graduation requirements). At times, even whole schools or districts are divided along these lines (Anyon, 1981, 1997).

Social Justice as the Foregrounding of Everyday Knowledge

A second widely held perspective on socially just/social justice subject-matter pedagogy eschews the development of expert knowledge as a goal of subject-area instruction on the grounds that expert knowledge derives from mainstream perspectives on the world. This mainstream knowledge—whether historical or scientific, mathematical or literary—is thought to shut down possibilities for other forms of knowledge to be generated or to send implicit messages to students about the value of their community or home knowledge (Roth & Lee, 2005). Researchers and theorists working from this perspective do not necessarily dismiss expert knowledge but they take the stance that disciplinary learning should begin with youth and/or community concerns, knowledge, and practice as a way of making the learning of disciplinary knowledge more accessible to youth (Alvermann & Hagood, 2000; Alvermann, Moon, & Hagood, 1999; Barton, 2001; Civil & Bernier, 2006; Elmesky, 2001; Gutiérrez, Rymes, & Larson, 1995; Gutstein, 2006; O. Lee, 1999; O. Lee & Fradd, 1998; Moje, Ciechanowski, et al., 2004; Seiler, 2001; Yerrick, 2000), relevant or responsive to youth interests (Ladson-Billings, 1994; C. D. Lee, 2001; C. D. Lee & Majors, 2003; Moje & Hinchman, 2004), or equal in value to disciplinary knowledge (Gee, 2005; Hull & Schultz, 2002; Mahiri, 2003).

Social Justice as Access to Useable Disciplinary Knowledge and Ways of Knowing

A third perspective is that of socially just/social justice education in the subject-matter areas as providing students with access to useable, everyday knowledge about the disciplines, knowledge that allows young people to evaluate ideas and act as informed citizens in the world. Although this perspective perhaps seems similar to the perspective on starting with youth knowledge, in fact, this perspective does not necessarily situate disciplinary learning in what youth already know and do. The goal of this perspective is, first and foremost, to teach disciplinary knowledge; researchers operating from this perspective, however, distinguish themselves from those who hold the perspective that socially just subject-matter instruction provides access for all students to expert knowledge.

This perspective is often referred to as providing youth with a type of literacy, despite the fact that such studies only minimally make specific reference to the processes and practices associated with making sense of or producing disciplinary (or other) texts. For example, the Association for the Advancement of Science (AAAS) developed benchmarks for what they refer to as "scientific literacy," which they defined as

Being familiar with the natural world and respect for its unity; being aware of some of the important ways in which mathematics, technology, and the sciences depend upon one another; understanding some of the key concepts and principles of science; having a capacity for scientific ways of thinking; knowing that science, mathematics, and technology are human enterprises, and knowing what that implies about their strengths and limitations; and being able to use scientific knowledge and ways of thinking for personal social purposes. (Rutherford & Ahlgren, 1990, p. x)

Norris and Phillips (2002) referred to this sense of subject-matter literacy as the "derived" sense of literacy, a focus on useable knowledge that does not attend to the role of language and texts in developing this useable and applied knowledge of a given discipline. Some scholars, however, argue that such a focus diminishes the power of this construct as a form of socially just pedagogy (Eisenhart, Finkel, & Marion, 1996; Leinhardt, 1994; Norris & Phillips, 2002, 2003; Wineburg & Martin, 2004). Although a focus on usable disciplinary knowledge may provide opportunities for all students to learn something about the discipline, and is thus socially just, such a focus alone may not provide opportunities for the development of informed citizens who understand how arguments are made and challenged in and through oral and written language of the disciplines and who can take action against societal injustices (or even on their own behalf; Wineburg & Martin, 2004). Norris and Phillips (2002) are most persuasive in this regard, citing theoretical and empirical studies to argue,

If scientific literacy is conceived only as knowledge of the substantive content of science, there is a risk that striving to learn the elements of that content will define our goals without any appreciation for the interconnection among the elements of content, their sources, and their implications. . . . When it is also recognized that science is in part constituted by text and the resources that text makes available, and that the primary access to scientific knowledge is through the read of texts, then it is easy to see that in learning how to read such texts a great deal will be learned about both substantive science content and the epistemology of science. (pp. 236–237)

Social Justice as Access to Knowledge Via
Access to Ways of Producing Knowledge

The final perspective that I will address in this review argues for a view of subject-matter instruction in which access to ways of producing knowledge is at the heart of social justice. The focus on ways of producing knowledge is distinct from ways of knowing, in that ways of producing knowledge evokes the need for a tool of some type, namely, the tool of language. Both oral and written language are the focus of this perspective, with a particular emphasis on how young people might be apprenticed into the nuanced differences in producing knowledge via written language across multiple disciplines. To be sure, this perspective recognizes the importance of understanding the accumulated knowledge of each discipline but also argues that knowing how to produce knowledge—and thereby how to critique its production— is where power in the disciplines lies, in part because it provides access to content knowledge and in part because it provides access to the discourse communities of the disciplines who produce that knowledge. In other words, some of the power of knowledge comes from being an active part of its production rather than from merely possessing it. Some theorists and researchers would even argue that a student of discipline does not really know the discipline unless she or he knows how to produce knowledge—with some facility—in it. Of the study of history, for example, Leinhardt (1994) argued,

> History is layered, and the teaching of it, like other subjects, involves not only a process of acquiring the stuff of the discipline but acquiring a particular rhetorical stance toward it. The artifacts of any given course (multiple texts, documents, discussions, and required essays) and the roles of the teachers and students are unique. (p. 218).

These same theorists will acknowledge that this awareness is not always at a conscious, or metacognitive, level but that is it is employed in the common acts of disciplinary knowledge production, nonetheless (Wineburg, 2003; Yore, Hand, & Prain, 2002). As Wineburg (2003) illustrated, he had the opportunity to observe an English literature scholar reading a narrative account before an audience of historians. The literature scholar gave the text a dramatic reading, imbuing historical figures with character attributes. Historians in the audience, Wineburg observed, were disturbed by the lack of information about authorship, or attribution. Wineburg argued that historians were disturbed by the reading because their disciplinary processes require that the first step in reading historical narratives is to determine who wrote the text or provided the account (i.e., determining attribution) and then to situate the text in a particular historical context. So enculturated were the historians in their disciplinary practices and processes of text reading that they could not bear to listen to what they viewed as an inappropriate reading.

From this perspective, then, subject-matter instruction depends as much on teaching the ways of engaging with disciplinary language and text as it does on teaching mainstream disciplinary knowledge or even habits of mind. It does not ignore either disciplinary knowledge or habits of mind but argues that a primary tool for accessing both lies in language. In addition, texts—especially written texts—inscribe disciplines with particular types of knowledge. Moreover, the acts of reading and writing—even in the most generic sense (i.e., apart from the unique work of reading and writing within disciplines)—involve complex cognitive processes that are mediated by largely taken-for-granted cultural practices. Reading, for example, is more than the simple process of decoding words and assigning meaning; reading involves decoding, to be sure, but also requires knowledge of semantics, syntax, text structures, linguistic features, purposes for reading, and rhetorical devices. Reading depends heavily on the content knowledge one brings to a text. Reading depends on one's motivation, and the outcomes of reading include more than just comprehension or extraction of information but also interpretation, analysis, critique, and application. The intricacies of learning to encode and decode, interpret and apply, and comprehend and critique specialized symbol systems demand particular attention in subject-matter instruction.

Thus, in what follows, I examine studies that use the fundamental sense of literacy (Norris & Phillips, 2002) to refer to acts of and practices surrounding the reading and writing of disciplinary written texts. However, the view of disciplinary literacy is a complicated one, and thus I review the variety of forms of disciplinary literacy theory and pedagogy, outlining strengths, areas for development, and ultimately, possible contributions to a conception of socially just subject-matter instruction that produces social justice.

DISCIPLINARY LITERACY THEORY AND RESEARCH

Often, when examining subject-matter instruction, education theorists and researchers explore concepts such as content knowledge, pedagogical knowledge, and of course, pedagogical content knowledge (Shulman, 1986), a construct that brings together a focus on the content of the subject-matter area, with methods and practices for teaching that content. In this review, the pedagogical content knowledge (PCK) of interest is that which revolves around how teachers develop practices for teaching and learning from texts in their disciplines, as well as how teachers develop practices for teaching youth to read, write, navigate across, and critique multiple texts of the disciplines. In this case, the construct of pedagogical content knowledge might well be expanded to include not only pedagogical practices for teaching content but also pedagogical practices for teaching the linguistic, cognitive, and cultural text-based practices and processes associated with a discipline. In a sense, then, teachers need not only to develop pedagogical content knowledge but also pedagogical process/practice knowledge. For many scholars (including Shulman, who proposed the idea of PCK), the notion of processes and practices is likely to be subsumed or understood within the term "content," but I want to tease out this idea here to underscore a particular point: Subject-matter learning is not merely about learning the stuff of the disciplines, it is also about the processes and practices by which that stuff is produced. Rather than use the cumbersome, if appropriate, phrase "pedagogical content/practice/process knowledge," however, I refer to this construct as disciplinary literacy pedagogy.

What does that phrase "disciplinary literacy pedagogy" mean? A number of variations on the phrase exist. One definition, for example, can be found on The Institute for Learning website (http://www.instituteforlearning.org/dl.html) of the Learning Research and Development Center at the University of Pittsburgh:

This approach to teaching and learning integrates academically rigorous content with discipline-appropriate habits of thinking. The driving idea is that knowledge and thinking must go hand in hand. To develop deep conceptual knowledge in a discipline, one needs to use the habits of thinking that are valued and used by that discipline. To develop strategic and powerful discipline-specific habits of thinking, one needs to be directed by one's content knowledge. For students to become literate in a particular discipline, they must grow in both dimensions simultaneously. The ultimate goal of Disciplinary Literacy is that all students will develop deep content knowledge and literate habits of thinking in the context of academically rigorous learning in individual disciplines.

A number of empirical studies have offered warrant for the idea that readers approach texts in different ways depending on the reader's purpose or goals for reading them, the reader's disciplinary commitments and practices, the nature of the text (its structure, its genre, etc.), the context in which the texts were generated, and the context in which the texts are being read. For example, as illustrated in a previous section, the same piece of historical narrative could be approached in different ways depending on the disciplinary (or other) context in which the text is being read or written. Wineburg's analysis suggests, in fact, that a text identified as a historical narrative may even lose that identity if read by someone other than a historian. Historical narrative—a primary source perhaps—could be data in the hands of a historian, literary narrative to be performed in the hands of a dramatist, literary narrative to be critiqued in the hands of a literary theorist, and interesting background information that provides context for explaining natural phenomena in the hands of a chemist (or other natural scientist).

Consequently, history educators who work from disciplinary literacy perspectives argue that deep subject-matter learning in historical studies requires students to think analytically and critically about the contexts in which texts or ideas were produced. Readers must examine texts for attribution, that is, the reader must ask such questions as, "Who wrote the text? What was the writer's background? What was the writer's perspective or standpoint?" Next, they ask what other sources corroborate or challenge the evidence provided from the first source (Wineburg, 2003). Leinhardt, Stainton, and Virji (1994) argue that producing historical accounts revolves around engaging in a dialogue that considers "surviving evidence about the past and existing analytical, theoretical, and political concerns in the present" (p. 14) with the work of production depending heavily on explanation and reasoning, both of which require attention to questions of purpose, evidence, chronology, causality, and contexts. The historical process, according to Leinhardt (1994), revolves around building a compelling case or narrative that integrates evidence, chronology, and cause to both support and generate hypotheses.

Scientific literacy theorists argue, by contrast, that school science typically requires students to bring practices of prediction, observation, analysis, summarization, and presentation to their science reading (as well as to writing and oral language practices; O. Lee & Fradd, 1998; Lemke, 1990). To learn science well, argue many science educators, students of science must learn to predict explanations for natural events or phenomena; hypothesize about those predictions based on the best available information (often found in written texts); design, carry out, and record results of investigations; draw conclusions about those results in relation to their hypotheses and the existing literature; and communicate their findings to others (Blumenfeld, Marx, Patrick, & Krajcik, 1997; Hand, Wallace, & Yang, 2004; Palincsar & Magnusson, 2001). Moreover, Lemke (1990) illustrated ways in which the discourse of science as inscribed in both oral and written language represents a specialized system of language that rests heavily on themes and concepts that are not immediately apparent to a novice science learner (see also Eisenhart et al., 1996). Learning science, then, means learning those themes and how to recognize the themes in oral and written language about the phenomenon of interest.

The study of English literature, which often appears to draw from everyday language and generic literacy processes, actually requires yet again another set of reading skills. Typically, the task of reading literature revolves around interpreting figurative language, recognizing symbols, irony, and satire (C. D. Lee, 2001) in texts that are situated in historical contexts, contexts of different social, cultural, and political systems. In addition to recognizing and interpreting symbols and themes in texts, students of English literature also must identify literary devices that signal emotions, motives, or goals and develop and demonstrate an understanding of how an author constructs a world that the reader simultaneously enters and stands apart from through various narrative devices (C. D. Lee & Spratley, 2006).

Finally, in examining the literate demands in mathematics, Bass (2006) writes,

Mathematics does involve substantial amounts of conventional text, not least in the form of dreaded word problems, but also in its extensive use of ordinary language, in both informal and technical ways. Further, mathematical relations and equations, even when expressed with technical notation (symbols, diagrams, etc.), are themselves a form of text, meaningful and articulable propositions, and their comprehension demands skills of literacy not entirely unlike those required for other kinds of textual sense making. Indeed, literacy for the student of mathematics entails being able to navigate flexibly back and forth between two or more language systems—academic mathematics language, school language, and common out-of-school languages (including one's home language). (p. 3)

Bass goes on to articulate an even more nuanced point about text in mathematics; he argues that "truth in mathematics resides not in the outside world, but in the very concepts of mathematics itself and *in the language used to express and manipulate them* [italics added] (Bass, 2006, p. 3). Thus, the texts of mathematics depend heavily on accuracy and precision in both their production and consumption. The words, terms, symbols, and diagrams (the heart of a mathematical symbol system, according to Bass) of mathematics must be used with precision to generate new knowledge. According to Bass, "The practices of doing mathematics are in significant measure the practices of precise and supple use of language, in a variety of forms" (p. 3). Similar to Bass, Lemke (2003) argued that mathematics is composed of multiple semiotic systems that both convey and produce meaning. Each of these systems can be read independently, but in mathematical reasoning, these systems are typically interdependent.

This range of definitions of disciplinary literacy presents a number of important differences in the practices and processes of the disciplines, but each perspective shares a focus on text, language, and other symbol systems. Some of the perspectives explicitly attend to cognition, others to culture and cultural practices of the disciplines and of the learners. Given this range of definitions of, or related to, disciplinary literacy, it seems worth exploring how disciplinary literacy pedagogy is conceptualized in the literature in relation to text, language, culture, and cognition and how, if at all, the different conceptualizations might contribute to teaching for social justice in the subject-matter areas of secondary schools.

ANOTHER WAY TO SLICE IT

The Role of Language, Cognition, and Culture in Disciplinary Literacy Pedagogy

An important distinction among the studies reviewed is that some studies appeared to conceptualize literacy as cognitive processes, whereas others were grounded in notions of disciplinary literacy as cultural practices. These categories, although useful for analytic purposes, are of course, much messier in real life. In many cases, the authors blur those boundaries, sometimes without explicitly situating their work within one or the other foci. Wineburg's (1991) work is a classic example; although Wineburg situates his work as studying the cognitive or epistemological processes of historians and adolescent students of history, his research reveals a way in which cognitive processes of both groups are culturally mediated. The discomfort he noted among the historians he studied as they listened to a culturally inappropriate reading of history text, for example, provides evidence of the cultural, that is, shared, normed, and taken-for-granted, nature of the work that historians do when they read. Their lack of metacognition about their reading habits suggests that these practices were culturally instantiated, supporting the sociocultural perspective that cognition is culturally mediated.

The same messiness of categorization could be noted for the line between work that focuses on cognitive processes and that which focuses on rhetorical strategies or between the work focusing on rhetorical strategies and cultural practices. That is, where does cognition stop and rhetorical strategizing start? Is the practice of rhetoric mediated by culture or cognition? Similarly, any focus on language analysis raises the same questions: Are the language differences analyzed in texts functions of epistemology or culture, and where is the line between the two?

Finally, it should be noted that many scholars are represented in more than one category. The work of Annemarie Palincsar is a good example of movement across categories due to Palincsar's evolving perspectives over time. Her early work focused on cognitive strategy instruction, specifically reciprocal teaching (Palincsar & Brown, 1984), as a way of supporting comprehension of content area (and other) texts. As she pursued her research agenda, Palincsar became interested in the role of discourse in cognitive strategy instruction in the content area of science (Collins, Palincsar, & Magnusson, 2005). Palincsar's recent work has focused on developing science texts for students to read and respond to as a way of enculturating elementary and secondary students into scientific ways of thinking (Palincsar & Magnusson, 2001) and on the development of technology tools that scaffold reading and writing in science. Such shifts in perspective can be detected in the work of several of the scholars; hence, the same scholars may be represented in several categories of disciplinary literacy research and theory.

These categories, although not tidy or stable, can be useful in highlighting different aspects of disciplinary literacy. Examining the points of convergence and divergence may generate possibilities for productively merging the pedagogical implications of disciplinary literacy theory and research and thus producing socially just and social justice subject-matter instruction. Thus, in what follows, I review four distinct patterns I noted in my review across disciplinary, literacy, and subject-matter studies. These include disciplinary literacy conceived as (a) teaching cognitive literacy processes, (b) teaching epistemological processes of the disciplines, (c) teaching linguistic processes of the disciplines, and (d) teaching linguistic and discursive navigation across cultural boundaries.

Disciplinary Literacy Pedagogy as Teaching
Cognitive Literacy Processes

This category, labeled Cognitive Literacy Processes, has a long history of research, stemming from the content-area literacy work of Harold Herber (1970), who promoted the idea of teaching cognitive strategies for making sense of text to adolescents as they progressed through middle and high school. Herber and his students fought an uphill battle of convincing other literacy researchers, the secondary school teaching force, and education policymakers that reading skill continues to develop throughout adolescence. For some education researchers, this idea was understood as reading to learn, and it was argued that literacy instruction needed to shift from learning to read (or write) in the lower grades to reading (or writing) to learn in the upper grades. In practice, however, the strategies developed and tested by content area reading researchers were focused on continued development in learning to read, premised on the argument that the texts of secondary school content areas such as science, social studies, and mathematics required different kinds of reading skills from those young people had learned in earlier grades, where narrative texts dominated. Thus, a host of cognitive strategies were developed, applied, and tested in a variety of secondary school settings, such as Ogle's K-W-L (What I *K*now, What I *W*ant to Know, and What I *L*earned; Ogle, 1986) to Palincsar and Brown's (1984) reciprocal teaching and Guthrie, Wigfield, and Perencevich's (2004) Concept-Oriented Reading Instruction. These various strategies have been reviewed by a number of scholars (Alvermann & Moore, 1991; Bean, 2000; Moore & Readence, 2001; Phelps, 2005) but are not always thought of as disciplinary literacy strategies. Instead, they are conceived of as cognitive strategies for text processing, with the assumption that they can be applied to any text, whether rooted in the disciplines or found in everyday life.

For example, Palincsar and Brown's (1984) Reciprocal Teaching is a classic and oft-cited example of a cognitive strategy designed to model for students how to ask questions of text in a way that supports comprehension of the text while also drawing from what students might be interested in as they read. The strategy builds on four activities that encompass the range of skills—or functions, as Palincsar and Brown label them—mature readers engage in as they read any kind of text. These skills or functions include understanding the purposes of reading, activating background knowledge, allocating attention, evaluating content, self-monitoring, and drawing and testing inferences. The particular activities Palincsar and Brown identified as critical were summarizing, questioning, clarifying, and predicting. Through extensive teacher modeling and student practice, students learn how to engage in these activities and take ownership for asking and answering their own questions of text.

This teaching-learning strategy stands out among cognitive literacy strategies because the authors have emphasized several key aspects of instruction that move the process from one of intensive teacher scaffolding to learner self-regulation. These aspects include explicit modeling, guided practice, and sustained enactment of the strategy. In effect, the strategy was conceptualized as a teacher practice rather than as a stand-alone strategy to be inserted into otherwise stable curriculum (Sutherland, Moje, Cleveland, & Heitzman, 2006). In addition, the strategy embeds possibilities for building on student interest and on being responsive to students' ideas about texts because in allowing students to generate questions of texts, their interests are not only uncovered but also are addressed. Thus, Reciprocal Teaching can be considered an early form of responsive teaching; although it is not specific about responding across culture or disciplinary difference, it does, nevertheless, make a place for student interest in the process of learning to develop and articulate questions about texts.

Finally, Reciprocal Teaching, when tested in controlled settings, showed positive effects on student learning (Brown & Palincsar, 1982; Palincsar & Brown, 1984). A number of interrelated studies, albeit conducted with small sample sizes, showed the possibilities for student reading and learning growth when reading and thinking strategies were modeled and scaffolded (Palincsar & Brown, 1984). Specifically, the results of the original studies of reciprocal teaching demonstrated significant progress among students in the Reciprocal Teaching treatment condition in producing accurate main idea questions and summaries and in constructing summaries in their own words rather than simply reading verbatim from texts. Students also appeared to be able to transfer these skills to different classroom reading tasks, although transfer across different kinds of disciplinary texts is not addressed by the Reciprocal Teaching studies.

In addition, working from cognitive literacy strategy perspectives, but motivated by the question of how to guide literacy strategy development while also engaging student readers, Guthrie and colleagues (Guthrie et al., 2004) have developed and tested a teaching practice that builds on cognitive literacy strategies and students' interests and engagement while also connecting to disciplinary content. Concept-Oriented Reading Instruction (CORI) was designed specifically to capitalize on and build student engagement in both reading and disciplinary learning by engaging students in text-based research around phenomena of interest in their everyday lives. CORI is enacted routinely with four stages during which the students (a) observe a phenomenon and then personalize it, or connect to their own lives or questions; (b) search for and retrieve information (thus necessitating text search strategies as well as scientific research strategies); (c) comprehend and integrate the information across multiple sources, both textual and human; and finally, (d) communicate what they have learned to others, thus necessitating literacy strategies to scaffold the development of summary and report writing skills.

Most of the CORI work published to date has been developed and tested at the elementary level and, as such, the disciplinary aspects remain at basic levels (Guthrie et al., 1996; Guthrie et al., 2004). Nonetheless, CORI is unique among cognitive literacy strategies because it does connect the practices of literate engagement to the content of particular disciplines. More important, the findings of CORI in terms of literacy skill development are positive, with students showing both increased engagement in learning content concepts and improved reading and writing skills.

As should be obvious from these two exemplar studies, the primary focus of the cognitive literacy strategy research has been on the application of cognitive literacy strategies designed for primary grades' learners to the range of subject areas present in middle grades and secondary school settings (see, e.g., Biancarosa & Snow, 2004). Many of these strategies have demonstrated promise for supporting secondary school students' comprehension of texts and have been widely cited among recent reviews of useful secondary school literacy teaching strategies (Alvermann & Moore, 1991; Phelps, 2005).

In particular, one notable aspect of work in cognitive literacy strategies that has not been as well recognized is the potential in many of these strategies to support efforts to teach subject matter in socially just ways. Cognitive literacy strategies, while not explicitly attentive to cultural difference and responsiveness, are based in reading theories that recognize—and indeed highlight—the role of the reader and, to a lesser extent, the context of the reading situation. Interactive models of reading (Rumelhart, 1994) argue explicitly for the interaction of the reader and text, and more recent conceptions of comprehension processes put forward by the RAND Comprehension Study Group (Snow, 2002) include attention to the specific reading activity and to context. Given the attention placed by these perspectives on readers' prior knowledge, perspective, and bias, it is appropriate to claim that, in theory, these strategies both support cognitive skill development and recognize and build on who students are as people. With more attention to how these strategies and practices should acknowledge cultural experiences and differences among readers and writers, these strategies could be leveraged to produce socially just subject-matter pedagogy in the sense that they can provide opportunities for youth to learn to independently access and evaluate texts.

What is missing, however, from the cognitive strategies work is attention to the specific demands of the practices—and thus, the texts—of the disciplines. Recent work among content-area literacy researchers has begun to attend to disciplinary-specific demands (Bulgren, Deshler, & Lenz, in press; Conley, in press; Guthrie et al., 2004; Hynd-Shanahan & Shanahan, in press; Schoenbach, Greenleaf, Cziko, & Hurwitz, 1999; Yore, Bisanz, & Hand, 2003; Yore & Treagust, 2006), but a focus remains on how to develop cognitive text processing strategies as a means of enhancing subject-area learning. In addition, a number of these studies are conducted at the upper elementary and middle-school levels, leaving the difficult question of what it means to offer subject-matter instruction that supports reading and writing of the increasingly complex texts demanded for subject-matter learning in the upper secondary-school grades.

The research program of Rafaella Borasi and Majorie Siegel (Borasi & Siegel, 2000; Borasi, Siegel, Fonzi, & Smith 1998; Siegel, Borasi, & Fonzi, 1998) represents an interesting bridge between the Cognitive Literacy Strategies category of disciplinary literacy research and the next disciplinary literacy category I present, that of Disciplinary Epistemologies. Borasi and Siegel (2000) describe the goal of their Reading to Learn Mathematics for Critical Thinking (RLM) study as the analysis of how and to what degree mathematics teaching and learning could be supported by the use of "rich math texts" (p. 9) that were scaffolded through the use of cognitive reading strategies designed to support students' sense-making of texts. Thus, the RLM approach was specifically embedded in a particular type of disciplinary text but was not designed to foster specific reading strategies related to mathematics texts. What Borasi and Siegel (2000) learned, however, was that multiple texts make up mathematics classrooms, above and beyond the planned rich math texts. Such texts might include student journals, textbooks, charts and graphs, class notes, and the like. These texts serve a variety of purposes, or "functions" (Siegel et al., 1998), including to (a) make thinking public, (b) get or provide models and other tools for conducting inquiry or producing representations of thinking, (c) obtain information necessary for informed decision making, (d) complicate thinking or raise new questions for exploration, and (e) push student inquiry. Based on their findings of extended analysis of classroom narratives, Borasi and Siegel make two strong claims: First, students' readings of the rich math texts provided, as well as of other classroom texts, were bolstered by the specific cognitive strategies they taught. Second, how students read in mathematics classrooms depended largely on the functions or purposes for which they read, suggesting that cognitive literacy strategies, although valuable, cannot be applied in generic ways across all forms of texts. This finding ties directly to work represented in the next category, which focuses on how the epistemological underpinnings of a given discipline shape acts of reading, writing, and communication.

Disciplinary Literacy Pedagogy as Teaching Epistemological Processes of the Disciplines

This second group of disciplinary literacy researchers and theorists[1] reverses, in some sense, the cognitive/subject-matter relationship, working within the disciplines to assess the cognition or thinking processes necessary for making sense of disciplinary texts (Bain, 2006; Goldman, 1997; Leinhardt & Young, 1996; VanSledright & Kelly, 1998; Wilson & Wineburg, 1988; Wineburg, 1991; Yore et al., 2002). Following Wineburg (1991), I label this perspective the Disciplinary Epistemological perspective, although the focus on epistemology seems to me to be largely cognitive, with the cultural norms and practices of the disciplines only an implicit thread in much of the work. These research programs are less interested in generic cognitive strategies and more interested in one or more of three foci: (a) specifying the cognition of members of the disciplines as they either comprehend or produce oral and written texts (Leinhardt, 1989; VanSledright & Kelly, 1998; Wineburg, 1991; Young & Leinhardt, 1998), (b) comparing those cognitive processes of members of the disciplines to learners in the subject-matter areas (Collins et al., 2005; Hand, Hohenshell, & Prain, 2004; Hand, Pain, Lawrence, & Yore, 1999; Hand, Wallace, et al., 2004; Palincsar & Magnusson, 2001), and (c) applying those cognitive processes to educational practice (Hynd-Shanahan, Holschuh, & Hubbard, 2004; C. D. Lee, 2005; Moje, 2006).

What is highlighted in any of those three strands is how members of a discipline think and how that thinking shapes the texts they produce or how they access the texts of others for disciplinary purposes. This line of work, in fact, has at times been critiqued as focusing too heavily on the work of disciplinarians, suggesting that the pedagogical goal is to turn every student into little historians, scientists, or mathematicians (little work has been conducted in this area in either mathematics or English language arts). In point of fact, very little evidence in the actual writing of these scholars supports that claim; in general, these scholars argue for studying and teaching the cognitive processes by which members of the discipline produce knowledge to more deeply learn the concepts of the discipline and to learn to reason through. Leinhardt (1994) commented specifically on this critique:

Mindfulness in teaching and learning is an important goal of education in the United States. It should be the goal of history education as well. However, the movement to teach more than rote memorization to everyone, not just the elite, is a relatively new concept, dating from around 1900, when educators turned their attention from goals of teaching basic facts to goals of reasoning with facts. (p. 253)

Thus, the argument from this perspective on disciplinary literacy is that learning disciplinary concepts via learning how knowledge is produced and consumed within the disciplines can be applied to life as a citizen of the world. As citizens, these scholars argue, we all need critical listening and reading skills to make informed decisions and critical speaking and writing skills to communicate our decisions. Critical reading, however, cannot be conceived in generic terms; one must understand not only the concepts of disciplines but also how evidence is used to arrive at and warrant those concepts. Informed participation in society, they argue, demands knowledge of how knowledge is produced in many domains of study.

Work on the role of disciplinary epistemologies in reading texts of the disciplines tends to be situated in studies of history learning. Wineburg's (1991) study launched this line of work by illustrating the "breach" that exists between how practicing historians read and how high school students of history. Specifically, Wineburg employed think-aloud protocols as eight historians and eight high school students read historical documents (not textbooks and not historical analyses) from the Battle of Lexington, which marks the start of combat in the Revolutionary War. The protocols revealed distinct differences in the ways historians and students of history approached the texts, with historians "sourcing," or seeking attribution as a way of previewing a text, highlighting subtexts and intertextual connections, and revisiting perspective and context of the written document as they monitored their comprehension. Students, by contrast, engaged in few of those practices, even as they enacted what might be considered appropriate comprehension strategies from the Cognitive Literacy Strategies perspective. In other words, historians applied ways of knowing—or epistemological stances—to their text reading; high school students of history did not. Wineburg also studied each group's reading of history classroom textbooks and found that although the students accepted the history textbooks without much critique, the historians rated them as less trustworthy than a piece of historical fiction. As a result of his analysis, Wineburg wrote, "If we ask, 'What does it mean to comprehend a historical text?' and rely exclusively on what generic comprehension tests tell us, we may learn a great deal about reading, but not much about history" (p. 516). Since then, Wineburg's argument has been extended by a number of adolescent literacy scholars to suggest that we may not even know much about reading at the secondary school level (e.g., Leinhardt et al., 1994; e.g., Wineburg, 1998; Yore et al., 2002) because the act of reading in adolescence is typically situated in specialized domains, both in and out of school. Moreover, it can be argued that Wineburg's argument is one of producing socially just pedagogy. Near the conclusion of his piece—and in several subsequent articles (e.g., Wineburg & Martin, 2004)—Wineburg articulated a view of critical reading that could emanate from close study of how members of disciplines (or any specialized domain) read and produce the texts they care about:

The view of text described here is not limited to history. Language is not a garden tool for acting on inanimate objects but a medium for swaying minds and changing opinions, for rousing passions or allaying them. This is a crucial understanding for reading the newspaper, for listening to the radio, for evaluating campaign promises, or for making a decision to drink a Nutrasweet product based on research conducted by the Searle Company. If students never learn to see the difference between the "Contras" and the "freedom fighters," between "Star Wars" and the "Strategic Defense Initiative," between "terrorists" and "members of the PLO," if they think of these terms as neutral appellations rather than charge symbols tapping different meaning systems, they become easy marks for sellers of snake oil of all persuasions. (p. 519)

This study, and a number of others, documented the practices and knowledge of practicing members of the disciplines (Leinhardt, 1989, 1993; Leinhardt & Smith, 1984; Wilson & Wineburg, 1988; Wineburg & Wilson, 1991), of expert teachers of different subject matters (Bain, 2000), and of children and youth (Afflerbach & VanSledright, 2001; VanSledright & Kelly, 1998).

Wineburg's (1991) point is especially critical when considering the critique of history and other disciplinary textbooks offered by a number of scholars. Paxton (1999), for example, has argued that the lack of authorial voice in most history textbooks produced in the United States contributes to a lack of critical reading skill on the part of adolescent (and child) history learners. These youth learn to take up history as a series of undisputed facts rather than as a practice of constructing an evidence-based account of events shaped by the author's perspective, background, and temporal location, among other factors. The "deafening silence" to which Paxton refers implicates not only an explanation for lack of student engagement in upper-level disciplinary learning but also a serious social justice concern. As J. D. Anderson (1986) has argued, U.S. history textbooks present a particular perspective on Black history in the United States, a perspective that can be challenged through close reading of multiple primary source documents. Without, however, access both to multiple and varied texts and to opportunities to learn to read those texts critically—as a historian or other disciplinarian might—the goal of socially just subject-matter pedagogy is threatened, regardless of how many opportunities one provides to learn expert or everyday content knowledge.

Robert Bain's (2006) work takes up these analyses of students' and historians' different reading and writing processes for application in classroom and teacher education practice. As a historian and 25-year veteran of high school history teaching, Bain studied his own world history teaching (Bain & Ellenbogen, 2001) as he attempted to jump "into the breach" by teaching students the practices of historians as they engaged with classroom texts. In presenting his findings, Bain was careful to point out that his analysis of 76 ninth-grade students' processes in learning to analyze and question classroom and historical texts should be not be read as causal claims regarding the impact of his instruction. Nevertheless, he offered student reflections on their learning as evidence of learning and changes in their thinking, as in this interview excerpt:

> This class taught me not to just believe something is right just because the teacher says it or if it's in a textbook. I now think and even perhaps act like a historian. If I disagree with something the teacher or the book says I can listen carefully or read through to check for internal consistency. Internal consistency is important especially when I'm listening to a teacher because if he/she contradicts themselves, it would be hard for me to know what is correct. Also, if a teacher says something which I think is wrong, I can corroborate with other sources to check which was correct. By far the most important thing I learned was not just to accept what is being said but check to see if it corresponds with what I had previously learned. Honestly, through this course, I have become a better thinker. (pp. 2106–2107)

In work beyond his own classroom, Bain (2000) has developed a classroom digital tool—the Virtual Curator and Virtual Expedition—that guides Detroit high school students as they explore museum text resources and locate relevant information. The digital tool frames their reading and research in questions of the discipline of history (specifically in the history of the great migration and urbanization of the 20th century) and provides scaffolds that push students to pose questions and to corroborate, contextualize, and analyze the sources and information they uncover at disciplinarily appropriate points in their reading and narrative construction process.

Leinhardt (1993) also has studied the implications for pedagogy of the breach between the text-based practices of historians and the text-based practices of students of history but has focused her analyses on how teachers construct explanations in practice that serve as models for students of the kinds of thinking required to make sense of and produce historical texts. Leinhardt argued that the two main tasks of students of history are learning to explain and learning to reason and specifically distinguishes between explaining in a discipline such as mathematics and explaining in history, claiming that both the questions that prompt explanations and the explanations that answer them are distinct in terms of form. In classroom-based studies, Leinhardt and colleagues (T. H. Anderson & Armbruster, 1984; Schleppegrell, Achugar, & Oteíza, 2004) traced two different kinds of explanations teachers made, what they referred to as "blocked" and "ikat" explanations. Blocked explanations are those that refer to particular events and have an initiation and conclusion that is relatively simple to identify. Ikat explanations, by contrast, are those that are woven throughout a discussion of ideas and that ebb and flow with new information added as that information is uncovered in the process of study.

What makes Leinhardt's analysis of how explanations occur in the history classroom especially interesting is the model that they serve—or do not serve—for the development of student explanations in historical writing. As a number of scholars of text note (Leinhardt et al., 1994), the textbooks students typically have at their disposal do not always display the most precise explanations by disciplinary standards. If much of even expert history teaching follows the ikat model of explaining, then how is it that students learn to read and produce the concise, data-based explanations that are accepted in the disciplines (and demanded on many state assessments)?

Leinhardt's (1994) analysis traced how expert teachers (who work from different stances) modeled over time the structures, forms, themes, and devices necessary for explaining. In addition, these teachers also modeled the particular features of reasoning in history. Most important, perhaps, is that Leinhardt documented these expert teachers making opportunities for students to take over much of the oral discourse of the classroom, thus providing scaffolded opportunities for students to practice these features of reasoning, which according to Leinhardt's analysis of historians' thinking (Hand et al., 1999; Hand, Wallace, et al., 2004), include strong narrative skill, evidential exhaustivity, hypotheses generation and assessment, and the ability to contextualize hypotheses and claims. One of the most critical findings of this work is the role that oral explaining—with both teachers and students participating— played in the development of what Leinhardt refers to as mindfulness among the students of history she observed.

In terms of disciplinary text production, the work of Brian Hand and colleagues in science stand as exemplars of the Disciplinary Epistemology perspective (see also Palincsar & Magnusson, 2001). Hand and colleagues began from a largely cognitive stance of applying writing strategies to the production of science texts, developing what they termed the Science Writing Heuristic (SWH; Akkus, Gunel, & Hand, in press). According to Hand and colleagues, the SWH is more than a cognitive literacy tool; rather, it structures the work of writing and reasoning so that it parallels the writing and reasoning of scientists. In particular, the SWH both builds on and supports a number of features of scientific work—such as the collaborative and constructive nature of science research—as students are led through a cycle of investigation, communication of initial results, revising and clarifying claims and reasoning, and refining explanations for phenomena. In this sense, the SWH is similar to other scientific and historical explanation writing rubrics (Moje, Peek-Brown, et al., 2004; Young & Leinhardt, 1998), although Hand and colleagues argue that the SWH makes a link from the "informal, expressive writing modes that foster personally constructed science understandings and more formal, public writing modes that focus on canonical forms of reasoning in science" by guiding students through the writing of scientific reports on inquiry done in classrooms (Akkus et al., in press). Perhaps most salient, the SWH offers students the following categories, which reflect a disciplinary attitude toward text production that is markedly different from those highlighted in historical text production: (a) Beginning ideas: What are my questions? (b) Tests: What did I do? (c) Observations: What did I do? (d) Claims: What can I claim? (e) Evidence: How do I know? Why am I making these claims? (f) Reading: How do my ideas compare with other ideas? and (g) Reflection: How have my ideas changed? Thus, the

SWH, with roots in Cognitive Literacy perspectives, has developed over time to represent the Disciplinary Epistemologies of science and to scaffold student writing by making explicit those epistemologies.

In multiple studies of various configurations of the SWH and other writing-to-learn strategies (e.g., SWH used in comparison to traditional instruction, rhetorical writing strategies used to guide informal science writing) with different age groups and in different fields of scientific study (i.e., chemistry, general science, biology), Hand and colleagues have documented that when offered the SWH and supported by teacher instruction in the process of science inquiry activities, students across a range of ages produce more complex and effective science texts than do students in traditional science instructional settings (Hand et al., 1999; Hand, Prain, & Yore, 2001; Hand, Wallace, et al., 2004; Hand, Yang, & Bruxvoort, in press). In one recent study, Hand et al. (in press) produced both quantitative analyses demonstrating that students' writing and science learning had improved from pre- to postinstruction and qualitative analyses that found students' understanding of rhetorical strategies for communicating science to be more developed than that of students who had not received the science-writing-to-learn instruction the researchers had offered.

Another version of the Disciplinary Epistemological perspective work draws heavily from work in the field of rhetoric and composition. This branch of work examines how writers in the disciplines and students of the disciplines make sense of their writing tasks, considering concepts such as purpose, goals, audience, and resulting form in the production of disciplinary writing (e.g., Greene, 1994; e.g., Johns & Swales, 2002; Parkinson & Adendorff, 2004). In many ways, this work closely represents that of Hand's work in disciplinary epistemology and writing. However, work informed by rhetorical perspectives operates less from a perspective that the production of disciplinary text requires knowing how members of the discipline think and more from the perspective that regardless of discipline, a writer must understand the goals of the writing task, the perspectives and interests of the target audience, and strategies for persuasive writing to write a piece of text effectively. Greene's (1994) analysis of student writers of history texts, for example, demonstrates a rhetorical take on the writing of history texts.

Using think-aloud protocols, Greene examined how 15 junior- and senior-level undergraduate students, 4 of whom were history majors, interpreted and enacted the writing tasks assigned to them in a university history course. Students were randomly assigned to one of two conditions: report writing or problem-based writing. Prior knowledge assessments were used as a covariate in analyzing the qualitative changes in knowledge displayed by the students, and observations for the course of an entire semester, interviews with the course professor, and think-aloud protocols conducted with three other practicing historians provided background for analyzing the students' responses. Greene's analyses demonstrated that students who wrote reports interpreted the assignment as required them to draw from the sources provided for them. They rarely included references to outside knowledge. Those who wrote problem-based essays attempted to integrate prior knowledge with the source material provided.

Greene's major finding, however, was that the context of the course shaped the students' rhetorical moves in key ways, that is, students unsurprisingly wrote for the professor as audience, whereas the practicing historians, despite recognizing that they were playing a role in a research study, wrote for other historians in the field. With these findings, Greene underscored the importance of considering the rhetorical strategies of students in a disciplinary setting and, in particular, of attending to how those strategies are shaped by students' interpretation of context and audience. From a disciplinary literacy perspective, Greene's work raises an important question: Just how does a teacher—whether secondary or postsecondary—engage novices to the discipline in understanding the disciplinary context and assumptions to which they are writing (or that shape their reading)? It is one thing to teach students the cognitive processes of reading and writing like historians, but what is the role of context and cultural practice, especially those of the classroom as context and working for grades as academic cultural practices?

Overall, one fairly common element of the Disciplinary Epistemological perspective of disciplinary literacy research is a focus on bringing to consciousness the cognitive work of the disciplines. In other words, this work connects to the more generic content-area literacy focus on teaching youth strategies and on teaching them to be metacognitive about their reading processes. The focus on developing metacognition about one's disciplinary reading and writing processes—although advocated by all four of the different perspectives outlined here—represents a curious irony. Specifically, the studies that examined the reading or writing processes of members of the disciplines typically represented them as having little conscious awareness of their ways of knowing and, particularly, of approaching texts (Wineburg, 1991; Yore et al., 2002, provide the most obvious example of this point). When thinking aloud with a text or when interviewed about their approaches to writing, the processes of the members of the discipline became clear, but these disciplinary scholars were not necessarily conscious of their approaches to texts. This point raises the question about the role of explicitness in any of these approaches, a point particularly relevant when considering the question of how to build both socially just pedagogical approaches and approaches that produce social justice in society. A reasonable argument could be made that the explicitness, or the making of such epistemology public (see C. D. Lee, 2001), is not the means by which such processes or practices are learned. It could be argued that such learning requires apprenticeship in text practices of the disciplines over time. By contrast, it also could be argued that such explicit, conscious attention is necessary to enable youth from many different backgrounds and experiences to navigate discourse communities and to make decisions about the value and worth of claims made from various disciplinary perspectives and that making the thinking and text practices of the disciplines public is necessary for socially just subject-matter pedagogy.

The question of explicitness is especially important because at times the focus on the cognitive or epistemological processes of the disciplines has the effect of reifying these ways of knowing as the only means for sense-making in particular disciplines, suggesting that it is somehow natural or innate for people who study a particular subject to think in particular ways. A number of these theorists and researchers do, in fact, acknowledge the role that the disciplinary community has in shaping how people think inside the community, thus suggesting that these processes are artifacts of cultural practices, and yet, the links from culture to cognition and back again often tend to be left implicit. Students are encouraged to think, talk, read, and write as members of the discipline might, but they are not explicitly asked to examine how those cognitive processes for navigating texts are artifacts of the discipline as a group of people, oriented toward a particular purpose. As a result, students often articulate beliefs such as those of the sophomore chemistry students interviewed in an ethnography of literacy practice in the chemistry classroom (Moje, 1995). Their views on the differences between literacy in chemistry and literacy in English class (which they offered unprompted except for the question, "What do you think of when you think of literacy?") included comments such as,

You're basically taking out main ideas of the paragraphs and just putting it in, just writing it in your own words. What they've said, you're just writing it. . . . In English [class] you're using more of your head. You're not really necessarily summarizing, except for books for something. Usually in English you're using your own creativity and imagination. (cited in Moje, 1995, pp. 362–363)

In sum, the students in my study talked about the subject area differences as if these distinctions were normative and to be questioned. Building on this point, it seems critical to mention that few, if any, of the Disciplinary Epistemology studies name their pedagogical starting place as resting in the knowledge and text practices that young people bring to classrooms. Instead, the work, by and large, operates from the stance of uncovering the text processes of members of the disciplines.

A final point about this category of disciplinary literacy pedagogy is that, by and large, work in this category does not highlight the role of language except insofar as it is necessary to learn to process the different language cues (e.g., subtexts, technical vocabulary, contextual or temporal cues, place names) demanded by the discipline. The work of linguistic analysis is reserved for another category of disciplinary literacy pedagogy, which I review in the next section.

Disciplinary Literacy Pedagogy as Teaching Linguistic Processes of the Disciplines

This branch of disciplinary literacy pedagogy focuses squarely on language processes, at times, but not always, tied to specific disciplinary processes. One line of language-based research, that of systemic functional linguistics (Halliday & Matthiessen, 2004), has gained prominence in subject-matter instructional research because of its precision in clarifying how subject-matter learning is dependent on language. Coffin (2006) writes that a basic goal of a functional linguistic model of language and learning is that it provide student with "access to, and control of, the written texts of mainstream education, for example, a persuasive essay, a laboratory report, or a critical review of an artwork of literary text" (pp. 413–414). Similar to the cognitive research done in content literacy processes and in disciplinary learning, Coffin argues that functional linguistics seeks to "bring to consciousness (both for teachers and students) the way in which such texts are linguistically structured and shaped and the way in which writers draw on grammar and lexis (i.e., vocabulary) to create different communicative effects" (p. 414). In one study, Coffin (2006) examined the linguistic features of secondary school history texts read and written by students and found three dominant genres demanded for successful writing in the classes: recording, explaining, and arguing genre. She also found that students were expected to use more technical language, to engage in more abstract writing, and to use linguistic processes such as nominalization (the translation of verb forms into noun forms through the process of collapsing actions, results, and logical connectors, much as I have done in this clause).

As a result of her analyses, Coffin (2006) developed a professional development intervention in which 17 history teachers worked with Coffin and other linguistic specialists to integrate the teaching of these genre-specific language practices to secondary school students. The teaching-learning cycle they developed included three phases: deconstruction, in which students analyze model texts for unique linguistic features; joint construction, in which teacher and students produce a protypical history text according to the uncovered linguistic features they analyzed in phase one; and independent construction, during which students work individually or in small groups. Coffin and colleagues then examined the results in an observational, pre-/postdesign intervention, in which the 17 teachers carried out the procedures they had collaboratively developed during professional development. Although not a controlled experiment or quasi-experiment, the results of the study suggest some promise for the approach, with students' abilities to recontextualize information increasing. However, Coffin notes that the gains were seen at the level of whole text rather than at the grammatical level. What's more, without more specific information about the measures by which gains were assessed, these results should be considered with caution.

Schleppegrell and colleagues (Schleppegrell & Achugar, 2003; Schleppegrell et al., 2004) also have studied the linguistic features of academic language learning and argue that academic language (oral or written), in general, is different from everyday language in terms of (a) the density of information presented, (b) the level of abstraction of concepts, (c) the technical nature of concept presentation, (d) the use of multiple semiotic systems, (e) the structural conventions, and (f) the type of voice that dominates. In discipline-specific study, Scheppegrell and colleagues (2004), for example, analyze textbook passages to demonstrate to history teachers how they can support students in making sense of the abstractions, multiple semiotic systems, and organizational expectations unique to history texts. According to Schleppegrell and Achugar (2003), these pedagogical moves result in increased critical reading and text comprehension among students, although specific effects are not described. Findings from a large-scale study of professional development around these linguistic techniques are in development (Schleppegrell et al., 2004).

Similar to the Cognitive Literacy and Disciplinary Epistemology stances, the Functional Linguistics stance is extremely useful for highlighting the challenges of language embedded in all academic texts and the specific challenges and expectations unique to particular disciplines. SFL may, however, be currently missing some important opportunities to develop youth language. Because functional linguistics, as applied to subject-matter learning, has tended to focus on the abstraction, density, organization, and semiotic systems of academic language, it has not attended as closely to the abstractions, density, and multiple semiotic systems of everyday language and texts young people routinely use to make meaning and claim spaces and identities (Moje, 2000). Consider, for example, this text example drawn from the web magazine *Performance Auto & Sound* (http://www.pasmag.com/), read by young men (middle- and high-school age) in a study of youth literacy and culture in Detroit, Michigan:

The Touring exhaust is a single straight-through design specifically tuned for the 2.4L engine. It is made in the USA with 304 100% mandrel-bent Stainless Steel and features Corsas' patented Reflective Sound Cancellation (RSC) technology. What RSC means is that the muffler is designed with a paper running straight through the muffler that incorporates a full 360-degree air gap that allows sound pressure waves to escape. The waves are channeled and then returned to the gap 180 degrees out of phase, canceling specific unwanted sound frequencies, commonly referred to as drone.

From a linguistic standpoint, the lexical, grammatical, and structural demands of this everyday text are many. From the first sentence, which refers to a "Touring exhaust" (which one assumes to be a particular type, cued only by the use of the upper-case T) and a "straight-through" design (which remains undefined, although may be a concept that is easily visualized) for a "2.4L engine." Those not versed in the lexis of the automotive domain would, no doubt, appreciate the considerateness of the author in defining phrases such as "Reflective Sound Cancellation" and "drone," but even these definitions depend on a relatively abstract conceptualization of sound waves, pressure, phase, and frequencies. The text also provides multiple semiotic cues, with images of exhaust systems that are, in the full text, cued to particular aspects of the article. The text, of course, could be considered to represent a specialized domain, which underscores the idea that specialization is not only the purview of the academy and, by extension, that generality, concreteness, and personal voice also may be found in texts of the academy. This point suggests the important possible work that remains to be done from a Functional Linguistic disciplinary literacy perspective in analyzing a wide range of both everyday and academic texts. Attention to the linguistic features and demands of texts young people read and write in homes, peer groups, families, and other settings outside of school via a Functional Linguistics perspective could provide an opportunity to build on young people's existing prowess with language as a way of learning academic language and text processing. Scaffolding—perhaps via cognitive literacy strategies—helps students understand the different assumptions brought to bear on different texts by different audiences and authors, particularly disciplinary audiences and authors. Parkinson and Adendorff (2004) attempt to bridge this gap from the Functional Linguistics perspective by suggesting that students of physics analyze the linguistic features of popular science articles that, the authors claim, offer a hybrid of everyday and popular language and resist the reification of scientific findings that the authors suggest are features of both science textbooks and scientific research reports. Parkinson and Adendorff's suggestion represents one text-based possibility for drawing from the texts of youths' everyday lives. Research represented in the next category of disciplinary literacy research, however, attempts to take the cultural practices and cognitive processes of young people's everyday lives into account by more explicitly drawing from and expanding those practices and processes as a way of constructing bridging, navigational, and changed-oriented, subject-matter, instructional practices.

Disciplinary Literacy Pedagogy as Navigation Across Cultural Boundaries

As previously indicated, one view of socially just secondary school subject-matter instruction is that subject-matter instruction should begin with students' interests, knowledge, and practice as a way to teach them content knowledge (e.g., Alvermann et al., 1999; Alvermann & Hagood, 2000; Barton, 2001; Edwards & Eisenhart, 2002; C. D. Lee, in press; S. Lee & Roth, 2003; e.g., Mahiri, 1998; Moje, 2000; Morrell & Duncan-Andrade, 2003; Roth & Lee, 2005; Yerrick, 2000). The Cultural Navigation perspective on disciplinary literacy builds on such work but adds the important emphasis on both oral and written language, although this category of work does not always take language study to the degree offered by functional linguistics or rhetoricians, and neither does the Cultural Navigation perspective routinely situate academic learning in the cognitive processes and practices of the disciplines. Although many, but not all, of the theorists/researchers in this group reflect the link between the cultural and the cognitive, most start with young people's knowledge, text practices, and interests as a basis for teaching disciplinary text processes, emphasizing how these processes are shaped by the purposes, norms, and conventions of making knowledge in the disciplines. An additional important aspect of the Cultural Navigation perspective on disciplinary literacy revolves around providing opportunities for youth to practice navigating across the different cultural, discursive, or linguistic communities of secondary schooling and of their everyday lives. Thus, many of the Cultural Navigation studies are either interdisciplinary in nature or situate student learning in classroom and community projects with heavy text demands.

The focus in this area, then, tends to be on the linking of everyday to academic cultural text practices and cognitive text processes, but at more global levels than in the disciplinary literacy perspectives previously reviewed. An important additional focus tends to be on the critiquing of mainstream academic knowledge and of prying open a space for young people's everyday knowledge to be used to inform and expand mainstream academic knowledge.

The theoretical basis for this work stems from the argument that the subject-matter areas, or disciplines, can be viewed as spaces in which knowledge is produced or constructed rather than as repositories of content knowledge or information

(Foucault, 1972; Halliday & Martin, 1996; Luke, 2001). Even more important, knowledge production in the content areas needs to be understood as the result of human interaction. As such, knowledge production of the disciplines operates according to particular norms for everyday practice, conventions for communicating and representing knowledge and ideas, and ways of interacting, defending ideas, and challenging the deeply held ideas of others in the discipline. Disciplines, then, are no different as discourse communities than are students' everyday home discourse communities or peer group discourse communities. They are not immutable, they are not unchangeable, and they are not simply bodies of knowledge to be handed down from expert to novice.

Researchers working from the Cultural Navigation perspective argue that part of learning in the subject-matter area involves coming to understand the norms of practice for producing and communicating knowledge in the disciplines. Part of that learning also involves examining how subject-matter norms for practice are similar to and different from everyday norms for practice and that such practices are artifacts of human interaction rather than innate tendencies or processes inherent in the nature of the work. Such learning requires understanding deeply held assumptions or themes of the discipline (Lemke, 1990) as well as the ways of knowing, doing, and communicating in other discourse communities. More to the point, perhaps, this perspective argues that deep subject-matter learning is fostered by learning to be metadiscursive (see New London Group, 1996).

Another crucial task of subject-matter education from the Cultural Navigation version of disciplinary literacy pedagogy is one of teaching students not only the privileged discourses (see Delpit, 1988) but also when and why such discourses are useful, and how these discourses and practices came to be valued. For example, in Detroit middle-school science classrooms, teachers emphasize the scientific practices of data representation, analysis, and interpretation as they teach students how to write clear scientific explanations of phenomena (Moje, Peek-Brown, et al., 2004). Even as they engage in inquiry around the phenomena, these teachers help students learn the literate practices required to make scientific investigation meaningful. Together with students, for example, they have constructed criteria for producing scientific explanations, criteria that include (a) making a claim; (b) providing multiple pieces of evidence, drawn from experimentation or the past research of others; (c) reasoning through the evidence back to the claim; and (d) writing the explanation in precise and accurate language that "anyone interested in science should be able to understand." From the Cultural Navigation perspective, however, what we need to continue to develop is the scaffolding of students' understanding of when and why they would write in "precise and accurate language" (i.e., why precision matters in the cultural practices of science) and why those explanations are not the same explanations they might give to a friend on the street (i.e., why different kinds of precision, as well as different kinds of warrant, are valued among peers in everyday interaction; Moje, Peek-Brown, et al., 2004).

In other words, what is equally important to subject-matter learning and disciplinary literacy, from the Cultural Navigation perspective, is the act of providing opportunities for young people to examine how the norms of knowing, doing, and communicating are constructed. Each of these norms is not only an important aspect of doing the discipline but each norm also is socially constructed. That is, the norms are constructed, practiced, and enforced by people; they are not a set of immutable rules that can be questioned or changed. Indeed, members of the different disciplines and profession often reconstruct rules, especially in their day-to-day practices.

Many scholars have produced Cultural Navigation projects focused on disciplinary literacy with young students in classrooms across the United States (Fradd, Lee, Sutman, & Saxton, 2001; Gutiérrez et al., 1995; Gutiérrez et al., 1999; Gutiérrez et al., 2001; Gutiérrez & Rogoff, 2003; Heath, 1983; O. Lee & Fradd, 1998; Moll, 1992; Moll & Gonzalez, 1994; Moll & Greenberg, 1990; Warren, Ballenger, Ogonowski, Roseberry, & Hudicourt-Barnes, 2001; Warren, Rosebery, & Conant, 1989, 1994). These are important studies that have laid the groundwork for similar work at the secondary school subject-matter levels. The challenge for building on youth knowledge and connecting it to upper-grades disciplinary literacy learning, however, is not one to be underestimated. To date, the majority of the work done on connecting youth language and literacy practices to disciplinary language and literacy practices (not, I should underscore, connecting knowledge to knowledge but literacy to literacy) has been done in secondary English language arts and social studies (history or political science classrooms).

For example, Carol Lee (2001) is actively pursuing such pedagogical and curricular developments in her research program. Lee's construct of cultural modeling situates subject areas as cultures and seeks to tease out the demands of discourse in subject areas such as English. She then looks for spaces to link students' everyday discourses and practices specifically for the purpose of enhancing academic discourse and literate development. Studying in her own classroom, Lee demonstrated how a teacher with deep knowledge of students' backgrounds and ways with words could link those experiences and ways to the practices valued in the discipline.

C. D. Lee's earliest work (1993) documented gains in student learning when experimental groups whose everyday discursive practices (e.g., signifying, among other discourse practices) were leveraged to scaffold their learning of literary devices (e.g., metaphor, metonym, simile, irony) necessary for interpretation of canonical literature. These groups were compared to youth who were taught by learning the literary devices with no connection to their everyday means of interpreting and sense making, and Lee found that both the discursive skill and the abilities to interpret literature using mainstream literary devices of the experimental group were significantly superior to those of the control group.

In work that built on these findings, C. D. Lee (1995) analyzed the particular features of students' everyday discourse practices, examining how they mapped onto the discourse practices demanded for the reading of English literature, whether canonical or popular, and argued that drawing from students' existing discursive skill to scaffold the learning of disciplinary discursive and textual skill served as a form of "cognitive apprenticeship."

In more recent work (C. D. Lee, 2001, in press; C. D. Lee & Majors, 2003), Lee has argued that such work is actually "cultural modeling" in the sense that it serves as a way of mapping for students the connections and disjunctures between the discourse and text practices they know and value and those of another discourse community. In her work with Yolanda Majors (C. D. Lee & Majors, 2003), Lee maps the links between the discourse practices of a community hair salon and those of English classrooms to illustrate the possibilities for drawing on students' everyday culturally situated language, discourse, and text practices to produce socially just subject-matter pedagogy. Although Lee's applications of cultural modeling have been predominantly based in the English language arts disciplines, she argues that cultural modeling—or what I am calling disciplinary literacy as Cultural Navigation—can be applied to any subject-matter area but will first require a mapping of both youth cultural, text-based practices and disciplinary cultural, text-based practices.

Similarly, Ernest Morrell and colleagues (Morrell, 2002; Morrell & Collatos, 2003; Morrell & Duncan-Andrade, 2003) have demonstrated methods for enhancing what might be thought of as traditional print literacy and discursive skills while building critical literacy skills among adolescent learners. Morrell's work draws primarily from students' interests in and proficiencies with hip hop, popular film, and television and other available media texts to produce critical research projects. According to Morrell (2002), students who participated in his interventions around popular film "honed critical research skills, understood the relationship between literature, popular culture, and their everyday lives, and . . . translated their experiences in quality oral debates and expository pieces" (p. 75).

When engaging with television and media text, Morrell's research participants developed projects to examine mainstream media sources, completing interviews with representative mainstream media outlets. Morrell does not report findings in terms of standardized literacy or subject-matter gains but offers qualitative assessments of the students' developing agency and ability to think critically and take action, as well as their developing prowess with both popular everyday texts and the texts demanded by their secondary school classrooms. Morrell's work is situated primarily in the subject areas of English language arts and social studies.

Gutiérrez and colleagues (e.g., Gutiérrez, 2005) also have developed a prominent research agenda that revolves around developing third spaces that provide discursive bridges for young people to move back and forth from what Gutiérrez and colleagues refer to as the counterscripts of their everyday lives and funds of knowledge to the official scripts of the oral and written texts of their content classrooms. This research program has demonstrated that master teachers who can hear, understand, respect, and incorporate the counterscripts of youth can use those everyday language practices as resources for bridging and navigating the discourses of different disciplines to support student learning (Gutiérrez et al., 1995; Gutiérrez et al., 1999; Gutiérrez et al., 2001; Gutiérrez & Rogoff, 2003). Much of Gutiérrez's work, similar to Morrell's, is situated in the subject areas of the social studies and emphasizes critical action projects embedded in everyday life.

Very little work from a disciplinary literacy as Cultural Navigation perspective has been developed in upper-level science or mathematics. A number of important studies of cultural navigation from students' everyday knowledge to science knowledge have been conducted (e.g., Barton, 2001; Roth & Lee, 2005; Seiler, 2001; Yerrick, 2000), but these are not studies of making connections across text-based practices and processes. My own work offers a start at tracing the science-related everyday knowledge text practices of one group of youth in one large, urban area (Moje, Ciechanowski, et al., 2004), but our research explicitly notes the difficulty in making sustained connections from youth everyday knowledge to advanced science subject-matter learning and text practices in classrooms. Although my colleagues and I have offered a number of suggestions from our classroom and community-based research for providing opportunities to learn science text practices while also drawing on youth knowledge and text practices (Moje, Ciechanowski, et al., 2004; Moje, Collazo, Carrillo, & Marx, 2001; Moje & Hinchman, 2004; Moje, Peek-Brown, et al., 2004), these implications have yet to be tested in large-scale applications and the work of cultural navigation often takes a back seat to the work of learning science or specific disciplinary practices such as explanation writing.

The work of Greenleaf and colleagues in WestEd (Greenleaf, Schoenbach, Cziko, & Mueller, 2001) has been promising in that regard and is especially notable because it began with a focus on cognitive literacy strategies instruction and has begun to develop practices for cultural navigation as well. Similarly, although focused on younger groups of students, Warren, Rosebery, and colleagues at TERC (Rosebery, Warren, & Conant, 1992; Warren et al., 1989; Warren et al., 2001) have developed a number of culturally responsive, language-based science teaching practices that are compelling in regard to student engagement.

One notable exception to the focus on English language arts and social studies in connecting everyday to disciplinary literacy practices is the Algebra Project of Robert Moses and colleagues (Davis & West, 2000; Moses & Cobb, 2001; West & Davis, 2004). Moses uses the term "mathematical literacy" in what Norris and Phillips (2003) refer to as its derived sense, that is, in terms of building useable knowledge for the average citizen (rather than the elite knowledge of the mathematician). However, the work that Moses engages in with youth in the project draws on the mathematical symbol systems described by Bass (2006). The Algebra Project is unique, however, in its ability to provide students opportunities to navigate from multiple everyday semiotic forms to multiple mathematical forms. Consider, for example, this dynamic systems problem, described in West and Davis (2004):

Students construct a period-by-period record, in written and symbolic form, of the amounts of the drug taken, and the amounts of the drug in the body, then construct a symbolic form for the basic recursive relationship. Using graphing calculators, they plot the amount of the drug in the body at a particular interval compared to a previous interval (resulting in points that lie on a straight line) and plot the amount of the drug in the body over a sequence of intervals (resulting in points that approach a constant amount.) These activities are used to deepen students' understanding of linear relationship and introduce students to dynamic functions that reach steady state. (pp. 4–5)

According to Moses and Cobb (2001), the approach is situated in the idea that arithmetic, logic, and set theory are based in "regimentation of ordinary discourse." The curriculum follows what Moses refers to as a five-step process, much like that of the Language Experience Approach (Stauffer, 1965) in the sense that students are provided with group experiences and then discuss these experiences in ordinary language. These discussions often are bolstered by access to pictures, diagrams, and essays. Next, students' language is restructured into observational statements that can be tested for truth value and precision. These statements are eventually translated into the structures and symbolic representations used in conventional mathematics.

The variety of projects—and the routine application of such projects—allows Moses and teachers trained in the Algebra Project to mine students' experiences; to allow for ambiguity in language use as students develop the precision necessary for mathematical language use (Street, 2005); and to, over time, apprentice students into mathematical discourse and mathematically literate practice. The words *over time* are significant here; to date, the Algebra Project results are positive, with Jackson, Mississippi, Algebra Project students' pass rate on the mathematics portion of the state test improving from 33% to 55% when using the new materials and performing significantly better than non–Algebra Project students in the same school (West & Davis, 2005). Moses and colleagues predict that, with time, more students will perform at even higher levels.

Although each of these projects varies in important ways in theoretical and methodological orientations, the goals of the work are similar: to provide opportunities for children and youth to bridge, navigate, and/or reconstruct both everyday and academic discourses in ways that allow them to learn disciplinary concepts and literacy skills and practices, to achieve in school settings, and to make contributions to and changes in society. Just as with each of the other disciplinary literacy perspectives, Cultural Text Navigation has much to offer, but it also suffers from some weaknesses. Not surprisingly, these weaknesses are represented as strengths in the other perspectives. Specifically, Cultural Text Navigation perspectives tend to focus more on documenting and analyzing youth text and cultural practices and leave the text practices of the disciplines a bit more vague (Cultural Modeling and The Algebra Project stand as exceptions to this critique). The disciplines are clearly acknowledged in each perspective but close analyses are not typically offered as ways of clarifying for teachers and teacher educators how connections can be made from the everyday text practices of youth to the text practices they must engage in to learn at advanced levels in the disciplines. In addition, the focus on linguistic features of the discourse communities tends to be absent across these studies, with attention to language rendered in terms of discourse practices, or common ways of speaking, performing, reading, and writing, as opposed to specific examinations of the functional linguistic features of the text work done by youth and members of the disciplines.

DISCIPLINARY LITERACY PEDAGOGY

Toward Socially Just Subject-Matter Teaching for Social Justice

What can we conclude about the role that disciplinary literacy theory and research might play in developing subject-matter instruction that is not only socially just but also produces social justice? Based on this review, I would argue that the various forms of disciplinary literacy theory suggest implications for offering socially just, social justice subject-matter pedagogy. Disciplinary literacy theory and research—regardless of particular perspective—suggests possibilities for the development of rigorous subject-matter knowledge. This subject-matter knowledge is developed as a function of the development of ability to produce and represent knowledge in multiple forms, the ability to analyze how others have represented knowledge and therefore to assess truth claims, and with that analytic power in hand, the ability to challenge long-standing—even mainstream—claims to knowledge and, ultimately, to produce new knowledge that will benefit society. Moreover, certain forms of disciplinary literacy pedagogy bring together the focus on the tools for producing knowledge, expert subject-matter knowledge, and the knowledge that youth from a variety of backgrounds bring to their learning. But several issues need to be further examined for disciplinary literacy theory and research to inform the development of socially just, social justice subject-matter instruction.

First, subject-matter instruction that does not focus on the processes and practices involved in reading and writing disciplinary texts will not go far enough in developing a citizenry that can participate in decision making and in new knowledge production. It is not enough to talk about developing disciplinary literacy as useable knowledge for the average citizen. Producing and assessing knowledge in the disciplines and in everyday life relies heavily on one's ability to access, interpret, critique, and produce texts, both oral and written, on both paper and electronic media. Those youth who come to school with high levels of fundamental literacy skill (see Norris & Phillips, 2002) across a range of textual media will be more likely to participate not only in advanced disciplinary study but also in civic conversations and activities driven by the natural and social sciences, by mathematical processes, and by themes and concepts informed via the study of literature (not to mention the domains of visual arts, music, and sports and fitness). Across these different perspectives, scholars agree that knowing how to connect disciplinary knowledge to everyday knowledge is necessary but not sufficient for full societal access. People need to be able to navigate across disciplinary and everyday forms of representation, including print, numerals, and other inscribed symbols.

Second, disciplinary literacy pedagogy is not uniformly conceived; there are many different approaches to disciplinary literacy theory, research, and concomitant pedagogy, including a focus on (a) offering youth cognitive strategies to support comprehension and composition of complex texts; (b) uncovering and apprenticing youth to epistemological or cognitive processes of members of a given discipline; (c) teaching rhetorical and linguistic analysis and practices, with an emphasis on how language and thinking work within disciplinary traditions; and (d) revealing the cultural practices—or conventions and norms of the discipline—that mediate the cognitive processing work of disciplinary knowledge production and apprenticing youth to those practices by linking youth cultural practices and cognitive processes to those of the discipline.

Each of these four perspectives is represented by a burgeoning theoretical and research literature (of which I have barely scratched the surface). Yet, a number of questions remain for disciplinary literacy theorists and researchers, questions that represent promising areas for further study. The first question to consider is whether these four perspectives could be productively merged to afford the greatest possibility for socially just, social justice subject-matter (and literacy) learning. Consider an analysis made by one 16-year-old youth, Yolanda, when asked what made reading her school science text difficult, as part of an interview on literacy practices in and out of school:

Y: School books are really boring. They don't make sense. Like the biology book. You read the whole section and you're like, okay, you gotta read it four times just to understand it a little bit. It's confusing.
E: You can imagine everything and just fill in the blanks when you read [those] novels. But why can't you imagine what's going on when you're reading a school text?
Y: It's just written **the way adults read it**. . . . And they have the **knowledge** to do that . . . And they write it in **their own little language**. Like you said, there's different ways to write a sentence. . . . Well, they write it in **their language that only them can understand** because they graduated they have a diploma and everything. And we don't get that. The **words are big** that you're like, "Okay." You gotta go look it up. . . . You read the word and you try to **translate it in Spanish**. . . . And you try to translate it and you can't. . . . It's like, oh, it gives you a head ache . . . so it gets you brain dead. (Moje, 2006, p. 12)

This young woman was able to acknowledge the role that a number of factors play in her struggle to read—and be motivated by—school science texts: She named prior and expert knowledge, the linguistic and rhetorical styles of disciplinary experts ("the way adults read it"; "in their language that only them can understand"), the technical vocabulary of texts, the challenges of crossing two national languages, and motivation and interest, each a factor considered separately by the different research traditions reviewed here. Even more interesting, in earlier comments this same young woman offered a contrasting view of her out-of-school reading of texts steeped in topics she cared about and understood, written in language conventions she could access. She acknowledged the important role her mother played in her out-of-school reading, stating that her mother helped her read "words soooo big" (Moje, 2006, p. 12), underscoring the importance of the kind of social relationships and cultural (and linguistic) modeling Carol Lee refers to in her cultural modeling framework.

Just as Yolanda has done, disciplinary literacy researchers might consider weaving these foci together to contribute to deep subject-matter learning for social justice. By deep subject-matter learning, I refer to the kind of learning that not only provides opportunities for youth to learn with proficiency the established knowledge of a given field or disciplines but that also encourages youth to question, critique, and produce new knowledge within the disciplines. In addition, a socially just social justice pedagogy provides opportunities for such knowledge development without dismissing the value of students' everyday processes and practices.

A third question revolves around the effects of these different approaches to disciplinary literacy/subject-matter teaching. As illustrated in the review of the different approaches, although the theoretical and research literature on disciplinary literacy is extensive, it is scattered. In addition, although the studies are empirical, much of the writing is largely theoretical, making arguments for why the field should focus on literacy learning in the disciplines. What's more, within each of the four perspectives reviewed here, different (and sometimes multiple) methods and practices were studied. Finally, with the exception of the cognitive literacy strategies perspectives (studied mainly among primary grade children), very few studies of applications of these perspectives with young people in classrooms demonstrated learning gains in any standard way. In fact, a number of studies did not provide in-depth description of research methods, instruments, or procedures for measuring effects or of sample sizes. Thus, it is difficult to make definitive claims about the effects on student learning (across multiple dimensions) as a result of the research on disciplinary literacy. Although I was able to document exceptions to this concern (e.g., most of the cognitive literacy studies, Brian Hand's studies, Carol Lee's 1993 study, and the work of the Algebra Project), more work needs to be done to study effects, whether effects on the learning of mainstream conceptions of subject matter, critical stances on subject matter, conventional literacy skills, or critical literacy skills.

Unfortunately, the lack of studies of effects is most notable in the Cultural Navigation perspective; if, as many scholars who work from Cultural Navigation perspectives would be likely to argue, this perspective has the most power for developing the literacy skills and subject-matter learning of marginalized youth, then those of us who work from this perspective need to find ways to document the effects of Cultural Navigation practices. This is a challenging call because standard assessments typically do not measure the kinds of learning that Cultural Navigation purports to develop. Yet, these perspectives will not gain traction if researchers cannot document their positive impact in some way. In other words, disciplinary literacy researchers face a serious challenge to develop methods for documenting growth in innovative ways. In doing so, across all the disciplinary literacy perspectives, care needs to be taken to document the methods of research, including participant populations, temporal contexts of the work (was the study for a unit, a lesson, a year?), and instrumentation for analyzing student learning. In short, the field needs more studies that report studies and effects in precise and systematic ways.

A final question to consider is whether we really know enough about the literate processes and practices of the disciplines and of youth and their cultural groups to teach disciplinary literacy and to study the effects of such practice. The work of a number of literacy and disciplinary scholars reviewed here has paved the way for thinking about the literacy processes and practices of the disciplines; however, we need a more carefully detailed archaeology of the disciplinary practices, one that mines both the cognitive processes and the cultural practices that mediate those processes. Carol Lee (2005) has begun to develop such a framework for English literature as a discipline. However, the scope of such an enterprise suggests that this is not work for one scholar alone. The work that needs to be done is not only theoretical; empirical studies of how members of the disciplines communicate and think about their communication—similar to the work of Yore et al. (2002)—would do much to advance this field for developing work related to preservice teacher education (see also Hynd-Shanahan & Shanahan, in press). Drawing from this review and from similar questions posed to historians by Leinhardt (1994), some questions to consider posing to members of the disciplines in such studies might include how language is used in the work of the disciplines (e.g., as a mathematician, a historian, a literary theorist or writer, a chemist), the types of texts used or produced as part of their work, and the purposes for using or producing such texts. Questions also should examine audiences for disciplinary work; standards for warrant; and taboo words, phrases, or writing styles. Finally, it would be useful to ask what disciplinarians consider critical for novices to learn about the discipline.

Another valuable direction in empirical studies would revolve around how secondary subject-matter teachers, subject-matter teacher educators, and even youth themselves conceive of literate processes and practices in the subject-matter areas they teach. Similar questions to those offered for members of the discipline could guide survey, interview, or observational studies of what teachers, students, and teacher educators think about when they think of literacy teaching and learning in the discipline. In particular, it would be important to probe teachers regarding the kinds of texts they turn to or produce when teaching in their content areas and regarding their purposes for turning to or producing such texts. Such interviews also could raise questions about establishing purposes for disciplinary reading or writing for students and discussion of the teacher's role and responsibility, as well as challenges, in supporting student learning about disciplinary literacy and in developing students' literacy skills.

Finally, a parallel study might involve posing virtually the same set of questions—modified appropriately—to youth in relation to particular aspects of their everyday lives. That is, even as we need an archaeology of the disciplines, we also need deeper and broader understandings of youth cultures if disciplinary literacy pedagogy is to be both just and transformative. Although a number of excellent studies of youth culture are offered in the literature, most work on youth cultural practices is ethnographic in orientation and thus focuses on small groups of young people. Youth culture and youth literacy researchers are in danger of essentializing all young people on the basis of deep studies of a few. We thus need to continue to conduct youth cultural research using ethnography, focusing on practices and texts of ethnic and racial groups, families and communities, youth or peer groups, and popular culture, so that we can better link youth practices, content knowledge, and interest to those of the disciplines to produce deep, just, and transformative subject-matter instruction. But we need to develop connections among those ethnographic studies, seeking to understand how the local can be understood globally (Brandt & Clinton, 2002) and how such understandings—without essentializing—might inform practice in secondary school subject-matter areas. Modeled on the questions for members of the disciplines, questions for youth would ask how and why youth use reading and writing in their daily lives, how they set purposes for everyday reading, who are the audiences for their writing, if certain words or practices are considered taboo, and when and how they know to code switch across discourse boundaries. Sharing similar questions across ethnographic studies will enable the field to build strong youth cultural and literacy theories that can inform practice.

Documenting the points of departure and similarity in how language and text practices are engaged for a range of purposes across a range of contexts and a range of young people could move the field closer to implications for developing subject-matter pedagogy that builds on youth knowledge and their motivation to engage in text practices while also moving them forward to learning the ways of engaging with texts in other discourse communities and learning ways to change the texts and knowledge of their own and other communities. Such practice is not only socially just but also produces social justice as youth learn to navigate boundaries and question taken-for-granted knowledge, processes, and practices of different discourse communities.

In sum, scholars operating from any one of the disciplinary literacy perspectives work from the stance that to learn deeply in a subject matter, young people need to have access to the way that conventions of disciplinary knowledge production and communication can be routinely or more explicitly challenged and reshaped by other forms or practices of knowing; such knowledge gives young people the power to read critically across various texts and various disciplines. Such knowledge also gives them the power to draw from other funds of knowledge and discourse to raise challenges to what they learn in the disciplines. The more they interrogate their practices across all the funds, networks, or discourse communities they encounter in and out of school, the more youth can become critical readers and thinkers. It seems equally likely that the more the field can integrate the findings and pedagogical implications from the range of disciplinary literacy perspectives reviewed here, the better our chances of teaching with integrity. In this case, teaching with integrity involves developing secondary school subject-matter pedagogy that is socially just in its provision of opportunities to learn how to make sense of and produce the texts of different subject areas and teaches social justice as teachers guide youth in critiquing, challenging, and constructing knowledge in those disciplines and in everyday life.

NOTE

[1] These scholars do not necessarily identify as disciplinary literacy researchers. Indeed, they tend to operate as disciplinary specialists or as psychologists of learning. I have taken the liberty of identifying them as disciplinary literacy specialists because of their sustained attention to the texts and literate processes of the disciplines.

REFERENCES

Afflerbach, P., & VanSledright, B. (2001). Hath! Doth! Middle graders reading innovative history text. *Journal of Adolescent & Adult Literacy, 44*(8), 696–707.

Akkus, R., Gunel, M., & Hand, B. (in press). Comparing an inquiry based approach known as the science writing heuristic to traditional science teaching practices: Are there differences? *International Journal of Science Education.*

Alvermann, D. E., & Hagood, M. C. (2000). Fandom and critical media literacy. *Journal of Adolescent & Adult Literacy, 43*(5), 436–446.

Alvermann, D. E., Moon, J., & Hagood, M. (1999). *Popular culture in the classroom: Teaching and researching critical media literacy.* Newark, DE: International Reading Association/National Reading Conference.

Alvermann, D. E., & Moore, D. W. (1991). Secondary school reading. In R. Barr, M. L. Kamil, P. B. Mosenthal, & P. D. Pearson (Eds.), *Handbook of reading research* (Vol. 2, pp. 951–983). New York: Longman.

Anderson, J. D. (1986). Secondary school history textbooks and the treatment of Black history. In D. C. Hine (Ed.), *The state of Afro-American history: Past, present, and future* (pp. 253–274). Baton Rouge: Louisiana State University Press.

Anderson, T. H., & Armbruster, B. B. (1984). Content area textbooks. In R. C. Anderson, J. Osborne, & R. J. Tierney (Eds.), *Learning to read in American schools: Basal readers and content texts* (pp. 193–226). Hillsdale, NJ: Lawrence Erlbaum.

Anyon, J. (1981). Social class and school knowledge. *Curriculum Inquiry, 11*, 1–42.

Anyon, J. (1997). *Ghetto schooling: A political economy of urban education reform.* New York: Teachers College Press.

Bain, R. (2000). Into the breach: Using research and theory to shape history instruction. In P. Seixas, P. Stearns, & S. Wineberg (Eds.), *Teaching, learning and knowing history: National and international perspectives* (pp. 331–353). New York: New York University Press.

Bain, R. (2006). Rounding up unusual suspects: Facing the authority hidden in the history classroom. *Teachers College Record, 108*(10), 2080–2114.

Bain, R. B., & Ellenbogen, K. M. (2001). Placing objects within disciplinary perspectives: Examples from history and science. In S. Paris (Ed.), *Perspectives on object-centered learning in museums* (pp. 153–170). Hillsdale, NJ: Lawrence Erlbaum.

Ball, D., & Wilson, S. (1996). Integrity in teaching: Recognizing the fusion in the moral and intellectual. *American Educational Research Journal, 33*(1), 155–192.

Barton, A. C. (2001). Science education in urban settings: Seeking new ways of praxis through critical ethnography. *Journal of Research in Science Teaching, 38*(8), 899–917.

Bass, H. (2006). *What is the role of oral and written language in knowledge generation in mathematics? Toward the improvement of secondary school teaching and learning. Integrating language, literacy, and subject matter.* Ann Arbor: University of Michigan Press.

Bean, T. (2000). Reading in the content areas: Social constructivist dimensions. In M. L. Kamil, P. B. Mosenthal, P. D. Pearson, & R. Barr (Eds.), *Handbook of reading research* (Vol. 3, pp. 629–644). Mahwah, NJ: Lawrence Erlbaum.

Biancarosa, G., & Snow, C. E. (2004). *Reading next: A vision for action and research in middle and high school literacy. A report to the Carnegie Corporation of New York.* Washington, DC: Alliance for Excellent Education.

Blumenfeld, P. C., Marx, R. W., Patrick, H., & Krajcik, J. S. (1997). Teaching for understanding. In B. J. Biddle, T. L. Good, & I. F. Goodson (Eds.), *International handbook of teachers and teaching* (pp. 819–878). Dordrecht, the Netherlands: Kluwer Academic.

Borasi, R., & Siegel, M. (2000). *Reading counts: Expanding the role of reading in mathematics classrooms.* New York: Teachers College Press.

Borasi, R., Siegel, M., Fonzi, J., & Smith, C. (1998). Using transactional reading strategies to support sense-making and discussions in mathematics classrooms. *Journal for Research in Mathematics Education, 29*(3), 275–305.

Brandt, D., & Clinton, K. (2002). Limits of the local: Expanding perspectives on literacy as a social practice. *Journal of Literacy Research, 34*, 337–356.

Brown, A. L., & Palincsar, A. (1982). Inducing strategic learning from texts by means of informed, self-control training. *Topics in Learning and Learning Disabilities, 2*(1), 1–17.

Bulgren, J., Deshler, D. D., & Lenz, B. K. (in press). Engaging adolescents with learning disabilities in higher-order thinking about history concepts. *Journal of Learning Disabilities.*

Ciechanowski, K. E. M. (2006). *The everyday meets the academic: How bilingual Latino/a third graders use sociocultural resources to learn in science and social studies.* Unpublished doctoral dissertation, University of Michigan, Ann Arbor.

Civil, M., & Bernier, E. (2006). Exploring images of parental participation in mathematics education: Challenges and participation. *Mathematical Thinking and Learning, 8*(3), 309–330.

Coffin, C. (2006) *Historical discourse: The language of time, cause and evaluation.* London, UK: Continuum.

Collatos, A., Morrell, E., Nuno, A., & Lara, R. (2004). Critical sociology in K–16 early intervention: Remaking Latino pathways to higher education. *Journal of Hispanic Higher Education, 3*(2), 164–180.

Collins, K. M., Palincsar, A. S., & Magnusson, S. J. (2005). Science for all: A discursive analysis examining teacher support of student thinking in inclusive classrooms. In R. Yerrick & W. M. Roth (Eds.), *Establishing scientific classroom discourse communities: Multiple voices of teaching and learning research* (pp. 199–224). Mahwah, NJ: Lawrence Erlbaum.

Conley, M. (in press). *Content area literacy: Learners in context.* New York: Allyn and Bacon.

Davis, F. E., & West, M. M. (2000). *The impact of the algebra project on mathematics achievement.* Cambridge, MA: Lesley College, Program Evaluation & Research Group.

Delpit, L. D. (1988). The silenced dialogue: Pedagogy and power in educating other people's children. *Harvard Educational Review, 58,* 280–298.

Duschl, R. (2005). Foreword. In R. Yerrick & W. M. Roth (Eds.), *Establishing scientific classroom discourse communities: Multiple voices of teaching and learning research* (pp. ix–xi). Mahwah, NJ: Lawrence Erlbaum.

Edwards, L., & Eisenhart, M. (2002, November). *Middle school Latinas studying science: Using valued identities to enhance engagement.* Paper presented at the American Anthropological Association, New Orleans, LA.

Eisenhart, M., Finkel, E., & Marion, S. F. (1996). Creating conditions for scientific literacy: A re-examination. *American Educational Research Journal, 33*(2), 261–295.

Elmesky, R. (2001). *Struggles of agency and structure as cultural worlds collide as urban African American youth learn physics.* Unpublished doctoral dissertation, Florida State University, Tallahassee.

Foucault, M. (1972). *The archaeology of knowledge and the discourse on language.* New York: Pantheon Books.

Fradd, S. H., Lee, O., Sutman, F. X., & Saxton, M. K. (2001). Promoting science literacy with English language learners through instructional materials development: A case study. *Bilingual Research Journal, 25*(4), 479–501.

Gee, J. P. (1996). *Social linguistics and literacies: Ideology in discourses* (2nd ed.). London: Falmer.

Gee, J. P. (2005). Language in the science classroom: Academic social languages as the heart of school-based literacy. In R. Yerrick & W. M. Roth (Eds.), *Establishing scientific classroom discourse communities: Multiple voices of teaching and learning research* (pp. 19–37). Mahwah, NJ: Lawrence Erlbaum.

Goldman, S. R. (1997). Learning from text: Reflections on the past and suggestions for the future. *Discourse Processes, 23,* 357–398.

Gonzalez, N., Moll, L. C., & Amanti, C. (2005). *Funds of knowledge: Theorizing practices in households, communities, and classrooms.* Hillsdale, NJ: Lawrence Erlbaum.

Greene, S. (1994). Students as authors in the study of history. In G. Leinhardt, I. L. Beck, & C. Stainton (Eds.), *Teaching and learning in history* (pp. 137–171). Hillsdale, NJ: Lawrence Erlbaum.

Greenleaf, C., Schoenbach, R., Cziko, C., & Mueller, F. L. (2001). Apprenticing adolescent readers to academic literacy. *Harvard Educational Review, 71*(1), 79–129.

Guthrie, J. T., Meter, P. Z., McCann, A., Wigfield, A., Bennett, L., Poundstone, C., et al. (1996). Growth in literacy engagement: Changes in motivations and strategies during con-cept-oriented reading instruction. *Reading Research Quarterly, 31,* 305–325.

Guthrie, J. T., Wigfield, A., & Perencevich, K. C. (2004). *Motivating reading comprehension: Concept-oriented reading instruction.* Mahwah, NJ: Lawrence Erlbaum.

Gutiérrez, K. D. (2005). *Rethinking educational policy for English learners.* Washington, DC: Aspen Institute Congressional Forum.

Gutiérrez, K. D., Baquedano-Lopez, P., & Alvarez, H. H. (2001). Literacy as hybridity: Moving beyond bilingualism in urban classrooms. In M. L. Reyes & J. J. Halcon (Eds.), *The best for our children: Critical perspectives on literacy for Latino students. Language and lit-eracy series* (pp. 122–141). New York: Teacher's College Press.

Gutiérrez, K. D., Baquedano-López, P., Alvarez, H., & Chiu, M. M. (1999). Building a cul-ture of collaboration through hybrid language practices. *Theory Into Practice, 38*(2), 87–93.

Gutiérrez, K. D., & Rogoff, B. (2003). Cultural ways of learning: Individual traits or reper-toires of practice. *Educational Researcher, 32*(5), 19–25.

Gutiérrez, K. D., Rymes, B., & Larson, J. (1995). Script, counterscript, and underlife in the classroom: James Brown versus Brown v. Board of Education. *Harvard Educational Review, 65,* 445–471.

Gutstein, E. (2006). "The real world as we have seen it": Latino/a parents' voices on teaching mathematics for social justice. *Mathematical Thinking and Learning, 8*(3), 331–358.

Halliday, M. A. K., & Martin, J. R. (1996). *Writing science.* London: Taylor & Francis.

Halliday, M. A. K., & Matthiessen, C. M. I. M. (2004). *An introduction to functional gram-mar* (3rd ed.). London: Arnold.

Hand, B., Hohenshell, L., & Prain, V. (2004). Exploring students' responses to conceptual questions when engaged with planned writing experiences: A study with year 10 science students. *Journal of Research in Science Teaching, 41,* 186–210.

Hand, B., Pain, V., Lawrence, C., & Yore, L. D. (1999). A writing in science framework designed to enhance science literacy. *International Journal of Science Education, 21*(10), 1021–1035.

Hand, B., Prain, V., & Yore, L. D. (2001). Sequential writing tasks' influence on science learning. In P. Tynjala, L. Mason, & K. Lonka (Eds.), *Writing as a learning tool: Integrating theory and practice* (pp. 105–129). Dordrecht, the Netherlands: Kluwer.

Hand, B., Wallace, C., & Yang, E. (2004). Using the science writing heuristic to enhance learning outcomes from laboratory activities in seventh grade science: Quantitative and qualitative aspects. *International Journal of Science Education, 26,* 131–149.

Hand, B., Yang, O. E. M., & Bruxvoort, C. (in press). Using writing-to-learn science strate-gies to improve year 11 students' understandings of stoichiometry. *International Journal of Science Education.*

Heath, S. B. (1983). *Ways with words: Language, life, and work in communities and classrooms.* Cambridge, UK: Cambridge University Press.

Herber, H. L. (1970). *Teaching reading in the content areas.* Englewood Cliffs, NJ: Prentice Hall.

Hull, G., & Schultz, K. (Eds.). (2002). *School's out! Bridging out-of-school literacies with class-room practice.* New York: Teachers College Press.

Hynd-Shanahan, C., Holschuh, J. P., & Hubbard, B. P. (2004). Thinking like a historian: College students' reading of multiple historical documents. *Journal of Literacy Research, 36*(2), 141–176.

Hynd-Shanahan, C., & Shanahan, T. (in press). Content area reading/learning: Flexibility in knowledge acquisition. In K. B. Cartwright (Ed.), *Flexibility in literacy processes and instruc-tional practice: Implications of developing representational ability for literacy teaching and learning.* New York: Guilford.

Johns, A. M., & Swales, J. M. (2002). Literacy and disciplinary practices: Opening and clos-ing perspectives. *Journal of English for Academic Purposes, 1,* 13–28.

Ladson-Billings, G. (1994). *The dreamkeepers.* San Francisco: Jossey-Bass.

Ladson-Billings, G., & Tate, W. (1995). Toward a critical race theory of education. *Teachers College Record, 97,* 47–68.

Ladson-Billings, G. J. (1999). Preparing teachers for diverse student populations: A critical race theory perspective. In A. Iran-Nejad & P. D. Pearson (Eds.), *Review of research in education* (Vol. 24, pp. 211–247). Washington, DC: American Educational Research Association.

Lee, C. D. (1993). *Signifying as a scaffold for literary interpretation: The pedagogical implications of an African American discourse genre* (Vol. NCTE Research Report, No 26). Urbana, IL: National Council of Teachers of English.

Lee, C. D. (1995). A culturally based cognitive apprenticeship: Teaching African American high school students skills in literary interpretation. *Reading Research Quarterly, 30*(4), 608–630.

Lee, C. D. (2001). Is October Brown Chinese? A cultural modeling activity system for under-achieving students. *American Educational Research Journal, 38*(1), 97–141.

Lee, C. D. (2005). Reconceptualizing disciplinary literacies and the adolescent struggling reader: Placing culture at the forefront. *National Reading Conference.*

Lee, C. D. (in press). Every good-bye ain't gone: Analyzing the cultural underpinnings of classroom talk. *Qualitative Studies in Education.*

Lee, C. D., & Majors, Y. (2003). Heading up the street: Localized opportunities for shared constructions of knowledge. *Pedagogy, Culture and Society, 11*(1), 49–68.

Lee, C. D., & Spratley, A. (2006). *Reading in the disciplines and the challenges of adolescent literacy.* New York: Carnegie Corporation.

Lee, O. (1999). Science knowledge, world views, and information sources in social and cultural contexts: Making sense after a natural disaster. *American Educational Research Journal, 36*(2), 187–219.

Lee, O., & Fradd, S. H. (1998). Science for all, including students from non-English language backgrounds. *Educational Researcher, 27*(3), 12–21.

Lee, S., & Roth, W. M. (2003). Science and the "good citizen": Community-based scientific literacy. *Science, Technology, and Human Values, 28*(3), 403–424.

Leinhardt, G. (1989). Math lessons: A contrast of novice and expert competence. *Journal for Research in Mathematics Education, 20*(1), 52–75.

Leinhardt, G. (1993). Weaving instructional explanations in history. *British Journal of Educational Psychology, 63,* 46–74.

Leinhardt, G. (1994). History: A time to be mindful. In G. Leinhardt, I. L. Beck, & C. Stainton (Eds.), *Teaching and learning in history* (pp. 209–255). Hillsdale, NJ: Lawrence Erlbaum.

Leinhardt, G., & Smith, D. (1984). Expertise in mathematics instruction: Subject matter knowledge. *Journal of Educational Psychology, 77,* 247–271.

Leinhardt, G., Stainton, C., & Virji, S. M. (1994). A sense of history. *Educational Psychologist, 29*(2), 79–88.

Leinhardt, G., & Young, K. M. C. (1996). Two texts, three readers: Distance and expertise in reading history. *Cognition and Instruction, 14*(4), 441–486.

Lemke, J. L. (1990). *Talking science: Language, learning, and values.* Norwood, NJ: Ablex.

Lemke, J. L. (2003). Mathematics in the middle: Measure, picture, gesture, sign, and word. In M. Anderson, A. Saenz-Ludlow, S. Zellweger, & V. V. Cifarelli (Eds.), *Educational perspective on mathematics as semiosis: From thinking to interpreting to knowing* (pp. 215–234). Ottawa, Ontario, Canada: Legas.

Luke, A. (2001). Foreword. In E. B. Moje & D. G. O'Brien (Eds.), *Constructions of literacy: Studies of teaching and learning in and out of secondary schools* (pp. ix–xii). Mahwah, NJ: Lawrence Erlbaum.

Mahiri, J. (1998). *Shooting for excellence: African American and youth culture in new century schools.* Urbana, IL: The National Council of Teachers of English.

Mahiri, J. (Ed.). (2003). *What they don't learn in school: Literacy in the lives of urban youth.* New York: Peter Lang.

McKeown, M. G., & Beck, I. L. (1994). Making sense of accounts of history: Why young students don't and how they might. In G. Leinhardt, I. L. Beck, & C. Stainton (Eds.), *Teaching and learning in history* (pp. 1–26). Hillsdale, NJ: Lawrence Erlbaum.

Moje, E. B. (1995). Talking about science: An interpretation of the effects of teacher talk in a high school classroom. *Journal of Research in Science Teaching, 32,* 349–371.

Moje, E. B. (2000). To be part of the story: The literacy practices of gangsta adolescents. *Teachers College Record, 102,* 652–690.

Moje, E. B. (2006, March). Integrating literacy into the secondary school content areas: An enduring problem in enduring institutions. *Toward the improvement of secondary school teaching and learning: Integrating language, literacy, and subject matter.* Adolescent Literacy Symposium, University of Michigan, Ann Arbor.

Moje, E. B., Ciechanowski, K. M., Kramer, K. E., Ellis, L. M., Carrillo, R., & Collazo, T. (2004). Working toward third space in content area literacy: An examination of everyday funds of knowledge and discourse. *Reading Research Quarterly, 39*(1), 38–71.

Moje, E. B., Collazo, T., Carrillo, R., & Marx, R. W. (2001). "Maestro, what is 'quality'?" Language, literacy, and discourse in project-based science. *Journal of Research in Science Teaching, 38*(4), 469–496.

Moje, E. B., & Hinchman, K. A. (2004). Developing culturally responsive pedagogy for adolescents. In J. Dole & T. Jetton (Eds.), *Adolescent literacy research and practice* (pp. 331–350). New York: Guilford.

Moje, E. B., Peek-Brown, D., Sutherland, L. M., Marx, R. W., Blumenfeld, P., & Krajcik, J. (2004). Explaining explanations: Developing scientific literacy in middle-school project-based science reforms. In D. Strickland & D. E. Alvermann (Eds.), *Bridging the gap: Improving literacy learning for preadolescent and adolescent learners in grades 4-12* (pp. 227–251). New York: Carnegie Corporation.

Moll, L. C. (1992). Literacy research in community and classrooms: A sociocultural approach. In R. Beach, J. L. Green, M. L. Kamil, & T. Shanahan (Eds.), *Multidisciplinary perspectives in literacy research* (pp. 211–244). Urbana, IL: National Conference on Research in English and National Council of Teachers of English.

Moll, L. C., & Gonzalez, N. (1994). Critical issues: Lessons from research with language-minority children. *Journal of Reading Behavior, 26*(4), 439–456.

Moll, L. C., & Greenberg, J. (1990). Creating zones of possibilities: Combining social contexts for instruction. In L. C. Moll (Ed.), *Vygotsky and education* (pp. 319–348). New York: Cambridge University Press.

Moll, L. C., Veléz-Ibañéz, C., & Greenberg, J. (1989). *Year one progress report: Community knowledge and classroom practice: Combining resources for literacy instruction* (IARP Subcontract No. L-10, Development Associates). Tucson: University of Arizona Press.

Moore, D. W., & Readence, J. E. (2001). Situating secondary school literacy research. In E. B. Moje & D. G. O'Brien (Eds.), *Constructions of literacy: Studies of teaching and learning in and out of secondary schools* (pp. 3–25). Mahwah, NJ: Lawrence Erlbaum.

Morrell, E. (2002). Toward a critical pedagogy of popular culture: Literacy development among urban youth. *Journal of Adolescent & Adult Literacy, 46,* 72–77.

Morrell, E., & Collatos, A. (2003, April). *Critical pedagogy in a college access program for students of color.* Paper presented at the American Educational Research Association, Chicago.

Morrell, E., & Duncan-Andrade, J. (2003). What they do learn in school: Hip-hop as a bridge to canonical poetry. In J. Mahiri (Ed.), *What they don't learn in school: Literacy in the lives of urban youth* (pp. 247–268). New York: Peter Lang.

Moses, R., & Cobb, C. E. (2001). *Radical equations: Civil rights from Mississippi to the Algebra Project.* Boston: Beacon Press.

New London Group. (1996). A pedagogy of multiliteracies: Designing social futures. *Harvard Educational Review, 66,* 60–92.

Nieto, S. (1994). Lessons from students on creating a chance to dream. *Harvard Educational Review, 64*, 392–426.

Norris, S. P., & Phillips, L. M. (2002). How literacy in its fundamental sense is central to scientific literacy. *Science Education, 87*, 224–240.

Norris, S. P., & Phillips, L. M. (2003). The public understanding of science information: Communicating, interpreting, and applying the science of learning. *Education Canada, 43*(2), 24–27, 43.

Ogle, D. M. (1986). K-W-L: A teaching model that develops active reading of expository text. *The Reading Teacher, 39*, 564–570.

Palincsar, A. S., & Brown, A. L. (1984). Reciprocal teaching of comprehension fostering and comprehension-monitoring activities. *Cognition & Instruction, 1*(2), 117–175.

Palincsar, A. S., & Magnusson, S. J. (2001). The interplay of first-hand and text-based investigations to model and support the development of scientific knowledge and reasoning. In S. M. Carver & D. Klahr (Eds.), *Cognition and instruction: 25 years of progress.* (pp. 152–193). Mahwah, NJ: Lawrence Erlbaum.

Parkinson, J., & Adendorff, R. (2004). The use of popular science articles in teaching scientific literacy. *English for Specific Purposes, 23*, 379–396.

Paxton, R. J. (1999). A deafening silence: History textbooks and the students who read them. *Review of Educational Research, 69*(3), 315–339.

Phelps, S. F. (2005). *Ten years of research on adolescent literacy, 1994-2004: A review* (No. ED-01-CO-0011). Naperville, IL: Learning Point Associates.

Rosebery, A., Warren, B., & Conant, F. (1992). Appropriating scientific discourse: Findings from language minority classrooms. *Journal of the Learning Sciences, 2*(1), 1–04.

Roth, W. M., & Lee, S. (2005, April). *Rethinking scientific literacy: From science education as propaedeutic to participation in the community.* Paper presented at the Annual Meeting of the American Educational Research Association, Seattle, WA. (ERIC Document Reproduction Service No. ED478153)

Rumelhart, D. (1994). Toward an interactive model of reading. In R. B. Ruddel, M. R. Ruddell, & H. Singer (Eds.), *Theoretical models and processes of reading* (4th ed., pp. 864–894). Newmark, DE: International Reading Association.

Rutherford, F. J., & Ahlgren, A. (1990). *Science for all Americans.* New York: Oxford University Press.

Saunders, S. (2006). I'm just a Black woman troubling the status quo. In C. A. Stanley (Ed.), *Faculty of color teaching in predominantly White colleges and universities* (pp. 283–298). Bolton, MA: Anker.

Schleppegrell, M. J., & Achugar, M. (2003). Learning language and learning history: A functional linguistics approach. *TESOL Journal, 12*(2), 21–27.

Schleppegrell, M. J., Achugar, M., & Oteíza, T. (2004). The grammar of history: Enhancing content-based instruction through a functional focus on language. *TESOL Quarterly, 38*(1), 67–93.

Schoenbach, R., Greenleaf, C., Cziko, C., & Hurwitz, L. (1999). *Reading for understanding: A guide to improving reading in middle and high school classrooms.* New York: Jossey-Bass.

Seiler, G. (2001). Reversing the "standard" direction: Science emerging from the lives of African American students. *Journal of Research in Science Teaching, 38*(9), 1000–1014.

Shulman, L. S. (1986). Those who understand: Knowledge growth in teaching. *Educational Researcher, 15*(2), 4–14.

Siegel, M., Borasi, R., & Fonzi, J. (1998). Supporting students' mathematical inquiries through reading. *Journal for Research in Mathematics Education, 29*(4), 378–413.

Snow, C. B. (2002). *Reading for understanding: Toward a research and development program in reading comprehension.* Santa Monica, CA: RAND.

Stauffer, R. G. (1965). A language experience approach. In J. A. Kerfoot (Ed.), *First grade reading programs, perspectives in reading No. 5.* Newark, DE: International Reading Association.

Street, B. (2005). The hidden dimensions of mathematical language and litearcy. *Language and Education, 19*(2), 136–141.

Sutherland, L. M., Moje, E. B., Cleveland, T. E., & Heitzman, M. (2006, April). *Incorporating literacy learning strategies in an urban middle school chemistry curriculum: Teachers' successes and dilemmas.* Paper presented at the American Educational Research Association, San Francisco.

Valdes, G. (1998). The world outside and inside schools: Language and immigrant children. *Educational Researcher, 27*(6), 4–18.

Valenzuela, A. (1999). *Subtractive schooling: U.S.-Mexican youth and the politics of caring.* Albany: State University of New York Press.

VanSledright, B. A., & Kelly, C. (1998). Reading American history: The influence of multiple sources on six fifth graders. *Elementary School Journal, 98*, 239–265.

Wade, S. E., & Moje, E. B. (2000). The role of text in classroom learning. In M. Kamil, P. B. Mosenthal, R. Barr, & P. D. Pearson (Eds.), *The handbook of research on reading* (Vol. 3, pp. 609–627). Mahwah, NJ: Lawrence Erlbaum.

Warren, B., Ballenger, C., Ogonowski, M., Rosebery, A., & Hudicourt-Barnes, J. (2001). Rethinking diversity in learning science: The logic of everyday languages. *Journal of Research in Science Teaching, 38*, 1–24.

Warren, B., Rosebery, A., & Conant, F. (1989). *Cheche Konnen: Science and literacy in language minority classrooms (Report No. 7305).* Cambridge, MA: Bolt, Beranek & Newman.

Warren, B., Rosebery, A., & Conant, F. (1994). Discourse and social practice: Learning science in a language minority classroom. In D. Spener (Ed.), *Adult biliteracy in the United States* (pp. 191–210). Washington, DC: Center for Applied Linguistics.

West, M. M., & Davis, F. E. (2004). *The Algebra Project at Lanier High School, Jackson, MS: Implementation and student outcomes.* Cambridge, MA: Program Evaluation & Research Group, Lesley College.

West, M. M., & Davis, F. E. (2005). *Research related to the Algebra Project's intervention to improve student learning in mathematics: Report to state of Virginia department of education.* Cambridge, MA: Program Evaluation & Research Group, Lesley University.

Wilson, S. M., & Wineburg, S. S. (1988). Peering at history through different lenses: The role of disciplinary perspectives in teaching history. *Teachers College Record, 89*(4), 525–539.

Wineburg, S. S. (1991). On the reading of historical texts: Notes on the breach between school and the academy. *American Educational Research Journal, 28*(3), 495–519.

Wineburg, S. S. (1998). Reading Abraham Lincoln: An expert/expert study in the interpretation of historical texts. *Cognitive Science, 22*(3), 319–346.

Wineburg, S. S. (2003). Teaching the mind good habits. *The Chronicle of Higher Education,* p. B20.

Wineburg, S. S., & Martin, D. (2004). Reading and rewriting history. *Educational Leadership, 62*(1), 62.

Wineburg, S. S., & Wilson, S. (1991). Models of wisdom in the teaching of history. *History Teacher, 24*(4), 395–412.

Yerrick, R. K. (2000). Lower track science students' argumentation and open inquiry instruction. *Journal of Research in Science Teaching, 37*(8), 807–838.

Yore, L. D., Bisanz, G. L., & Hand, B. M. (2003). Examining the literacy component of science literacy: 25 years of language arts and science research. *International Journal of Science Education, 25*(6), 689–725.

Yore, L. D., Hand, B. M., & Prain, V. (2002). Scientists as writers. *Science Education, 10*, 672–692.

Yore, L. D., & Treagust, D. F. (2006). Current realities and future possibilities: Language and science literacy. Empowering research and informing instruction. *International Journal of Science Education, 28*(2–3), 291–314.

Young, K. M., & Leinhardt, G. (1998). Writing from primary documents: A way of knowing in history. *Written Communication, 15*(1), 25.

Chapter 2

Resisting Unlearning: Understanding Science Education's Response to the United States's National Accountability Movement

SHERRY A. SOUTHERLAND
Florida State University

LEIGH K. SMITH
Brigham Young University

SCOTT P. SOWELL
Cleveland State University

JULIE M. KITTLESON
The University of Georgia

The assessment head for the state Department of Education (DOE) travels across town to present a lecture to the university's science education faculty. His talk is on the state's science assessment and what the inclusion of this assessment in determination of AYP (adequate yearly progress) will mean for the state's teachers. The room feels a bit uncomfortable because DOE staff and professors seldom speak, formally or informally. There is much handshaking and elaborate introductions as the faculty work to make the DOE representative comfortable and as he networks for possible resources. His PowerPoint begins with, "All of us here share an overriding goal . . ." The faculty nod, content that the DOE staff person is working to create a sense of community. He continues, " . . . and that goal is to increase the performance of students in our state . . ." A hand shoots up. The DOE staff person tries to continue but the shaking hand will not go down. "Yes?" he asks. The owner of the hand quickly responds, "I hate to disagree with you so quickly but increasing performance is NOT our goal. Our job is to help teachers develop the knowledge and skills needed to better help their students learn science. If performance on some measure goes up, well so much the better." He retorts, "But isn't learning and increased performance the same thing?"

The scenario described above highlights conflicts between the science education research community and the educational climate associated with No Child Left Behind (NCLB, 2001). Our goal in this chapter is to explain the apparent failure to communicate between science education researchers, policy makers, and staff at state and district offices of education. Each group is a stakeholder in K–12 education. Policy makers specify courses of action to meet the needs of an educational system, state and district staff

Review of Research in Education
March 2007, Vol. 31, pp. 45–77
DOI: 10.3102/0091732X06299015

work to implement these policies, and science education researchers examine educational systems with the hope of proposing changes to better support learning. Ideally, research would complement and inform policy. However, the failure-to-communicate scenario above exposes a fundamental incommensurability between current educational policy and science education research. The timing of our analysis is particularly fortuitous because science is the latest discipline to be included in AYP for NCLB.

We invoke the idea of first-order/second-order change as described by Cuban (1988) to explain this failure to communicate. First-order change requires small alterations of or additions to existing practices (e.g., changes in texts, number of students in a classroom, length of day, equipment), basically any attempt to increase the effectiveness and efficiency of current schooling practices. In contrast, second-order change is meant to alter the fundamental patterns of schooling; these changes are much more radical and transformative because they challenge the structures and rules that constitute traditional schooling practices. Second-order changes "challenge the cultural traditions of schools" (Romberg & Price, 1983, p.159) and require fundamental changes in both teacher thinking and classroom practice. Thus, they are inherently more difficult to implement and sustain.

We argue that the science education reform efforts that began in the mid-1980s represent an attempt to enact second-order change. In contrast, the policy community, via NCLB, simply calls for change without guidelines to support teaching and learning. To comply with NCLB requirements, school districts often take the most expedient and efficient routes rather than support the kinds of teaching and learning environments that support reform-oriented recommendations. For instance, in reaction to the upcoming NCLB inclusion of science, we have seen schools employ after-school and weekend tutoring sessions where students who are underperforming are drilled on content. Doing more of what is typically done is akin to a first-order response. In contrast, the science education research community might support a reformulation of instruction that entails pulling examples of content from students' out-of-school lives or asking them to produce metacognitive maps/journals based on inquiries they have performed. An issue that is particularly frustrating is that the first-order changes associated with policy implementation require substantial time, money, and energy and these requirements shift resources away from the second-order changes desired by researchers.

Increasing performance on standardized tests constitutes a measure of effectiveness for certain communities, and these communities may respond to NCLB by making the existing system more efficient in terms of improving student performance. Many science educators, on the other hand, look toward scientific literacy as a sign of effectiveness. The science education research community will not, and should not, reverse its focus on scientific literacy for all to more efficient performance on standardized tests. Scientific literacy entails construing effective science teaching as a practice that results in students' construction of applicable, meaningful, and useful knowledge. We argue that scientific literacy is a framework that is more compelling than the diluted versions of science teaching and learning inspired by NCLB.

Although science education researchers find themselves working within a climate of first-order changes, we argue that our community must resist unlearning what decades of empirical research have taught us about effective science teaching and learning. We argue that we cannot ignore the need for fundamental, second-order changes simply because we are faced with a push for more short-term, less substantive alterations in science teaching. Finally, we argue that it is not enough to work within the current climate of first-order changes; instead, science educators must take a more active role in helping states, districts, and producers of textbooks and assessments to make our call for fundamental, second-order change intelligible and compelling.

SCIENCE FOR ALL AMERICANS

For decades, there have been a number of calls to reform science teaching and learning. Typically, these calls have been in response to a real or rhetorically expedient crisis invoked by policy makers (Klopfer & Champagne, 1990). In the mid-1980s, the crisis in question was reported in *A Nation at Risk: The Imperative for Educational Reform* (National Commission on Excellence in Education [NCEE], 1983). The authors of this report argued that educational mediocrity was endangering American "preeminence in commerce, industry, science and technological innovation" (p. 1). The political climate at that time "encouraged both careful examination of how students learn science and the assumptions about what science knowledge is most valued by society" (Collins, 1998, p. 712).

Two groups, the American Association for the Advancement of Science (AAAS) and the National Science Teachers Association (NSTA) (working in conjunction with the National Research Council [NRC]), responded to the public plea for science education reform. These groups established visions for science learners; standards for content, teaching, and assessment; and descriptions of systemic changes needed to enact these standards. AAAS took the lead in defining scientific literacy as the preeminent goal of science education, as described in *Science for All Americans: Project 2061* (AAAS, 1989). The NSTA/NRC group authored the *National Science Education Standards* (NRC, 1996), which describes standards for science teaching, professional development, assessment, content, programs, and systems.

The efforts of these two groups coalesced on a number of points that characterize the most current reform efforts in science education:

1. The goal of science education is to "prepare people to lead personally fulfilling and responsible lives" (AAAS, 1989, p. xiii); thus, the ultimate goal is democratic, in which education is seen as preparing students to become responsible citizens.
2. Democratic equality in science can be achieved by ensuring that students become scientifically literate. As described in *National Science Education Standards* (NRC, 1996), science literacy

means that a person can ask, find, or determine answers to questions derived from curiosity about everyday experiences. . . . Scientific literacy implies that a person can identify scientific issues underlying national and local decisions and express positions that are scientifically and technologically informed. A literate citizen should be able to evaluate the quality of scientific information on the basis of its source and the methods used to generate it. (p. 22)

3. Acquiring scientific literacy is no longer thought to be the goal for a select segment of the student population: "The world has changed in such a way that science literacy has become necessary for everyone, not just a privileged few: science education will have to change to make that possible" (AAAS, 1989, p. xvi).
4. Inquiry is central to science education reform. Students should understand how scientific inquiries are conducted and how these processes shape the knowledge produced. In addition, a classroom incarnation of inquiry should be one of the fundamental means through which students' science learning is accomplished.
5. Students bring knowledge with them into the classroom and build from this knowledge to construct new scientific understandings. Student science learning can be difficult, requiring a great deal of energy and support.
6. Finally, the changes called for do not entail a quick fix. Rather, they will involve a slow, laborious process that will require a long-term, sustained effort.

These ideas have shaped the efforts of the science education research community during the past decade. For the purpose of this chapter, we focus on five strands of science education research: student science learning, inquiry, the nature of science, diversity, and teacher education. In the following sections, we briefly summarize the central ideas within each of these areas and then discuss how researchers working in each of these areas have responded or refused to respond to NCLB.

STUDENT SCIENCE LEARNING

Much of the research in student science learning, which lies at the heart of science education reform, centers on recognizing the difficulties students have in learning science. Take, for example, students' understandings of the relationship between the earth and the sun:

While growing up, children are told by adults that the "sun is rising and setting," giving them an image of a sun that moves about the earth. In school, students are told by teachers (years after they have already formed their own mental model of how things work) that the earth rotates. Students are then faced with the difficult task of deleting a mental image that makes sense to them, based on their own observations, and replacing it with a model that is not as intuitively acceptable. This task is not trivial, for students must undo a whole mental framework of knowledge that they have used to understand the world. (NRC, 1997, chapter 4, p. 3)

The difficulty students have in learning science does not result from their lack of understanding. Rather, students bring preconceived notions about natural phenomena to science classes. Their everyday ways of thinking are often at odds with the scientific explanation being promoted in the classroom. The difficulty involves changing or reshaping students' conceptions (Duschl, Schweingruber, & Shouse, 2007).

Students' alternative ways of understanding the world—typically referred to as "misconceptions," "alternative conceptions," or "children's science"—captured the attention of innumerable science educators for more than two decades. Two reviews of thousands of such studies summarize this research (Pfundt & Duit, 1994; Wandersee, Mintzes, & Novak, 1994). It is thought that if science educators understood the nature of students' conceptions, then they would be in a better position to revise them.

Science Learning As Conceptual Restructuring

Although there are notable exceptions (e.g., Hammer, 1996), researchers who view science learning as conceptual restructuring understand science knowledge to exist in conceptual frameworks. Using this image, a learner's knowledge of a particular domain is described as a network of interrelated conceptions. Learning is characterized as a series of cognitive restructurings in which a learner's conceptual framework undergoes structural modifications or revisions (Duit & Treagust, 2003). Thus, learning is seen as a change in a preexisting conceptual framework (Chi, 1992). These changes can include the simple incorporation of new ideas into existing knowledge structures, a process referred to as accretion, addition, or weak restructuring. In cases where the new concept contradicts a preexisting one, a radical restructuring is required. Much of the research on learning in science education has focused on instances of radical restructuring; indeed, the field has paid less attention to more accretionary additions.

The research on students' understandings of science largely falls around two general lines: Piagetian notions of the learner interacting with physical phenomena and Vygotskian notions of learners constructing understandings based on making sense of group interactions. Until recently, research on science learning has largely focused on how individual learners accommodate novel scientific explanations of natural phenomena. For example, the conceptual change model (CCM; Posner, Strike, Hewson, & Gertzog, 1982; Strike & Posner, 1992) describes the process of an individual's learning in terms of patterns of paradigmatic changes in science (T. Kuhn, 1970). According to the original CCM, learners are understood to logically evaluate the utility of their conceptions to account for data or evidence. If a learner is unable to account for anomalous data, then a second, competing conception is sought. The learner then evaluates the competing conceptions, experiencing change only if the new conception is found to be superior in accounting for all current and future data.

The CCM has been critiqued for its inability to adequately account for the diverse pathways students use to construct a scientific understanding (Pintrich, Marx, & Boyle, 1993; Strike & Posner, 1992) because it ignores learning processes that are not in alignment with Western, linear, logical patterns of thought. This critique was echoed in the work of a host of researchers who worked to push past the rational, logical, strictly cognitive confines of this model (Alsop, 2005; Demastes-

Southerland, Good, & Peebles, 1995). These authors explain that goals, emotions, dispositions, and motivations interact with cognitive constructs to play a significant role in shaping learning.

The Role of The Group in Conceptual Restructuring

Based on the need to go beyond individual psychological accounts of learning to generate a better understanding of the richness of the classroom context, the social constructivist perspective, informed by the work of Vygotsky, has gained favor as researchers direct their attention to the manner in which groups of students generate shared explanations for scientific phenomena (Kelly & Green, 1998; Kittleson & Southerland, 2004; Moje, Collazo, Carrillo, & Marx, 2001). Just as the conceptual change model draws persuasive power by its links to knowledge construction in science, this perspective draws momentum from the idea that science knowledge is socially constructed (Alexopoulou & Driver, 1996; Roth, 1993). The social constructivist perspective closely attends to how the group makes sense of phenomena, focusing on the social sphere and attending to the manner in which the negotiation of individual ideas contributes to group meaning making.

A goal of the social constructivist framework is to understand the discursive practices students use when engaged in science. This requires understanding "how knowledge is constructed and how discourse processes, social actions, and cultural practices shape what counts as knowing and doing within a particular group" (Kelly & Green, 1998, p. 146). Toward these ends, numerous studies closely analyze the events transpiring within science discussions (Bianchini, 1997; Shepardson & Britsch, 2006) and focus on how students' social interactions shape the knowledge the class constructs. Other studies have investigated how this class construction becomes assimilated by the individual (Moje & Shepardson, 1998; Southerland, Kittleson, Settlage, & Lanier, 2005).

Learning As Developing Science Practice

There is a growing emphasis on science learning as a process of socialization into the culture of science, where science is viewed as a unique culture with particular ways of knowing. The purpose of science instruction is to provide students with experiences in scientific activities to shape their appropriation of scientific practices (Driver, Asoko, Leach, Mortimer, & Scott, 1994). Within much of this research, learning science involves learning to talk science (Lemke, 1990), which means learning how to engage in activities such as constructing explanations, drawing inference from evidence, and weighing the utility of explanations against evidence (Duschl et al., 2007). Supporting students' scientific literacy skills in a fundamental sense (Norris & Phillips, 2003) entails helping students develop the ability to negotiate science texts and knowledgeably communicate within the language of science (Yore, Bisanz, & Hand, 2003). Indeed, some scholars argue that science learning should be conceived primarily in terms of argument because enculturation into scientific discourse affords participation in science (Driver, Newton, & Osborne, 2000).

What would second-order changes in the area of student learning include? Beginning lessons by assessing students' prior knowledge and using that knowledge to frame the lesson would be a useful beginning (Atkin, Black, & Coffey, 2001). Recognizing the need for sustained, focused, individual, and group sense-making opportunities, as advocated by science education researchers, also would suggest a very different flow of lessons instead of those that emphasize rote memorization of a broad scope of material. Ensuring that assessments include multiple modalities for students to demonstrate their knowledge and skills (Duschl & Gitomer, 1997) as well as opportunities for students to apply their new knowledge to real-world situations also would be a form of second-order change.

INQUIRY

Inquiry has long been a term employed to describe quality teaching and learning in science (NRC, 1996, 2000; Schwab, 1962), and inquiry is one of the cornerstones of the current round of science education reform. This trend is not surprising given that scientists played a prominent role in its articulation (Rudolph, 2002). Clearly, the authors of science education reform documents draw parallels between how science is conducted and how students learn science (NRC, 2000):

Scientific inquiry refers to the diverse ways in which scientists study the natural world and propose explanations based on the evidence derived from their work. Inquiry also refers to the activities of students in which they develop knowledge and understanding of scientific ideas, as well as an understanding of how scientists study the natural world. (p. 23)

Meaningful learning in science is facilitated when students employ some of the same strategies scientists use: observing, questioning, examining research to determine what is known, planning and conducting investigations, constructing explanations based on those investigations, and communicating what they have learned.

Defining Inquiry

Despite its prominence in current reform efforts, Settlage (2003) asserts that the term "inquiry" has been "one of the most confounding terms within science education" (p. 34). There are at least three different usages of the term inquiry (R. D. Anderson, 2002): (a) science as inquiry, (b) learning as inquiry (the fundamentals of which were discussed in the previous section), and (c) teaching as inquiry (also known as "classroom-based inquiry"). This section will focus on the first and third meanings of inquiry.

Perhaps the most familiar notion of inquiry is that of inquiry as an investigative process. In this usage, "inquiry refers to the diverse ways in which scientists study the natural world and propose explanations based on the evidence derived from their work" (NRC, 1996, p. 23). It is this use that harkens back to the scientific method that many people experienced as learners. However, the portrait of inquiry as conveyed in the reforms is fundamentally different than this lock-step method. Instead, when students come to learn about science as a process of inquiry, they learn how scientists go about constructing explanations of natural phenomena and come to recognize that these methods are appropriate for questions posed in their own lives (Flick, 2003).

Learning about inquiry is distinct from using inquiry to teach science content. Indeed, the most prolific use of inquiry in science education surrounds its use as a teaching approach, largely because it is described as the "central strategy" to be employed when teaching science (NRC, 1996, p. 31). In this vein, inquiry has been used to describe a wide variety of curriculum projects and programs (Moss, Abrams, & Robb-Kull, 1998; Rivet & Krajcik, 2004), teaching techniques (McCarthy, 2005), and overall approaches to teaching science (Druva & Anderson, 1983; Lott, 1983).

To further assist in recognizing inquiry-based teaching, the reforms attempt to describe its central features (NRC, 1996, 2000). Using these features, a classroom event is considered to be some form of inquiry if it allows learners to (a) engage with scientifically oriented questions; (b) place priority on evidence, allowing them to develop and evaluate explanations that address scientifically oriented questions; (c) draw inferences from evidence to formulate explanations that address scientifically oriented questions; (d) evaluate their explanations in light of possible alternatives; and (e) communicate and justify their explanations.

Another approach to understanding classroom-based inquiry focuses more on the nature of the task and less on what the students are engaged in doing. Chinn and Malhotra (2002) distinguish between the nature of simple and authentic inquiry experiences. Simple experiments involve investigating the effect of a single independent variable on a single dependent variable accompanied by careful observations and descriptions guided by a specified procedure. In contrast, authentic experiences are ones in which questions are not necessarily determined, there is often more than one variable, procedures must be designed, and there is usually a need for multiple studies. Chinn and Malhotra argue that complex, authentic inquiry experiences should become a priority in science classrooms.

The Benefits of Classroom-Based Inquiry

The benefits associated with classroom-based inquiry involve developing the ability to approach and answer questions in a reasoned manner (relating to epistemology), enhancing students' content knowledge, and improving students' attitudes toward science.

Epistemological understandings. Epistemology relates to the "grounds on which we base our decisions about the acceptance or rejection of scientific knowledge claims" (Duschl, 2000, p. 188). A host of science education researchers assert that students should understand the processes by which scientific content is advanced (e.g., Chinn & Malhotra, 2002; Duschl & Grandy, 2005) because epistemological understandings are thought to enable thinking critically, solving ill-structured problems, and making judgments about knowledge claims (King & Kitchener, 1994; D. Kuhn & Weinstock, 2002). Understanding epistemological aspects of scientific knowledge is equated with a deep understanding of science. Current thinking suggests complex, authentic inquiry experiences, such as those advocated by Chinn and Malhotra (2002), are needed to facilitate epistemological development.

Greater content learning and improved attitudes toward science. Another rationale for the focus on classroom-based inquiry is tied to understandings of learning (Bransford, Brown, & Cocking, 2000). This research suggests that instruction that is more inductive, in which students are actively involved in the construction of explanations, will result in more meaningful, retrievable, and applicable knowledge. Thus, one would expect that inquiry-based teaching would aid student learning. However, the effectiveness of inquiry in engendering student learning has been inconclusive, with some studies suggesting marked improvement in students' test scores, whereas others report no significant increase (Marx et al., 2004).

Despite the articulated benefits of inquiry teaching, altering the way science has traditionally been taught in classrooms by implementing classroom-based inquiry requires teachers to drastically reenvision science teaching and learning and to make second-order changes in their practice. Clearly, this has affected efforts to induce teachers to enact classroom-based inquiry as described by science education reformers, and the results of these efforts have been mixed. Although some teachers have readily accepted inquiry as a way of teaching (Crawford, 2000; L. K. Smith, 2005), others have been more reluctant to teach science as inquiry (Davis, 2002; Laplante, 1997, L. K. Smith, 2005), and still other classroom teachers remain uncertain as to how to enact these second-order changes in the way they teach science (L. K. Smith, 2005). Moreover, because of the wide variety of interpretations of what classroom inquiry might look like, we should not be surprised that multiple studies have documented both preservice and inservice teachers' struggle to understand and to implement inquiry teaching (Crawford, Zembal-Saul, Munford, & Friedrichsen, 2005; Lee, Hart, Cuevas, & Enders, 2004; Windschitl, 2004), a challenge that will be discussed further in a section that follows. Indeed, it must be recognized that some in our community see inquiry as such a nebulous construct that it has become a hindrance to our reform efforts (Settlage, 2003), suggesting that our definitions of inquiry must be reconceived in terms of student learning outcomes so as to eliminate much of the confusion surrounding this construct.

NATURE OF SCIENCE AND SCIENTIFIC EPISTEMOLOGIES

One of the most consistent messages in reform is that deep conceptual knowledge of science includes understanding the nature of science (NOS), that is, knowledge about science in contrast to scientific knowledge (Duschl, 1990). NOS instruction includes the cultural practices of science, its presuppositions, methodological assumptions, goals, and boundaries, as well as the conventions underlying knowledge produced through science (Poole, 1996; M. U. Smith & Scharmann, 1999). An understanding of NOS serves scientific literacy because if one is expected to make informed personal and societal decisions, one must understand how science works.

The following are put forth as central tenets necessary to understand scientific knowledge:

Scientific knowledge is tentative; empirical; theory-laden; partly the product of human inference, imagination, and creativity; and socially and culturally embedded, and knowing about science involves understanding the distinction between observation and inference, the lack of a universal recipe like method for doing science, and the functions of and relationships between scientific theories and laws. (Lederman, Abd-El-Khalick, Bell, & Schwartz, 2002, p. 499)

These tenets are not meant to codify conceptions of scientific knowledge or settle debates about the nature of knowledge. Rather, these tenets are meant to describe aspects of NOS that are important to know to be a literate citizen, particularly for formal K–12 schooling. Other researchers working in this realm focus on scientific epistemologies; they focus on how science is done and the nature of the knowledge it produces, but without a tight focus on the individual acquisition of a small group of concepts. Researchers who focus on scientific epistemologies often closely examine practice as a means to understand that epistemology (e.g., Hammer & Elby, 2003; Kelly, 2004; Kittleson, 2006; Sandoval, 2005). Both NOS and scientific epistemological efforts focus our attention on the importance of knowledge about science as opposed to the historically narrow focus on scientific knowledge.

Because NOS figures prominently into curricular reform, there has been a wealth of research into teaching and learning NOS, including a substantial amount of research on preservice and inservice teachers' conceptions of NOS (e.g., Abd-El-Khalick & Lederman, 2000; Southerland, Johnston, & Sowell, 2006). It is well established that NOS conceptions are difficult for students to fully understand and that most teachers do not hold a sophisticated understanding of the nature of science (e.g., Abd-El-Khalick, 2001; Johnston, 2001; Lederman, 1992; Southerland, Gess-Newsome, & Johnston, 2003). Researchers argue that preservice and inservice teachers should explicitly and reflectively engage with NOS, and many researchers have designed activities (Cobern & Loving, 1998; Lederman & Abd-El-Khalick, 1998; M. U. Smith & Scharmann, 1999) as well as entire courses that target NOS conceptions (Loving & Foster, 2000; Southerland et al., 2006).

Research Instruments and NOS

Despite its prominence in reform, science educators continue to struggle with how to validly assess NOS knowledge. NOS assessments of the 1970s and 1980s were characterized by Likert-style, forced-choice questions (i.e., Aikenhead, Ryan, & Fleming, 1989; Rubba & Anderson, 1978). Lederman and O'Malley (1990), however, challenged paper-and-pencil assessments of learners' NOS conceptions, arguing that written means of expression mask students' underlying ideas. Lederman,

Wade, and Bell (1998) later explained that forced-choice multiple choice measures impose various portrayals of NOS onto participants and that qualitative measures provide the most appropriate descriptions of learners' NOS conceptions. Thus, much current NOS research relies heavily on qualitative assessment of learners' conceptions (via written responses and interviews). However, recently, researcher have begun to question the validity of a sole reliance on such interview strategies (Southerland, Johnston, Sowell, & Settlage, 2005). Other instruments designed to assess NOS understandings have been developed (e.g., Chen, 2006) and are essential for the continued development of this strand of research.

DIVERSITY

A resounding message of reform-oriented education is the following: "Science in our schools must be for all students: All students, regardless of age, sex, cultural or ethnic background, disabilities, aspirations, or interest and motivation in science, should have the opportunity to attain high levels of scientific literacy" (NRC, 1996, p. 20). Simply put, if our goal is that every student attains a useful level of scientific literacy, then we must come to better understand how to teach all students, particularly those who come from marginalized, traditionally underserved groups who tend to underperform on standardized measures of science learning (Kober, 2001; Norman, Ault, Bentz, & Meskimen, 2001). Traditional classroom practices, however, often share a genealogy with mainstream, middle-class, White populations. Science educators who focus on diversity examine what this means for teaching and learning science, especially for students of color, students whose first language is not English, and students who live in poverty. Given the existing achievement gaps for non-mainstream students, the research community continues to explore the best ways to engender scientific literacy for culturally, linguistically, and socioeconomically diverse student groups.

Although reform calls for science for all, scholars posit that reform documents themselves are largely blind to student and teacher difference. Science education researchers have taken up the task of exploring how the standards could actually be implemented within a multicultural theoretical framework. According to Rodriguez (1998), "the basic premise of multiculturalism is that all learners at any grade level must be provided with equitable opportunities for success" (p. 591). The distinction between equal and equitable science education is a fundamental one. Reform is not pushing us toward a "one size fits all" (Lynch, 2001) approach to the teaching and learning of science. Rather, it encourages equitable science teaching and learning. "Equitable instruction and assessment practices for diverse students involve consideration of their cultural and linguistic experiences in preparing them to function competently in the institutions of power as well as in their homes and communities" (Lee, 2001, pp. 499-500). This suggests that there is a need for teachers to be aware of who they are teaching, knowing the critical intersections between Western science, school science, and the cultural backgrounds of the students themselves.

Envisioning the attainment of the goal of science for all has pushed science education research toward exploring inclusive, multicultural science teaching and learning. Science education researchers have provided strong evidence of the importance of recognizing and bringing into play the linguistic and cultural resources students carry with them into the classroom (Lee, 2001, 2003; Warren, Ballenger, Ogonowski, Rosebery, & Hudicourt-Barnes, 2001). Much of science education research efforts have moved from an "add marginalized group and stir" model (such as ensuring more girls have access to upper-level science courses, an example of Cuban's first-order change) toward one that looks at the very nature of how school science instruction intersects with issues of student diversity (such as examining the curriculum to address areas of gender bias in a course, an example of Cuban's second-order change).

This latter model focuses on more nuanced issues of student and teacher identities (Barton, 1998; Brickhouse, Lowery, & Schultz, 2000; Carlone, 2003, 2005; Letts, 1999; Sowell, 2004), culturally relevant curricula (Parsons, Travis, & Simpson, 2005), instructional congruence (Lee & Fradd, 1998), and the role that everyday discourse plays in scientific meaning making (Southerland, Johnston, et al., 2005; Varelas, Pappas, & Rife, 2004; Warren et al., 2001).

The history of gender research illuminates our current approach to multicultural science education. Baker (2002), in a review of articles appearing in a leading journal in the field since the 1970s, described the history of gender equity in science education in this way:

> These studies were either psychological in orientation and used White male performance as the benchmark, or lacked explicit theoretical frameworks. . . . They were conducted under what I call the "My Fair Lady" framework, or "Why can't a woman be more like a man?" When there were differences or correlates, the White male model was the right model. (p. 660)

By the 1980s, a less mechanistic concern for diverse populations, including women, had emerged, with a stronger advocacy for getting more female students involved in science rather than simply explaining differences based on sex. However, "the psychological perspective still held sway, and no one was yet questioning whether the so-called problem of girls and science had less to do with the nature of girls and more to do with the nature of science" (Baker, 2002, p. 660). In the early 1990s, research began to challenge the nature of school science, and "fixing school science" took precedence over "fixing the girl science student." Baker notes that attention toward a multiplicity of difference (gender, race, class, ethnicity, etc.) that arose in the latter 1990s allowed connections between gender and other forms of social inequity. We argue that efforts toward understanding other markers of student difference (e.g., race, culture, or ability) have mirrored to some degree this pattern that Baker illustrates for gender.

Clearly, careful consideration of knowledge about science (NOS) is highly important as we look at student diversity and inclusion (Barton, 1998; Lee, 1997; Southerland & Gess-Newsome, 1999; Sowell, Southerland, & Blanchard, 2006). Understanding

NOS can be an important political tool to achieve more equitable science teaching (Southerland, 2000). If one goal of reform-minded NOS instruction is to provide students with an understanding of the boundaries of scientific knowledge and how science intersects and compares with other ways of knowing, then there are very pragmatic connections between reform messages and those within aspects of multicultural science education. We recognize the connections and contradictions between the students' everyday discourse and the cultural norms of science itself. Southerland, Johnston, et al. (2005) comment that researchers must "pay particular attention to potential incongruities between the cultural norms of science and those of the students from diverse settings" (p. 1035). This message has become central to the way in which we approach equity research.

The border-crossing literature (Aikenhead, 1996; Hodson, 1999) promotes facilitating students' moving between the cultures of science and of home and purposefully making those boundaries and crossings very transparent. Teachers must become proficient tour guides for their students' border-crossings, in effect becoming bilingual/bicultural individuals. As Lee (2003) points out, the teacher needs knowledge of both sides of that border: "science disciplines and students' languages and cultures" (p. 481). This approach facilitates a higher degree of instructional congruence, that is, the integration of students' everyday culture and language with the cultural and linguistic practices of science.

Diversity informs reform efforts by examining how certain groups of students interact with school science. Categories of difference, although perhaps falsely perceived as homogeneous, allow us to recognize when less equitable practices need to be addressed. Equity research in science education utilizes identity politics as a way of calling us out on inequitable classroom practices. Research in multicultural science education uses the productive tension between recognizing the achievement gaps for certain underserved student populations while at the same time working to better understand nuances and differences within those particular groups.

How would teachers enact second-order changes with regard to issues of diversity and equity? Thinking first and foremost about student identities, as well as the linguistic and cultural resources these students bring with them into the classroom, is key to keeping issues of diversity at the forefront of instructional planning. Planning for instruction that emerges from the lived experiences of the students is one way to engender a more harmonious relationship between classroom teaching and students' everyday lives. Thus, second-order changes place greater onus of change on science teaching and curricula (i.e., the culture of classroom science) than on the students themselves.

SCIENCE TEACHER EDUCATION

The overarching goal of science teacher education since the mid-1980s has been to radically change the way science is taught in classrooms. It has clearly been an era of reform intended to enact second-order change in both science curriculum and instruction at all grade levels. Having previously articulated the goals of reform in other sections of this discussion, we focus here on the challenges faced by science teacher educators in educating and supporting prospective and practicing teachers to actively engage students at all levels in learning foundational science concepts, the nature of science, and the processes of scientific inquiry.

There are many individuals within the science education research community who are "committed to the new vision for teaching and learning science" (Meadows, 2005, p. 1) offered via the reforms. Literally thousands of methods courses, research initiatives, curriculum development projects, professional development seminars, and other national and local efforts have been devoted to promoting the national standards and supporting teachers' enactment of them in the classroom (e.g., Luera & Otto, 2005). For much of the 1980s and 1990s, successful implementation of the reforms was most often attributed to prospective and practicing teachers' abilities to reconsider the way they think about science and science instruction (Gess-Newsome, Southerland, Johnston, & Woodbury, 2003). Recently, the conversation has broadened to focus on teachers' knowledge and beliefs as situated in contexts that shape the enactment of reforms. Despite the work of reform-minded science teacher educators, scientists, and policy makers, these efforts are far from uniform. L. K. Smith and Gess-Newsome (2004) suggest that efforts to attend to these standards by instructors of elementary science methods courses are not consistent across programs. Of the 56 methods courses (representing all geographic areas of the United States) described in their study, approximately 27% failed to emphasize inquiry-based science instruction enough to include mention of it in the course objectives, assignments, or assigned topics and readings. Likewise, some practicing science teachers at both the elementary and secondary levels embrace reform-oriented instruction in their classrooms, whereas others are either unable or unwilling to modify their curriculum or instruction to align more closely with current science initiatives (Crawford, 2000; Davis, 2002; L. K. Smith, 2005; L. K. Smith & Southerland, 2007).

Internally Imposed Barriers to Science Education Reform

R. D. Anderson (2002) posits that "much of the difficulty [in enacting reform] is internal to the teacher, including teachers' beliefs and values related to students, teaching, and the purposes of education" (p. 7). Teachers' subject matter knowledge and personal practical knowledge (see Clandinin, 1986) may affect if and how reforms are implemented (Laplante, 1997; Wallace & Kang, 2004). Even well-meaning teachers who value proposed changes and believe they are embracing radically new practices may not implement the intended reforms (Gess-Newsome et al., 2003; Southerland et al., 2003). Thus, as Craig (2006) suggests, teachers are not merely "implementers"; rather, they are "curriculum makers," using their knowledge to shape curriculum and instruction according to the perceived needs of their students.

There is some evidence that certain teachers may be more willing to embrace innovations than others due to intrinsic psychological attributes (Hopkins, 1990). The argument is that the cognitive development, psychological state, or "personalities" (McKibbin & Joyce, 1981, p. 254) of teachers, in combination with the general milieu of the school and the social movements of the times, allow some teachers to see possibilities for thinking about and implementing new ways of teaching. In contrast, other teachers fear and avoid the risks associated with change. In essence, this research contends that more abstract and cognitively complex teacher thinking allows for greater use of new educational ideas (Hopkins, 1990).

Other research (C. W. Anderson, 2003) suggests that one reason for the continued struggle to convince teachers to enact reform is "a fundamental incompatibility" between how teachers view science and the way science is portrayed in the reforms (p. 9). C. W. Anderson argues that, for teachers, "science provides an authoritative picture of how the world is" (p. 9). The epistemological stances that accompany these views (such as knowledge as final form, directly reflected by data, isolated from context) make adoption of the tenets of reform very difficult, a finding supported by a host of other researchers (Abell & Smith, 1994; Sandoval, 2003; Windschitl, 2003, 2004).

Teachers' beliefs about their ability to positively influence student learning through particular instructional interventions—beliefs that have come to be known as teacher self-efficacy (Tschannen-Moran, Hoy, & Hoy, 1998)—also influence their willingness to implement science education reform. Low teacher self-efficacy is characterized by teacher-centered science instruction; high teacher self-efficacy is more likely to result in the use of inquiry and more student-centered pedagogical practices (Ramey-Gassert, Shroyer, & Staver, 1996).

Both prospective and practicing teachers hold beliefs about science and what constitutes good science education. These beliefs are developed throughout years of experience as students in classrooms (Lortie, 1975) and in out-of-school contexts (L. K. Smith, 2005), and they are mediated by teachers' conceptions of self: as learners and knowers of science (Laplante, 1997; L. K. Smith, 2005) and as science teachers (Weld & Funk, 2005). These beliefs also are deeply held (Pajares, 1992) and guide teachers' selection of content and teaching methods (Abell & Smith, 1994; Brickhouse & Bodner, 1992; Gess-Newsome, 1999). Some teachers hold beliefs about appropriate instruction that can serve as barriers to reform; other educators hold beliefs that align closely with the tenets of reform and openly embrace inquiry-based instruction in their classrooms (L. K. Smith, 2005; L. K. Smith & Southerland, 2007). Based on this evidence, teacher preparation and teacher development programs have targeted teachers' science-related beliefs in efforts to change teaching practices. Some of these efforts suggest that science methods courses may influence preservice teachers' beliefs about what it means to teach and learn science (Abell & Bryan, 1997; Eick & Dias, 2005). However, studies that have examined the impact of professional development opportunities for practicing teachers describe wide differences in teachers' abilities to incorporate innovative teaching practices (Davis, 2002; Luft, 2001).

In addition to new instructional practices, science education reforms also ask teachers to implement innovative, reform-based assessment practices that make different and challenging demands of teachers' knowledge and skills. Similar to other pedagogical innovations, these changes may conflict with teachers' fundamental beliefs about science assessment (Matese, Griesdorn, & Edelson, 2002; L. K. Smith & Southerland, 2007), constraining teachers' response to calls for change.

Teachers' subject-matter knowledge may be another significant barrier to implementing classroom-based inquiry and other reform-based practices (Laplante, 1997; Wallace & Kang, 2004). Many teachers (both elementary and secondary) lack a conceptually rich or accurate understanding of the content they teach (Gess-Newsome, 1999). As a result, these teachers are likely to rely heavily on the textbook and worksheets and to cover the content in a sequential and isolated fashion (Carlsen, 1991). In contrast, because they have a more fluid and multifaceted understanding of their content, teachers with strong conceptual knowledge are more prone to adopt inquiry as a facet of their teaching.

Finally, aside from the influence of teachers' content knowledge and beliefs, enacting classroom-based inquiry requires a significant shift in teaching practices (Crawford, 2000; Windschitl, 2004). Although teachers come to the classroom with a wealth of pedagogical content knowledge (PCK), much of it is largely traditional (Davis, 2002). Because classroom-based inquiry requires a different kind of PCK, and this knowledge requires significant time to develop, it is frequently not seen in science classrooms.

Externally Imposed Barriers to Science Education Reform

In addition to the often-cited internal barriers, factors outside the teacher and teacher knowledge are found to play a role in the enactment of reforms. Externally imposed barriers or obstacles to reform often are tied to the "basic grammar of schooling" (Tyack & Cuban, 1995, p. 83) or the traditional way schools are structured or organized, including the way time and space are allocated and the splintering of knowledge into separate subjects. These and other institutional or organizational structures (e.g., the level of administrative support, available physical space or instructional materials, funding, and academic time devoted to planning and teaching) continue to have a significant impact on teachers' ability or inclination to think differently about science instruction and to change their practice (Abell & Roth, 1992; Sandall, 2003; Yore et al., in press).

Science teacher educators continue to face multiple challenges as they encourage teachers to think differently about science and science instruction. The form of science teaching described here exemplifies what Cuban refers to as second-order change because it asks teachers to turn from traditional recitation methods of "teaching as telling" and rote memorization of science content. Instead, teachers are asked to provide learning experiences that actively engage students in learning the substantive content of science through classroom-based inquiry, enabling them to understand the facts, principles, and theories of the discipline as well as the ability to comprehend, interpret, analyze, reason, and communicate about discipline-specific ideas. In short, classroom teachers are asked to develop scientifically literate individuals, an effort that will continue to require the sustained support of science teacher educators. However, as will be discussed, current accountability movements that spur states' and districts' adoptions of first-order changes play a powerful role in preventing the enactment of science educations' efforts at second-order reforms.

SCIENCE EDUCATION IN THE CONTEXT OF NCLB

Science teaching has recently taken a "back seat" to reading and math because "what gets taught in a classroom is largely determined by what gets tested" (Lee & Luykx, 2006, p. 28). Some elementary teachers, for example, report that their administrator is so eager to provide evidence of AYP in math and literacy that science has been completely removed from their curriculum, and some high school science teachers are required to explicitly drill math and reading skills in science class (Saka, 2007). Beginning in the 2007–2008 school year, however, schools must administer annual tests in science achievement at least once in Grades 3 to 5, 6 to 9, and 10 to 12. Some people hope that these assessments will prompt schools and school districts to align content standards with teaching practices (Hovey, Hazelwood, & Svedkauskaire, 2005). Others inside and outside the science education community have responded with a mixture of anticipation and dread. An article published in *Education Week*, for example, suggests that NCLB could "alter science teaching" by forcing schools to "cut back on some of the in-class experiments many teachers value" in favor of a more straightforward approach (Cavanagh, 2004, p. 1). Although this "straightforward approach" fits with common traditions of schooling and meshes well with many teachers' approaches to science instruction, it contradicts much of what we have learned through the past 20 years or more of research.

We understand NCLB to be an attempt to elicit first-order changes because it does not articulate clear goals for learners or explicitly describe any particular form of instruction or assessment. Given the lack of a clear vision for pedagogy and the limited nature of funding for the development of state standards and assessments, NCLB is not capable of instigating second-order changes. The structures within NCLB policy encourage schools to do more of what they have traditionally been doing: more rigor (in terms of scope of content, not depth of thought) as a route to greater student achievement. Quick fixes (first-order change) become far more imperative than exploring what is called for within science education research-based reform (second-order change).

We are reluctant to embrace NCLB because of its first-order nature, and this first-order nature plays out in two prominent ways: teachers' perceptions of assessments and the problematic nature of the accountability measures themselves. Many teachers view the national standards documents, the state science curricula, and the associated end-of-level tests to be conflicting (L. K. Smith & Southerland, 2007). Indeed, some teachers argue that the National Science Education Standards (NRC, 1996) describe an image of science that is incompatible with state-mandated curriculum and accountability measures that they perceive to be focused primarily or exclusively on content coverage. Accountability measures that focus on content are problematic because it is unclear how well these measures assess students' "walking around knowledge" of science (Brickhouse, 2006). Some of these assessments might measure practices such as the application of knowledge or the interpretation of data; however, it is important to recognize that each state has its own standardized assessment tool. Thus, there is likely a wide range of assessments employed around the nation.

Despite the NCLB legislation, funding for developing assessments is limited. Because of this, assessments are not continually revised in many states, preventing teachers from fully engaging with the yearly assessments. This lack of full engagement means that often teachers are not able to construct a robust understanding of the kinds of student learning to be assessed. In some states, teachers have been fined if they are caught examining the assessments firsthand (Aydeniz, 2007). Although such efforts may be attempts to prevent "teaching to the test," this isolation leaves teachers to teach to their understandings and/or worst fears about what the test might contain and targeting lower-level knowledge in their classrooms (L. K. Smith & Southerland, 2007). In addition, limited funding for professional development associated with assessments may drive teachers to cover a great deal of content in very little time, thus negating many of the instructional approaches supported in reform efforts. Given these interactions, there is a mismatch between reform efforts focusing on scientific literacy and the policy goals of NCLB.

With no clear direction from NCLB in terms of how teaching and learning should be approached in any reform-specific way—combined with the high-stakes nature of the assessment outcomes for administrators and teachers—districts, schools, and teachers may feel pressured to rely on traditional methods of teaching science. Collins (1998) describes that there are three tools of reform: content standards (descriptions of what should be learned), pedagogical standards (descriptions of how that content should be taught [NRC, 2000]), and assessment standards (descriptions of how student learning and the effectiveness of instruction is to be measured [Atkin et al., 2001]). However, the content standards are the only tool that features prominently in states' interpretation of NCLB. Thus, research areas that are adequately represented in the content standards, such as the nature of science, have enjoyed some degree of success in terms of their inclusion in many state standards. In addition, diversity has been influenced by NCLB because states are required to examine achievement levels of various groups of students. Research in teacher education also is becoming vigorous, at least in terms of understanding how science teaching is shaped by local, district, and state climates. Other aspects of science education research, such as learning theory, however, are poorly represented in the states' interpretations of content standards and thus have had limited responses to NCLB. In the following sections, we describe the uneven nature of the response of the various research communities.

Response of Learning Research to NCLB

The national content standards at the center of the science education reform effort have achieved some measure of success because science standards in most states have been restructured in response to them, although even the national efforts are sometimes criticized for being too broad in scope (Duschl et al., 2007). However, DeBoer (2002) explains that the states' "focus on testing has . . . led individual states to create curriculum standards that are more detailed and highly specified than the more general national content standards" (p. 413). If learning science was simply a process of accreting information or adding knowledge to already well-structured conceptual frameworks, such broad curricula might be congruent with the reforms. However, the difficulty of these more detailed and extensive state standards is that the shear amount of material to address in the school year often serves to prohibit a robust, clear, intensive treatment of foundational ideas. Wandersee and Fisher (2000) remind us that focusing on too many details prevents students from grasping the foundational ideas, or the "big picture," of the science they are studying. Indeed, Schmidt (2003; cited in Hovey et al., 2005) suggests that America's lackluster results in an international testing effort in science and mathematics (TIMSS) can best be explained by a school curriculum that is "a mile wide and an inch deep."

Implementing current learning theory focuses on understanding broad conceptual ideas and enculturation into the practices and discourses of science. From this perspective, learning is understood to be a long, complex process requiring an engaged learner. This conception of learning is at odds with the wide scope of the content curricula found in many states, their associated assessments, and the common pedagogical response to these extensive curricula (i.e., drilling months before the examination, wide content coverage to ensure student recognition of maximum amount of material, approaching science as a vocabulary exercise). There has been very little overt reaction by the science education community in response to NCLB because the two sides operate on almost incommensurate views of learning.

Response of Research Into Inquiry to NCLB

Not surprisingly, Wideen, O'Shea, Pye, and Ivany (1997) concluded that standardized examinations discourage teachers from using strategies that promote inquiry and active student learning. This trend is well recognized, and the science education community is attempting to address this, both by clarifying the meaning of and goals for inquiry (Adams, Undreiu, & Cobern, 2006; Grandy & Duschl, 2005) and disseminating that knowledge to teachers (Abrams, Southerland, & Silva, 2007). Beyond helping teachers understand inquiry, it is also important for our research community to demonstrate the efficacy of inquiry in terms of engendering student learning. Toward this end, numerous multiclassroom, large-scale studies are underway to empirically examine the effectiveness of inquiry (Blanchard, Southerland, & Granger, 2005; Cobern, Lederman, Schwartz, & Schuster, 2004).

Response of Nature of Science Research to NCLB

NCLB legislation may serve to formalize NOS into the school science cannon. *Systems for State Science Assessment* (Wilson & Bertenthal, 2005) includes NOS as a central aspect of science that needs to be assessed. In addition, the NOS also is being conceived by some researchers as scientific epistemology, with a focus on how NOS ideas play out in practice. This approach holds promise for taking NOS under-standings from potentially inert content knowledge to a form of knowledge students employ during science-related activities. From either perspective (NOS as cannon or scientific epistemologies), the ways of assessing NOS understandings required by large-scale assessments may trivialize and make overly simplistic what could be a rich, productive domain of study (Elby & Hammer, 2001).

Response of Diversity Research to NCLB

The area of science education research most affected by NCLB is diversity. One of the goals of NCLB is to reduce the achievement gaps between mainstream and nonmainstream students; this goal is shared by the science education research com-munity. Test scores of traditionally underserved students highlight achievement gaps. NCLB presupposes that holding schools/districts accountable for these achievement gaps through punitive funding policies will allow for enhanced learning for all students. However, Cochran-Smith (2005) describes that "new regulations requiring that graduation rates be included in NCLB accountability provisions are not being enforced, whereas incentives for removing low-scoring students are rigidly followed" (p. 102). In essence, there are negative consequences for schools with a wide demographic variety. An unintended consequence may involve pushing us back toward a deficit view of multiculturalism, a view that does not support teachers in validating and using the cultural and linguistic resources of nonmainstream students as foundational aspects of curricula and teaching strategies. Consequently, diversity from a NCLB framework actually becomes something negative to overcome as opposed to something positive with which to work.

Shaver, Cuevas, Lee, and Avalos (in press) describe elementary teachers' reactions to the current policy climate and its relation to the teaching/learning of science. In particular, they focus on the effects of policy on students who are English language learners (ELL) and students of low socioeconomic status (SES). In general, the teach-ers had positive perspectives on state and district science standards, seeing them as supportive guidelines for science instruction. However, they were less positive as they described how state assessment practices resulted in increased test preparation for those subject areas being tested, including reading, writing, and mathematics, and reduced instructional time for those subject areas not being tested, including science. Added to this were frustrations regarding the expectations for ELL students to take and pass the Florida Comprehensive Assessment Test (FCAT) without accommoda-tions. The researchers point to the accountability climate as a factor that reduces teacher agency regarding the success of their students, in particular those students who have been traditionally underserved by the existing system.

NCLB can be seen as pushing us to be more difference blind in that the policy pro-motes seemingly academically rigorous traditional teaching, teaching that has strongest commonalities with the language and cultural practices of mainstream students. NCLB prevents states from ignoring this problem because it clearly requires states to focus on achievement gaps. However, the emphasis on broad content knowledge that is seen in most states' science content standards renders states' responses to NCLB largely devoid of emphasis on the cultural aspects of science content. This is in direct contradiction to research on equitable science education that highlights the importance of recognizing and honoring cultural aspects of science teaching and learning. Although NCLB requires states to address achievement gaps, the manner in which it has been implemented largely prevents states from substantively addressing the underlying reasons for these gaps.

In terms of teacher quality, we also see a mismatch between what is known via research into diversity and the structures imposed by NCLB. Whereas science education places value on a wide range of teacher knowledge (science content knowledge, pedagogical knowledge, students' prior knowledge and experiences, pedagogical content knowledge), which is recognized to include teacher knowledge of student diversity, NCLB places higher priority on how much science content a teacher knows. "The [Highly Qualified Teacher] definition focuses almost exclusively on subject matter and ignores pedagogy and other professional knowledge and skills" (Cochran-Smith, 2005, p. 101). A synthesis of the most recent research in science education has shown that equitable science teaching practices require much more than simple content knowledge. Work at the Ch'eche Konnen Center for Science Teaching and Learning, for instance, introduced the idea "repertoires of practice" into the field of science education. Rosebery (2004) describes repertoires of practice as "what people do and what they say about what they do. It is the practices they engage in, what they do as a result of their involvement in particular communities" (p. 2). In terms of science teaching, important repertoires of practice include the cultures of science, the classroom, the school, and the broader culture of the teaching profession. Content knowledge, then, is just one of many necessary sources of teacher knowledge.

To sum, although NCLB does focus attention on achievement gaps of particular demographics groups, the limited funding does not provide schools with the resources necessary to meet the accountability standards it imposes, promising greater consequences for nonmainstream students than their mainstream counterparts (Lee & Luykx, 2006).

Response of Teacher Education Research to NCLB

NCLB has intensified the focus on science educators. We have become attuned to the number of science teachers, particularly those designated as "highly qualified teachers." Work that focuses on issues of teacher attrition have gained a new salience, both within and outside our community. Ingersoll (2003) points out that science teachers leave for a variety of reasons, including lack of student motivation, inadequate time, intrusions on teaching time, and poor administrative support.

In addition to these analyses of the teacher population, there is a growing body of teacher education research that focuses on the way in which teachers respond to their state's implementation of NCLB legislation (Aydeniz, 2007; Luft et al., 2007; Saka, 2007; Shaver et al., in press; L. K. Smith & Southerland, 2007). Indeed, standardized testing within high-stakes testing programs currently serve as "a dominant force in the current streams of thought and politic" shaping K-12 education (Huber & Moore, 2002, p. 18). For example, heightened accountability through mandated high-stakes testing has discouraged teachers from implementing reform-based science instruction in their classrooms (Yerrick, Parke, & Nugent, 1997) and have led to a number of other negative consequences, including what Settlage and Meadows (2002) describe as the "trivialization of science instruction" (p. 116), where the emphasis is placed primarily on "the acquisition of isolated facts rather than broad conceptual understanding" (L. K. Smith & Southerland, 2007). In short, teachers are hard pressed to enact the second-order changes of science education reform because of the intensified need to show demonstrable student gains on state-produced examinations.

REJECTING UNLEARNING AND THE CHALLENGES OF MEANINGFUL WORK WITHIN NCLB

We could conceivably raise test scores in science without substantively influencing who engages in science either professionally or as a citizen or enhancing the quality of that engagement. Tests are only a proxy for those competencies that we really value. Some tests are certainly better proxies than others. But none of them are the actual competencies that are the aim of scientific literacy. While there may be a time when it is justifiable to use test scores as a proxy for the competencies we value, we need to be very critical of our measures and cognizant of the need to keep real educational assessment as close to the actual competencies as we can. (Brickhouse, 2006, p. 3)

Conflicting Views Between NCLB and the Science Education Community

This quote by the former editor of one of the premier research journals in science education cogently explains the failure to communicate introduced at the outset of this discussion; it describes the reaction of a sizable portion of the science education community to the prospect of meaningful work and meaningful learning within the context of NCLB. We argue that completely meshing the efforts of the science education research community to improve science education with those of NCLB would require science educators to unlearn much of what we have come to understand and value throughout the past decades of science education research.

In terms of what counts as the gold standard of research methodology under NCLB, the methodological push asks us to use largely traditional, quantitative, experimental, or quasi-experimental research methods that yield prescriptions for action. This narrow perspective of what counts as good research shapes the questions one may legitimately pursue and would represent a radical shift in the current practice of science education research. The studies we have cited in our synthesis of research employ a broad spectrum of methods, from ethnographies to hierarchical linear modeling. Indeed, scholars in our field are currently engaged in diverse types of inquiries requiring very different methodologies, all in an effort to inform our understanding of science teaching and learning and to improve science education for all students.

However, NCLB would limit such efforts, supporting the use of only a fraction of those methods, thereby limiting the kinds of questions deemed legitimate and ultimately ignoring the more important questions of how research and education "contribute to the well-being of students, teachers, and communities" (Hostetler, 2005, p. 16). Hence, this push is asking us to move backward in time 20 years or more in terms of what is considered appropriate, limiting our focus only to test scores as opposed to how science teaching affects all students' access to scientific knowledge, their participation in a democracy, and ultimately their quality of life.

In terms of what counts as a highly qualified science teacher, again NCLB pushes us to focus on merely a subsection of the rigorous knowledge, skill, and disposition bases our field recognizes as important to the craft of science teaching. Where NCLB emphasizes content knowledge above all else, we also recognize the need for pedagogical content knowledge, broader pedagogical knowledge, knowledge of student learning patterns within the field of study, high expectations for all learners, recognition of the need for equity in the teaching of science, and multiple repertoires of practice. Again, the emphasis of NCLB in terms of what is needed for teacher quality asks us to ignore much of what the research of the past 20 years has revealed as fundamentally essential for science teaching.

We understand the particular atmosphere of science education in the United States to be the result of the interaction of a number of factors related to NCLB: the high stakes nature of accountability, the limited funds available for the construction of assessments that can measure the competencies we value, and the manner in which the national science content standards have been adopted while the pedagogical and assessment standards have failed to be accommodated by the same systems. This atmosphere makes it very unlikely that the second-order reforms we have worked toward can come to fruition because real science literacy seems to have taken a back seat to performance to weak proxies.

Acknowledging Our Responsibilities as Science Educators

What, then, is the hope for meaningful work within this context? As we have described to this point, much of the science education community has continued their work, ignoring or possibly rejecting the changing atmosphere of schools, because we are unwilling to unlearn. Perhaps some have been hoping that conditions will change as the political climate of the nation changes; perhaps some have been working to support pockets of science education reform within the broader national system (Barab & Luehmann, 2003; Rivet & Krajcik, 2004).

Because NCLB does not include science until 2007, the research on this area is very limited. We hope that more research, such as the work of Marx et al. (2004) and Shaver et al. (in press), that focuses on the success of reform in the climate of accountability will emerge as NCLB becomes part of policy and practice in science education. There is a growing body of research suggesting that our push toward second-order change is not intelligible given the states' overwhelming emphases on first-order remedies. Thus, many of us have isolated our work and our professional development efforts to those pockets in which a productive discussion is eased, ignoring that which is out of our control.

As Julie Kittleson (2005) recently asked at a meeting dedicated to reflecting on the state of science education research, "To whom are science education researchers responsible? Are we responsible only to ourselves?" (p. 2). Our answer is that researchers' blind eye approach to the state of science schooling is fundamentally irresponsible. Although we are not willing to reject what we know from the science education reform movement and the large body of research that has been accomplished in response to it, we argue that science educators are responsible for making real efforts to change what happens in schools. As Settlage (2006) describes, taking a "scholarly stance" is important but insufficient. We must "proceed with a sense of purpose" in "intellectually informed activity" (p. 4).

To do this, to own up to our responsibilities, scholars must develop new sensibilities and skills that will facilitate the enactment of the vision of science literacy for all. Perhaps most important, we must learn to better communicate between and across different populations; we must assume the role of "border crossers" or "border crossing" (see Sandholtz & Finan, 1998), and not only across the researcher-teacher border (a boundary spanning that many of us have come to see as a critical part of our work). We also must be willing to move across a number of professional borders (i.e., researcher-administrator, researcher-parent, researcher-policy maker, researcher-test producer). We use the term "border-crossing" very deliberately here as we see moving between professional communities as kin to moving across cultures, suggesting that we can no longer afford to think in terms of us and them but instead need to work to be active in many spheres if these communities are to inform one another in any real way.

To facilitate this border crossing, science educators also must accept work within our local, state, and national context as an essential aspect of our work to better articulate and propagate a realizable vision of meaningful science teaching and learning, that is, we understand assessment and accountability to be fundamental aspects of learning. Indeed, we echo Collins's (1998) contention that reform is about appropriate standards, related pedagogical practices that are based in and respond to our understanding of student learning, while recognizing that assessment is a visceral aspect of such change. Instead of ignoring standardized assessments or railing against what we perceive to be their misuses, we must offer up meaningful alternative assessments to what we understand to be weak proxies. These alternatives can then serve as models of how to adequately measure students' knowledge and skills in ways that are in alignment with the second-order reforms we seek.

In tandem, if second-order reforms in science education are to be supported, then we advocate that science educators must weigh in on the adequacy of textbooks and other curricula in terms of how well or how poorly they support reform-based instruction. Again, this should be with an eye to suggesting models of what textbooks that adequately support reform-based instruction may look like.

Science education researchers also must become more active in the development of sound educational policy, on all levels, by engaging in activities such as working to lobby the legislature, participating in school board meetings, and writing editorials for newspapers. But, as Windschitl (2006) points out, in these roles we must move past our familiar scripts (such as that played out in the opening vignette) and work to forge productive discussions—shared meanings—grounded in classroom scenarios. It is not enough to develop a body of knowledge about teaching and learning. Instead, we must work to make this knowledge intelligible, useful, and available for others, in particular when these others are in powerful positions to enact legislative or school change.

We recognize that much of what we're advocating is for science educators and scholars to reconceptualize our work. In addition to our efforts in research, teacher education, and the education of children and youth, we argue for an additional component to our work. Much of this work, this professional border crossing, will not profit our careers in any proximal way. Indeed, working across communities often represents a significant investment of time and energy, time and energy no longer available to our more familiar (and professionally recognized) scholarly activity. However, Kittleson's (2005) query resonates, "To whom are science educators responsible?" We contend that we are responsible not only to the community of scholars in terms of furthering our understandings of the processes involved in the teaching and learning of science but we are also responsible to our wider society in terms of working to allow this knowledge to inform and shape the patterns of science teaching and learning.

ACKNOWLEDGMENTS

Our thanks to Okhee Lee, Steve Oliver, and the anonymous reviewers for their insights into earlier versions of this chapter.

REFERENCES

Abd-El Khalick, F. (2001). Embedding nature of science instruction in preservice elementary science courses: Abandoning scientism, but . . . *Journal of Science Teacher Education, 12*(3), 215–233.

Abd-El-Khalick, F., & Lederman, N. G. (2000). Improving science teachers' conceptions of the nature of science: A critical review of the literature. *International Journal of Science Education, 22*(7), 665–701.

Abell, S. K., & Bryan, L. A. (1997). Reconceptualizing the elementary science methods course using a reflection orientation. *Journal of Science Teacher Education, 8*(3), 153–166.

Abell, S. K., & Roth, M. (1992). Constraints to teaching elementary science: A case study of a science enthusiast student teacher. *Science Education, 76*(6), 581–595.

Abell, S. K., & Smith, D. C. (1994). What is science? Preservice elementary teachers' conceptions of the nature of science. *International Journal of Science Education, 16*(4), 475–487.

Abrams, E., Southerland, S. A., & Silva, P. (Eds.). (2007). *Inquiry in the classrooms: Challenges and opportunities.* Greenwich, CT: Information Age.

Adams, B. A. J., Undreiu, A., & Cobern, W. W. (2006). *The presence of inquiry in science education: What do we know? . . . and what don't we know yet?* Paper presented at the annual meeting of the National Association for Research in Science Teaching San Francisco, CA.

Aikenhead, G. S. (1996). Science education: Border crossing into the subculture of science. *Studies in Science Education, 27*, 1–52.

Aikenhead, G., Ryan, A., & Fleming, R. (1989). *Views on science-technology-society* (from CDN.mc.5). Saskatoon, Canada: Department of Curriculum Studies, University of Saskatchewan.

Alexopoulou, E., & Driver, R. (1996). Small-group discussion in physics: Peer interaction modes in pairs and fours. *Journal of Research in Science Teaching, 33*(10), 1099–1114.

Alsop, S. (2005). *The affective dimensions of cognition: Studies from education in the sciences.* the Netherlands: Kluwer Academic.

American Association for Advancement of Science. (AAAS). (1989). *Science for all Americans: Project 2061.* Washington, DC: Author.

Anderson, C. W. (2003, March). *Difficulties with inquiry in science classrooms.* Paper presented at the meeting of the National Association for Research in Science Teaching, Philadelphia.

Anderson, R. D. (2002). Reforming science teaching: What research says about inquiry. *Journal of Science Teacher Education, 13,* 1–12.

Atkin, J. M., Black, P., & Coffey, J. (2001). *Classroom assessment and the national science education standards.* Washington, DC: National Academy Press.

Aydeniz, M. (2007). *Understanding the challenges of implementing assessment reform in science classrooms: A case study of science teachers, conceptions and practices of assessment.* Unpublished doctoral dissertation, Florida State University, Tallahassee.

Baker, D. (2002). Where is gender and equity in science education? *Journal of Science Teacher Education, 39,* 659–663.

Barab, S., & Luehmann, A. (2003). Building sustainable science curriculum: Acknowledging and accommodating local adaptation. *Science Education, 87,* 454–467.

Barton, A. C. (1998). Teaching science with homeless children: Pedagogy, representation, and identity. *Journal of Research in Science Teaching, 35,* 379–394.

Bianchini, J. (1997). Where meaning making, equity, and context intersect: Student learning of science in small groups. *Journal of Research in Science Teaching, 34,* 1039–1065.

Blanchard, M., Southerland, S. A., & Granger, D. E. (2005). *A quantitative study of inquiry-based versus traditional science teaching methods.* Multi-University Reading, Mathematics, and Science Initiative, Learning Systems Institute, Tallahassee, FL.

Bransford, J., Brown, A., & Cocking, R. (2000). *How people learn: Brain, mind, and experience & school.* Washington, DC: National Academy Press.

Brickhouse, N. W. (2006). Editorial: Celebrating 90 years of *Science Education*: Reflections on the gold standard and ways of promoting good research. *Science Education, 90*(1), 1–7.

Brickhouse, N., & Bodner, G. M. (1992). The beginning science teacher: Classroom narratives of convictions and constraints. *Journal of Research in Science Teaching, 29*(5), 471–485.

Brickhouse, N. W., Lowery, P., & Schultz, K. (2000). What kind of a girl does science? The construction of school science identities. *Journal of Research in Science Teaching, 37,* 441–458.

Carlone, H. (2003). (Re)producing good science students: Girls' participation in high school physics. *Journal of Women and Minorities in Science and Engineering, 9*(1), 17–34.

Carlone, H. (2005, October). *Science identity in science education: Possibilities and complexities.* Paper presented at the Science Education at the Crossroads Conference, Storrs, CT.

Carlsen, W. S. (1991). Questioning in classrooms: A sociolinguistic perspective. *Review of Educational Research, 61,* 157–178.

Cavanagh, S. (2004). NCLB could alter science teaching. *Education Week.* Retrieved June 30, 2006, from http://www.edweek.org/ew/articles/2004/11/10/11science.h24.html?r&levelId+1000&levelId=1000. Chang, C., & Mao, S. (1999). Comparison of Taiwan science students' outcomes with inquiry-group versus traditional instruction. *The Journal of Educational Research, 92*(6), 340–346.

Chen, S. (2006). Development of an instrument to assess views on nature of science and attitudes toward teaching science. *Science Education, 90*(5), 803–819.

Chi, M. T. H. (1992). Conceptual change within and across ontological categories: Examples from learning and discovery in science. In R. N. Giere (Ed.), *Minnesota studies in the philosophy of science: Vol. XV. Cognitive models of science* (pp. 129–186). Minneapolis: University of Minnesota Press.

Chinn, C. A., & Malhotra, B. A. (2002). Epistemologically authentic inquiry in schools: A theoretical framework for evaluating inquiry tasks. *Science Education, 86*(2), 175–218.

Clandinin, D. J. (1986). *Classroom practice: Teacher images in action.* Philadelphia: Falmer.

Cobern, W., Lederman, N., Schwartz, R., & Schuster, D. (2004). *An experimental efficacy study of science achievement and attitude development amongst 8th grade students using an inquiry, integrated science-mathematics-engineering model of instruction.* Retrieved July 7, 2006, from http://drdc.uchicago.edu/offhm/index.html?http://www.nsf.gov/award-search/showAward.do?AwardNumber=0437655.

Cobern, W., & Loving, C. (1998). The card exchange: Introducing the philosophy of science. In W. McComas (Ed.), *The nature of science in science education: Rationales and strategies* (pp. 73–82). Dordrecht, the Netherlands: Kluwer Academic.

Cochran-Smith, M. (2005). No child left behind: 3 years and counting. *Journal of Teacher Education, 56*(2), 99–103.

Collins, A. (1998). National science education standards: A political document. *Journal of Research in Science Teaching, 35*(7), 711–727.

Craig, C. J. (2006). Why is dissemination so difficult? The nature of teacher knowledge and the spread of curriculum reform. *American Educational Research Journal, 43*(2), 257–293.

Crawford, B. A. (2000). Embracing the essence of inquiry: New roles for science teachers. *Journal of Research in Science Teaching, 37*(9), 916–937.

Crawford, B., Zembal-Saul, C., Munford, D., & Friedrichsen, P. (2005). Confronting prospective teachers' ideas of evolution and scientific inquiry using technology and inquiry-based tasks. *Journal of Research in Science Teaching, 43*(6), 613–637.

Cuban, L. (1988). A fundamental puzzle of school reform. *Phi Delta Kappan, 69*(5), 341–344.

Davis, K. S. (2002). "Change is hard": What science teachers are telling us about reform and teacher learning of innovative practices. *Science Education, 87*(1), 3–30.

DeBoer, G. (2002). Student centered teaching in a standards based world: Finding a sensible balance. *Science & Education, 11*(4), 405–417.

Demastes-Southerland, S., Good, R., & Peebles, P. (1995). Students' conceptual ecologies and the process of conceptual change in evolution. *Science Education, 79*(6), 637–666.

Driver, R., Asoko, H., Leach, J., Mortimer, E., & Scott, P. (1994). Constructing scientific knowledge in the classroom. *Educational Researcher, 23*(7), 5–12.

Driver, R. A., Newton, P., & Osborne, J. (2000). Establishing the norms of scientific argumentation in classrooms. *Science Education, 84*(3), 287–312.

Druva, C. A., & Anderson, R. D. (1983). Science teacher characteristics by teacher behavior and by student outcome. *Journal of Research in Science Teaching, 20*(5), 467–479.

Duit, R., & Treagust, D. F. (2003). Conceptual change: A powerful framework for improving science teaching and learning. *International Journal of Science Education, 25*(6), 671–688.

Duschl, R. A. (1990). *Restructuring science education: The importance of theories and their development.* New York: Teacher's College Press.

Duschl, R. A. (2000). Making the nature of science explicit. In R. Millar, J. Leach, & J. Osborne (Eds.), *Improving science education: The contribution of research* (pp. 187–206). Philadelphia: Open University Press.

Duschl, R. A., & Gitomer, D. H. (1997). Strategies and challenges to change the focus of assessment and instruction in science classrooms. *Educational Assessment, 4*(1), 37–73.

Duschl, R. A., & Grandy, R. (2005, February). *Reconsidering the character and role of inquiry in school science: Framing the debates.* Paper presented at Inquiry Conference on Developing a Consensus Research Agenda, New Brunswick, NJ.

Duschl, R. A., Schweingruber, H., & Shouse, A. W. (2007*). Taking science to school: Learning and teaching science in grades K-8.* Washington, DC: National Academy Press.

Eick, C., & Dias, M. (2005). Building the authority of experience in communities of practice: The development of preservice teachers' practical knowledge through coteaching in inquiry classrooms. *Science Education, 89*(3), 470–491.

Elby, A., & Hammer, D. (2001). On the substance of a sophisticated epistemology. *Science Education, 85,* 554–567.

Flick, F. B. (2003, March). *Inquiry as cognitive process.* Paper presented at the annual meeting of the National Association for Research in Science Teaching, Philadelphia.

Gess-Newsome, J. (1999). Secondary teachers' knowledge and beliefs about subject matter and their impact on instruction. In J. Gess-Newsome & N. G. Lederman (Eds.), *Examining pedagogical content knowledge: The construct and its implications for science education* (pp. 51–94). Dordrecht, the Netherlands: Kluwer.

Gess-Newsome, J., Southerland, S. A., Johnston, A., & Woodbury, S. (2003). Educational reform, personal practical theories, and dissatisfaction: The anatomy of change in college science teaching. *American Educational Research Journal, 40*(3), 731–767.

Grandy, R., & Duschl, R. (2005). *Reconsidering the character and role of inquiry in school science: Analysis of a conference.* Paper presented at the annual meeting of the International History, Philosophy, Sociology and Science Teaching Conference, Leeds, England.

Hammer, D. (1996). Misconceptions or P-Prims: How may alternative perspective of cognitive structure influence instructional perceptions and intentions. *The Journal of the Learning Sciences, 5,* 97–127.

Hammer, D., & Elby, A. (2003). Tapping epistemological resources for learning physics. *The Journal of the Learning Sciences, 12*(1), 53–90.

Hodson, D. (1999). Going beyond cultural pluralism: Science education for sociopolitical action. *Science Education, 83*(1), 775–796.

Hopkins, D. (1990). Integrating staff development and school improvement: A study of personality and school climate. In B. Joyce (Ed.), *ASCD yearbook: Changing school culture through staff development* (pp. 41–67). Alexandria, VA: Association for Supervision and Curriculum Development.

Hostetler, K. (2005). What is "good" education research? *Educational Researcher, 34*(6), 16–21.

Hovey, A., Hazelwood, C., & Svedkauskaire, A. (2005). *Critical issue: Science education in the era of No Child Left Behind. History, benchmarks, and standard.* North Central Regional Education Laboratories. Retrieved July 1, 2006, from http://www.ncrel.org/sdrs/areas/issues/content/cntareas/science/sc600.htm#references.

Huber, R. A., & Moore, C. J. (2002). High stakes testing and science learning assessment. *Science Educator, 11*(1), 18–23.

Ingersoll, R. (2003). *Is there really a teacher shortage?* Consortium for Policy Research in Education, University of Pennsylvania. Retrieved, July 12, 2006, from http://www.gse.upenn.edu/faculty/ingersoll.html.

Johnston, A. T. (2001). *A conceptual change analysis of nature of science conceptions: The deep roots and entangled vines of a conceptual ecology.* Unpublished doctoral dissertation, The University of Utah, Salt Lake City.

Kelly, G. J. (2004, April). *Toward an empirical program of epistemology in science education.* Paper presented at the annual meeting of the American Educational Research Association, San Diego, CA.

Kelly, G., & Green, J. (1998). The social nature of knowing: Toward a sociocultural perspective on conceptual change and meaning making. In B. Guzzetti & C. Hynd (Eds.), *Perspectives on conceptual change* (pp. 145–182). Mahwah, NJ: Lawrence Erlbaum.

King, P. M., & Kitchener, K. S. (1994). *Developing reflective judgment: Understanding and promoting intellectual growth and critical thinking in adolescents and adults.* San Francisco: Jossey Bass.

Kittleson, J. M. (2005, October). *Responsibility in the face of accountability.* Paper presented at Science Education at the Cross Roads, Storrs, CT.

Kittleson, J. M. (2006). *Epistemological beliefs and epistemological practices in elementary science education.* Unpublished doctoral dissertation, University of Delaware, Newark.

Kittleson, J., & Southerland, S. A. (2004). The role of "discourse" in group knowledge construction: A case study of engineering students. *Journal of Research in Science Teaching, 41*(3), 267–293.

Klopfer, L. E., & Champagne, A. B. (1990). Ghosts of crisis past. *Science Education, 74*(2), 133–154.

Kober, N. (2001). *It takes more than testing: Closing the achievement gap.* Washington, DC: Center on Education Policy.

Kuhn, D., & Weinstock, M. (2002). What is epistemological thinking and why does it matter? In B. K. Hofer & P. R. Pintrich (Eds.), *Personal epistemology: The psychology of beliefs about knowledge and knowing* (pp. 121–144). Mahwah, NJ: Lawrence Erlbaum.

Kuhn, T. (1970). *The structure of scientific revolutions* (2nd ed.). Chicago: University of Chicago Press.

Laplante, B. (1997). Teachers' beliefs and instructional strategies in science: Pushing analysis further. *Science Education, 81,* 277–294.

Lederman, N. G. (1992). Students' and teachers' conceptions of the nature of science: A review of the research. *Journal of Research in Science Teaching, 29*(4), 331–359.

Lederman, N. G., & Abd-El-Khalick, F. (1998). Avoiding de-natured science: Activities that promote understandings of the nature of science. In W. McComas (Ed.), *The nature of science in science education: Rationales and strategies* (pp. 83–126). Dordrecht, the Netherlands: Kluwer Academic.

Lederman, N. G., Abd-El-Khalick, F., Bell, R. L., & Schwartz, R. S. (2002). Views of nature of science questionnaire (VNOS): Toward valid and meaningful assessment of learners' conceptions of nature of science. *Journal of Research in Science Teaching, 39*(6), 497–521.

Lederman, N. G., & O'Malley, M. (1990). Students' perceptions of tentativeness in science: Development, use, and sources of change. *Science Education, 74*(2), 225–239.

Lederman, N. G., Wade, P., & Bell, R. L. (1998). Assessing understanding of the nature of science: A historical perspective. In W. F. McComas (Ed.), *The nature of science in science education* (pp. 331–350). Dordrecht, the Netherlands: Kluwer Academic.

Lee, O. (1997). Scientific literacy for all: What is it and how can we achieve it? *Journal of Research in Science Teaching, 34*(3), 219–222.

Lee, O. (2001). Culture and language in science educating: What do we know and what do we need to know? *Journal of Research in Science Teaching, 38*(5), 499–501.

Lee, O. (2003). Equity for linguistically and culturally diverse students in science education: A research agenda. *Teachers College Record, 105*(3), 465–489.

Lee, O., & Fradd, S. H. (1998). Science for all, including students from non-English-language backgrounds. *Educational Researcher, 27*(4), 12–21.

Lee, O., Hart, J. E., Cuevas, P., & Enders, C. (2004). Professional development in inquiry-based science for elementary teachers of diverse student groups. *Journal of Research in Science Teaching, 41*(10), 1021–1043.

Lee, O., & Luykx, A. (2006). *Science education and student diversity.* New York: Cambridge University Press.

Lemke, J. (1990). *Talking science.* Norwood, NJ: Ablex.

Letts, W. J. (1999). Teaching science/learning gender: Preservice elementary curriculum discourse. An anti-essentialist approach to gender-inclusive science. *Gender and Education, 13*(3), 275–290.

Lortie, D. (1975). *Schoolteacher: A sociological study.* Chicago: University of Chicago Press.

Lott, G. W. (1983). The effect of inquiry teaching and advance organizers upon student outcomes in science education. *Journal of Research in Science Teaching, 20*(5), 437–451.

Loving, K., & Foster, A. (2000). The religion in the science classroom issue: Seeking graduate student conceptual change. *Science Education, 84,* 445–468.

Luera, G. R., & Otto, C. A. (2005). Development and evaluation of an inquiry-based elementary science teacher education program reflecting current reform movements. *Journal of Science Teacher Education, 16*(3), 241–258.

Luft, J. (2001). Changing inquiry practices and beliefs: The impact of an inquiry-based professional development programme on beginning and experienced secondary science teachers. *International Journal of Science Education, 23*(5), 517–534.

Luft, J., Roehrig, G., Brown, M., Fletcher, S., Kern, A., & Puthoff, E. (2007). *Beginning secondary science teachers in different induction programs: Findings from the pilot year.* Submitted for review.

Lynch, S. (2001). "Science for all" is not equal to "one size fits all": Linguistic and cultural diversity and science education reform. *Journal of Research in Science Teaching, 38*(5), 622–627.

Marx, R. W., Blumenfeld, P. C., Krajcik, J. S., Fishman, B., Soloway, E., Geier, R., et al. (2004). Inquiry-based science in the middle grades: Assessment of learning in urban systemic reform. *Journal of Research in Science Education, 41*(10), 1063–1080.

Matese, G., Griesdorn, J., & Edelson, D. C. (2002). *Teacher beliefs about assessment in inquiry-based science: Research to inform professional development.* Paper presented at the annual meeting of the American Educational Research Association, New Orleans, LA.

McCarthy, C. B. (2005). Effects of thematic-based, hands-on science teaching versus a textbook approach for students with disabilities. *Journal of Research in Science Teaching, 42*(3), 245–263.

McKibbin, M., & Joyce, B. R. (1981). Psychological states. *Theory Into Practice, 19*(4), 248–255.

Meadows, L. (2005, October). *Vision & reality: Sustaining teacher change.* Paper presented at Science Education at the Crossroads, Storrs, CT.

Moje, E., Collazo, T., Carrillo, R., & Marx, R. (2001). "Maestro, what is 'quality'?" Language, literacy, and discourse in project-based science. *Journal of Research in Science Teaching, 38,* 469–498.

Moje, E. B., & Shepardson, D. P. (1998). Social interactions and children's changing understanding of electric circuits: Exploring unequal power relations in "peer"-learning groups. In B. Guzzetti & C. Hynd (Eds.), *Perspectives on conceptual change* (pp. 225–234). Mahwah, NJ: Lawrence Erlbaum.

Moss, D. M., Abrams, E. D., & Robb-Kull, J. (1998). Can we be scientists too? Secondary students' perceptions of scientific research from a project-based classroom. *Journal of Science Education and Technology, 7*(2) 149–161.

National Commission on Excellence in Education. (NCEE). (1983). *A nation at risk: The imperative for educational reform.* A report to the nation and the Secretary of Education United States Department of Education by the National Commission on Excellence in Education. Retrieved June 30, 2006, from http://www.goalline.org/Goal%20Line/NatAtRisk.html.

National Research Council. (NRC). (1996). *National science education standards.* Washington, DC: National Academy Press.

National Research Council. (NRC). (1997). *Science teaching reconsidered: A handbook.* Washington, DC: National Academy Press.

National Research Council. (NRC). (2000). *Inquiry and the national standards in science education.* Washington, DC: National Academy Press.

No Child Left Behind Act. (NCLB). (2001). Pub. L. No. 107–110, 115 Stat. 1425. Retrieved June 30, 2006, from http://www.ed.gov/legislation/ESEA02.

Norman, O., Ault, C., Bentz, B., & Meskimen, L. (2001). The black-white achievement gap as a perennial challenge of urban science education: A sociocultural and historical overview with implications for research and practice. *Journal of Research in Science Teaching, 38*(10), 1101–1114.

Norris, S. P., & Phillips, L. M. (2003). How literacy in its fundamental sense is central to scientific literacy. *Science Education, 87*(2), 224–240.

Pajares, M. F. (1992). Teachers' beliefs and educational research: Cleaning up a messy construct. *Review of Educational Research, 62*(3), 307–322.

Parsons, E. C., Travis, C., & Simpson, J. S. (2005). The Black cultural ethos, students' instructional context preferences, and student achievement: An examination of culturally congruent science instruction in the eighth grade classes of one African American and one Euro-American teacher. *The Negro Educational Review, 56*(2, 3), 183–203.

Pfundt, H., & Duit, R. (1994). *Bibliography: Students' alternative frameworks and science education* (4th ed.). Keil, Germany: Institute for Science Education at the University of Keil.

Pintrich, P. R., Marx, R. W., & Boyle, R. A. (1993). Beyond cold conceptual change: The role of motivational beliefs and classroom contextual factors in the process of conceptual change. *Review of Educational Research, 63*, 167–199.

Poole, M. (1996). " . . . for more and better religious education." *Science and Education, 5*, 165–174.

Posner, G. J., Strike, K. A., Hewson, P. W., & Gertzog, W. A. (1982). Accommodation of a scientific conception: Towards a theory of conceptual change. *Science Education, 67*(4), 489–508.

Ramey-Gassert, L., Shroyer, M. G., & Staver, J. R. (1996). A qualitative study of factors influencing science teaching self-efficacy of elementary level teachers. *Science Education, 80*(3), 283–315.

Rivet, A. E., & Krajcik, J. S. (2004). Achieving standards in urban systemic reform: An example of a sixth grade project-based science curriculum. *Journal of Research in Science Teaching, 41*(7), 669–692.

Rodriguez, A. J. (1998). Strategies for counterresistance: Toward sociotransformative constructivism and learning to teach science for diversity and for understanding. *Journal of Research in Science Teaching, 35*(6), 589–622.

Romberg, T. A., & Price, G. G. (1983). Curriculum implementation and staff development as cultural change. In G. Griffin (Ed.), *Staff development: 82nd yearbook of the National Society for the Study of Education* (pp. 154–184). Chicago: University of Chicago Press.

Rosebery, A. (2004, May). *Some thoughts about culture and the preparation of science teachers for urban classrooms.* Wingspread conference on Urban Science Education, Racine, Wisconsin.

Roth, W. M. (1993). Construction sites: Science labs and classrooms. In K. Tobin & D. Tippins (Eds.), *The practice of constructivism in science education* (pp. 145–170). Hillsdale, NJ: Lawrence Erlbaum.

Rubba, P., & Anderson, H. (1978). Development of an instrument to assess secondary school students' understanding of the nature of scientific knowledge. *Science Education, 62*(4), 449–458.

Rudolph, J. (2002). *Scientists in the classroom: The cold war reconstruction of American science education.* New York: Palgrave Macmillian.

Saka, Y. (2007). *What happens to our reform minded beginning science teachers?* Unpublished doctoral dissertation, Florida State University, Tallahassee.

Sandall, B. R. (2003). Elementary science: Where are we now? *Journal of Elementary Science Education, 15*(2), 13–30.

Sandholtz, J. H., & Finan, E. C. (1998). Cooperating teachers' perspectives on the student teaching triad. *Journal of Teacher Education, 49*(2), 108–119.

Sandoval, W. (2003). The inquiry paradox: Why doing science doesn't necessarily change ideas about science. In C. P. Constantinou & Z. C. Zacharia (Eds.), *Proceedings of the Sixth International Computer-Based Learning in Science Conference 2003* (pp. 825–834). Nicosia, Cyprus.

Sandoval, W. (2005). Understanding students' practical epistemologies and their influence on learning through inquiry. *Science Education, 89*(4), 634–656.

Schmidt, W. H. (2003, February 6). *International perspective.* Presentation made at the Secretary's Summit on Mathematics, Washington, DC. Retrieved July 1, 2006, from http://www.ed.gov/rschstat/research/progs/mathscience/schmidt.html.

Schwab, J. (1962). The teaching of science as enquiry. In *The teaching of science* (pp. 1–103). Cambridge, MA: Harvard University Press.

Settlage, J. (2003, January). *Inquiry's allure and illusion: Why it remains just beyond our reach.* Paper presented at the annual meeting of the National Association for Research in Science Teaching, Philadelphia.

Settlage, J. (2006, September). Prospects of pragmatism: The generation of science education adventurist. Plenary session at Science Education at the Crossroads, Ogden, UT.

Settlage, J., & Meadows, L. (2002). Standards-based reform and its unintended consequences: Implications for science education within America's urban schools. *Journal of Research in Science Teaching, 39*(2), 114–127.

Shaver, A., Cuevas, P., Lee, O., & Avalos, M. (in press). Teachers' perceptions of policy influences on science instruction with culturally and linguistically diverse elementary students. *Journal of Research in Science Teaching.*

Shepardson, D. P., & Britsch, S. J. (2006). Zones of interaction: Differential access to elementary science discourse. *Journal of Research in Science Teaching, 43*(5), 443–466.

Smith, L. K. (2005). The impact of early life history on teachers' beliefs: In-school and out-of-school experiences as learners and knowers of science. *Teachers and Teaching: Theory and Practice, 11*(1), 5–36.

Smith, L. K., & Gess-Newsome, J. (2004). Elementary science methods courses and the National Science Education Standards: Are we adequately preparing teachers? *Journal of Science Teacher Education, 15*(2), 91–110.

Smith, L. K., & Southerland, S. A. (2007). Reforming practice or modifying reforms? Elementary teachers' response to the tools of reform. *Journal of Research in Science Teaching, 43*(3).

Smith, M. U., & Scharmann, L. C. (1999). Defining versus describing the nature of science: A pragmatic analysis for classroom teachers and science educators. *Journal for Research in Science Teaching, 83,* 493–509.

Southerland, S. A. (2000). Epistemic universalism and the shortcomings of curricular multicultural science education. *Science and Education, 9,* 289–307.

Southerland, S. A., & Gess-Newsome, J. (1999). Preservice teachers' views of inclusive science teaching as shaped by images of teaching, learning, and knowledge. *Science Education, 83,* 131–150.

Southerland, S. A., Gess-Newsome, J., & Johnston, A. (2003). Portraying science in the classroom: The manifestation of scientists' beliefs in classroom practice. *Journal of Research in Science Teaching, 40,* 669–691.

Southerland, S. A., Johnston, A., & Sowell, S. (2006). Describing teachers' conceptual ecologies for the nature of science. *Science Education, 90*(5), 874–906.

Southerland, S. A., Johnston, A., Sowell, S., & Settlage, J. (2005). *Perhaps triangulatin isn't enough: A call for crystallization as methodological reference in NOS research.* Paper presented at the annual meeting of the American Educational Research Association, Montreal, Canada.

Southerland, S. A., Kittleson, J., Settlage, J., & Lanier, K. (2005). Individual and group meaning making in an urban, third grade classroom: Red fog, cold cans, and seeping vapor. *Journal of Research in Science Teaching, 42*(9), 1032–1061.

Sowell, S. (2004). *Doing gender/teaching science: A feminist poststructural analysis of middle school science teachers' identity negotiations.* Unpublished doctoral dissertation, Florida State University, Tallahassee.

Sowell, S., Southerland, S. A., & Blanchard, M. (2006, May). *Who are the "they" in "They say . . . ?" Finding fruitfulness of nature of science within an urban context.* Paper presented at the annual meeting of the National Association for Research in Science, San Francisco.

Strike, K. A., & Posner, G. J. (1992). A revisionist theory of conceptual change. In R. Duschl & R. Hamilton (Eds.), *Philosophy of science, cognitive psychology, and educational theory and practice.* Albany: State University of New York Press.

Tschannen-Moran, M., Hoy, A. W., & Hoy, W. K. (1998). Teacher efficacy: Its meaning and measure. *Review of Educational Research, 68,* 202–248.

Tyack, D., & Cuban, L. (1995). *Tinkering toward utopia: A century of public school reform.* Cambridge, MA: Harvard University Press.

Varelas, M., Pappas, C. C., & Rife, A. (2004). Dialogic inquiry in an urban 2nd grade classroom: How intertextuality shapes and is shaped by social interactions and conceptual understandings. In R. Yerrick & W. -M. Roth (Eds.), *Establishing scientific classroom discourse communities: Multiple voices of research on teaching and learning* (pp. 139–168). Mahwah, NJ: Lawrence Erlbaum.

Wallace, C. S., & Kang, N. (2004). An investigation of experienced secondary science teachers' beliefs about inquiry: An examination of competing belief sets. *Journal of Research in Science Teaching, 41*(9), 936–960.

Wandersee, J. H., & Fisher, K. M. (2000). Knowing biology. In K. M. Fisher, J. H. Wandersee, & D. Moody (Eds.), *Mapping biology knowledge* (pp. 39–54). Dordrecht, the Netherlands: Kluwer.

Wandersee, J. H., Mintzes, J. J., & Novak, J. D. (1994). Research on alternative conceptions in science. In D. L. Gabel (Ed.), *Handbook of research on science teaching and learning* (pp. 177–210). New York: Macmillan.

Warren, B., Ballenger, C., Ogonowski, M., Rosebery, A. S., & Hudicourt-Barnes, J. (2001). Rethinking diversity in learning science: The logic of everyday sense-making. *Journal of Research in Science Teaching, 38*(5), 529–552.

Weld, J., & Funk, L. (2005). "I'm not the science type": Effect of an inquiry biology content course on preservice elementary teachers' intentions about teaching science. *Journal of Science Teacher Education, 16*(3), 189–204.

Wideen, M. F., O'Shea, T., Pye, I., & Ivany, G. (1997). High-stakes testing and the teaching of science. *Canadian Journal of Education, 22*(4), 428–444.

Wilson, M. R., & Bertenthal, M. W. (Eds.). (2005). *Systems for state science assessment.* Washington, DC: National Academies Press.

Windschitl, M. (2003). Inquiry projects in science teacher education: What can investigative experiences reveal about teacher thinking and eventual classroom practice? *Science Education, 87*(1), 112–143.

Windschitl, M. (2004). Folk theories of "inquiry": How pre-service teachers reproduce the discourse and practices of an atheoretical scientific method. *Journal of Research in Science Teaching, 41*(5), 481–512.

Windschitl, M. (2006). Why we can't talk to one another about science education reform. *Phi Delta Kappan, 87*(5), 348–355.

Yerrick, R., Parke, H., & Nugent, J. (1997). Struggling to promote deeply rooted change: The "filtering effect" of teachers' beliefs on understanding transformational views of teaching science. *Science Education, 81,* 137–159.

Yore, L. D., Bisanz, G. L., & Hand, B. M. (2003). Examining the literacy component of science literacy: 25 years of language arts and science research. *International Journal of Science Education, 25*(6), 689–725.

Yore, L., Henriques, L., Crawford, B., Smith, L. K., Zwiep, S., & Tillotson, J. (in press). Selecting and using inquiry approaches to teach science: The influence of context in elementary, middle & secondary schools. In E. Abrams, S. A. Southerland, & P. Silva (Eds.), *Inquiry in the classrooms: Challenges and opportunities.* Greenwich, CT: Information Age.

Chapter 3

Queering Foundations: Queer and Lesbian, Gay, Bisexual, and Transgender Educational Research

Cris Mayo

University of Illinois at Urbana-Champaign

Since the beginning of the modern homophile movement, gay people have made education of themselves and heterosexuals central to their political project. That dedication to education can be seen in the first lesbian periodical, *The Ladder* (October 1956–December 1966), which included in its frontispiece a series of statements of purpose, including

Education of the variant, with particular emphasis on the psychological, physiological and sociological aspects, to enable her to understand herself and make her adjustment to society in all its social, civic and economic implications—this to be accomplished by establishing and maintaining as complete a library as possible of both fiction and non-fiction literature on the sex deviant theme; by sponsoring public discussions on pertinent subjects to be conducted by leading members of the legal, psychiatric, religious and other professions.

For all its talk of adjustment, the authors in *The Ladder* also were deeply interested in creating what lesbians could be, questioning social norms, and debating critical features of gender and sexuality oppression. As much as it is now current practice to distinguish between the beginnings of the lesbian and gay movement as essentialist and our newer approaches as social constructionist (a parallel gesture also is made in writings about research in education on sexuality), this is often an oversimplification. Far from celebrating essential differences among genders and sexualities, early radical lesbian feminist writing underscored the provisional and political definition of sexual minority status. In the words of the Radicalesbians (1973), "lesbianism is the rage of all women condensed to the point of explosion" (p. 240). Shifting ideas about sexuality from psychological identity to political statement, they began a move that was further complicated by attention to the intersections of identity. As the Black lesbian antiracist feminist group the Combahee River Collective (1984) put it, although their particular goal was "the development of integrated analysis and practice based upon the fact that the major

Review of Research in Education
March 2007, Vol. 31, pp. 78–94
DOI: 10.3102/0091732X06298013
© 2007 AERA. http://rre.aera.net

systems of oppression are interlocking" (p. 210), they simultaneously recognized that "the only people who care enough about us to work consistently for our liberation is us" (p. 212). In other words, although much recent discussion has developed around the difference between lesbian and gay studies—supposedly an approach that centralizes demanding visibility, interrogating bias, and illuminating lesbian and gay presence—and queer theory—supposedly an approach more poststructurally interested in inter-sectionalities of difference and disturbing foundational ideas about gender, sexuality, and transgression—these easy distinctions wind up falling apart under close scrutiny, whether one is examining the history of the movements or the brief history of educational research in minority sexualities. Similar to debates over essentialism versus constructionism, it turns out that there is quite a bit of radical problematization of foundational concepts in writings from the gay and lesbian liberation movement and the homophile movement. It turns out, to a large degree, things have been queer all along.

This chapter will first briefly examine general trends and shifts in lesbian, gay, bisexual, and transgender (LGBT) and queer educational research in the past two decades. Then, I will turn to a discussion of one overarching theme—that of the place of coming out in LGBT and queer research in educational foundations. In this examination of research involving questions around coming out and space, I will draw on a wide range of published research as well as some observations from my own research on queer youth. I intend these accounts to show that youth are as involved in the complexity of questions researchers ask as the researchers themselves. In a sense, the turn to queer theory has enabled a theoretical coming out for educational researchers and LGBT and queer youth alike, giving us all a chance to examine the practices of theorization that organically develop from experience as well as highlighting the centrality of theory to research.

Early research on LGBT issues in education sought to complicate the theoretical ground of work on—or work that ignored—sexuality. Included in these early 1990s (if such recent literature can be considered early) discussions of lesbian and gay issues in education was a concern that without looking at gender bias and inflexibility of gender roles one cannot fully understand the operation of homophobia (Sapon-Shevin & Goodman, 1992; Sears, 1992), without critically examining heterosexism and masculinity one cannot address homophobia (Friend, 1995; Nayak & Kehily, 1997), without being cautious about the exclusions we enact when we begin to address lesbian and gay issues or see them represented in textbooks we will simply replicate the inequalities we critique (Whatley, 1992b), and without examining the political context of our discussions we will continue to find it difficult to discuss pleasure in sex education classes (Whatley, 1992a).

Recently, some researchers have suggested that older research focused on the obstacles facing LGBT youth, whereas newer work examines their resiliency and agency (Blackburn, 2004; Bochenek & Brown, 2001; Bohan, Russell, & Mont-gomery, 2002; Gray, 1999; Kosciw & Cullen, 2001, Muñoz-Plaza, Quinn, & Rounds, 2002; Savin-Williams, 1990, 2005; Talburt, 2004). Of course, these calls for a reexamination of the discourse of LGBT youth risk point to the constraints that

LGBT/queer youth face; otherwise, why would they even need to be resilient? Might one also look at earlier work critiquing institutional, social, and political barriers to LGBT flourishing as themselves statements of agency? After all, critique is agency. Still, where early work critiqued notions of sexuality that ignored LGBT existence and advocated for recognition of LGBT students, teachers, parents, and families, newer work begins the work of critiquing ideas that have been central to LGBT politics and using queer theory to point out the limits of a politics of visibility that implicitly demands intelligibility and to caution against the exclusionary tendencies of identity categories, even oppositional ones.

Queer theory works the verb "to queer" to centralize the constant need for critical attention to the processes of subjectification, whereby particular meanings of identity come to form potentially limiting understandings of identities, practices, and communities. But queer theory, similar to LGBT studies, is concerned with examining places in dominant discourses that are particularly open to the play of meanings that make change, however momentary, possible. Queer theory, then, is as concerned with the press of normative power in dominant culture as it is in queer subcultures themselves, concerned not only with the limits of discourse around queerness but the limits of discourse in general. Work troubling the metaphor of the closet and coming out (Rasmussen, 2004), pointing to the problematic tendency for gay and queer to collapse into White and male and the need to challenge White masculinity (Pinar, 2003), and arguing that queerness itself sets up an unattainable ideal, forever transgressive and unknown but somehow also something to aspire to, all point to the effect queer theory has had on scholarship on sexual minorities. Queer theory now expands well beyond LGBT to queer heterosexuality (Rodriguez & Pinar, 2007), gender identity, gender formation and sex assignment, processes of racial identification and community formation and maintenance, as well as a variety of other issues that intersectionally form the diversity of sexualities. In an even broader claim to queer theory's particular relevance for education, Deborah Britzman (1995) argues,

To work within gay and lesbian theories, then, allows for the consideration of two kinds of pedagogical stakes. One has to do with thinking ethically about what discourses of difference, choice, and visibility mean in classrooms, in pedagogy, and in how education can be thought about. Another has to do with thinking through structures of disavowal within education, or the refusals—whether curricular, social, or pedagogical—to engage a traumatic perception that produces the subject of difference as a disruption, as the outside to normalcy. (p. 152)

Even as introducing queer subject and LGBT issues inevitably queers the presumed heterosexual organization of educational practice and institutions, much work in LGBT issues in education is less interested in the theoretical nuance of queerness than in attempting to make those institutions more accountable to LGBT members. Bridging research with immediate practical application, a variety of books address ending homophobia in education, is an especially challenging task given cultural taboos against youth sexuality and sexuality in general (Kissen, 2002; Lipkin, 2004; Sears & Williams, 1997). Other articles and collections trouble the easy-sounding solutions and conceptions underlying attempts at making schools safer by adding sexuality to diversity programs (Blount & Anahita, 2004; Britzman, 1995, 1997; Bryson & de Castell, 1993; de Castell & Bryson, 1997; Harwood, 2004; Martindale, 1997; Mayo, 2002, 2004b; Rasmussen, 2004, 2006; Rofes, 2004; Talburt, 2004). Britzman (1995), for instance, has argued that queer theory disrupts the normalcy of education, maintains the difficulty of education, and because it is meant to provoke, cannot be easily integrated into education as usual.

The disruption of education's normalcy effected by the integration of LGBT issues also are examined in research on the ethics of teaching in a diverse, democratic context. Whether as a mobilizing example or an extended illumination of a theoretical point, foundations of education has recognized the centrality of queer difference to key pedagogical, research, and policy issues. Especially in work examining the collision between religious commitments and democratic, inclusive classrooms, gay issues appear to be flashpoints for controversy (Applebaum, 2003; Feinberg, 1998). As Boler (2004) argues, too often, pedagogical invitations to self-disclosure seem to encourage "thinly veiled" expressions of hate speech (pp. 9–10). She argues for an "affirmative action" pedagogy that recognizes the historical limitations on minority speech and encourages us to challenge not only the spoken prejudices of students but to consider the kinds of classroom practices that may make it harder for queer teachers to be out (Boler, 2004, p. 12). Applebaum (2003) argues that public school educators cannot hide behind religious convictions to support their homophobia but instead must engage in reasonable practices grounded in democratic values.

In addition, book-length studies of policy implications of homosexuality and nonnormative heterosexuality bring together educational policy analysis, cultural history, and studies of representation to highlight the tensions that sexuality raises in school communities. Studies include examinations of policy, controversy, and representational disputes about teen pregnancy and abstinence-only education (Levine, 2002; Mayo, 2004a; Pillow, 2004), safe schools policy and legislation (MacGillivray, 2004), civil rights law disputes and queer youth (Filax, 2006), HIV/AIDS (Mayo, 2004a; Patton, 1996; Silin, 1995), gay–straight alliance policies (Miceli, 2005; Perrotti & Westheimer, 2001), and experiences of sexual minority members of school communities living under particular policies and laws (Birden, 2005). In addition, large-scale surveys of school climate undertaken by the Human Rights Watch (Bochenek & Brown, 2001) and the Gay, Lesbian, and Straight Educators' Network (GLSEN; 2005), as well as collections of LGBT adult memories of school (Jennings, 1998), LGBT teacher and student accounts of school experience (Woog, 1995), ethnographies of queer youth (Gray, 1999), collections of queer youth narratives (Bello, Flynn, Palmer, Rodriguez, & Vente, 2004; Sonnie, 2000), and qualitative research on gay parents' experiences with schools (Casper & Schultz, 1999), all combine nuanced personal experiences with examinations of the organizational and policy context of public schools. Other work builds the specifics of queer critique into methodological and epistemological approaches to research and policy (Capper,

1999; Dilley, 1999; Honeychurch, 1996; Kumashiro, 2002; Leck, 2000; Sears, 1993; Talburt, 1999; Unks, 1995). In addition, research and writing on school communities and LGBT issues also can be found in leadership and administration, particularly important because of the impact that school leaders can have on school climate and the difficulties LGBT administrators may face (Fryand & Capper, 2003). Although schools have been organizationally structured to keep out gender and sexual dissenters, educational professions have nonetheless been populated by "gender transgressors" (Blount, 2000, p. 83) and sexual minorities (Lugg, 2003).

Even though I've begun with the gesture of similarity across the decades of sexual minority research in education, LGBT writing in social foundations has gone from instance on existence and care for particular concerns of LGBT students to discursive analysis of the production of heterosexuality and queerness in curricula and policy and materialist analysis of queer bodies in straight institutions or research practices. In other words, we might say that research and writing has gone from demands for recognition, respect, and rights to discourse to psychoanalytic theory, poststructural theory, and new materialist theorization of bodies, although not in any easily supersessionist way. Although tensions do remain between approaches to educational research on sexual minorities, those dynamics also are mirrored in most work in queer research. Some researchers may emphasize the rupture entailed by queer presence, the overwhelming power of normalcy, and still also remark on the moments of ordinariness in queer and sexual minority lives. Other researchers point to the desire for unlabeled normality among a younger generation of people involved in same-sex relationships, to the point where they do not want to identify as gay (Savin-Williams, 2005). Even in those accounts of what has been called the postgay generation, those same young people also point to the pressures on them to conform to the norm and the difficulty that poses for their attempts to live ordinary lives. LGBT studies and queer writing, then, are caught in the same simultaneous gestures toward ubiquity and uniqueness, mundane and transgressive, comfort and critique that other work on a variety of oppositional minority groups has traced.

THE PROBLEM OF "OUT"

One of the difficulties for researchers of sexual minorities has been determining exactly whom it is they are researching and how those research participants might be identified. The most easily identified members of sexual minorities are "out," that is, they self-consciously and publicly identify as a member of a sexual minority group and thus can be contacted, observed, and collaborated with on research projects. For some researchers, "outness" is a potential problem. How can we know the limitations of our studies if we can only research LGBT students who are in some way known to us? How do we reckon with the fact that their very outness makes them a specific subset? Not every researcher sees this as necessarily an obstacle, but nonetheless, the realization that there are a variety of ways of being queer, engaging in same-sex relations without identifiying as LGBT, and a host of other complications to the issue means that studying anything around sexuality is complicated affair. Ginsburg (1998) points out the limitations imposed by research protocols and the delicacy of the subject. Not only do the youth involved need to be out to be recognized by the researcher but because parental approval is necessary for studying youth, the parents need to be supportive of their out gay/lesbian children to be willing to give permission. Other researchers who find themselves stymied by district and parental approval requirements turn instead to writing about the problematics of that process rather than actually doing their initial school-based research (Donelson & Rogers, 2004). For Savin-Williams (2005), the focus on out gay and lesbian youth is equivalent to studying Black youth only by studying "Afrocentric advocates" or studying young women only by studying "feminists" (p. 180). Although much of his work complicates the variety of aspects of sexuality entailed in self-definition, this remark too simply tracks outness with political belief. Youth are not only out along different political trajectories but the spaces and times in which they are out vary considerably, as do the meanings they attach to their outness. For some, being out means provocation and disruption, for others being out represents an authentic expression of one aspect of their sense of self. From my own experiences, I know that observing the gay–straight alliance with no openly gay members is not the full story. Outside of adult view, members are out to one another and not even the reassurances of a sympathetic researcher will alter the generational split or the lack of comfort in being out outside of a friendship network. The difficulty, then, in doing research on "just out" gay youth is magnified as one understands the complexity of sexual identity and the different ways youth embody and experience their identities in different spaces and times. Not only are researchers more likely to get parental approval from youth who already have parental approval for their identities but they are likely to be unwilling to put youth not out to parents at risk by trying to study them. This very situation—where youth are uncomfortable and feel put at risk by research protocols intent on protecting them via parental oversight—ought to be a dynamic that deserves its own research. The problem, of course, is that the very youth one might want to interview about their feelings of risk from parental knowledge are themselves unable to speak in either direction. They cannot explain themselves to researchers and they are not willing to explain themselves to their parents. This is not meant to indicate that they are unable to be out and active within their peer groups or at community events but rather to complicate common definitions of "out." Being out is not a settled issue, it is not dependent on political ideology, and it is not an indication of either complete safety or utterly unlivable risk. Rather, being out is a complex series of negotiations, a complicated set of weighed consequences and benefits, as well as a way of creating spaces for possibilities with others.

Because space, knowledge, and sexuality are closely linked, theoretical, as well as empirical, research grapples with the meaning and place of sexual identity, activity, and community. Sometimes in their attempt to get at the complex interaction of public/private, discussions seem less to complicate the relationship of these analytic categories than to stumble over the contradictory influences that the public/private distinction has for queer youth. In some of this theoretical muddle, the tendency to overdeconstruct appears to set aside writers concerned with the context of here and now. Bryson (2002) worries about such tendencies to deconstruct minority sexual identity, asking,

What does it mean to carry out a deconstructive ontological project within a realm that looks . . . like a battlefield littered with wounded bodies and peopled with proud men and women who have put their lives, careers, family affiliations and the like on the line for just the right to lay claim, and proudly, to lesbian and gay identity? (p. 376)

Although visibility alone does not tell the full story of sexual identities, activities, or communities, there is a tendency for critique of coming out to turn into a too ready dismissal of the constitution of sexuality under systems of meaning that simultaneously rely on intelligibility and are drawn to obscure gestures and meanings not quite capable of being articulated. For instance, Rasmussen (2006, p. 153) problematizes coming out because it freezes identities that queer theory insists are in flux. Without maintaining a critical analysis of claims to identity, notions of sexuality concretize and slide into claims of essential difference, neglecting to critically examine the social context in which they are formed. In a dialogue about coming out and deconstructing identity, Bromley (2005) troubles queer deconstructive practices of disrupting narratives of identity, arguing instead that because "to identify as 'queer' in school is to fight against societal norms of the heterosexual world" (p. 30), disrupting queer identities then disrupt queer potential for critique. Part of the problem of queer critique is not so much the degree of scrutiny to which one puts sexual identity—Rasmussen and Bromley agree on that—but rather where one stops the time of sexuality. Bromley, in a very short rejoinder to Rasmussen's cautions on coming out and subjectification, is not so much arguing for strategic essentialism, where the complex processes of subjectification are sidestepped to make political statements, but rather arguing that even in processes of critical negotiation there are moments when one necessarily engages in critique of one's self and critique of a context in which the stopped time of that self encounters an obstacle. Critical examination of social context and subjectivity can be simultaneous, but at one point in time, one must say something beyond the observation that all is process. As Silin (1995) explains, writing in the context of HIV/AIDS, constructing narratives of experience help give one a sense of an audience, a "reason to repeat the story" (p. 1), even as one is suspicious of the process of narrativization. However necessary a fiction they are, narratives are also themselves sites of critique, especially as those narratives are bound together with political questions about coming out and hiding, knowledge and ignorance (Silin, 1995, p. 9).

Loutzenheiser and MacIntosh (2004) observe that more kids are coming out as queer, but they are concerned that normative forces frame the coming out process in ways that diminishes the agency of coming out. They argue that when youth come out in an atmosphere of heteronormativity, "their private lives are made public and unwittingly become the central mechanism of their *publicness*" (p. 152). They then contend that queer kids are outed, too, by the absence of representation in the classroom. In other words, they point to the constraints of narratives and practices of heteronormativity that can overwhelm queer critique or constrain queer presence.

CONTRADICTIONS AND QUEERNESS

The debate over deconstruction and theoretical troubling of key concepts around queerness helps to underscore the dilemmas of writing and research on queer youth. We are at a classic moment in identity/postidentity politics where we are finding ourselves without a way to negotiate competing desires for research: the first to examine experiences of youth, the second to be cautious about what we mean by "experience" (Scott, 1993), or youth, or queer. Qualitative accounts of queer youth are grappling not only with the problems of representation—too much emphasis on obstacles, not enough on resiliency; too much emphasis on self-conscious identity, not enough on same-gender practices— but also the generational inconsistencies and shifts in queer identity. Researchers and researched alike are continually coming up against the limits of language, concepts, and identity positions to adequately describe themselves. Queer youth who are out and politically active begin to sound exasperated at academics who want to remind them of their constructedness, not only because those identities are hard-won and the processes of constructing in opposition are often quite clear to them but also because identities are useful strategies. Other youth who do not want to be labeled or engage in political activity appear equally baffled that anyone would try to label themselves by a term of derision. In other words, on both sides of the youth political spectrum, there is dissatisfaction with categories of meaning that currently structure and disrupt the contemporary political context and simultaneously, on both ends of the spectrum, a clear understanding of the cost of identifying as queer. For some youth, this means an enthusiastic embrace of the term, whereas for others, it means a retreat into the happy limbo of nonidentity.

Other strategies of identification also include particular school-based pressures as well as student creativity. Boldt (1996) traces a complex process of contradictory understandings of gender identity and public gender crossings in elementary students. She details situations where athletic ability or desire to play with girls created a context in which a girl and boy, respectively, were able to identify with and be identified as boy and girl. In some contexts, other students seemed eager to continue the cross-identification, although Boldt also pointed out that there were moments when the other students objected. She suggests that these, often simultaneously held, supportive and critical ideas about gender crossing may be an indication that students are trying to figure out what adults want them to say: "How to play the school game?" (Boldt, 1996, p. 124). In other words, youth in schools are themselves unsure which space they occupy—are they supposed to be creative, conformist, or both? For Britzman and Gilbert (2004), writing in the context of HIV/AIDS education, questions about identity and narrative in education raise the issue of the time of education. Because education is caught between the past and aims toward the future, they contend that education ought to be more hospitable to possibilities not yet formed. Cautioning against overconfidence in our ability to pedagogically craft such possibilities, Bryson and de Castell (1993) note how difficult it is to intervene in the "production of 'normalcy' in schooled subjects" (p. 285).

Because of the complications involved in theorizing subjectivity as a critical yet constrained process, and the desire to begin to research accounts of how that process works in specific contexts, research is increasingly interested in the space and time of critical engagement with sexuality (Britzman & Gilbert, 2004; Mayo, 2004a; Pillow, 2004; Rasmussen, 2006). Examining how queer youth stumble through their own complex engagement with the meaning of space may help to demonstrate how knowledge, self-representation, and social recognition warps and relies on the public/private distinction, itself reliant on particular meanings attached to particular spaces. A repeated theme in interviews done with queer youth and supportive faculty is the intermittency and instability of being out and how different social and spatial contexts shift the possibilities for being out, being recognized as out, needing to strategize invisibility, and so on. For students in one gay advocacy group, being out at school was a private act in the sense that did not involve their families or adult community members. When the possibility that their school-based outness would develop into a wider form of being out via media coverage of a planned demonstration, the youth decided as a group that they could not afford that kind of publicity. In other words, within the school context they were able to be publicly known by classmates and the rest of the school community as out, but they felt the broader community's knowledge would have entailed difficulty in maintaining parental support; extended family ties; and racial, ethnic, immigrant, and religious community membership (C. Mayo, personal communication, 2005). In another, very different example, two White lesbian students who were out at school felt nonetheless much more out when at queer community events and preferred that form of publicity, choosing adult queer events as opposed to school-sponsored, queer-supportive events that they felt were not particularly supportive (C. Mayo, personal communication, 2004). In their case, the public of the school was insufficient to fully support their needs for queer community participation and recognition of their queer identity. They could be out only to the extent that their schoolmates understood what that meant, and to them, it was incomplete knowledge and thus incomplete outness. Other students have gone further and said that they have no desire to be out at school at all, that the space is too confining and they would rather enact their queer identities only in queer community outside of school (C. Mayo, personal communication, 2005). For these students, the school community is simultaneously too public, in that being out opens one to harassment, and too private, in that one cannot easily mingle with other members of one's community, there is no reason to bother expending energy to be out in a context where few other people share that identity or would even understand it.

OUT IN SPACES

Different spaces also affect the contours of outness. For Black queer youth in a community center context, being out to one another in more public contexts was facilitated by their use of "Gaybonics." (Blackburn, 2005). This strategy of developing a form of communication that drew on Black and queer community traditions not only gave them a way to maintain their outness to one another but provided a pleasurable way to express their identities in wider public areas without being fully intelligible to outsiders (Blackburn, 2005). Being out, then, was being out to those in the know and being strategically unintelligible for protection against those who might not react kindly to the knowledge. In their public personas, then, they were private; in their outness, they were still in as well. Space becomes not just a place but a relationship within a space as well and relational aspects of identity can trouble the easy distinction between public and private spaces. Furthermore, some of the spectacle of membership may become something of an invitation to belonging.

This combination of provocation and pleasurable speculation seems to be one way that youth work through the complexity of public and private. Students in many contexts engage in pleasurable speculation about the sexuality of other students (C. Mayo, personal communication, 2004–2006). Although there is much theoretical work on the problems on unintelligibility and abjection (Butler, 1993), the game of speculation shows that one of the operations of desire, same sex or otherwise, entails wonderment about possibilities, close reading of signs that may provide clues, and an understanding that all of sexual attraction is not explicit. Queer and questioning youth look for the subtle signs as well as clear markers, and as Gilbert (2004) argues about the relationship between novel reading and sex education, they use their interpretive skills not only because they have to living under a regime of silence but also because they live in a context of myriad attractions. Although there is a lack of explicit discussion of pleasure in the official curriculum, schools are places where youth produce and experience pleasure. In his discussion of Black gender-nonconforming young men, McCready (2004) points out the process whereby one Black queer youth converts what clearly appears to be a harassing context into "his peers' way of flirting with him." Antoine defuses—or engages—his harassers by repositioning them as in relation to him. As he puts it, "[When someone says] 'I can't see myself being with a dude.' That's still thinking about it" (McCready, 2004). Antoine, in other words, sees his role in provoking these discussions and reads antagonistic interest as primarily interest, understanding that any other kind of interest would entail risk for his antagonists. Similar to the role of teasing and playing in early forays into heterosexuality (Thorne, 1995), Antoine sees that publicity about desire is risky, especially in a context where sexual identity is implicated in racial and gender identity, but that those gestures are nonetheless made by other young Black men as willing to strategize ways to think about the intersections of race, gender, and sexuality as Antoine does.

Still, there are also ample reasons to be concerned that educators' understandings of being out have been oversimplified and neglect to account for the multiple ways in which students experience and are recognized by their identities, not only sexuality alone but sexuality through vectors of race, ethnicity, class (Collins, 2004; Connell, 1999; Crowley, 1999; Duncan, 2005; Leck, 2000; Mayo, 2004a; McCready, 2004; Pallotta-Chiarolli, 1999; Pillow, 2004; Pinar, 2003; Sears, 1995, 1997; Snider, 1996; Wilson, 1996), gender (Bochenek & Brown, 2001; Leck, 2000; Mayo, 2004a; McCready, 2004; Pillow, 2004; Quinlivan & Town, 1999; Wilkerson, 2002), and disability (Wilkerson, 2002). Leck (2000) points out the links between race/ethnicity and public recognition of nonnormative sexuality and/or gender performance, arguing that the stakes of such opting out may be higher urban youth of color, not only because of homophobic threats but because of potential isolation from ethnic or racial groups. This isolation may be more the result of perceived identification with White gay norms rather than specifically an indication of levels of homophobia in communities of color. Ross (2005) has argued that the closet needs to be understood as a raced metaphor because Black communities may be very supportive of Black gay men without any public exchange of explicitly spoken information. He contends that explicit coming out, in those contexts, works as an insult to its audience: They already know perfectly well that there are Black gay men in their communities, so the implication of coming out is to criticize a falsely conceived ignorance (p. 180). In other words, there are forms of being known as gay that do not entail being out in a White, conventional sense. Wilson (1996) demonstrates the complex interaction between a supportive group of Cree elders watching her dance male steps while a younger community member objected to her gender nonconformity. She details her own process of coming to understand the place of Two-Spirit people in her communities, seeing that she was accepted in public contexts in her youth but had to also move in contexts where her gender nonconformity and sexuality were not acceptable. To whom one is out, then, is an important feature of outness and one may be (or want to be) simultaneously out to supportive and in to unsupportive people.

In school contexts, though, Anderson (1997) argues that too often the invisibility— or at least the perceived invisibility— of lesbian and gay youth enables school leaders to neglect them. Capper (1999) reports that straight administrators do not believe that their sexuality affects their leadership practices, whereas LGBT students give very clear examples of how this is so, including greater attention to multiple forms of diversity and an understanding of the visibility and invisibility of identities. Schools as organizational structures, then, may thwart coming out. Or, as heteronormative organizations, schools may out students without their consent. Parental notification policies intent on involving parents in school-based harassment situations may be one route of unintentional "outing by policy." One district has had to change its policy on reporting in school harassment to parents, a policy adopted to ensure that racist and ethnocentric harassment and violence was not being ignored by school administrators, because reporting homophobic harassment and violence to parents can out a student not ready to be out (C. Mayo, personal communication, 2006). Transgender youth also report insensitivity of teachers and school personnel who call them by their birth names and thus out their birth genders to classmates (Grossman & D'Augelli, 2006, p. 112). School personnel also mistakenly assume that a student's willingness to join a special program or group for queer youth, or even choose to attend a school for lesbian and gay youth, may indicate that they are out to their parents. In one situation, a school staff member outed a student to her parent by commenting that the group the student was in was for lesbians and gays when the student had not previously explained that to her mother (Misa, 2006).

Researchers, concerned that students may not understand the full implications of having their name in print and thus being out to a different sort of public, also may decide not to use research subjects' names even after youth have asked them to do so (Allen, 2006).

Students' decision to be out changes not only their relationship to themselves and their negotiation of spaces but it also changes their feeling of belonging to the school community. For some students in a gay–straight alliance, being out and working to ensure their group's continued existence in the face of objections from the school board gave them a strong sense of belonging and commitment to improving their school (Lee, 2002). Students, frustrated at the dilemmas of being out and available to take on all questions about sexuality, may respond with Day of Silence activities, making the question of public identity one for non-gay or non-out students to have to deal with (Mayo, 2004b). For students of color, the overwhelmingly White context of gay supportive groups in schools, groups that do not interrogate their practices of racist exclusion, are a barrier to participation in gay–straight alliances and show the effect of patterns of school segregation on the development of queer community (McCready, 2004).

GLOBALIZATION AND OUTNESS

Although this chapter has tracked differences in the concept of "out" across times, spaces, identity categories, and age, increasingly, work on globalization and transnationality complicates the picture further. The global focus of the *Journal on Gay and Lesbian Issues in Education* edited by James T. Sears has provided an important venue not only for research on sexualities in a global and transnational context but for conversations among researchers across the globe. Examining the global context of sexuality highlights tension between what Katie King (1989) has called "globalized gay" identity and local forms of same-sex desire. Parallel to this distinction between globalized and local identity are global and local sources of homophobia, including local justifications for homophobia that, in the Zimbabewan context for instance, blame colonialism for homosexuality and argue that gayness is not indigenous (Goddard, 2005). Other forms of homophobia seem to emerge from a critique of United States–dominated commercialization and commodification.

Just as queer youth in the United States increasingly find images of themselves through participation in online communities, gay people unable to find a large enough community in which to be out in their local, real space may find the space to be out online (Fann, 2005). In some ways, reliance on queer virtual space can deeply trouble our ideas about identity and outness. As queers of many locations find themselves making virtual community, they disturb, as do other kinds of cybercommunities, the usual boundaries of time and space. On the other hand, as much as some of these virtual interactions may appear to give promise to isolated LGBT youth in the United States or queers of all sorts in other spaces and nations, those interactions still rely on access to computers—very often necessitating knowledge of

Ginsburg, R. W. (1998, Winter). Silenced voices inside our schools. *Initiatives, 58*, 1–15.

Goddard, K. (2005). Commentaries. In J. Sears (Ed.), *Gay, lesbian, and transgender issues education: Programs, policies, and practices* (pp. 52–56). New York: Harrington Park Pre

Gray, M. L. (1999). *In your face*. Binghamton, NY: Hawthorn.

Grossman, A. H., & D'Augelli, A. R. D. (2006). Transgender youth: Invisible and vulne ble. *Journal of Homosexuality, 51*, 111–128.

Harwood, V. (2004). Subject to scrutiny: Taking Foucauldian geneaologies to narratives youth oppression. In M. L. Rasmussen, E. Rofes, & S. Talburt (Eds.), *Youth and sexua ties: Pleasure, subversion, and insubordination in and out of schools* (pp. 85–107). New Yor Palgrave Macmillan.

Honeychurch, K. G. (1996). Researching dissident subjectivities: Queering the grounds theory and practice. *Harvard Educational Review, 66*, 339–356.

Jennings, K. (1998). *Telling tales out of school: Gays, lesbians, and bisexuals revisit their scho days*. Los Angeles: Alyson Press.

King, K. (1989, January). Local and global: AIDS activism and feminist theory. *Came Obscura*, pp. 79–100.

Kissen, R. (Ed.). (2002). *Getting ready for Benjamin: Preparing teachers for sexual diversity the classroom*. Lanham, MD: Rowman & Littlefield.

Kosciw, J. G., & Cullen, M. K. (2001). *The GLSEN 2001 national school climate survey: Th school-related experiences of our nation's lesbian, gay, bisexual, and transgender youth*. Nev York: Gay, Lesbian, and Straight Educators Network.

Kumashiro, K. (2002, Spring). Against repetition: Addressing resistance to anti-oppressiv change in the practices of learning, teaching, supervising, and researching. *Harvard Educa tional Review, 72*(1), 67–92.

Leck, G. M. (2000, May). Heterosexual or homosexual? Reconsidering binary narratives on sexual identities in urban schools. *Education and Urban Society, 32*, 324–348.

Lee, C. (2002, February). The impact of belonging to a high school gay/straight alliance. *High School Journal*, pp. 13–26.

Levine, J. (2002). *Harmful to minors: The perils of protecting children from sex*. Minneapolis: University of Minnesota Press.

Lipkin, A. (2004). *Beyond diversity day: A q & a on gay and lesbian issues in schools*. Lanham, MD: Rowman & Littlefield.

Loutzenheiser, L. W., & MacIntosh, L. B. (2004, Spring). Citizenships, sexualities, and edu- cation. *Theory Into Practice, 43*, 151–158.

Lugg, C. A. (2003). Sissies, faggots, lezzies, and dykes: Gender, sexual orientation, and a new politics of education? *Educational Administration Quarterly, 39*(1), 95–134.

MacGillivray, I. K. (2004). *Sexual orientation and school policy*. Boulder, CO: Rowman & Littlefield.

Martindale, K. (1997). *Unpopular culture: Lesbian writing after the sex wars*. Albany: State University of New York Press.

Mayo, C. (2002). Education by association: Shortcomings of discourses of privacy and civil- ity in anti-homophobia education. In R. Kissen (Ed.), *Getting ready for Benjamin: Prepar- ing teachers for sexual diversity* (pp. 81–90). Boulder, CO: Rowman & Littlefield.

Mayo, C. (2004a). *Disputing the subject of sex: Sexuality and public school controversy*. Boulder, CO: Rowman & Littlefield.

Mayo, C. (2004b). The tolerance that dare not speak its name. In M. Boler (Ed.), *Democratic dialogue in education: Disturbing silence, troubling speech* (pp. 33–47). New York: Peter Lang.

McCready, L. T. (2004, Spring). Understanding the marginalization of gay and gender non-conforming Black male students. *Theory Into Practice, 43,* 136–143.

Miceli, M. (2005). *Standing out, standing together: The social and political impact of gay-straight alliances.* New York: Routledge.

Misa, C. M. (2006). *Marginalized multiplicities: The journeys of Chicana/Latina lesbian and bisexual high school students.* Unpublished dissertation.

Mufioz-Plaza, C., Quinn, S. C., & Rounds, K. A. (2002, April). Lesbian, gay, bisexual, and transgender students: Perceived social support in the high school environment. *High School Journal,* pp. 52–63.

Nayak, A., & Kehily, M. J. (1997). Masculinities and schooling: Why are young men so homophobic? In D. L. Steinberg, D. Epstein, & R. Johnson (Eds.), *Border patrols: Policing the boundaries of heterosexuality* (pp. 138–161). London: Cassell.

Pallotta-Chiarolli, M. (1999). Diary entries from the "teachers' professional development playground": Multiculturalism meets multisexualities in Australian education. *Journal of Homosexuality, 36,* 183–205.

Patton, C. (1996). *Fatal advice: How safe-sex education went wrong.* Durham, NC: Duke University Press.

Perrotti, J., & Westheimer, K. (2001). *When the drama club is not enough: Lessons from the safe schools program for gay and lesbian students.* Boston: Beacon.

Pillow, W. (2004). *Unfit subjects: Educational policy and the teen mother.* New York: Routledge.

Pinar, W. F. (2003). Queer theory in education. *Journal of Homosexuality, 45,* 357–360.

Quinlivan, K., & Town, S. (1999). Queer pedagogy, educational practice and lesbian and gay youth. *Qualitative Studies in Education, 12,* 509–524.

Radicalesbians. (1973). The woman identified woman. In A. Koedt, E. Levine, & A. Rapone (Eds.), *Radical feminism* (pp. 240–245). New York: Quandrangle.

Rasmussen, M. L. (2004, Spring). The problem of coming out. *Theory Into Practice, 43,* 144–150.

Rasmussen, M. L. (2006). *Becoming subjects: Sexuality and secondary schooling.* New York: Routledge.

Rodriguez, N., & Pinar, W. (Eds.). (2007). *Queering straight teachers: Discourse and identity in education.* New York: Peter Lang.

Rofes, E. (2004). *Youth and sexualities: Pleasure, subversion, and insubordination in and out of schools.* New York: Palgrave Macmillan.

Ross, M. B. (2005). Beyond the closet as raceless paradigm. In E. P. Johnson & M. G. Henderson (Eds.), *Black queer studies: A critical anthology* (pp. 161–189). Durham, NC: Duke University Press.

Sapon-Shevin, M., & Goodman, J. (1992). Learning to be the opposite sex: Sexuality education and sexual scripting in early adolescence. In J. T. Sears (Ed.), *Sexuality and the curriculum: The politics and practices of sexuality education* (pp. 89–105). New York: Teachers College Press.

Savin-Williams, R. C. (1990). *Gay and lesbian youth: Expressions of identity.* New York: Hemisphere Publishing Group.

Savin-Williams, R. C. (2005). *The new gay teenager.* Cambridge, MA: Harvard University Press.

Scott, J. (1993). The evidence of experience. In H. Abelove, M. A. Barale, & D. M. Halperin (Eds.), *The lesbian and gay studies reader* (pp. 397–415). New York: Routledge.

Sears, J. T. (1992). The impact of culture and ideology on the construction of gender and sexual identities: Developing a critically based sexuality curriculum. In J. T. Sears (Ed.), *Sexuality and the curriculum: The politics and practices of sexuality education* (pp. 139–156). New York: Teachers College Press.

Sears, J. T. (1993). Credibility in teacher education: Dilemmas of faculty, students, and administrators at Indiana University. *Journal of Curriculum Theorizing, 10*(3), 109–151.

Sears, J. T. (1995). Black-gay or gay-Black? In G. Unks (Ed.), *The gay teen* (pp. 135–157). New York: Routledge.

Sears, J. T. (1997). Centering culture: Teaching for critical sexual literacy using the sexual diversity wheel. *Journal of Moral Education, 26,* 273–284.

Sears, J. T., & Williams, W. L. (Eds.). (1997). *Overcoming heterosexism and homophobia: Strategies that work.* New York: Columbia University Press.

Silin, J. G. (1995). *Sex, death, and the education of children: Our passion for ignorance in the age of AIDS.* New York: Teachers College Press.

Snider, K. (1996). Race and sexual orientation: The (im)possibility of these intersections in educational policy. *Harvard Educational Review, 66,* 294–302.

Sonnie, A. (2000). *Revolutionary voices: A multicultural queer youth anthology.* Los Angeles: Alyson Books.

Talburt, S. (1999). Open secrets and problems of queer ethnography: Readings from a religious studies classroom. *Qualitative Studies in Education, 12,* 525–539.

Talburt, S. (2004, Spring). Constructions of LGBT youth: Opening up subject positions. *Theory Into Practice, 43,* 116–121.

Thorne, B. (1995). *Gender play: Girls and boys at school.* Brunswick, NJ: Rutgers University Press.

Unks, G. (Ed.). (1995). *The gay teen: Educational practice and theory for lesbian, gay, and bisexual adolescents.* New York: Routledge.

Whatley, M. (1992a). Commentary: Whose sexuality is it anyway? In J. T. Sears (Ed.), *Sexuality and the curriculum: The politics and practices of sexuality education* (pp. 77–78). New York: Teachers College Press.

Whatley, M. (1992b). Images of gays and lesbians in sexuality and health textbooks. In K. M. Harbek (Ed.), *Coming out of the classroom closet: Gay and lesbian students, teachers, and curricula* (pp. 197–211). New York: Harrington Park Press.

Wilkerson, A. (2002, Fall). Disability, sex radicalism, and political agency. *National Women's Studies Association Journal, 14,* 33–57.

Wilson, A. (1996). How we find ourselves: Identity development and two-spirit people. *Harvard Educational Review, 66,* 303–317.

Woog, D. (1995). *School's out: The impact of gay and lesbian issues on America's schools.* Boston: Alyson Press.

Chapter 4

Contesting the Model Minority and Perpetual Foreigner Stereotypes: A Critical Review of Literature on Asian Americans in Education

JENNIFER C. NG
University of Kansas

SHARON S. LEE
YOON K. PAK
University of Illinois at Urbana-Champaign

Student: "Asians are threatening our economic future . . . We can see it right here in our own school. Who are getting into the best colleges, in disproportionate numbers? Asian kids! It's not fair."
Teacher: "Uh . . . That certainly was an unusual essay . . . Unfortunately, it's racist."
Student: "Um . . . are you sure? My parents helped me."
—Garry Trudeau, *Doonesbury*, March 17, 1988, cited in Wu (2002, p. 39)

The Asian American[1] presence in schools, as captured by cartoonist Garry Trudeau here, has a compelling grasp on the public imagination. Scholars (Dong, 1995; Wu, 2002) have utilized the pointed cartoon strip to emphasize the criticality of understanding how insidious and pervasive is the myth of Asian Americans as model minorities, especially in education. The Asian American model minority image is alluring yet troubling. On one hand, the supposed academic achievement of Asian Americans is used as a beacon to highlight the prototypical American success story, a group to be admired and emulated by others. At the same time, however, it is used to produce a heightened sense of fear, particularly in schools, where the Asian "horde" will take over the classrooms to raise test scores and ruin the grading curve, resulting in a new form of "White flight" (Hwang, 2005). These concerns exist at the K–12 level as well as in the realm of higher education admissions, as captured by Trudeau. In either case, one thing remains clear: Asian Americans are cast outside the peripheries of normalcy.

Review of Research in Education
March 2007, Vol. 31, pp. 95–130
DOI: 10.3102/0091732X06298015
© 2007 AERA. http://rre.aera.net

An understanding of how racial meanings have been constructed about Asian Americans, or how they have been racialized (Omi & Winant, 1994), requires a departure from a Black/White racial binary. Legal scholar Ancheta (2000) considers how anti-Asian discrimination is distinctly different from anti-Black subordination. He writes, "The racialization of Asian Americans has taken on two primary forms: racialization as non-Americans and racialization as the model minority" (p. 44). This outsider racialization constructs Asian Americans as foreign-born outsiders. In the realm of education, this construction extends to the view of Asian Americans as "forever foreigners" (Tuan, 1998), where the permanency of equal status as citizens cannot be fully realized.

Asian American racialization as both the model minority and the foreigner exists within larger racial discourses. C. Kim (1999) posits a theory of "a field of racial positions" that considers how Asian Americans have been racialized relative to Whites and Blacks and how racialization is more complex than a hierarchy with Whites on top, Blacks on the bottom, and other groups in between (p. 106). Kim's field of racial positions involves at least two axes (superior/inferior and insider/foreigner), which acknowledges the different ways that groups are racialized. Asian Americans are "racially triangulated" vis-à-vis Whites and Blacks through two interrelated processes of "relative valorization" (Whites valorizing Asian Americans relative to Blacks) and the process of "civic ostracism" (Whites constructing Asian Americans as foreign and Other, p. 107).

The model minority and foreigner images emerge in research on Asian Americans in K–12 schooling (Lei, 1998) and higher education (S. S. Lee, 2006; Suzuki, 2002). Both Lei and S. S. Lee discuss how these representations play off each other and are interconnected, placing Asian Americans in a vulnerable racial position, ostracized from both the White majority and causing racial tensions with other minorities (primarily African Americans). Placed within the confines of the Black/White discourse, Asian Americans have been inexactly situated in comparison to Whites and Blacks rather than understood as racialized in distinct ways. The representations of Asian American students as models and foreigners also uphold the racial status quo, which marginalizes students of color (Jo, 2004; S. J. Lee, 2006; Lei, 1998).

Although researchers have uncovered the more complex ways that Asian Americans are racialized, Asian Americans continue to be cast as interlopers in a Black/White racial discourse; being neither Black nor White, Asian Americans rarely gain visibility and voice as racial minorities. Scholars in the fields of history (Takaki, 1998), English (Lowe, 2000), anthropology (Manalansan, 2000, 2003), sociology (Kibria, 2002; C. Kim, 1999; Min, 1996; Tuan, 1998), ethnic and gender studies (Espiritu, 1997; R. Lee, 1999), and law (Ancheta, 2000; Wu, 1995) have critically examined the complexities of Asian American experiences and challenged the ways that the public has falsely imagined them. The field of education, however, has lagged behind these theoretical advances. There is great foundational knowledge to be gleaned from other disciplines in addressing the educational concerns and needs of Asian American students.

The specter of Asians and Asian Americans as the yellow peril and the model minority has a long history. First invoked during the 19th century to create comparative labor advantage between and among the railroad barons to yield high profit through the cheapest labor force, Chinese workers were typically fashioned as the model against which other immigrant groups, such as the Irish, should aspire (Takaki, 1998; Wu, 1995). When the Chinese Exclusion law of 1882—stemming from the fear of the "Yellow Peril," as popularized by novelist Jack London— curtailed further migration of Chinese, attention started to shift to the growing population of Japanese immigrants along the West Coast (Daniels, 1988). Again, although seemingly admired for their ability to cultivate difficult arid lands, they were then shunned and despised for their success in agriculture. At the outbreak of World War II, Japanese immigrants and Americans were incarcerated for fear of disloyalty and espionage.

In the 1960s, during the Civil Rights movement, the image of Asian Americans seemed to improve, in relation to African Americans and other racial minority groups who sought equal rights and protection under the law; at this time, newspaper headlines hailed Chinese and Japanese Americans as the model minority. Popular magazines such as *Time* and *Newsweek* highlighted their Confucian-style "rugged individualism"; Asians did not need government support to make it in U.S. society. As numerous Asian Americanists have noted throughout the years (Cheng & Yang, 2000; Osajima, 2000), the purposeful ways in which Asians were heralded for their success was a direct attack against African Americans in their outspoken quest for equality in the 1960s and against a critique of institutional and structural racism. Such pernicious and unfounded comparisons between the races only served to create fissures that continue to exist today and support a message of individual effort as a primary means to overcome racism, erasing the existence of structural barriers.

Contemporary characterizations of Asian Americans reveal the persistence of the foreigner and model minority stereotypes in mainstream culture and more educated, professional communities. In 2002, for example, the popular young adult clothing company Abercrombie & Fitch launched a line of T-shirts intended to add humor and levity to its fashion that featured slant-eyed, Asian characters pulling rickshaws and working in laundromats (Gliona & Goldman, 2002). Notions of Asian American foreignness also are evident in educational discussions. In his 1999 *Phi Delta Kappan* essay titled "The Demise of the Asian Math Gene," for example, Gerald Bracey speculated on the role of Confucian ideals behind Asian American educational success as well as the impact of poorer, rural, and less literate homeland factors resulting in Asian American juvenile delinquency. Even more recently, Bracey (2005) wrote about the "spelling gene" that children of Indian ancestry must possess, helping them win five of the last seven Scripps National Spelling Bees. Bracey (citing Joseph Berger from *The New York Times*) explained that preparing for spelling bees is especially compatible with the "rote learning methods of their homeland" where people "do not regard champion spellers as nerds" (p. 92). However, concluding that Indian parents may be even more single-minded than American parents who want their children to succeed in extracurricular endeavors, Bracey stated, "I couldn't help thinking of those years of mono-maniacally obsessive preparation as a form of child abuse" (p. 92). These representations reinforce ideas that Asian Americans are culturally (and even genetically) distinct from the rest of America and that their narrow focus on achievement is not completely praiseworthy.

Theories about Asian "Otherness" can be applied to educational discussions. Cultural theorist Said's (1978) influential work on the theory of Orientalism also provides ample thought for how the Occident has imagined the place of the Orient as a means for dominance and control, including the means of representation as reified into the daily structures of institutions such as education. Indeed, the power of the Western gaze to focus on its cultural superiority over others has led to the continued belief and resultant policies maintaining the status quo. As Rizvi and Lingard (2006) write,

> Orientalism is best understood as a system of representations, a discourse framed by political forces through which the West sought to understand and control its colonized populations. It is a discourse that both assumes and promotes a fundamental difference between the Western "us" and Oriental "them." It is a manner of regularized interpreting, writing about and accounting for the Orient, dominated by imperatives, perspectives, and ideological biases politically marshaled to self-justify imperial conquests and exploitation. In this sense, the Orient is an imagined place that is articulated through as an entire system of thought and scholarship. (p. 296)

As Rizvi and Lingard (2006) note, the influence of Said to education and educational policies comes from one's perceived notions of how the Other lives. In this example, and through our years of teaching experiences, we find that a number of educators still come to the classroom with a priori assumptions about the profound foreignness of their Asian American students. It is that sense of profound cultural difference that underlies the model minority stereotype as well.

One dangerous strain in educational research that perpetuates the construction of Asian Americans as profoundly different relates to explanations for their academic success. All too often, cultural explanations are offered. For example, our initial perusal of research related to Asian American students revealed a troubling tendency to rely on particular cultural characteristics, such as the Confucian norms, to primarily account for the academic achievement of Asian Americans (Pearce, 2006; Zhou, 2000). The tenor of these conclusions presumes Asian American educational achievement, when in fact these studies do not acknowledge Asian Americans' bimodal performance, which includes students performing below the norm (Hune & Chan, 1997). Pang, Kiang, and Pak (2004) have indicated the great diversity of ethnicities that constitute Asian Pacific Americans (APA) and assert that creating monolithic truths based on two or three high-achieving ethnicities does a disservice to everyone. Yet the continued emphasis on educational research that presumes and highlights the academic achievement of Asian Americans creates a wedge between other racial minority groups. Coupled with this, Asian American success discourse is a presumption of African American and Latino academic underachievement. Critical historians (Anderson, 1998, 2004a, 2004b; Span & Anderson, 2005; Williams, 2005) have provided ample evidence for the persistence of educational attainment by African Americans since the time of slavery to counter current misconceptions and cultural deficit models in which African Americans do not value education. Yet the implicit and sometimes explicit academic comparisons between the high-achieving Asians with the low-achieving African Americans persists and only serves to maintain White privilege. This binary erases the experiences of Asian Americans who do not achieve and also the experiences of African Americans, Latinas/Latinos, and Native Americans who do achieve. As aptly phrased by S. J. Lee (1996), the model minority stereotype is a hegemonic device to desensitize the public about the deep and troubling history of race relations in the United States; schools and educators become implicated in the process.

Our discussion here is not to deny or ignore the population of high-achieving Asian American students per se, but basing conclusions on specific Asian cultural practices and beliefs limits our understanding of how particular racialized groups in the United States adopt certain adaptive strategies to deal with racism and how education is seen as one of the few means to gain social capital. Members of a racialized group can come to internalize the myths about cultural difference themselves without examining the larger structural formations of how racism is lived in the everyday (see, e.g., Abboud & Kim, 2005). The structural barriers that have been placed to impede larger-scale achievement among all students, therefore, require further investigation.

There are several aims of this literature review. At its basic level, our goal is to provide readers with content knowledge of the educational research on Asian Americans, highlighting important findings and key studies in the field. The educational literature on Asian Americans is a growing field; it is our goal to identify themes and trends and look to important future directions as a whole, specifically examining the collective effect of a wide range of studies rather than focusing on a singular work or narrow subfield. Through the review, our second goal is to reveal the severely limited representations of Asian Americans as model minorities and cultural foreigners in educational research. The educational community needs to critically assess these representations and understand the deleterious impact they have on Asian American students and faculty/teachers. Our third goal is to examine new directions of research that show the complexity of Asian American identities and experiences, which cannot be simply reduced to individual merit or cultural value alone. As Lowe (2000) points out, Asian Americans are a heterogeneous and hybrid group who defy easy categorization. By employing intersectional approaches, this research refuses to reduce Asian Americans to simplistic caricatures but shows how the myriad factors of ethnicity, language, gender, culture, socioeconomic status, sexuality, and the like affect Asian American experiences. At the same time, we recognize that although we seek to contest racialized representations, they continue to be highly salient in our society—we cannot easily dismiss them as mere ideological fabrications. Our final goal is thus to listen to the voices of Asian American students and teachers as they

themselves struggle to make sense of racialized expectations and messages and negotiate their own experiences. Because racism persists toward Asian Americans and is
evident in simplistic notions, we embrace an antiracist approach. As Osajima
(1995a) articulates, although postmodern interpretations offer a lens through which
to appreciate the rich complexity of Asian Americans, they do not adequately address
the necessity of political unity to challenge anti-Asian racism. Thus, our analysis is
one that does not abandon the concepts of race and racism but seeks to center Asian
American voices and experiences in negotiation and resistance to these structures.

This article also provides a cautionary note for educational researchers interested
in pursuing research on Asian Americans. History shows there are sometimes pitfalls
to researching this population.[2] During the early 20th century, sociologist Robert
Park spearheaded academic research on Asian immigrants and Asian Americans,
work that fueled scholars' obsessions with Oriental success, driving a subsequent
generation of researchers to embark on a path to uncover explanations for the phenomenon rather than asking if the phenomenon actually existed (H. Yu, 2001).
Showcasing Oriental success also was reflected in intercultural education school curricula in the 1930s and 1940s (Pak, in press). In a similar vein, there also exists a tendency to treat the unsuccessful Asian American groups as so profoundly different,
from a cultural standpoint, that no clear means of acculturation can exist (see, e.g.,
Faderman 1999; Fadiman,1998; Walker-Moffat, 1995). They can only exist as foreigners who need intermediaries, presumably the well-meaning, White (female),
middle-class researcher, to gain legitimacy (Depouw, 2006). This critique is not
intended to solely implicate or denigrate research performed by White researchers
about non-White subjects but to point out that we all need to maintain reflexive
practices about how our own positionality inserts itself in what we do.

ASIAN AMERICANS IN K–12 RESEARCH

Understanding Asian American Experiences Through the Lens of Cultural Difference

A great deal of the educational literature on Asian Americans discusses their experiences and needs through the lens of "cultural difference" (Sleeter & Grant, 2003).
As Lei (2006) explains, one strength of this approach is that it provides educators
with a body of literature from which to develop an understanding of Asian Americans. By discussing Asian Americans as members of distinct and stable cultural
groups, such research provides factual descriptions and concrete recommendations
in various regards.

Sometimes, Asian Americans are cast pan-ethnically, and other times, focus is given
to particular ethnic or regional groups. For example, each chapter in the book *Asian
American Education: Prospects and Challenges* (Park & Chi, 1999) features the detailed
immigration, sociocultural, and linguistic experiences of an ethnic group to "provide a
sense of how each group is faring," illuminate the "unique educational issues, needs,
and challenges faced by the group," and provide "practical and insightful suggestions"

for teachers and others working with Asian American students (p. viii). More concise summaries of different behaviors and values also can be found in literature reviews such as that of Mathews (2000), who describes the cultural patterns of South and Southeast Asians with respect to family relationships, respect for age, social interaction, communication style, family expectations of success, humility, school situations, decision making, and socialization barriers, as well as their accompanying implications for teaching (see also Adler, 1998, on Japanese Americans). Suggestions for working with Asian parents and families also have been compiled, encouraging teachers to show respect for immediate and extended family members, provide opportunities to share differences in U.S. and Asian schools and society, and consider Asian parents' English proficiency (e.g., G. Lee & Manning, 2001a, 2001b). Scholars also have offered their recommendations for instructional strategies and curriculum best suited for Asian American children (Chiang, 2000).

However, although this literature provides educators with straightforward and quick overviews about various aspects of working with Asian Americans, it tends to treat the group monolithically and is thereby unable to get at the more complicated realities of Asian American identities and experiences. Some authors express their awareness of this tendency by providing the following caveat:

> Prototypic Asian American parents and families do not exist. Just as all parents and families differ, Asian American parents differ by educational backgrounds, linguistic ability, socioeconomic status, acculturation, and demographic region, just to name representative examples. Educators need to be wary when referring to "Asian American" parents and families. (G. Lee & Manning, 2001b, p. 23)

Yet the essentializing effect of such an approach is difficult to balance, perpetuating stereotypes about Asian American foreignness and endorsing the goal of assimilation (Lei, 2006). The working premise of many of the studies reviewed is to attend to the needs of relatively recent Asian immigrant students (Park & Chi, 1999). The idea that Asian Americans belong to stable and distinct cultures leads to conclusions such as, "Obedience, silence, and nonassertiveness are *normal* traits for most South Asian and Southeast Asian school children," "they do not *normally* initiate conversation, and they are comfortable with silence," and "behaviors such as timidity, overdependence, and lack of initiative can be manifestations of the *cultural* traits of students from South Asian and Southeast Asian families" (Mathews, 2000, pp. 103–104, italics added).

Paradoxically, the cultural distinctiveness of Asian Americans has served as an explanation for both their notable educational success as well as for their increasing rates of juvenile delinquency. On one hand, researchers have sought to identify the positive cultural components leading to Chinese American students' high educational achievement to develop programs that could prompt similar cultural shifts in individual students from other racial/ethnic backgrounds. Pearce (2006) argues, "By gaining a better understanding of the factors that aid some Chinese Americans in realizing academic success, we can identify methods for ameliorating the situation among underachieving groups" (p. 76). On the other hand, a growing body of literature examines how the notion of profound cultural difference contributes to the "ideological Blackening" (Ong, 1996) of Southeast Asians. In particular, this characterization supports an image of Southeast Asians who do not culturally value education, grouping them in the same racialized categories as African Americans (Depouw, 2006; S. J. Lee, 2006).

New Conceptualizations: Intersections and Negotiations

As Coloma (2006) notes, a different paradigm of educational research on Asian Americans takes an intersectional approach, examining the ways in which race intersects with other identities such as sexuality, gender, and class. Coloma notes that this approach is innovative because by revealing the complexities of people's actual experiences, it avoids overgeneralizations and essentialist interpretations. Educational research on Asian American experiences revealing the complex interplay of various factors highlights real experiences and gives voice to Asian American students as they negotiate externally imposed racial expectations.

Innovative research showing the complexities of Asian American experiences takes this approach. For example, examining Asian American identity formation as a dynamic process shaped by intergroup relations illustrates the complexity of the classification, especially because identity is a developmental concept reflecting an individual's sense of self derived from a feeling of belonging or commitment to one's own group as well as an acculturative concept indicating the way an individual relates to other groups and society at large (Shrake & Rhee, 2004). S. J. Lee's (1996) study of Academic High provides a rich example of the varied identifications Asian American students constructed as they sought to make sense of their position in the racial minefield in their school. Korean-identified students who socialized primarily with other Korean-identified students tried to befriend White students and adopt American behaviors for status and avoided contact with African American students; Asian-identified students who adhered firmly to a belief in fairness and meritocracy admired but remained socially distant from White students and rationalized their experiences with racism as temporary difficulties; new wavers who adopted an oppositional stance to school engaged the racially charged exchange of insults with African American students who were tracked in the same classes and lived in the same neighborhoods as they did while incorporating some designators of street culture; and Asian American–identified students who challenged the supposed superiority of Whites questioned the truthfulness of the model minority stereotype and sought alliances with students of other racial groups. Considering the meaningfulness that Asian American students attach to different reference subgroups thus generates insight into the many dimensions of the identifier (see also S. J. Lee, 2001, 2005).

The tendency to essentialize Asian Americans also can be countered by disaggregating data, and researchers such as Baker, Keller-Wolff, and Wolf-Wendel (2000) have found that such practices add explanatory value to statistical models. While recognizing the constraints of available large-scale data sets and the need to maintain subgroup sample sizes, Baker et al. used the 1998 National Educational Longitudinal Study (NELS) data to assess the extent to which commonly used racial/ethnic classifications appropriately represented their constituent subgroups with respect to academic achievement. They concluded that some subgroups may not be accurately represented by their common aggregate classification. For example, the high mathematics achievement of Asian Americans overall was problematized when disaggregation indicated that there was a range in outcomes from Pacific Islanders who performed 6.83 points below White students to West Asian students who performed 8.45 points above White students (p. 524). Not only was the variation in outcomes among subgroups wide, but the inclusion of West Asian individuals from Iranian, Afghan, and Turkish backgrounds under the rubric "Asian" in this data set reveals problems with conceptualizing Asian American educational experiences. West Asian students' experiences are arguably quite distinct from Chinese, Japanese, Korean, Filipino, and Indian students, for example, who have a shared history of being racialized as non-White.[3]

The intersectionally nuanced experiences of particular ethnic groups also have been captured in qualitative studies. Through observations and interviews, Goto (1997) situates the seemingly inconsistent and contradictory social and academic behavior of Chinese American high school students in a web of peer relationships, including "nerds," "normal people," and "homeboys." Rather than endure the racialized stereotype of being nerds singularly focused on their academic achievement, these students positioned themselves strategically so as not to be too popular or too high performing and remain comfortably anonymous. In this way, students in Goto's study lived up to their expressed preference for maintaining harmonious friendships with others rather than foster relationships characterized by individual competition and status. Goto (1997) concludes, "Asian students, particularly adolescents, may be more concerned about a localized form of mobility—the ability to move about between different peer groups, reinforcing friendships and not making enemies" (p. 82).

Identity goes beyond ethnicity. Baker et al. (2000) also recommend considering students' varying English language proficiency, socioeconomic status, and generational status. S. J. Lee (2006) reiterates this point, arguing that the various identities and intersections of identities that shape Asian American experiences include not only social class, ethnicity, and generation but also gender. Some of the most insightful contemporary research adopts such an integrated perspective.

Lew's (2004) work examines the relationship between ethnicity and class and documents the effects of limited social capital and weak ethnic ties on working-class Korean students' decisions to drop out of high school. Respondents in her study reported feeling isolated and ill-equipped to make decisions about their academic futures because their parents worked long hours and were unable to provide them with the firsthand guidance necessary to do well in school. Furthermore, they attended underresourced schools where their teachers and counselors provided minimal and sometimes inaccurate advice. By internalizing feelings of their low status, Lew found that these students negotiated their racial and ethnic identities differently than other Asian American students who maintained strong ethnic community connections or had wealth. Instead, most Korean dropouts in Lew's study developed oppositional perspectives and "aligned their shared experiences of racism and low socio-economic status with other low-income minority peers—Blacks, Hispanics, and Asians" (Lew, 2004, p. 318).

Louie (2001) found similar effects in her study of Chinese immigrant parents' expectations, strategies, and investments in their children's education. Whether middle or low income, the parents in Louie's study reported emphasizing the value of education not only because of their traditional cultural values but because of the availability of postsecondary education in the United States compared to their respective countries of origin, potential monetary returns for a college degree in the American labor market, and as a form of protection against the effects of perceived racial discrimination. However, middle-class Chinese parents whose livelihood was derived through their participation in the mainstream economy secured information about different educational options from their friends, teachers, and other school administrators. As a result, they were able to enroll their children in private schools, secure financial aid if necessary, or even move to neighborhoods with reportedly excellent schools. In contrast, the low-income Chinese parents in Louie's study worked primarily within the more limited ethnic economy of restaurants and garment factories and therefore relied on informal ethnic networks to learn about school reputations and specialized entrance examinations. Typically, these informants were also immigrants who had resided in the United States longer and were economically more secure.

Although advances are being made in educational scholarship, thorough consideration of issues related to the intersection of race, gender, and sexuality are still relatively scant. For example, Lei (2003) documents how the identities of Southeast Asian male students were constructed at Hope High School through racialized and gendered regulatory discourses and normative representations. Because these students were often quiet, teachers viewed them variously as model students, secretive, gang-like, and clannish. Compared to the masculine ideal of White, European American men, these students were viewed as small and weak. As a result, students typically socialized in groups with other Southeast Asian young men who could provide them with protection from harassment if needed, and they all appeared tough to outside observers because they had adopted markers of urban, hip-hop culture. The result, as Lei (2003) points out, is that

> By being in a group, the Southeast Asian American males created a defense barrier that protected them from potential harassment. The same barrier, however, served to maintain a lack of communication and understanding between the Southeast Asian American male students and the rest of the school. (p. 176)

In describing her earlier study, S. J. Lee (2006) also found that "the messages (boys) receive from school, popular culture, and the larger society is that they are too short, too quiet, and too Asian. In short, they learn that they lack the qualities associated with hegemonic masculinity" (p. 24). Researchers such as Shrake and Rhee (2004) explain, however, that Asian American adolescent girls may become quickly assimilated into a more egalitarian American culture and society, thereby heightening the tensions between familial and societal expectations and leading to psychologically internalized distress such as depression or anxiety. The extent of Asian American students' acculturation also seems to be related to their level of personal self-esteem (Rhee, Chang, & Rhee, 2003). These issues warrant further consideration because they affect not only Asian American students' self-concept but also shape significant social and familial interactions.

Asian American Families: Embodying the Complexities of Experience

Representations of Asian Americans as the model minority and foreigner support a simplistic discourse of the Asian family as a hub of distinct and positive cultural values that embrace education, hard work, and family cohesion. However, a more in-depth analysis is needed to understand how culture is shaped and contested. The issue of a culture gap does arise within Asian families, particularly in the form of inter-generational conflict between immigrant parents and U.S.-born children; often, immigrant parents dichotomize Asian culture with American culture and interpret their children's behaviors as a rejection of their family traditions. Second- and later-generation Asian American children therefore struggle to define their own culture, and their experiences of living in the United States are often affected by the reality of anti-Asian racism. Research on Asian American families reveals the complexities and conflicts that can arise as culture is contested and constantly recreated.

Cultural differences within an immigrant family can result in tension. For instance, the student respondents in Louie's (2001) study from working-class families reported that their parents utilized more authoritarian styles of interaction, which they believe fostered ineffective communication. Qin (2006) further explored the parent-child relations of two Chinese immigrant families, one from the middle class and one from the working class. Although the family relationships differed according to how much time parents were able to spend with their children instead of working outside the home and the quality of direct assistance given to support their children's educations, the children ultimately became alienated from their parents in both cases. Qin (2006) attributes this estrangement to "dissonant acculturation" whereby,

Parents tend to compare their children's behaviors with those of children in China or their own experiences growing up, immigrant children increasingly compare their parents with the American parents they see in movies or parents of their friends, who emphasize more communication and freedom, and less control in their relationship with children. (p. 173)

Qin found parent-child alienation to be more acute during adolescence and the financial demands placed on the low-income parents further exacerbated the problem.

S. J. Lee's (2001) study of Hmong American high school students provides additional detail about the ensuing difficulties involved in bridging cultural gaps between parents and their children. She examines one and a half–generation students (those born abroad and in the United States for 3 to 8 years) and second-generation (U.S.-born) students. By retaining more of the "traditional Hmong values" (those that parents and teachers defined as putting high importance on education and family obligations), teachers and parents both perceived one and a half–generation children to be model students. This view stemmed from the parental belief that Hmong culture provided children with a type of protection against becoming too Americanized and reinforced the belief that "[a] good kid will go back to the culture." These one and a half–generation children remained relatively isolated from other children in the school, and because they were able to compare their experiences of discrimination in the United States with the difficulties they endured in their native country, they were more willing to overlook instances of racism and focus on the positive aspects of living in the United States. American-born, second-generation Hmong students in S. J. Lee's study, however, were seen as bad kids because they wore baggy clothes resembling gang attire, insisted on exercising their independence from authority, and rebelled against their parents' strict rules forbidding dating. In these instances, parents lamented what they saw as the loss of their children to American ways. Conversely, the children expressed skepticism with the idea that education would lead to upward social mobility because they saw discrimination as a persistent feature of living in the United States. These children struggled to make sense of their experiences amid competing cultural messages and racialized realities.

Other studies examining ethnicity and generational status have found that language loss and language differences between Asian immigrant parents and their children may have significant negative effects on family relations and other aspects of children's health and social development because language is a measure of acculturation. Using data from the 1997–1998 World Health Organization Study of Health Behavior in School Children, S. M. Yu, Huang, and Schwalberg (2002) documented an association between students who did not speak English at home and higher health risks, such as not wearing seat belts, higher psychosocial risks such as feeling marginalized at school and experiencing difficulty making new friends, and higher parental risks such as feeling unsupported when trying to deal with school and personal problems (pp. 193–194). These adolescents also reported more frequent incidents of illness, including dizziness, headaches, and stomachaches.

The process of language loss typically occurs in three generations or less, resulting in children who have little or no working knowledge of their parents' and grandparents' native language and cultural traditions. Researchers have attributed this phenomenon to the assimilative pressures of culturally and linguistically dominant groups over others as well as perceptions of linguistic inferiority internalized by minority individuals and affecting their social identity. Given the adverse direct and indirect effects of language loss described above and denigration of bilingual and bicultural identities, it is important to consider possible strategies for fostering language resilience among native biliterate Asian American youth. Tse (2001) argues that "schools alone have limited ability to revitalize threatened languages" because resisting the process requires broader involvement with peer groups that use the heritage language, institutions that value the language, and parents who speak the language and encourage its use. Reinforcing the vitality of a language—its status and prestige as shaped by various social, political, cultural, and psychological influences—and involvement in rich literacy environments and experiences is essential.

Asian American Teachers and Teachers of Asian American Students

Asian Americans are clearly underrepresented in the teaching profession, constituting only 1% to 1.2% of all K–12 teachers across the country, with an average enrollment of eight preservice teachers each in certification programs across the country (Gordon, 2000). These numbers are disproportionate to the participation of Asian Americans in higher education as well as the workforce at large and are perhaps best explained by immigration status and selective career planning (Rong & Preissle, 1997). Existing research provides several explanations for why Asian Americans are reluctant to become teachers, including the negotiation of racial barriers and messages of racial expectations.

Based on student-led interviews with members of the Asian American community, Gordon (2000) offers four main reasons for their low interest in teaching. First, respondents cited the spoken and unspoken pressures they felt from their parents, family, and community to secure positions of high status and income. Because of culturally internalized values such as deference toward elders and maintaining family harmony, these respondents felt obliged to enter occupations in medicine or engineering that would "enhance the image of [their] family" (p. 184). Second, regardless of their ethnic origins, all of Gordon's respondents identified with traditional Chinese views on the significance of education and the near perfection necessary in those individuals who aspired to become teachers. Respondents feared the responsibility and potential incompetence they might experience in educating someone else's child, rendering them "discouraged before they [tried]" (p. 186). Third, respondents voiced concerns about having to work outside their comfort zones with students whose backgrounds were unfamiliar, maintain classroom discipline and order, and perhaps be ridiculed for their lack of English proficiency. They also worried about having to share their personal opinions and experiences publicly. Last, because the respondents saw little value in matching Asian American children with Asian American teachers, they did not feel compelled to enter the teaching profession. In fact, respondents expressed their specific desire to be accepted as "normal" and "feared that Asian teachers would reach out to Asian students in a different way, thereby stigmatizing, isolating, or favoring those students" (p. 190).

Gordon's (2000) study and related work (Gordon, 1997, 2005; also see Asher, 2002, on the cultural influences shaping Indian American students' career choices) provide numerous cultural insights into why Asian Americans may avoid becoming teachers, but their research is based primarily on first- or second-generation Asian immigrants whose retention of their traditional values is still strong and readily compare their American educational experiences and notions of success to those "in their home countries" (Gordon, 2000, p. 176). Other researchers have emphasized the more complex economic, demographic, political, sociocultural, psychological, and educational factors contributing to the shortage of Asian American teachers. Rong and Preissle (1997) point out that ethnic-enclave professions that many Asian Americans enter, such as engineering, computer science, medicine, and the hard sciences, help them not only limit social interaction with others to "save face" against cultural awkwardness but provide spaces where they can be judged more meritocratically on their mastery of objective skills and shield themselves from racial discrimination. Rong and Preissle (1997) further note that Asian American teachers view their experiences as different from other teachers with respect to parents' expectations, teacher-student relationships, and teachers' expectations of students. Asian American teachers "believed that they [were] a marginal minority, invisible in school, and that the school curriculum [was] irrelevant to Asian American life experiences and to their culture" (pp. 282–283).

Regardless of whether there is inherent value in race-matched teaching, Asian American teachers represent part of the growing diversity in the United States and have a role in modeling democratic free thinking and increasing both students' and teachers' knowledge and positive interaction among different cultural groups (Jorgenson, 2000). Given the heterogeneity within the community, Asian American teachers also may be especially able to identify with the needs and concerns of Asian American children, and their bicultural perspectives are a significant asset. More scholarship that considers the complexities of Asian American identity and career choice is needed. For example, Tang's (2002) study comparing Asian American, Chinese, and Caucasian American college students' career choices found that acculturation was a significant factor in career selection. Chinese respondents were most likely to enter occupations based on family expectations, and Caucasian American students were most likely to enter occupations based on their individual desires. Asian American respondents tended to fall in between these two groups, varying according to the extent of their acculturation. This finding is interesting, especially in light of Rong and Preissle's (1997) point that most minority teachers are native born.

The invisibility of Asian Americans across key aspects of public education such as curriculum and staffing is problematic because it fosters the neglect of Asian American students' complex identities, experiences, and educational needs. It also perpetuates their marginality within traditional discussions of race premised on a Black/White framework of society. Kiang (2004) notes that K–12 curriculum lacks significant content on Asia. Exacerbating this situation is high-stakes testing that has officially defined the curriculum students that should learn and excluded content about Asian Americans. These omissions affect all students and can reinforce Asian American stereotypes. S. J. Lee and Kumashiro (2005) note,

All students pick up social messages from what is included and what is excluded from the curriculum. Both AAPI and non-AAPI students are affected when issues related to AAPI history and culture are not taught in our schools. When Asian American and Pacific Islander (AAPI) histories are not taught as part of U.S. history the implicit message is that AAPIs are not real Americans, thereby contributing to the stereotype that AAPIs are perpetual foreigners. (pp. 15–16)

According to Kiang (2004), Asian American studies (AAS) programs in higher education are significant—albeit underutilized—educational, cultural, and institutional assets that can contribute meaningfully in efforts to address these issues through a minimum of six interventions at the K–12 level: to assist in the development of curriculum, to raise awareness through teacher professional development, to facilitate classroom research and advocacy, to examine the long-term effects of AAS on teachers, to support the involvement of Asian American parents and families, and to mentor Asian American youth in school and community settings.

The impact of multicultural education in teacher preparation programs also must be considered because most teachers are White and have limited prior experience with Asian American children whose numbers have doubled to represent 4.2% of the total current student population (Goodwin, 2002). Whereas certain multicultural approaches can reinforce teachers' beliefs about distinct group differences or merely focus on the feel-good outcomes of human relations, other approaches can foster deeper knowledge about the historical and contemporary experiences of a racial/ethnic group, promote the individual and collective diversity that exists in society, and critically examine and transform existing systems of inequality and discrimination (Sleeter & Grant, 2003). An essential first step is that teachers must be trained to recognize the presence and range of experiences had by Asian American children in schools. In reviewing teacher education textbooks, Goodwin (2002) found that terms such as "children of color," "diverse children," "culturally and linguistically diverse students," and "minority children" tended to be used interchangeably with "immigrant children." This conflation of terminology makes it difficult for teachers to really understand or begin to address Asian American students' educational identities and needs.

Perceptions of Asian Americans as foreigners and the model minority curtail genuine progress. Pang (1997) emphasizes the need for teachers who work with Asian American students to care about the whole child, including not only their educational but also social and psychological needs. Achieving such an end requires helping teachers critically examine their own racial identity development (Carter, 2000; Carter & Goodwin, 1994) and prejudices (Pang & Park, 2003) to then build a foundation of knowledge on which to work most appropriately and effectively with Asian American youth.

ASIAN AMERICANS IN HIGHER EDUCATION RESEARCH

The general understanding of Asian Americans in higher education is also one of high achievement, with a specific tenor of their overrepresentation at elite, prestigious universities. This discourse is particularly visible in the debate about affirmative action because critics of these race-conscious policies hold Asian Americans up as exemplars of individual effort and hard work. However, scholars are embarking on the important task of deconstructing these representations and revealing the complicated, intersectional realities of Asian American college students and faculty.

Representations

A significant body of research critically examines the representation of Asian Americans in higher education, particularly in the context of affirmative action admissions policies. Much of the research on Asian Americans in higher education relates to the admissions controversy of the 1980s where Asian American activists charged that campus administrators had placed a cap on Asian American enrollment at elite universities such as Brown; Yale; Princeton; Cornell; Stanford; University of California, Los Angeles (UCLA); and University of California, Berkeley. From 1983 to 1986, Asian American enrollments at these schools remained steady and were lower than White admissions despite the increasing size of the Asian American applicant pool. Nakanishi (1989) and Wang (1988) detail the statistical disparity in admissions, changing admissions policies that discriminated against Asian American applicants, and the rationale offered by some administrators that Asian Americans were overrepresented at these campuses.

By far the most thorough examination of the admissions controversy and the shifting representations of Asian Americans in the political discourse is by Takagi (1992), who documents that although the investigation initially focused on charges that Asian American applicants were being denied admission in favor of Whites, by 1989, the image of the model minority reemerged as the debate turned to affirmative action admissions as the real culprit for Asian American rejection. Takagi notes that as Asian Americans were lauded as the new victims of affirmative action, they became an important political tool used by those who sought to repeal race-conscious policies.

During the admissions controversy, the image of Asian Americans as models separated them from other minority groups, grouping them with Whites as victims of affirmative action. At the same time, the image of Asian American students as foreign and the yellow peril taking over campuses also was evoked in the discourse of Asian American overrepresentation, which implied that Asian American student numbers had to be limited because they did not contribute to diversity because they were all the same (S. S. Lee, 2006). The tenuous position of Asian Americans and their representation in affirmative action has been examined as the 1990s witnessed a repeal of affirmative action. For instance, Omi and Takagi (1996) show how in the 1990s in California, Asian Americans were consistently depicted as victims of affirmative action, claimed by the political Right and abandoned by the Left who did not know what to do with a minority group that did too well.

This representation of Asian Americans is the result of a limited Black/White framework in which "minority" and "high achievement" seem to be incompatible concepts and, as a result, reifies the idea that Asian Americans are no longer minorities. Asian Americans have been "de-minoritized" (S. S. Lee, 2006) and scholars point out that Asian American are now routinely ignored. Osajima (1995b) discusses how Asian American college students struggle to prove that they are still minorities as they are rendered invisible, their academic and student services needs unmet. Inkelas (2003a, 2003b) describes Asian Pacific Americans as "diversity's missing minority"; analyses of APA student attitudes on affirmative action reveal that students feel marginalized by admissions policies that do not offer them underrepresented minority benefits or majority legacy benefits (Inkelas, 2003a; Louie, 2004). To capture this frustration, Inkelas (2003a) describes these students feeling as if they are in a racial "no-man's land" (p. 635). Such theoretical constraints limit the ways in which non-Black minorities experience higher education.

Although the admissions controversy itself is now more than 20 years old, the issues relating to Asian Americans as the model minority persist today and remain a challenge to higher education researchers who seek to deconstruct this simplistic representation. Vigilance regarding these representations is necessary to gain an accurate understanding of Asian Americans in higher education. Two levels of research seek to reveal a more accurate understanding of Asian Americans in higher education and their persistent needs—macrolevel studies that examine administrative policies and aggregate statistics and microlevel studies that highlight Asian American students' experiences and voices.

Macrolevel Studies: Deconstructing Representations

Large-scale statistical studies of Asian American students have a common mantra: disaggregate. Once data is separated along ethnicity, gender, and a host of other variables, a more complex picture is revealed. Hsia's (1988) work is a comprehensive quantitative analysis of Asian American achievement in education and occupation that persists and remains salient today. Despite their educational success, Asian Americans face barriers of access to higher education and economic parity. Hsia also discusses the limitations of aggregate data given the wide diversity of experiences under the Asian American rubric, such as along ethnic lines (Southeast Asian students having higher high school drop-out rates) and academic discipline. One of Hsia's most consistent findings is that Asian American students score lower on achievement tests measuring verbal aptitude and score higher on quantitative and math tests than do Whites. This finding is consistent across ethnic groups and even after several generations in the United States (with the exception of a small proportion of socioeconomically and educationally advantaged Asian Americans).

Similar themes were discovered in later studies by Hsia and Hirano-Nakanishi (1995) and Escueta and O'Brien (1991), who disaggregated data to reveal that Southeast Asian American groups experience lower rates of high school completion than other Asian American subgroups and that Asian Americans are concentrated in business and physical science fields. The most comprehensive and recent examination of disaggregate data by Hune and Chan (1997) critiques the model minority myth and points to structural barriers and opportunities that have enabled APAs to excel in some areas of higher education but not in others. The strength of this research is the critical analysis of data that reveal the bimodal nature of APA educational achievement (with high rates of both college completion and high school dropouts), a gender gap, and ethnic disparity (Southeast Asians and Pacific Islanders at the lower spectrum). APA achievement in disciplines also is uneven, with higher representation in sciences and math along all levels of education through the doctorate degree. Hune and Chan advocate for additional research on this diverse group.

Research also shows that academic persistence remains an issue, despite images of their success. As disaggregated data shows, Yeh (2004–2005) argues that research needs to focus on non–East Asian American subgroups to identify barriers to low academic persistence rates due to immigrant/refugee status, academic underpreparedness, first-generation college status, language barriers, low socioeconomic status, family demands and obligations, and cultural adjustment. In addition, institutional barriers include marginalization and racism on campus, cultural barriers to effective student services, model minority stereotype pressures, and lack of financial aid.

Community Colleges

Statistical studies of Asian American students in community colleges also identify persistent barriers for this population and challenge the image of Asian American model minority students concentrated at elite universities. Limited research has been conducted on Asian American students in community colleges, despite the fact that a 1990 study found that 40% of Asian American students in higher education were in 2-year community colleges (Kiang, 1992, p. 98) and that according to the 2000-2001 U.S. Census, APAs made up 15% of all students enrolled in 2-year institutions (Lew, Chang, & Wang, 2005, p. 64). Because of this lack of research, Lew et al. (2005) call APA students in community colleges the "overlooked minority."

Local studies, however, reveal that APA students in community colleges face significant barriers. Kiang's (1992) study of students at a public urban university (whose demographics are shared with local community college students) revealed that Asian American students had high rates of working part-time, lower retention rates than White students, and frustrations with language barriers, family obligations, and anti-Asian racism. Kiang also discovered that AAS courses provided a supportive learning environment for these students, who began to see themselves reflected in the curriculum. X. Yang and Rendon's (1994) study of Asian students in North Carolina's community college system revealed that Asian students were more strongly influenced by the advice of their families and friends as opposed to informational literature or college recruiters. In addition, obstacles to attending community college involved greater job and family obligations, which limited Asian students' time. Makuakane-Drechsel and Hagedorn (2000) examined Hawaiian students at four community colleges in Oahu and identified predictive variables for academic persistence that included cumulative grade point average, financial aid, and average credit hours. These findings point to specific challenges in ensuring a wider access to and persistence in community colleges for Asian American and Pacific Islander (AAPI) students.

In addition to access and persistence issues, Lew et al. (2005) cite studies that APA community college students report dissatisfaction with faculty, discrimination and marginalization on campus, and a lack of APA faculty representation. These studies reveal that APA students struggle on community college campuses, and they highlight the reality that a significant proportion of APA college students are overlooked when the focus is on the Asian American model minority at elite universities.

Student Affairs Policies and Implications

Research in student affairs related to Asian American college students is a growing field. Several studies examine university policies and student services and how they affect Asian American students.[4] The persistent model minority myth is discussed in particular to the ways in which it perpetuates barriers to effective services for Asian American students. For instance, a study by Liang and Sedlacek (2003) found that White student affairs practitioners held stereotypical positive attitudes toward Asian American students (seeing them as nonthreatening, technically inclined, and hard working), yet at the same time, the practitioners did not express sensitivity to Asian American students in regard to family obligations or academic pressures. The authors challenge practitioners to be more vigilant of stereotypes and to be more culturally sensitive.

Delucchi and Do (1996) demonstrate how the model minority myth can lead to higher education's indifference of Asian Americans as victims of racial intolerance and compromised services. Using a University of California campus as a case study, the authors reported how administrators would not characterize the harassment of a Vietnamese American student as racially motivated, whereas racist incidents against African Americans were quickly defined as such. The authors point out how the model minority stereotype kept administrators from recognizing when Asian American students were victims of racism on campus.

The process by which Asian American students might internalize the model minority stereotype is revealed in a study by R. Yang, Byers, Ahuna, and Castro (2002), who proposed that Asian American students might avoid seeking Asian American targeted services if they internalized the model minority stereotype. They found that Asian American students who reported valuing their family backgrounds used ethnic specific services more often, whereas those who disidentified with their cultural heritage did not, which might point to attempted acculturation or an acceptance of the model minority myth.

Several researchers also have examined Asian American student identity development and related psychological issues. Kawaguchi (2003), Alvarez (2002), and Kodama, McEwen, Liang, and Lee (2002) propose identity development models for Asian American students, cautioning that Asian Americans are diverse and may be at different stages at different times. Understanding identity development can help assist student affairs practitioners in providing the most appropriate services. Research also shows that pan-Asian identity and student activism assist APA students in coping with and combating ignorance and discrimination and developing a stronger commitment to their communities (Inkelas, 2004; Rhoads, Lee, & Yamada, 2002).[5]

Asian American Student Experiences and Voices

What are Asian American college students' experiences in reality? This section will highlight research findings that focus on these experiences and voices to uncover a complicated and diverse picture, one that challenges simplistic stereotypes of the model minority and shows how Asian Americans are still racialized as culturally foreign and distinct. Asian American experiences also are best understood using an intersectional approach.

Campus Climate

Campus climate is a rich field, and Asian American students are included in several studies. A significant body of work produced from the 1980s to the 2000s from a student affairs/counseling psychology perspective on campus climate included some coverage of Asian American students. These studies' findings include the fact that minority students (including Asian Americans) report greater social alienation than White students at predominantly White institutions (Jones, Castellanos, & Cole, 2002; Loo & Rolison, 1986), that Asian students who experienced racism on campus had lower social adjustment (LeSure, 1994), that Asian American negative perceptions of campus climate were correlated with self-reported levels of depression (Cress & Ikeda, 2003), and that Asian American students reported experiences with stereotypes and prejudice and dissatisfaction despite academic satisfaction and persistence (Bennett & Okinaka, 1990; Loo & Rolison, 1986). Although, in general, Asian American students did not report levels of discrimination as high as African American students, their reports of being singled out, stereotyped, or harassed were significant and higher than that of White students (Ancis, Sedlacek, & Mohr, 2000; Asian Pacific American Education Advisory Committee, 1990; LeSure, 1994; Mack, Tucker, & Cha, 2000). Incidents range from racial slurs and fights (Alvarez & Yeh, 1999) to subtle comments that single out Asian Americans or ignore them (Woo, 1997). These incidents are underreported by Asian American students as well and implications are discussed to improve student services (Kotori & Malaney, 2003).

Furthermore, Rohrlick, Alvarado, Zaruba, and Kallio (1998) insightfully demonstrate that the model minority's presumption that APA students all do well and do not need any assistance (as evidenced by persistence and statistical numbers) renders APA students invisible. Despite this perception, their study at the University of Michigan in 1996 found that APA students reported gaining less from their education, reported a less favorable campus climate than White students, and less overall satisfaction with campus life. Rohrlick et al. (1998) conclude,

When measured by enrollment, retention, college grades, and graduation rates, Asian/APA students appear to be among the most successful students on our campus. It is incongruous, then, to find that their assessment of their undergraduate experience is less positive than other students, and troubling that their greatest differences occur in areas central to the University's mission, such as the development of writing and communication skills, gains in critical thinking, and experiences with faculty in the classroom. The initial comparison of responses suggests that APA students have a different experience on our campus than do White students—and one that is less positive. *If that is true, then it certainly challenges the myth that has grown out of the model minority image: that is, all we have to do is enroll APA students, and they will thrive on campus.* These results suggest that we need to revisit that assumption. (p. 9, italics added)

Although some of these studies are dated and indicative of heightened anti-Asian sentiment in the late 1980s and mid 1990s, the findings show that Asian Americans report an alienating campus climate and support the argument that they are not similar to Whites. In addition, even high-achieving Asian American students who persist and achieve academically still face these alienating environments where they are racialized as Others, a reality that needs to be addressed.

Complexities of Asian American Experiences: College Choices, Asian American Student Voices, and Families

Asian American students are diverse. Several studies examining Asian American college students' choices reveal ethnic diversity and a push for research on ethnic subgroups. There are a host of many complex factors affecting Asian American students' choice of college major; variation was found along ethnic lines, gender, and psychological measures such as locus of control (Song & Glick, 2004). Simpson (2001) also found that Asian American students were more influenced by maternal guidance and high school English courses in choosing between a technical or public service/liberal arts program. Teranishi, Ceja, Antonio, Allen, and McDonough (2004) examined the impact of class and ethnicity on college choice for APA students using data from UCLA's Cooperative Institutional Research Program in 1997. The authors found that Southeast Asians and Chinese were more often from families earning less than $24,999 a year. In addition, larger proportions of Chinese and Koreans attended highly selective colleges than Filipinos or Southeast Asians. Filipinos and Southeast Asians from the lowest income were more likely to choose a college because it was close to home, and they expressed more major financial concerns about college than did other groups. Along with Japanese students, they also were twice as likely to apply to only one campus, whereas Chinese and Koreans in the sample were likely to apply to five or more colleges.

Socioeconomic status affects groups differently and warrants more research. For instance, Teranishi et al. (2004) found that Chinese students had the highest rates of attending private colleges, but only at the highest socioeconomic levels. This finding is just one example of how intersectional approaches can go beyond a superficial examination of racial or ethnic differences. Louie's (2004) ethnographic study takes this exciting approach as she examines how race, immigration, gender, and class affect the understanding of higher education for Chinese students from well-off suburbs and from the ethnic enclave of Chinatown. Additional research needs to examine specific subgroups in the APA population given this diversity.

Other studies reveal the complexity of Asian American student experiences and attitudes that involve the intersectionality of a number of variables. Inkelas (2003a, 2003b) examined APA college students' attitudes toward affirmative action at a large, public, midwestern university. In a large-scale survey, Inkelas (2003b) conducted quantitative regressions to determine factors that lead to APA support for affirmative action. She found that a complicated web of interrelated factors were relevant, including academic major (humanities or social sciences), gender (women supported affirmative action more than did men), informal conversations with peers about diversity, participation in diversity programming, and racial/ethnic identity. Inkelas reveals that attitudes are complicated and interrelated and affected by ideology and college experiences.

The representation of Asian Americans as the model minority and foreigner projects an understanding of distinct (i.e., non-Western) Asian culture that highly values family cohesion, deference to authority, and education. Just as K–12 research reveals more complicated family relations that question these presumptions, higher education researchers who examine the Asian American family reveal a different reality.

Although family expectations may be high for Asian American students, the pressures also result in high demands and intergenerational conflict. For instance, Gloria and Ho (2003) examined measures of noncognitive dimensions of perceptions of university climate and social support in the college adaptation of APA students in the Southwest. They found that APA students might not see their family support as completely positive given the pressures that parental expectations can bring (APA students reported using peer support more often than family support). Osajima (1991) also found these pressures in his qualitative study of Asian American college students and the "hidden injuries of race." Osajima documents how Asian American students expressed persistent experiences with racism and highly complicated family relationships that challenge a model minority image of strong Asian families with high educational expectations. Although students credited family support and expectations as influencing their educational aspirations, they also expressed frustration and compromised familial relationships due to these expectations. Work by R. Lee, Su, and Yoshida (2005) examines the various strategies Asian American college students used to cope with intergenerational conflict. This research complicates the idea of perfect Asian American families.

What about the famed Asian American family values of education? Louie's (2004) work examines the role of the Chinese family in conveying messages about higher education and, more important, how Chinese American children make sense of these messages in developing their own views of higher education and their possibilities of socioeconomic mobility. Unlike the model minority image that depicts Asians as "honorary Whites," she finds instead that race is highly salient and both suburban and enclave Chinese parents frame education as a way to buffer the effects of racial discrimination. Parents emphasize that their children must work hard because racism closes off equal access to opportunities. Children were aware of structural barriers for their advancement and expressed uncertainty about their future. Kibria's (2002) study of second-generation Chinese and Korean American young adults revealed similar views of education as a strategy to cope with racism.

Despite this awareness of structural barriers to advancement due to race, Louie (2004) also found that students internalized and embraced an ethnic-cultural script that attributed educational achievement (or lack thereof) to the Chinese family. Chinese parents (and Asian parents in general) were seen as more strict and emphasized education and hard work, giving Chinese children a distinct advantage over other groups. This attribution is troubling because it persisted despite the students' nuanced and critical analyses of the model minority stereotype, awareness of foreigner racialization, and belief in structural barriers to advancement along racial and socioeconomic lines.

Kibria's (2002) study also revealed similar attitudes, with some of her respondents embracing the idea of Asian cultural values of hard work in their rejection of affirmative action and in contrasting themselves with other racial minorities. Interpreting the model minority stereotype and the messages of Asian family values as positive, Kibria (2002) concludes, "Fueled by the very fact of their racialized marginality, Asian Americans *may ironically affirm the stereotype of themselves as a model minority in an effort to ease their own path of integration into American society*" (p. 206, italics added). These studies point to the ways in which representations are negotiated and can be internalized, particularly for second-generation Asians with immigrant parents. Future work should examine if a more heightened critical perspective emerges in later generations and the ways in which Asian Americans contest or accept these messages.

Faculty Issues

Research on Asian American faculty and administrators reveals similar representations of faculty as model minorities who are passive, hard-working, and nonconfrontational, for example, and foreigners whose cultural differences are so great they are incapable of leadership. Nakanishi (1993) and Hune and Chan (1997) highlight the issues of APA faculty and administrators, including the underrepresentation of APA faculty as administrators, the concentration of faculty in sciences and engineering, and the greater concentration of Asian foreign nationals among faculty than native-born Asian Americans (a finding that points more to educational opportunity abroad than in the United States for Asians). Hune and Chan also point out APA faculty struggle with lower tenure rates, especially for Asian American women who also face a gender gap, with APA men serving in three out of four faculty positions (p. 57). Asian American faculty who conduct research in AAS or other ethnic or gender studies fields also face marginalization for work that is seen as not objective or rigorous (Chan, 2005; Nakanishi, 1993).

Asian American women face additional stereotypes and barriers due to sexism and an image of Asian women as exotic and submissive. General collections reveal rich data on the experiences of women of color faculty (TuSmith & Reddy, 2002; Vargas, 2002). These collections are all written from the perspective of women of color and their struggles establishing authority, credibility, and objectivity in the classroom. Hune's research (1997, 1998) on APA women in higher education greatly adds to this literature, citing racialized and gendered stereotypes of the exotic Dragon Lady, lowered tenure rates for Asian American women, and their underrepresentation at upper administrative levels.

The experiences of Asian women faculty also are outlined in a recent edited collection by Li and Beckett (2006). This collection features a range of studies and personal narratives of Asian and Asian American women struggling with marginalization due to racism and sexism, establishing credibility as nonnative English speakers, securing tenure and promotion, building mentoring and networking relationships, balancing multiple roles and value systems, and constructing positive identities. Several contributors speak to the issue as nonnative English-speaking Teachers of English to Students of Other Languages (TESOL) professors and the privilege that nativity brings in the largely White field. Another important theme is the resistance these women face by students, including Asian students themselves who internalize racism and sexism that results in their greater deference to White male professors. While highlighting voices of nonnative English speakers, this collection reveals barriers for Asian and Asian American women faculty.

Additional research examines tenure battles of Asian American faculty (Minami, 1990; Nakanishi, 1990). Cho (1997) also discusses how racialized sexual harassment is a real barrier for APA women faculty, who face stereotypes of being exotic, sexual objects. She discusses two major court battles of APA women who fought racialized sexual harassment in academia and the ways in which the institutions defended their harassers.

The quantitative data of Asian American faculty and administrative representation in higher education is beginning to be addressed. For example, the Committee of 100 (2005) examined the representation of APAs in the top quartile of higher education institutions and found that APAs are underrepresented in the top administrative positions of president, provost, or chancellor (most APA presidents were at community colleges, in the University of Hawaii system, or at for-profit institutions). The committee's report card raises questions as a starting point for additional research.

A more thoroughly researched study by S. M. Lee (2002) sets out to determine if Asian American faculty face a glass ceiling in higher education. Using salary as the dependent variable, Lee found that although initially there was no significant difference between Asian and White faculty salaries (thus negating a glass ceiling effect), upon further investigation, problematic differences did emerge, including different effects from gaining tenure, publication productivity, and service. In addition, native-born Whites benefited more from being native, whereas native-born Asians did not yield the same benefits. Hence, Lee concludes that there was some support for and against the existence of a glass ceiling.

APAs are highly underrepresented as chief executive officers in higher education. Chan and Wang (1991) and Hune and Chan (1997) point out that Asian American faculty are not identified as potential administrators and are not mentored to take these positions. Stereotypes of Asian Americans as not having the right leadership style because they are quiet or passive evokes ideas of their foreignness. Although they are the model minority and are hard working, there is something else that keeps them from being fully embraced by the majority at the highest levels of higher education; hence, they continue to be marginalized.

The Field of Asian American Studies

The field of AAS, part of a larger ethnic studies movement, emerged in the late 1960s as a product of student demands for a more inclusive curriculum and campus. Although challenges remain in institutionalizing the discipline (Chan, 2005; Chang, 1999; Endo & Wei, 1988), research has shown that AAS makes the curriculum more relevant to Asian American students. For example, in his study of APA students at a public urban university, Kiang (1992) discovered that AAS courses provided a supportive learning environment for these students who began to see themselves reflected in the curriculum. In addition, AAS advances research and teaching that educates others about Asian American experiences and deconstructs simplistic representations. Scholars have pointed to the important ways that the field of AAS and ethnic studies transforms the curriculum and "democratizes" higher education (Hune, 1995), providing exemplary principles for general education such as interdisciplinary approaches and pedagogy that reach diverse students (Chang & Kiang, 2002). It is precisely through the intellectual contributions by scholars in AAS that educators can now begin to see the interconnections between the school lives of students and how we are all embodied within larger sociohistorical contexts. Educators and higher education administrators need to see the intellectual rigor such programs like ethnic and gender studies bring to academic institutions by engaging in the fundamental tenets of intellectual diversity and freedom. Such programs serve unique functions for racial minority students, but they also provide needed services to all students by reflecting the realities of our society.

One of the continuing challenges in institutionalizing AAS is the fact that many educators and administrators have difficulty discerning between Asian studies and AAS, ultimately conflating the two. Although another area of transnational studies has emerged that bridges the two, they are each very distinct fields and areas of study that should not be confused (Hune, 2001). The fact that AAS is commonly mistaken for Asian studies and rarely mistaken for American studies points to the persistent notion that Asian Americans are foreigners and not part of U.S. history. Dismantling one's conception of Asian-ness as foreignness is a step in the right direction.

CONCLUSION AND IMPLICATIONS FOR FUTURE RESEARCH

Representations of Asian Americans are highly political and manufactured to support a stance, as in the case of affirmative action, and distract us from understanding the diversity of Asian American experiences (Chang & Kiang, 2002). For those who embrace a model minority image, it is easy to disregard Asian American students in favor of more pressing minority students who may still be more visibly underrepresented. Although these disparities for groups such as African Americans, Latinas/Latinos, and Native Americans are pressing concerns, Asian Americans should not be excluded based on statistics alone. Research presented here reveals not only a wide variation of experiences, needs, and outcomes along ethnic lines but also a more complicated situation in which Asian American students struggle to interpret and negotiate the racial and cultural demands of identity development, family relations, college access and retention, campus racial climate, and an invisibility in education policies.

As for any group of students, viewing Asian American students through a particular ideological lens has powerful implications for school policies. For example, through critical race theory, Teranishi (2002) examined racial climate for APA students in four California public high schools. He found that teachers and counselors expected Chinese students to be the model minority with high educational aspirations, hence tracking them into college preparatory programs. Conversely, Filipino students reported that they were viewed and treated as gang members and tracked into vocational programs, without college counseling. By centering these students' voices, Teranishi found that the different stereotypes they faced affected their racial, ethnic, and academic identities and ultimately affected their postsecondary aspirations.

It is a critical time to better understand the educational needs of Asian Americans. High-stakes testing at the state and federal level overlooks Asian American students by lumping them in the aggregate. The 2001 No Child Left Behind (NCLB) Act does not require ethnic disaggregation of student performance, thus masking Asian American ethnic and socioeconomic variation. Kiang (2004) discusses these issues in regard to the Massachusetts Comprehensive Assessment System, the mandatory standardized tests assessing English, math, and science/technology. In schools with the highest concentrations of Southeast Asian students, the mean scaled scores for Asian students at the 10th-grade level was failing compared to other districts where Chinese and Indian students were passing. We do not see this reality if we focus on the aggregate.

High-stakes testing also poses tremendous educational obstacles for nonnative speakers of English, a particular problem for Asian immigrant students. Genishi, Stires, and Yung-Chan (2001) caution against the narrowing effects of NCLB on teachers' instructional practices with English-language learners at the prekindergarten levels and they demonstrate the positive effects of embedding early literacy development within meaningful social and cultural contexts. S. J. Lee and Kumashiro (2005) note that although research shows it takes 4 to 9 years to achieve second-language fluency, NCLB guidelines require English Language Learners (ELLs) be tested in English and language arts after only 3 years. NCLB also requires students with limited English proficiency to still take the math portions of tests with no hiatus. Although some may surmise that math performance is not affected by language proficiency, Wright (2006) critically examines the barriers for immigrant students learning math. Schools bear the brunt of providing bilingual instruction, which is primarily in Spanish—a disadvantage for Asian immigrant students. Students' ability to catch up with their peers depends on their prior education before coming to the United States and their school's resources; although students are entitled to linguistic accommodation in taking tests, some schools lack the resources to provide it. Wright also demonstrates that the vocabulary in math problems (particularly in complex word problems and in advanced computations that require abstract reasoning) poses significant barriers for English-language learners and requires a more advanced language proficiency than presumed.

The state of Asian Americans in higher education is also facing a critical time. In January 2003, Congressman Wu (Oregon) introduced H.R. Bill 333 to amend the Higher Education Act, which would designate "Asian American and Pacific Islander–serving institutions" and provide federal dollars to help recruit and retain AAPI students (Laanan & Starobin, 2004). Such legislation challenges the presumption that APA college students do not need assistance. In addition, the continued debates about affirmative action in the wake of the 2003 Supreme Court Michigan cases *Gratz v. Bollinger* and *Grutter v. Bollinger* (and the representations of Asian Americans in the debate) have led to legal articles that examine the ways in which diversity has been narrowly defined to exclude Asian American students (Choy, 2005; Gee, 2004; Wu, 1995). Legal scholars such as Cho (1998, cited in Asian Pacific American Law Students Association Symposium, 1998) also have argued that parity cannot be the sole measure for lack of discrimination. Asian American overrepresentation in higher education is an obscuring image that evokes the yellow peril and essentializes a diverse Asian American population as all the same.

Research highlighting Asian American students' voices, identities, choices, and families reveals complicated realities that involve a variety of factors beyond simply ethnicity or race. New educational research takes primarily an intersectional approach, introducing other sectors of identity.[6] For instance, Joshi (2006) has studied the interplay of religious and racial identity for Indian Americans; Kumashiro (2001, 2004) has examined how students and activists negotiate race and sexuality; Palmer (2001) introduces new research on how gender and racial bias affect Korean young women adoptees' racial identity development and educational experiences as well as how transcultural adoption affects their identity in distinct ways; and studies by Poon-McBrayer and Garcia (2000) and Parette and Huer (2002), respectively, explore the process of referring, assessing, and placing Asian American students with learning disabilities in special education programs and working with Asian American families whose children have augmentive or alternative communication needs. These intersectional approaches assert the multiplicity and hybridity of the Asian American experience.

However, we cannot deny that racism exists and that Asian Americans must negotiate and challenge racially constraining representations. This reality is evident by the fact that even high-achieving Asian American groups such as East Asians and South Asians, who may appear to be the model minority, remain either not fully integrated or seen as White. In this way, it is necessary to understand and examine the ways in which race continues to affect Asian American students, ways that are not captured by statistics or notions of parity alone. Racialization of foreignness and alienation are not measured by statistics and may not emerge in rates of academic persistence or grade point average. More nuanced understandings of race and racializations in education are needed to see the real experiences of Asian American students as they negotiate inequitable and discriminatory social structural conditions. This understanding is critical to seeing Asian Americans in their full complexity and diversity and to avoid essentialist notions of culture that feed into an Othering discourse. It is only through these approaches that we can begin to truly contest pernicious representations of the model minority and foreigner, generating a more accurate understanding of Asian Americans in their full diversity and humanity.

NOTES

[1] We use the term "Asian American" in reference to individuals of Asian descent in the United States (Chinese, Japanese, Korean, Indian, Filipino, Vietnamese, and other Southeast Asian groups) who have been racialized and grouped as Asian in policy and legislation. There is great variation in the research literature as to use of the term Asian American or Asian Pacific American (APA) in describing this community. When referencing other studies, we use the term chosen by the author; we are aware that an uncritical inclusion of Pacific Islander Americans within the Asian American rubric runs the risk of marginalizing and conflating this group, which has distinct histories (Diaz, 1994; Kauanui, 2005). For this reason, when we refer to this population, we use the term "Asian American."

[2] The historical literature on Asian American education is sparse. Educational historian Eileen Tamura (2001) provides an alarming look at how the major publication within the field, the *History of Education Quarterly*, published only one essay and one book review related to Asian American educational history within a 10-year period (1990-1999). Of equal import is another finding that "only 15.1 percent of the essays and essay reviews (given all the publications within the ten year period) and an even smaller 9.5 percent of the book reviews focused on issues of race and ethnicity, most of which were on African Americans, followed by European Americans, and then Native Americans" (p. 65). Important contributions to the field include Tamura's (2003) edited special issue of the *History of Education Quarterly*, Pak (2002), Asato (2005), Okihiro (1999), and Austin (2004). Aside from specific texts devoted to Asian American educational experiences, most notably the edited book by Nakanishi and Nishida (1995) and Weinberg (1997), which include brief histories of some of the major Asian ethnic groups, the field of educational history needs to develop more inclusive scholarship that reflects the changing nature of students' lives in the latter half of the 20th century.

[3] Research on West Asian students is also an important topic to study, and the racialization of Americans of Middle Eastern descent is becoming a pointed issue, particularly after the events of September 11, 2001. Still, for purposes of this article, we are focusing on Asian American experiences as defined in Note 1.

[4] An important contribution to this field is the special journal issue of *New Directions for Student Services* (Vol. 97) edited by McEwan, Kodama, Alvarez, Lee, and Liang (2002) titled *Working With Asian American College Students*.

[5] Psychological research on Asian American college students is also a burgeoning field, examining the impact of the model minority stereotype and bicultural pressures on mental health (see Cheryan & Bodenhausen, 2000; B. Kim & Omizo, 2005).

[6] It is important to note that it was not until 1952 that full citizenship to all Asian groups was granted. Given that fact, as well as that the majority of Asian immigration to the United

States occurred post-1965, including the resettlement of Southeast Asian refugees in the 1970s and 1980s, we are in the midst of creating a new generation of critical scholars in Asian American studies.

REFERENCES

Abboud, S. K., & Kim, J. Y. (2005). *Top of the class: How Asian parents raise high achievers— and how you can too.* New York: Berkeley Publishing Group.

Adler, S. M. (1998). *Mothering, education, and ethnicity: The transformation of Japanese American culture.* New York: Garland.

Alvarez, A. (2002). Racial identity and Asian Americans: Supports and challenges. In M. McEwan, C. Kodama, A. Alvarez, S. Lee, & C. Liang (Eds.), *Working with Asian American college students: New directions for student services* (Vol. 97, pp. 33–43). San Francisco: Jossey-Bass.

Alvarez, A., & Yeh, T. (1999). Asian Americans in college: A racial identity perspective. In D. Sandhu (Ed.), *Asian and Pacific Islander Americans' issues and concerns for counseling and psychotherapy* (pp. 105–119). Commack, NY: Nova Science Publishers.

Ancheta, A. (2000). *Race, rights and the Asian American experience.* New Brunswick, NJ: Rutgers University Press.

Ancis, J., Sedlacek, W., & Mohr, J. (2000). Student perceptions of campus cultural climate by race. *Journal of Counseling and Development, 78*(2), 180–185.

Anderson, J. D. (1998). *The education of Blacks in the South, 1860-1935.* Chapel Hill: University of North Carolina Press.

Anderson, J. D. (2004a). Crosses to bear and promises to keep: The jubilee anniversary of Brown v. Board of Education. *Urban Education, 39*(4), 359–372.

Anderson, J. D. (2004b). The historical context for understanding the test score gap. *Journal of Public Management & Social Policy, 10*(1), 2–22.

Asato, N. (2005). *Teaching Mikadoism: The attack on Japanese language schools in Hawaii, California, and Washington, 1919-1927.* Manoa: University of Hawaii Press.

Asher, N. (2002). Class acts: Indian American high school students negotiate professional and ethnic identities. *Urban Education, 37*(2), 267–295.

Asian Pacific American Education Advisory Committee. (1990). *Enriching California's future: Asian Pacific Americans in the CSU.* Report of the APA Education Advisory Committee, Office of the Chancellor, California State University.

Asian Pacific American Law Students Association Symposium. (1998). Rethinking racial divides: Asian Pacific Americans and the law. *Michigan Journal of Race and the Law, 4*, 187–240.

Austin, A. (2004). *From concentration camp to campus: Japanese American students and World War II.* Urbana: University of Illinois Press.

Baker, B. D., Keller-Wolff, C., & Wolf-Wendel, L. (2000). Two steps forward, one step back: Race/ethnicity and student achievement in education policy research. *Educational Policy, 14*(4), 511–529.

Bennett, C., & Okinaka, A. (1990). Factors related to the persistence among Asian, Blacks, Hispanic, and White undergraduates at a predominantly White university: Comparisons between first and fourth year cohorts. *Urban Review, 22*(1), 33–60.

Bracey, G. W. (1999). The demise of the Asian math gene. *Phi Delta Kappan, 80*(8), 619–620.

Bracey, G. W. (2005). And now, the Indian spelling gene. *Phi Delta Kappan, 87*(1), 92.

Carter, R. (2000). Reimagining race in education: A new paradigm from psychology. *Teachers College Record, 102*(5), 864–897.

Carter, R. T., & Goodwin, A. L. (1994). Racial identity and education. *Review of Research in Education, 20*, 291–336.

Chan, S. (2005). *In defense of Asian American Studies: The politics of teaching and program building.* Urbana: University of Illinois Press.

Chan, S., & Wang, L. (1991). Racism and the model minority: Asian Americans in higher education. In P. Altbach & K. Lomotey (Eds.), *The racial crisis in American higher education* (pp. 43–68). Albany: State University of New York Press.

Chang, M. (1999). Expansion and its discontents: The formation of Asian American Studies programs in the 1990s. *Journal of Asian American Studies, 2*(2), 181–206.

Chang, M., & Kiang, P. (2002). New challenges of representing Asian American students in U.S. higher education. In W. Smith, P. Altbach, & K. Lomotey (Eds.), *The racial crisis in American higher education: Continuing challenges for the twenty-first century* (Rev. ed., pp. 137–158). Albany: State University of New York Press.

Cheng, L., & Yang, P. (2000). The "model minority" stereotype deconstructed. In M. Zhou & J. Gatewood (Eds.), *Contemporary Asian America: A multidisciplinary reader* (pp. 459–482). New York: New York University Press.

Cheryan, S., & Bodenhausen, G. (2000). When positive stereotypes threaten intellectual performance: The psychological hazards of "model minority" status. *Psychological Science, 11*(5), 399–402.

Chiang, L. H. (2000). Teaching Asian American students. *Teacher Educator, 36*(1), 58–69.

Cho, S. (1997). Converging stereotypes in racialized sexual harassment: Where the model minority meets Suzie Wong. In A. Wing (Ed.), *Critical race feminism* (pp. 203–220). New York: New York University Press.

Choy, V. (2005). Perpetuating the exclusion of Asian Americans from the affirmative action debate: An oversight of the diversity rationale in Grutter v. Bollinger. *U.C. Davis Law Review, 38*, 545–571.

Coloma, R. (2006). Disorienting race and education: Changing paradigms on the schooling of Asian Americans and Pacific Islanders. *Race, Ethnicity, and Education, 9*(1), 1–15.

Committee of 100. (2005). *Asian Pacific American (APAs) in higher education report card.* New York. Retrieved August 24, 2006, from http://www.committee100.org/publications/publications_edu.htm

Cress, C., & Ikeda, E. (2003). Distress under duress: The relationship between campus climate and depression in Asian American college students. *NASPA Journal, 40*(2), 74–97.

Daniels, R. (1988). *Asian America: Chinese and Japanese in the United States since 1850.* Seattle: University of Washington Press.

Delucchi, M., & Do, H. (1996). The model minority myth and perceptions of Asian Americans as victims of racial harassment. *College Student Journal, 30*(3), 411–414.

Depouw, C. (2006). *Negotiating race, navigating school: Situating Hmong American university student experiences.* Unpublished dissertation, University of Illinois at Urbana-Champaign.

Diaz, V. (1994). To "P" or not to "P"? Marking the territory between Pacific Islander and Asian American studies. *Journal of Asian American Studies, 7*(3), 183–208.

Dong, S. (1995). "Too many Asians": The challenge of fighting discrimination against Asian Americans and preserving affirmative action. *Stanford Law Review, 47*, 1027–1057.

Endo, R., & Wei, W. (1988). On the development of Asian American Studies programs. In G. Okihiro, S. Hune, A. Hansen, & J. Liu (Eds.), *Reflections on shattered windows: Promises and prospects for Asian American studies.* Pullman: Washington State University Press.

Escueta, E., & O'Brien, E. (1991). Asian Americans and higher education: Trends and issues. *Research Briefs, 2*(4), 1–10. (ERIC Document Reproduction Service No. ED381103)

Espiritu, Y. (1997). *Asian American women and men: Labor, laws, and love.* Thousand Oaks, CA: Sage.

Faderman, L. (1999). *I begin my life all over: The Hmong and the American immigrant experience.* Boston: Beacon.

Fadiman, A. (1998). *The spirit catches you and you fall down*. New York: Farrar, Straus, and Giroux.

Gee, H. (2004). From Bakke to Grutter and beyond: Asian Americans and diversity in America. *Texas Journal on Civil Liberties and Civil Rights, 9*, 129–158.

Genishi, C., Stires, S. E., & Yung-Chan, D. (2001). Writing in an integrated curriculum: Prekindergarten English language learners as symbol makers. *Elementary School Journal, 101*(4), 399–416.

Gliona, J. M., & Goldman, A. (2002). *Answering protests, retailer to pull line of T-shirts that mock Asians*. Retrieved April 22, 2002, from atlatimes.com/archives

Gloria, A., & Ho, T. (2003). Environmental, social, and psychological experiences of Asian American undergraduates: Examining issues of academic persistence. *Journal of Counseling & Development, 81*(1), 93–105.

Goodwin, A. L. (2002). Teacher preparation and the education of immigrant children. *Education and Urban Society, 34*(2), 156–172.

Gordon, J. A. (1997). Teachers of color speak to issues of respect and image. *Urban Review, 29*(1), 41–66.

Gordon, J. A. (2000). Asian American resistance to selecting teaching as a career: The power of community and tradition. *Teachers College Record, 102*(1), 173–196.

Gordon, J. A. (2005). In search of educators of color. *Leadership*, pp. 30–35.

Goto, S. T. (1997). Nerds, normal people, and homeboys: Accommodation and resistance among Chinese American students. *Anthropology and Education Quarterly, 28*(1), 70–84.

Hsia, J. (1988). *Asian Americans in higher education and at work*. Hillsdale, NJ: Lawrence Erlbaum.

Hsia, J., & Hirano-Nakanishi, M. (1995). The demographics of diversity: Asian Americans and higher education. In D. Nakanishi & T. Nishida (Eds.), *The Asian American educational experience: A source book for teachers and students* (pp. 249–258). New York: Routledge.

Hune, S. (1995). Opening the American mind and body: The role of Asian American studies. In D. Nakanishi & T. Nishida (Eds.), *The Asian American educational experience: A source book for teachers and students* (pp. 322–328). New York: Routledge.

Hune, S. (1997). Higher education as gendered space: Asian American women and everyday inequities. In C. Ronai, B. Zsembik, & J. Feagin (Eds.), *Everyday sexism in the third millennium* (pp. 181–196). New York: Routledge.

Hune, S. (1998). *Asian Pacific American women in higher education: Claiming visibility and voice*. Washington, DC: Association of American Colleges and Universities.

Hune, S. (2001). Asian American studies and Asian Studies: Boundaries and borderlands of ethnic studies and area studies. In J. Butler (Ed.), *Color-line to borderlands: The matrix of ethnic studies* (pp. 227–239). Seattle: University of Washington Press.

Hune, S., & Chan, K. (1997). Special focus: Asian Pacific American demographic and educational trends. In D. Carter & R. Wilson (Eds.), *Minorities in higher education: Fifteenth annual status report: 1996-1997* (pp. 39–67, 103–107). Washington, DC: American Council on Education.

Hwang, S. (2005, November 19). The new White flight. *The Wall Street Journal*, p. A1.

Inkelas, K. (2003a). Caught in the middle: Understanding Asian Pacific American perspectives on affirmative action through Blumer's group position theory. *Journal of College Student Development, 44*(5), 625–643.

Inkelas, K. (2003b). Diversity's missing minority: Asian Pacific American undergraduates' attitudes towards affirmative action. *Journal of Higher Education, 74*(6), 601–639.

Inkelas, K. (2004). Does participation in ethnic cocurricular activities facilitate a sense of ethnic awareness and understanding? A study of Asian Pacific American undergraduates. *Journal of College Student Development, 45*(3), 285–302.

Jo, J. (2004). Neglected voices in the multicultural America: Asian American racial politics and its implications for multicultural education. *Multicultural Perspectives, 6*(1), 19–25.

Jones, L., Castellanos, J., & Cole, D. (2002). Examining the ethnic minority student experience at predominantly White institutions: A case study. *Journal of Hispanic Higher Education, 1*(1), 19–39.

Jorgenson, O. (2000). *The need for more ethnic teachers: Addressing the critical shortage in American public schools.* Retrieved August 28, 2000, from http://www.tcrecord.org (ID No. 10551).

Joshi, K. (2006). *New roots in America's sacred ground.* Piscataway, NJ: Rutgers University Press.

Kauanui, J. K. (2005). Asian American studies and the "Pacific question." In K. Ono (Ed.), *Asian American studies after critical mass* (pp. 123–143). Oxford, UK: Blackwell.

Kawaguchi, S. (2003). Ethnic identity development and collegiate experience of Asian Pacific American students: Implications for practice. *NASPA Journal, 40*(3), 13–29.

Kiang, P. (1992). Issues of curriculum and community for first-generation Asian Americans in college. *New Directions for Community Colleges, 80,* 97–113.

Kiang, P. (2004). Linking strategies and interventions in Asian American Studies to K–12 classrooms and teacher preparation. *International Journal of Qualitative Studies in Education, 17*(2), 199–225.

Kibria, N. (2002). *Becoming Asian American: Second-generation Chinese and Korean American identities.* Baltimore: The Johns Hopkins University Press.

Kim, B., & Omizo, M. (2005). Asian and European American cultural values, collective self-esteem, acculturative stress, cognitive flexibility, and general self-efficacy among Asian American college students. *Journal of Counseling Psychology, 52*(3), 412–419.

Kim, C. (1999). The racial triangulation of Asian Americans. *Politics and Society, 27*(1), 105–138.

Kodama, C., McEwen, M., Liang, C., & Lee, S. (2002). An Asian American perspective on psychosocial student development theory. In M. McEwan, C. Kodama, A. Alvarez, S. Lee, & C. Liang (Eds.), *Working with Asian American college students: New directions for student services* (Vol. 97, pp. 45–60). San Francisco: Jossey-Bass.

Kotori, C., & Malaney, G. (2003). Asian American students' perceptions of racism, reporting behaviors, and awareness of legal rights and procedures. *NASPA Journal, 40*(30), 56–76.

Kumashiro, K. (Ed.). (2001). *Troubling intersections of race and sexuality: Queer students of color and anti-oppressive education.* Lanham, MD: Rowman & Littlefield.

Kumashiro, K. (Ed.). (2004). *Restoried selves: Autobiographies of queer Asian/Pacific American activists.* New York: Harrington Park Press.

Laanan, F., & Starobin, S. (2004). Defining Asian American and Pacific Islander–serving institutions. *New Directions for Community Colleges, 127,* 49–59.

Lee, G., & Manning, M. L. (2001a). Treat Asian parents and families right. *Education Digest, 67*(4), 39–45.

Lee, G., & Manning, M. L. (2001b). Working with Asian parents and families. *Multicultural Education, 9*(1), 23–25.

Lee, R. (1999). *Orientals: Asian Americans in popular culture.* Philadelphia: Temple University Press.

Lee, R., Su, J., & Yoshida, E. (2005). Coping with intergenerational family conflict among Asian American college students. *Journal of Counseling Psychology, 52*(3), 389–399.

Lee, S. J. (1996). *Unraveling the model minority stereotype: Listening to Asian American youth.* New York: Teachers College Press.

Lee, S. J. (2001). More than "model minorities" or "delinquents": A look at Hmong American high school students. *Harvard Educational Review, 71*(3), 505–529.

Lee, S. J. (2005). *Up against Whiteness: Race, school, and immigrant youth.* New York: Teachers College Press.

Lee, S. J. (2006). Additional complexities: Social class, ethnicity, generation, and gender in Asian American student experiences. *Race, Ethnicity, and Education, 9*(1), 17–28.

Lee, S. J., & Kumashiro, K. (2005). *A report on the status of Asian American and Pacific Islanders in education: Beyond the "model minority" stereotype.* Washington, DC: National Education Association of the United States Human and Civil Rights.

Lee, S. M. (2002). Do Asian American faculty face a glass ceiling in higher education? *American Educational Research Journal, 39*(3), 695–724.

Lee, S. S. (2006). Over-represented and de-minoritized: The racialization of Asian Americans in higher education. *InterActions: UCLA Journal of Education and Information Studies, 2*(2), Article 4. Retrieved from http://repositories.cdlib.org/gseis/interactions/vol2/iss2/art4

Lei, J. (1998, April 13-17). *(Op)posing representations: Disentangling the model minority and the foreigner.* Paper presented at the AERA annual meeting, San Diego, CA.

Lei, J. (2003). (Un)necessary toughness? Those "loud Black girls" and those "quiet Asian boys." *Anthropology and Education Quarterly, 34*(2), 158–181.

Lei, J. (2006). Teaching and learning with Asian American and Pacific Islander students. *Race, Ethnicity, and Education, 9*(1), 85–101.

LeSure, G. (1994, August 22). *Ethnic differences and the effects of racism on college adjustment.* Paper presented at the annual convention of the American Psychological Association, Toronto.

Lew, J. (2004). The "other" story of model minorities: Korean American high school dropouts in an urban context. *Anthropology and Education Quarterly, 35*(3), 303–323.

Lew, J., Chang, J., & Wang, W. (2005). UCLA community college review: The overlooked minority. Asian Pacific American students at community colleges. *Community College Review, 33*(2), 64–84.

Li, G., & Beckett, G. (2006). *"Strangers" of the academy: Asian women scholars in higher education.* Sterling, VA: Stylus.

Liang, C., & Sedlacek, W. (2003). Attitudes of White student services practitioners toward Asian Americans. *NASPA Journal, 40*(3), 30–42.

Loo, C., & Rolison, G. (1986). Alienation of ethnic minority students at a predominantly White university. *Journal of Higher Education, 57*(1), 58–77.

Louie, V. (2001). Parents' aspirations and investment: The role of social class in the educational experiences of 1.5- and second-generation Chinese Americans. *Harvard Educational Review, 71*(3), 438–474.

Louie, V. (2004). *Compelled to excel: Immigration, education, and opportunity among Chinese Americans.* Stanford, CA: Stanford University Press.

Lowe, L. (2000). Heterogeneity, hybridity, multiplicity: Marking Asian American differences. In M. Zhou & J. Gatewood (Eds.), *Contemporary Asian America: A multidisciplinary reader* (pp. 677–696). New York: New York University Press.

Mack, D., Tucker, T., & Cha, S. (2000, August 4-8). *Inter-ethnic relations on campus: The color of hatred.* Paper presented at the annual conference of the American Psychological Association, Washington, DC.

Makuakane-Drechsel, T., & Hagedorn, L. (2000). Correlates of retention among Asian Pacific Americans in community colleges: The case for Hawaiian students. *Community College Journal of Research and Practice, 24,* 639–655.

Manalansan, M. (Ed.). (2000). *Cultural compass: Ethnographic explorations of Asian America.* Philadelphia: Temple University Press.

Manalansan, M. (2003). *Global divas: Filipino gay men in the diaspora.* Durham, NC: Duke University Press.

Mathews, R. (2000). Cultural patterns of south Asian and southeast Asian Americans. *Intervention in School and Clinic, 36*(2), 101–104.

McEwan, M., Kodama, C., Alvarez, A., Lee, S., & Liang, C. (Eds.). (2002). *Working with Asian American college students: New directions for student services* (Vol. 97). San Francisco: Jossey-Bass.

Min, P. G. (1996). *Caught in the middle: Korean communities in New York and Los Angeles.* Berkeley: University of California Press.

Minami, D. (1990). Guerilla war at UCLA: Political and legal dimensions of the tenure battle. *Amerasia Journal, 16*(1), 81–107.

Nakanishi, D. (1989, November/December). A quota on excellence? The Asian American admissions debate. *Change,* pp. 38–47.

Nakanishi, D. (1990). Why I fought. *Amerasia Journal, 16*(1), 139–158.

Nakanishi, D. (1993). Asian Pacific Americans in higher education: Faculty and administrative representation and tenure. In C. Turner, M. Garcia, A. Nora, & L. Rendon (Eds.), *Racial and ethnic diversity in higher education* (pp. 370–375). Needham Heights, MA: Simon & Schuster.

Nakanishi, D., & Nishida, T. (Eds.). (1995). *The Asian American educational experience: A source book for teachers and students.* New York: Routledge.

Okihiro, G. (1999). *Storied lives: Japanese American students and World War II.* Seattle: University of Washington Press.

Omi, M., & Takagi, D. (1996). Situating Asian Americans in the political discourse on affirmative action. *Representations, 55,* 155–162.

Omi, M., & Winant, H. (1994). *Racial formation in the United States: From the 1960s to the 1990s* (2nd ed.). New York: Routledge.

Ong, A. (1996). Cultural citizenship as subject-making: Immigrants negotiate racial and cultural boundaries in the United States. *Current Anthropology, 37*(5), 737–762.

Osajima, K. (1991). Breaking the silence: Race and the educational experiences of Asian American college students. In M. Foster (Ed.), *Readings on equal education: Qualitative investigations into schools and schooling* (Vol. 11, pp. 115–134). New York: AMS Press.

Osajima, K. (1995a). Postmodern possibilities: Theoretical and political directions for Asian American Studies. *Amerasia Journal, 21,* 79–87.

Osajima, K. (1995b). Racial politics and the invisibility of Asian Americans in higher education. *Educational Foundations, 9*(1), 35–53.

Osajima, K. (2000). Asian Americans as the model minority: An analysis of the popular press image in the 1960s and 1980s. In M. Zhou & J. Gatewood (Eds.), *Contemporary Asian America: A multidisciplinary reader* (pp. 449–458). New York: New York University Press.

Pak, Y. (in press). *Wherever I go, I will always be a loyal American: Schooling Seattle's Japanese Americans during World War II.* New York: Routledge Falmer.

Pak, Y. (in press). We are already multicultural: Why policy and leadership matter. In R. Joshee & L. D. Johnson (Eds.), *Multicultural education policy in Canada and the United States: Symbol and substance.* Vancouver, BC: University of British Columbia Press.

Palmer, J. (2001). Korean adopted young women: Gender bias, racial issues, and educational implications. In C. Park, A. Goodwin, & S. Lee (Eds.), *Research on the education of Asian and Pacific Americans* (pp. 177–204). Greenwich, CT: Information Age Publishing.

Pang, V. O. (1997). Caring for the whole child: Asian Pacific American students. In J. J. Irvine (Ed.), *Critical knowledge for diverse teachers and learners* (pp. 149–188). Washington, DC: AACTE Publications.

Pang, V. O., Kiang, P., & Pak, Y. (2004). Asian Pacific American students: Fighting overgeneralizations. In J. A. Banks (Ed.) & C. A. McGee Banks (Assoc. Ed.), *Handbook of research on multicultural education* (2nd ed., pp. 542–563). San Francisco: Jossey-Bass.

Pang, V. O., & Park, C. D. (2003). Examination of the self-regulation mechanism: Prejudice reduction in pre-service teachers. *Action in Teacher Education, 25*(3), 1–12.

Parette, P., & Huer, M. B. (2002). Working with Asian American families whose children have augmentative and alternative communication needs. *Journal of Special Education Technology, 17*(4), 5–13.

Park, C. C., & Chi, M. M. (Eds.). (1999). *Asian American education: Prospects and challenges.* Westport, CT: Bergin & Garvey.

Pearce, R. R. (2006). Effects of cultural and social structural factors on the achievement of White and Chinese American students at school transition points. *American Educational Research Journal, 43*(10), 75–101.

Poon-McBrayer, K. F., & Garcia, S. B. (2000). Profiles of Asian American students with LD at initial referral, assessment, and placement in special education. *Journal of Learning Disabilities, 33*(1), 61–71.

Qin, D. B. (2006). "Our child doesn't talk to us anymore": Alienation in immigrant Chinese families. *Anthropology and Education Quarterly, 37*(2), 162–179.

Rhee, S., Chang, J., & Rhee, J. (2003). Acculturation, communication patterns, and self-esteem among Asian and Caucasian American adolescents. *Adolescence, 38*(152), 749–768.

Rhoads, R., Lee, J., & Yamada, M. (2002). Panethnicity and collective action among Asian American students: A qualitative case study. *Journal of College Student Development, 43*(6), 876–891.

Rizvi, F., & Lingard, B. (2006). Edward Said and the cultural politics of education. *Discourse: Studies in the Cultural Politics of Education, 27*(3), 293–308.

Rohrlick, J., Alvarado, D., Zaruba, K., & Kallio, R. (1998, May 17–20). *From the model minority to the invisible minority: Asian and Pacific American students in higher education research.* Paper presented at the annual forum of the Association for Institutional Research, Minneapolis, MN.

Rong, X. L., & Preissle, J. (1997). The continuing decline in Asian American teachers. *American Educational Research Journal, 34*(2), 267–293.

Said, E. (1978). *Orientalism.* New York: Vintage Books.

Shrake, E. K., & Rhee, S. (2004). Ethnic identity as a predictor of problem behaviors among Korean American adolescents. *Adolescence, 39*(155), 601–622.

Simpson, J. (2001). Segregated by subject: Racial differences in the factors influencing academic major between European Americans, Asian Americans, and African, Hispanic and Native Americans. *Journal of Higher Education, 72*(1), 63–100.

Sleeter, C., & Grant, C. (2003). *Making choices for multicultural education: Five approaches to race, class, and gender* (4th ed.). New York: John Wiley.

Song, C., & Glick, J. (2004, December). College attendance and choice of college majors among Asian American students. *Social Science Quarterly, 85*(5), 1401–1421.

Span, C., & Anderson J. D. (2005). The quest for "book learning": African American education in slavery and freedom. In A. Hornsby, Jr., D. P. Aldridge, & A. M. Hornsby (Eds.), *A companion to African American history* (pp. 295–311). Malden, MA: Blackwell.

Suzuki, B. (2002). Revisiting the model minority stereotype: Implications for student affairs practice and higher education. In M. McEwan, C. Kodama, A. Alvarez, S. Lee, & C. Liang (Eds.), *Working with Asian American college students: New directions for student services* (Vol. 97, pp. 21–32). San Francisco: Jossey-Bass.

Takagi, D. (1992). *The retreat from race: Asian American admissions and racial politics.* New Brunswick, NJ: Rutgers University Press.

Takaki, R. (1998). *Strangers from a different shore: A history of Asian Americans.* Boston: Little, Brown.

Tamura, E. (2001). Asian Americans in the history of education: An historiographical essay. *History of Education Quarterly, 41*(1), 58–71.

Tamura, E. (Ed.). (2003). A special issue on Asian American educational history. *History of Education Quarterly, 43*(1).

Tang, M. (2002). A comparison of Asian American, Caucasian American, and Chinese college students: An initial report. *Journal of Multicultural Counseling and Development, 30*(2), 124–134.

Teranishi, R. (2002). Asian Pacific Americans and critical race theory: An examination of school racial climate. *Equity and Excellence in Education, 35*(2), 144–154.

Teranishi, R., Ceja, M., Antonio, A., Allen, W., & McDonough, P. (2004). The college-choice process for Asian Pacific Americans: Ethnicity and socioeconomic class in context. *Review of Higher Education, 27*(4), 527–551.

Tse, L. (2001). Resisting and reversing language shift: Heritage-language resilience among U.S. native biliterates. *Harvard Educational Review, 71*(4), 676–707.

Tuan, M. (1998). *Forever foreigners or honorary Whites? The Asian ethnic experience today.* New Brunswick, NJ: Rutgers University Press.

TuSmith, B., & Reddy, M. (Eds.). (2002). *Race in the college classroom: Pedagogy and politics.* New Brunswick, NJ: Rutgers University Press.

Vargas, L. (Ed.). (2002). *Women faculty of color in the White classroom: Narratives on the pedagogical implications of teacher diversity.* New York: Peter Lang.

Walker-Moffat, W. (1995). *The other side of the Asian American success story.* San Francisco: Jossey-Bass.

Wang, L. (1988). Meritocracy and diversity in higher education: Discrimination against Asian Americans in the post-Bakke era. *Urban Review, 20,* 189–209.

Weinberg, M. (1997). *Asian American education: Historical background and current realities.* Mahwah, NJ: Lawrence Erlbaum.

Williams, H. (2005). *Self-taught: African American education in slavery and freedom.* Chapel Hill: University of North Carolina Press.

Woo, D. (1997). Asian Americans in higher education: Issues of diversity and engagement. *Race, Gender & Class, 4*(3), 122–143.

Wright, W. (2006). Catching up in math? The case of newly-arrived Cambodian students in a Texas intermediate school. *Texas Association for Bilingual Education Journal, 9*(1), 1–22.

Wu, F. (1995). Neither Black nor White: Asian Americans and affirmative action. *Third World Law Journal, 15,* 225–284.

Wu, F. (2002). *Yellow: Race in America beyond Black and White.* New York: Basic Books.

Yang, R., Byers, S., Ahuna, L., & Castro, K. (2002). Asian American students' use of a university student-affairs office. *College Student Journal, 36*(3), 448–470.

Yang, X., & Rendon, L. (1994). A profile of Asian students in North Carolina community colleges. *Community College Review, 22*(1), 19–33.

Yeh, T. (2004-2005). Issues of college persistence between Asian and Asian Pacific American students. *Journal of College Student Retention, 6*(1), 81–96.

Yu, H. (2001). *Thinking Orientals: Migration, contact, and exoticism in modern America.* Oxford, UK: Oxford University Press.

Yu, S. M., Huang, Z. J., & Schwalberg, R. H. (2002). Association of language spoken at home with health and school issues among Asian American adolescents. *Journal of School Health, 72*(5), 192–198.

Zhou, M. (2000). Social capital in Chinatown: The role of community-based organizations and families in the adaptation of the younger generation. In M. Zhou & J. Gatewood (Eds.), *Contemporary Asian America: A multidisciplinary reader* (pp. 315–335). New York: New York University Press.

Chapter 5

Policies on Free Primary and Secondary Education in East Africa: Retrospect and Prospect

MOSES OKETCH
CAINE ROLLESTON
Institute of Education, University of London

This chapter reviews the evolution of education policies in the East African region in a historical context. The focus is on the formulation of policies for access to primary and secondary education in Kenya, Uganda, and Tanzania since their independence in the 1960s. We ask the following questions: What led to those policies and how were they funded? What was the role, if any, of the international community? What were the politics and underpinning philosophy surrounding the formulation of those policies and have the policies changed over time, and if so why?

In recent years, several countries in sub-Saharan Africa have (re)introduced the Free Primary Education (FPE) policy in line with both Education For All (EFA) and Millennium Development Goals (MDGs) international agendas. Three East African countries—Kenya, Uganda, and Tanzania—are among them. All three countries are often held up as success stories in the implementation of FPE policies and in all of them, implementation of FPE policies is already leading to new policies for access to secondary education. But the idea of a universal primary education system is not new to these countries. Efforts have been made to expand access to education ever since they gained their independence from British colonial rule in the early part of the 1960s. Yet, still, there are those with no access, those who are excluded after initial entry, those at risk of dropout, and a majority excluded from any form of secondary education.

The three countries have common characteristics and historical backgrounds. For example, few of their population had access to education at all levels in the past, and hence, each faced similar educational and literacy challenges at the time of their political independence in the 1960s. Kenya declared a campaign for Universal Primary Education (UPE) free of charge as a long-term objective in 1963. Tanzania followed in 1967, and Uganda, although lukewarm in its desire to expand primary education, nonetheless experienced improved access from the time of independence in 1962 until the late 1970s when internal political conflict and war caused serious

Review of Research in Education
March 2007, Vol. 31, pp. 131–158
DOI: 10.3102/0091732X06298014
© 2007 AERA. http://rre.aera.net

disruption (Bogonko, 1992; Ssekamwa & Lugumba, 2001). All three have over time been characterized by Consortium for Research on Education Access, Transition and Equity (CREATE) zones of exclusion (i.e., those with no access, those who are excluded after initial entry, those at risk of dropout, and those excluded from secondary education). They have similarly announced and implemented new policies for FPE following the international and internal pressure leading to the reintroduction of multiparty politics in the late 1990s (Stasavage, 2005). However, the three countries have had different experiences with the implementation of both UPE in the 1960s and FPE in the 1990s and have differed in the philosophies underpinning their education expansion more generally.

Sharing common borders, the three countries came together to form the East African Community (EAC), a loose federation as a political vehicle to pursue common goals in the 1960s. The community broke down in 1977 following philosophical differences in their development strategies. Tanzania and Uganda followed a socialist model of development, symbolized by the late President Nyerere's "Ujamaa" model, whereas Kenya adhered to capitalism in practice (although referred to "African socialism" in development strategy policy documents). Faced with similar challenges, partly as a result of policies of economic liberalization under Structural Adjustment Programmes (SAPs), the EAC was revived in the 1990s to provide a common platform from which to address common problems.

The rest of this chapter is organized as follows: First, we discuss policies and action taken by governments of the three countries in the immediate postindependence era in relation to expanding access to those who had been excluded by the colonial education policies. Second, we present the formulation of those policies again in relation to how and whom they benefited. Third, we discuss implementation strategies and processes of those policies. Fourth, we discuss their institutionalization, replicability, and financial sustainability. Fifth, we outline the implications of these policies for the poorest groups. Sixth, we provide an overview of recent policies on access to secondary education and ask whom they have benefited and how the excluded groups can be reached. The conclusion follows.

IMMEDIATE POSTINDEPENDENCE POLICIES ON ACCESS

Independence and education were intertwined in all three East African countries. Tanzania was the first to attain independence in 1961 and Julius Nyerere, the founding president, having been a teacher himself, placed emphasis on secondary education for the nation's development. Uganda followed in 1962 and there too Milton Obote, the founding president, immediately emphasized the need to expand education to meet national development needs, although priority was given to secondary education. Kenya gained independence a year after Uganda in 1963 and Jomo Kenyatta's Kenya African National Union (KANU) Government did not hesitate to declare education one of its key priorities for national development, with emphasis placed on the development of secondary and tertiary education (Bogonko, 1992). The three countries adhered to a 1961 agreed framework at a conference held in

Addis Ababa and sponsored by the United Nations Educational, Scientific and Cultural Organization (UNESCO). The conference had set the tone and prioritized the expansion of secondary and tertiary education. This was for the key practical reason of meeting human resource requirements at that time.

Although prioritization of education policy driven by labor force needs immediately followed independence, the three governments identified ignorance and illiteracy as two of the problems they needed to tackle through education. This essentially implied expanding primary education. Consequently, access to education immediately became synonymous with development and its provision preoccupied the three governments. Moreover, access had been problematic during colonial administration because there were many Africans who were simply denied entry to education both for practical and political reasons. Practically, the rural subsistence economy may not have required much education. Politically, an educated population may not have served the interests of the colonial system. A few who managed to gain entry to primary education could not go beyond 4 years of education because access was controlled through the Grade IV examination. Access to secondary education was extremely limited and those who managed to reach it regarded themselves the cream of the African population. Often they were rewarded with immediate employment in the civil service, an opportunity that immediately set them apart from the rest of the population. Given the obvious benefits that accrued to those who had accessed secondary education, the demand for it became very high. However, access to secondary education required that one had to access primary education first. Thus, the demand for primary education was driven by the benefits attached to secondary education. Education immediately became an issue of disagreement between the Africans and the colonial governments and was used as a theme to fight for political independence. Once independence was attained, expanding access to those who had been excluded by the colonial administration became an important means of gaining full legitimacy and of reassuring the people that political independence was not a sham (Bogonko, 1992). A number of policies were pursued to facilitate rapid access.

An immediate policy initiative in the three countries toward expanding access for Africans was to abolish racial school systems that had existed during the colonial period and to integrate them into one national education system. However, this action did not expand access for the majority who had been excluded because fees remained a barrier. What it did was to open access to the emerging African political elites who could afford to pay the fees charged in what had been well-equipped, formerly Europeans-only schools. The next step that improved access in Kenya and Tanzania was the abolition of the Grade IV examination, although fees remained a barrier to many poor households. In Uganda, the situation was already better because there was a policy of 6 years of uninterrupted primary education and of 2 years at junior secondary, which was open to all who could pay for it. This had placed Uganda ahead of both Kenya and Tanzania in terms of transition to some form of secondary education, although in reality very few managed to go beyond primary education (Bogonko, 1992).

Tanzania championed the idea of a federal East African country and her leader Julius Nyerere had been willing to delay Tanzania's attainment of independence by 1 year if this would facilitate the formation of such a community. Kenya and Uganda were, however, lukewarm to the idea and, hence, independence was ultimately attained by each country separately (Southall, 1974). Still, the spirit of an East African Community remained and the leaders of the newly independent countries felt that a common education would be instrumental to the achievement of this goal. Moreover, by the time of independence, the only university available in the region and shared by the three countries was the University of East Africa at Makerere in Uganda. The need to have a uniform education system was therefore one of practical necessity if the countries were to share the university in an effort to quickly meet their labor needs. Admission to the university had to be based on some agreed uniform or equivalent years of primary and secondary education. To deal with this problem, Nyerere, Kenyatta, and Obote, as heads of state in each of the three countries, called for a common 7-year primary education cycle. Consequently, by 1964, Kenya had scrapped the Grade IV examination and the former primary and intermediate courses were replaced by one consolidated 7-year primary course that was fully implemented in 1966 (Bogonko, 1992). This resulted in a rapid increase in the number of children proceeding to the Kenya Preliminary Examination (KPE) taken at the end of the primary cycle from 62,000 in 1964 to 133,000 in 1966 (Kenya, MEARS, 1964–1966, cited in Bogonko, 1992). Uganda also introduced changes leading to the merging of the 6-year primary education and the 2-year junior secondary into one 7-year primary education system by 1967. This had a significant impact on access because "formerly only about one out of three or four primary-school pupils obtained places in junior secondary school" (Bogonko, 1992).

Tanzania followed in 1966 when the Grade IV examination was scrapped in towns and then in rural areas in 1973 (Morrison, 1976, cited in Bogonko, 1992). Bogonko (1992) argues that Tanzania's separate treatment of rural and urban education reflected the scant attention paid to the expansion of primary education for the masses. The policy that was openly supported in Tanzania was the expansion of secondary and tertiary education believed to have been more useful for economic development than primary education. Tanzania's behavior also seems to have been in line with the recommendations reached at the 1961 Addis Ababa Conference where expansion of secondary education to meet "manpower" needs was prioritized over access to primary education.

The uniform system of education continued in the three countries until Kenya changed its education system to an 8-year primary, 4-year secondary, and 4-year university education (8 + 4 + 4) system in 1984 (Bogonko, 1992).

In terms of impact on access and in relation to CREATE zones, the integration of racial schools into one national education system and the elimination of the Grade IV examination led to improvements in access to primary education for Africans who had been excluded during the colonial period. Although government policy placed emphasis on the expansion of secondary education for manpower purposes, it was at the primary level "where education experienced the most tremendous and most unprecedented growth of all in terms of both the number of schools and of pupils" (Bogonko, 1992, p. 25).

In Kenya, enrollment at primary level increased by 23.3% between 1964 and 1968 from 980,849 to 1,209,680. This rose even further such that by 1983 nearly 93% of school-age pupils were enrolled, up from less than 60% in 1963. Enrollment in 1983 stood at 4.3 million pupils. The highest rates of growth were witnessed between 1970 and 1974 following the announcement that school fees had been abolished, first in semiarid areas and for needy cases throughout the country and second for the first 4 years in 1974 throughout the country (Bogonko, 1992; Buchmann, 2001).

Tanzania followed suit in 1969 in response to the pressure from local and Tanganyika African National Union (TANU) leaders to expand access. Expansion of government-aided schools had been restricted by government policy, which placed emphasis on secondary education. The only significant expansion of access that was allowed, following pressure by political and community leaders, was that of unaided schools. The decision to restrict government expansion of primary educa-tion seriously affected access. It was Neyerere's speech during the launch of the sec-ond National Development Plan (1969–1974) in which he lamented low levels of primary enrollment in Tanzania as "unacceptable to a country which claims to be building socialism" that triggered a change in policy that saw Tanzania achieve uni-versal primary education in 1977 (Bogonko, 1992).

Uganda also attempted to expand access to education for her citizens, but achieve-ments were fewer than in Kenya and Tanzania. Between 1964 and 1982, primary-school enrollment in Uganda rose by only 166%. During the same period, the corresponding increases in Kenya and Tanzania were 327% (from 980,849 to 4,184,602) and 523% (from 633,678 to 3,312,799), respectively. In the 1970s, the annual average growth of primary-school pupils was 6% for Uganda, 12% for Kenya, and 16% for Tanzania (Bogonko, 1992; also see Ssekamwa & Lugumba, 2001).

Further analysis of expansion of access after independence based on gender indi-cates that the three countries considered the issue of gender seriously in their plans for educational expansion. At independence in each of the three countries, girls' share in total enrollment was less than 40%. This was low in relation to female pro-portion of the total population in each of the three countries, which stood at more that 50%. According to Bogonko (1992), progress was made in enrolling girls. For instance, in Kenya, girls' share of total enrollment rose from 34% in 1963 to 46% and 48% in 1975 and 1986, respectively. In Tanzania, it increased from 36% of the total primary school enrollment in 1962 to 42% and 50% in 1974 and 1986, respec-tively. In Uganda, enrollment of girls increased from 37% of total enrollment in 1965 to 40% and 44% in 1974 and 1983, respectively. Bogonko (1992) attributes progress to constant appeals to parents by the government in each of the three coun-tries to disengage in cultural beliefs that acted as barriers for girls.

Although each of the three countries attempted to encourage equal access for both girls and boys, Tanzania moved fastest. By 1986, Tanzania had more girls than boys enrolled at the primary level by .05%. Kenya closely followed Tanzania with 48% of her primary enrollment being girls. Uganda lagged behind both Tanzania and Kenya. However, in spite of these gains, girls were still underrepresented at the primary level. Figure 1 shows the progress made in bridging the gender gap in primary enrollment in Kenya between 1964 and 1995. Plotted on the vertical axis is the Gender Parity Index (GPI). At independence in 1963, there were only 55 girls for every 100 boys enrolled. This has since improved tremendously throughout the years. Somerset (2006) attributes improvements in the GPI during the first decade of independence to changing parental attitudes toward the education of daughters rather than overt government policy targeting girls. The abolition of formal school fees in 1974 accelerated what had already been a steady social trend such that between 1973 and 1975, the GPI went up from 77 to nearly 85. Where fees had been a barrier to access, girls were the most affected (Somerset, 2006). The abolition of the building levy in 1979 also gave a boost to the GPI, although this was much smaller compared to the 1974 government policy to abolish formal fees. The (re)introduction of the FPE policy in 2003 may have improved the GPI but the figures were not available to the authors at the time of this review.

Although there was tremendous growth in education in Tanzania and Kenya in the 1960s and 1970s, economic growth in the late 1970s was less positive. This affected the government's ability to successfully sustain a policy of universal and free primary education. Uganda had already experienced turbulent political leadership following coups and countercoups that affected its education system in the early part of the 1970s. The mid-1980s into the 1990s featured little in terms of expansion of access to primary education. The gains that had been made in the 1960s and 1970s were eroded following the implementation of economic SAPs promoted by the World Bank and International Monetary Fund (IMF; Galabawa, 2001; Mukudi, 2004; Vavrus, 2005). The World Bank and IMF had considered SAPs as a necessary policy for readjusting and revitalizing African economies. SAPs were to achieve this by reducing the role of the state and improving that of the market in determining economic activities and policies. In the social sectors such as health and education, SAPs introduced demand management policy (Oketch, 2003). Consequently, the education sector was seriously affected when cost-sharing was introduced and parents were asked to carry some of the burden of educating their children. Enrollment declined and only picked up again following a new drive to achieve EFA by 2015 and the announcement of FPE was by each of the three countries. Uganda was the first to declare and implement FPE in 1997. Tanzania followed in 1999, and Kenya in 2002.

FORMULATION AND IMPLEMENTATION OF UPE POLICIES

Kenya

The KANU campaign in the 1960s and its manifesto included the provision of universal primary education upon attainment of independence (Bogonko, 1992). The First National Development Plan (1964–1969) highlighted the need to expand education and noted that "education and national development are so closely related

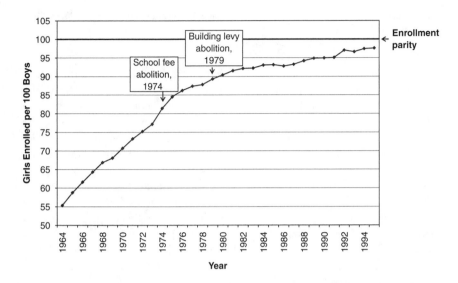

**FIGURE 1   Kenya: Representation of Girls in Primary School
Enrollments, 1964–1995**

Source. Somerset (2006).
Note. Girls enrolled per 100 boys, all grades.

in a developing country that it is almost impossible to speak of one without the other" (Republic of Kenya, 1964, p. 305; Republic of Kenya's *National Development Plan* [DP], 1964–1969). Sessional Paper No. 10 of 1965 also included education as an instrumental part of Kenya's development strategy but pointed out that emphasis should be placed on the economic value rather than social value of education. Education was to be "regarded as the principal means of relieving the shortage of skilled manpower and equalizing economic opportunities among all citizens" (Republic of Kenya, 1964, p. 305; Republic of Kenya's DP, 1964–1969). Provision of universal primary education was nonetheless identified as the first of the three long-range objectives for Kenya's educational program. The other two were to ensure availability of enough places at the secondary and higher levels to educate those with recognized abilities and to organize the educational system to meet the manpower needs of the country (Republic of Kenya, 1964; Republic of Kenya's DP, 1964–1969). The government in its first 5-year National Development Plan (1964–1969) noted that the movement toward universal primary education would not only satisfy the demand by the *wananchi* (citizens) for this level of education but was instrumental for unity and cohesion of the nation. UPE was associated with widespread literacy, which the government linked to overall development and national stability. The following statement in the National Development Plan (1964–1969) sums up the government's view:

Widespread literacy opens up many avenues of mass communication as an effective means of keeping people well informed on national, African and world problems, as well as on local affairs. An informed citizenry is necessary if a democratic African socialist state is to develop. (p. 305)

Although the government recognized the importance of primary education along these lines, it was not ready to create any illusion that it would provide it free of charge in the short term. It is clearly stated in the National Development Plan (1964–1969) that "primary education is largely a local responsibility" (p. 306) and that although the achievement of universal primary education remained the policy of the government, for purely economic reasons, the development of primary education could not be given "as high priority as secondary, technical and higher education" (p. 306). This continued as the official government policy during the second 5-year National Development Plan (1970–1974) but it was made clear that it remained impossible to provide free primary education for all. To signal the priority placed on secondary education, the government scrapped fees for advanced secondary education, otherwise known as Forms V and VI, in low-cost schools and reduced them in what were high-cost, formerly purely European schools. This was aimed at increasing the supply of middle-level and high-level manpower but in itself also fueled the demand for the lower levels of education (Republic of Kenya, 1964, p. 307; Republic of Kenya's DP, 1964–1969).

The belief in a link between education and economic development, as evident in the first 5-year National Development Plan (1964–1969) and in subsequent National Development Plans (1970–1974; 1974–1978; 1979–1983; 1984–1988; 1989–1993; 1997–2001; 2002–2008) as well as in the Sessional Paper No. 10 is another factor that triggered policies of Universal Primary Education. Although it was believed that true economic value of education could only be realized through the expansion of secondary education, the government was sympathetic to the view of the Kenya Education Commission Report of 1964–1965 (Republic of Kenya, 1964: Ominde Commission Report) that primary education was fast becoming a minimum basic educational requirement. The Kenya Education Commission (Ominde Commission) had also recommended the abolition of racially segregated schools and strongly advised that the government should take full charge in the formulation of education policies. The Commission's views were taken on board and were reflected in the emphasis that the government placed on the expansion of primary education in practice (although in policy terms, priority was on the expansion of secondary and tertiary education to meet manpower needs).

The government believed that education could be a means to mitigate the inequalities that had existed during the colonial period (Republic of Kenya, 1964; Republic of Kenya's DP, 1964–1969). The colonial government had not provided education to regions that were of low potential such as semiarid areas. Neither did Christian missionaries provide or build schools in regions that had already experienced Arabic and/or Islamic influence such as the coastal parts of Kenya. These regions therefore had lower access to all levels of formal Western education at the time of independence in the 1960s. Education in the postcolonial era, then, was to be a tool for inculcating loyalty to the state, a sense of national unity, and a means of teaching African values (Republic of Kenya, 1964; Republic of Kenya's DP, 1964-1969). Its access by all citizens was important if these goals were to be achieved. The disparities between regions also necessitated the need to formulate policies for universal education.

The ruling KANU party had committed itself to free primary education by the end of the decade and in 1971 a presidential decree had abolished tuition fees in the most geographically disadvantaged areas and, in 1973, in all areas for Grades I to IV with a uniform fee of Sh.60 (US$80 pence) imposed for Grades V, VI, and VII throughout the country (Republic of Kenya, 1964; Republic of Kenya's DP, 1974–1978). It was anticipated that these measures would result in a significant increase in enrollment in primary education. However, the financial and logistical implications of these policies had not been subjected to close scrutiny, leading to a priorities rethink by the Ministry of Education in 1974 owing to a staggering rise in pupil enrollment. Although school fees had been abolished, no countermeasures were put in place to replace lost revenue, and consequently, primary schools resorted to the use of a building levy that in most cases turned out to be higher than the school fees charged previously. Enrollments initially doubled in most districts but fell back to their original levels following the introduction of the building levy (Muthwii, 2004).

The fourth National Development Plan (1979–1983) was released under new political leadership. Jomo Kenyatta, Kenya's founding President, died in August 1978 and was replaced by Daniel Arap Moi, his Vice President. Moi continued in the steps of his predecessor under the KANU banner of *Fuata Nyayo* (follow the footsteps) by maintaining universal primary education as a standing educational objective of his new government. Although UPE had not been achieved, enrollment had grown from less than 50% in 1963, the year Kenya gained independence, to more than 85% by 1978 (Republic of Kenya, 1979; Republic of Kenya's DP, 1979-1983). However, the language had shifted from that of emphasizing secondary education to that of recognizing primary education as the foundation of economic and national development. The following statement illustrates this, "The primary stage of education is the most important for any child since it is here that basic knowledge is given to the child and foundations for an economically productive and satisfying life are laid" (Republic of Kenya, 1979, p. 154; Republic of Kenya's DP, 1979-1983). For once, the national education policy was in agreement with the international goal. The Plan brought forward what had been steady UPE progress by stating the government's objective to provide universal primary education of 7 years, free of charge to all children of primary-school age. The government also aimed to abolish building and other school funds in primary schools and to provide free milk to primary school children throughout the country (Republic of Kenya, 1979; Republic of Kenya's DP, 1979–1983). Enrollment patterns in Figure 2 illustrate alternate periods of relative stability and those of sudden change. Sudden change reflects response to

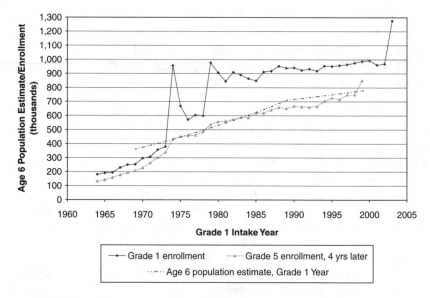

FIGURE 2   Kenya: Age 6 Population Estimates, Grade 1 Intakes and Grade 5 Survivors, 1964 to 2003

Source. Somerset (2006)

government initiatives such as the abolition of formal school fees in 1974, the scrapping of the building levy in 1979, and the reintroduction of free primary education policy in 2003 (Somerset, 2006).

Similar to Kenyatta, who had used the UPE campaign as a means of assuring the citizens that independence was not a sham, Moi also seemingly used UPE as a way of reassuring the people of Kenya that he would continue along the steps of the founding president and that people should not panic at the change of leadership. There was a shift in policy however in the way secondary education was to be organized. The government announced that it would only allow modest expansion in secondary education to correct the imbalance between districts and between boys and girls (Republic of Kenya, 1979; Republic of Kenya's DP, 1979–1983).

During Moi's leadership, primary education continued to experience rapid growth, with Kenya achieving near universal primary education by the 1990s. Kenya's achievement in the development of basic education was a showcase among sub-Saharan African countries at the World Conference on Education for All in 1990. However, in the years that followed, many of the gains made were lost or reversed for a number of reasons, including economic decline and the introduction of "cost-sharing." Enrollment and participation rates at the primary level declined between 1990 and 2000 and transition and completion rates stagnated. Gross enrollment at the secondary level also declined and gender and regional disparities widened, whereas children with special needs remained underenrolled. With this background, the National Alliance Rainbow Coalition (NARC) Government, which was elected in 2002, pledged to provide free primary education for all in its 2002 manifesto (OWN and Associates, 2004).

Consequently, Kenya (re)introduced free primary education in 2003 with a view to establishing "universal primary education" and meeting the EFA and MDG target of universal access by 2015. An interim target of a net enrollment rate of 85% was established for 2005 (Vos, Bedi, Kimalu, Manda, & Nafula, 2004). Free primary education again became an election pledge and was launched as a policy in 2003 when tuition fees and levies were abolished (Muthwii, 2004). Throughout the 1990s, enrollment had already increased by more than 27% and gender parity in enrollment had almost been attained (Vos et al., 2004). Stasavage (2005) argues that rapid expansion in access to primary education in recent years in Kenya as in Uganda and Tanzania are linked to the (re)introduction of democratic elections in these countries, his point being that when leaders are subjected to competitive politics they tend to initiate policies that are popular with the electorate. Such was the case in the 1960s when independence was achieved in the three countries under multiparty politics. However, the newly elected leaders moved quickly to amend the constitution to outlaw multiparty politics within the first decade of independence in a bid to curb any opposition to their leadership and dictatorship. The cold war is said to have helped this scenario to sustain itself for decades. However, with the end of the cold war, internal as well as international pressure gained momentum and these constitutions were repealed. Stasavage (2005) argues that it is possible that causation flows between school enrollment and democratization in both directions owing to the increased incentive for democratic governments to expand education for a population to which they are accountable and to the possibility that democracy is more sustainable in countries with a better-educated population. Indirect effects of education such as income redistributive effects also may be associated with enabling democracy. Presidential popularity is also said to be higher in countries with a recent significant increase in primary school attendance, and attendance rates have been found to be significant in explaining a proportion of cross-national variation in presidential popularity levels. The conclusion may be that African democracies provide more primary education than nondemocracies (Stasavage, 2005).

King (2005) discusses a number of trade-offs that are emerging between basic and postbasic educational provision in the context of Kenya. These relate to issues of quality, access, and inequality; the provision of other social services; the development of productive employment opportunities; and the evolution of international and donor development policy alongside that of the Kenyan government. He notes that despite a shift in international development thinking toward poverty reduction and Universal Primary Education in the 1990s and a heavy reliance by Kenya on donor assistance for recurrent education expenditure, Kenya retains its commitment to a broad-based educational strategy that makes reference to links with the labor market, economic growth and wealth creation, and the informal employment sector.

From the 1980s, Kenya's support for diversified schools and their work orientation had been at odds with international thinking that emphasized high returns to primary education and basic education expansion. The poverty perspective has become evident in Kenyan policy, particularly since the externally driven Poverty Reduction Strategy Paper (PRSP), which focuses on the provision of essential social services for low-income groups, including primary education. This agenda has encouraged the identification of inequities in the Kenyan education system, particularly concerning cost-sharing, and measures such as bursaries for the most disadvantaged in the education system have been put in place. However, moves in the international agenda more recently for education and development toward more comprehensive approaches have brought international and Kenyan policy into greater coincidence. Kenya continues to emphasize wealth creation, the micro and small enterprise sectors, skills, and technology. But the 2004 and 2005 sectorwide approaches (SWAPs) developed in conjunction with external partners also make reference to these aspects of a more comprehensive approach and King suggests that the Kenya Education Sector Support Programme (KESSP) may represent a strategic compromise between external and internal development priorities in Kenya (King, 2005).

Uganda

Uganda did not have as successful an experience with the expansion of primary education as Kenya and Tanzania. For example, enrollments in public primary schools rose from 524,867 in 1964 to 720,127 in 1970 and then to 1,036,920 and 1,582,009 in 1976 and 1982, respectively (Bogonko, 1992). A number of factors are associated with Uganda's less impressive performance. They include a lack of funds, long distances from schools in the sparsely populated areas, a substantial proportion of unqualified teachers, and the military rule of Idi Ami (1971–1979). However, Bogonko (1992) argues that these issues were equally prevalent in both Kenya and Tanzania, especially the first three setbacks, leaving it only possible therefore to suggest that the main reason lay in Ugandan leadership's lack of commitment to expand free primary education. Furthermore, Uganda devoted less of her budget toward primary education in comparison with Kenya and Tanzania.

Castle Education Commission, the first commission established by the newly independent government of Uganda, debated a range of issues affecting the education system and made its recommendations to the government in 1963, but nothing on the list of changes that were recommended reflected even vaguely the idea of universal primary education free of charge. Apart from suggesting that primary education should last 7 years instead of 6, the Commission dwelled mostly on the curriculum and the quality of education. This has prompted Ssekamwa and Lugumba (2001) to note that "the Commission's suggestion that concentration be on increasing the quality of primary education, in circumstances where many primary school-age pupils had no opportunity to go to school, just could not be accepted" (p. 149).

In the early years following independence, Ugandan education devoted a large proportion of expenditure to the postprimary stages of education serving manpower requirements of the administration. Despite attempts to introduce reforms aimed toward UPE, this situation continued into the 1980s, resulting from negative political and economic climates (Avenstrup, Liang, & Nellemann, 2004). Under the leadership of President Yoweri Musoveni, who came to power in 1986 after waging a bloody civil war against the government of Milton Obote, the Education Policy Review Commission (EPRC) was established in 1987 and, following consultations, recommended implementing UPE in 1989. A government White Paper followed in 1992 and reforms in preparation for UPE began in 1993, including teacher and management development, curriculum and assessment reform, development of instructional materials, and new arrangements for progress monitoring. Enrollment figures did not grow substantially until 1996 when the first direct presidential election was held in Uganda.

Musoveni campaigned on a UPE platform, pledging primary education for the first four children in every family. On being elected, he began the implementation of UPE in 1997. A nationwide enumeration exercise was undertaken and the government committed itself to providing tuition fees for four children per family, instructional materials, basic physical facilities, and teachers' salaries and training. Gross enrollment rates (GERs) rose from 77% in 1996 to 137% in 1997, and net enrollment rose from 57% to 85%. Enrollment in Grade 1 increased threefold and girls accounted for 47% of enrollments by 1999. Growth in the number of schools was not so rapid and average numbers of pupils per school doubled between 1980 and 1999. The pupil:teacher ratio rose from 37.62 pupils per teacher in 1996 to 51.83 in 1997 and 63.63 in 1999. The percentage of trained teachers, however, increased. Teachers' pay increased between 1989 and 1999, although it remained difficult for them to make ends meet. In 1997, the drop-out rate was reported to be 6% and the repetition rate 11% (Avenstrup et al., 2004).

It appears, and as argued by Stasavage (2005), that free primary education was a result of the transition to democratic politics. Political demand rather than rational planning seemingly triggered UPE in Uganda and the policy was consequently implemented without time for detailed planning and in the absence of sufficient data. Skepticism was prevalent and pointed to potential problems of finance, sustainability, and educational quality. There was little time to mobilize funding and make adequate budgetary preparations or to undertake necessary structural and organizational reforms to develop capacity for massive expansion. Avenstrup et al. (2004) have described the results as "access shock." The burden of large increases in enrollment resulted in overcrowding, multiple shifts, teacher and material shortages, and a rise in overage students. For example, the GER rose from 68% to 123% in the 1st year of UPE and enrollment rose 240% in 6 years. In spite of these shortcomings, access improved considerably and the effect on the poor was particularly marked. Access among the poorest quintile was almost as high as that of the richest quintile (Avenstrup et al., 2004; Deininger, 2003). Confidence in the government's ability to provide education rose and some private resources were freed up with the abolition of fees. But access shock also resulted in worsening of many other indicators, including the student:teacher ratio and the ratio of resources including classrooms to students. Drop-out rates increased and the survival rate fell from 59% to 37%. Dropout is explained by factors such as early marriage or pregnancy, the need to work, disability or illness, failure, repetition, and lack of interest. Avenstrup et al. (2004) suggest that where these factors are student related they may indicate falling educational quality, which also may result from such factors as increasing teacher absenteeism due to stress.

UPE presented considerable challenges in Uganda in 1999, where approximately 19% of the population was of primary school age. The existing education system had not undergone fundamental change since independence in 1962 and remained highly selective with respect to progression. War and civil strife, poor facilities and resources, a lack of planning, urban–rural disparities, poor teacher training, high user costs, overemphasis of academic examinations, lack of data, inefficiency of management, lack of relevance in curricula, and a limited government budget were identified as key difficulties of the existing system (Ministry of Education and Sports, Uganda, 1999).

Since 1962, enrollments had been expanding, although the number of schools was not correspondingly increased and both gross domestic product (GDP) and education spending as a proportion of the national budget declined in the period 1971–1985. Primary education at this time reached approximately 50% of Ugandan children in the age group. Financially, the bulk of the burden was met by parents, indicating strong demand but also excluding the poor who frequently dropped out long before the end of the primary cycle if they enrolled at all. Conditions in schools were poor and often deteriorating.

Parents in Uganda are considered to value education highly and continued to send children to school in periods of considerable hardship. There is a strong tradition of community support for schools and in 1991 parental contributions made up 90% of recurrent and capital expenditure for primary education. Lack of funds was the principal reason why out of school children were not enrolled, although in some pastoral communities UPE did not precipitate the high enrollment growth seen elsewhere owing to a greater perception of the opportunity costs. Political will was a key factor in the progress of UPE in Uganda, particularly in overcoming opposition, which focused on the inability of the educational infrastructure to cope with the burden of such a dramatic rise in numbers. UPE also was enabled by primary education reforms and projects already in progress, including the Teacher Development and Management System, Instructional Materials Unit, assessment reform, and the Improving Educational Quality research project. These initiatives provided support to UPE in terms of teacher training; school and cluster organization; teaching materials; community support; and a reorientation toward formative assessment, action research, and educational quality. In addition, decentralization policy begun in 1997 brought the administration and management of schools closer to the point of delivery by strengthening the role of the district administration with the aim of increasing accountability and responsiveness. The abolition of fees was announced for four children per household during the first phase of UPE in Uganda and to all children in the second phase. These were implemented nationally. In the first phase, UPE resulted in access shock at the school level as enrollments increased by 58% in the 1st year of the initiative in the absence of adequate infrastructural expansion and increases in teacher and materials supply. UPE substantially increased schools' reliance on Kampala for funds and much of the necessary funding did not reach the schools immediately (Grogan, 2006).

Tanzania

In Tanzania, the growth in primary education was outside government planning and contradicted the government stand on the expansion of primary education. It was not funded by the central TANU government. The growth was largely due to self-help efforts and pressure from the Tanganyika African Parents Association (TAPA) to the endeavors of the Local Education Authorities (LEAs) and to politicians (Bogonko, 1992). The people of Tanyanyika, having gained independence, did not want to retain anything that resembled restrictions that had been placed on African education during the colonial period. So, if the government was not going to provide education to the Africans, the people of Tanzania were going to take it upon themselves to provide it to advance their way of economic and social life. Unrelenting demand from pressure groups sterilized the government's policy to arrest the expansion of primary education. "The outcome was the opening of many unaided primary schools by TAPA and by many LEAs, notably in Kilimanjaro, Bukoba and Rungwe" (Morrison, 1976, pp. 137, 145–155, cited in Bogonko, 1992, p. 26). Pressure against restrictions on expanding schools saw enrollment grow by 22% from 59,000 in 1965 to 72,000 in 1967, with aided schools only accounting for 6% of this growth (Bogonko, 1992). But as noted by Bogonko (1992), "admittedly, the percentage increases in the latter schools decreased from 12 in 1965 to 1 in 1969" (p. 26).

Tanzania did not prioritize expansion of primary education before the Arusha Declaration (February 1967) because it was believed that "no direct economic benefits flowed from primary school development" (Bogonko, 1992, p. 26). According to Bogonko (1992), the first two Development Plans (1961–1964; 1964–1969) were aimed at restraining expansion of primary education. This, however, did not actually result in stopping expansion from taking place. Pressure from TAPA and from local TANU leaders, combined with high social status attached to education, led to a situation of contradiction between what the government policy prescribed and what was actually practiced. It therefore became "difficult to arrest expansion" (Bogonko, 1992, p. 26). The demand for education was so great that even before the 1967 Arusha Declaration, growth in primary school enrollment had superseded all previous records. For example, enrollment figures increased in the period 1956–1961 by 26%, whereas in the period 1961–1966 they increased by 54% (Morrison, 1976, cited in Bogonko, 1992).

Almost as many children in 1971 as in 1961 failed to get places in primary schools. As noted by Nyerere (1973), "this . . . infuriated President Nyerere to the extent that, on introducing the second 5-year National Development Plan (1969–1974) on May 28, 1969, he called it 'unacceptable to a country which claims to be building social-ism'" (p. 86, cited in Bogonko, 1992, pp. 26–27). It is ironic that the same government that had placed restrictions on the expansion of primary education was now admitting failure to expand primary education and cautioned against indulging in self-congratulation about what Tanzanians had achieved in education. This presidential warning triggered a shift in policy that led to rapid expansion of aided primary schools. By 1974, aided schools registered unprecedented growth of 16.5% from 1,106,387 in 1973 to 1,288,886 in 1974 (Bogonko, 1992). This increased even further by 52.1% in 1977 when enrollment went up to 2,973,487 from 1,288,886 in 1974. By 1977, Tanzania had achieved UPE and enrollment growth continued until 1982, when for the first time since Nyerere's warning it declined to 3,512,799 from 3,538,183 pupils in 1981 (Bogonko, 1992). As noted by Galabawa (2001), Tanzania had effectively achieved free UPE ahead of the target date agreed at the Addis Ababa Conference.

Under Nyerere's leadership, the Musoma Resolution became the framework for a "miracle" of enrollment growth. Expansion was achieved with little donor assistance and denominational schools were nationalized, giving the government almost sole responsibility for provision. The organizational structure of the TANU Party facilitated central direction and top-down control. Fees were abolished and government spending grew as communities were mobilized in an effective drive to provide access for all.

The economic background, however, was one of little growth as Tanzania experienced a prolonged economic crisis in the 1970s and mid-1980s that, along with the associated policy responses, led to the inability to sustain progress toward EFA (Galabawa, 2001). African socialism as the development strategy pursued by Nyerere encouraged heavy state control of economic activities, which in the long-run led to the isolation of Tanzania by international investors and from Foreign Direct Investment (FDI). Gross enrollment rates (GERs) rose from 39.1% in 1970 to 98.0% in 1980 and then fell to 77.7% in 2000. Rates of dropout and repetition for the same years were 0.9%, 2.0%, and 6.6%. Absolute numbers in primary education were increasing despite fluctuations in the GER, doubling between 1975 and 1990 and rising a further 38% from 1990 to 2000. Population growth remained fairly high (2.7% in 1995) and the dependency ratio also was high, with 53% of the population being younger than age 18 in 1995. Female enrollment rates fluctuated from 83.2% in 1985 to 77.6% in 1999, although the drop-out rate was higher for boys than for girls (Galabawa, 2001).

Beginning in the mid-1980s, Tanzania was increasingly affected by HIV/AIDS, which raised the dependency ratio, causing a fall in demand for education and taking the lives of many teachers (Galabawa, 2001). Internationally imposed SAPs brought wide-ranging economic and educational reforms emphasizing private sector provision and financial efficiency. The Economic Recovery Programme of 1989-1993 dismantled the central system of state control and moved toward a free-market orientation. In education, cost-efficiency measures were introduced alongside cost-sharing initiatives and the development of nonstate provision. As a result, the balance of financial burden shifted away from the government and toward parents, which resulted in growing inequality of access at all levels along with disparities of quality (Galabawa, 2001; Vavrus, 2005).

The disenabling environment of SAPs raised the out of school numbers as costs rose and parental incomes fell. Poor macroeconomic conditions in Tanzania thwarted self-reliance and government tax revenues in Tanzania were low compared to neighboring countries throughout the period, even by 2000. Despite a similar proportion of government spending being allocated to education as in Kenya and Uganda, spending as a proportion of GNP was much lower at only 2.3% in 1990 compared to the East African average of 5.12%. Notably, Tanzania spent 5.0% of GNP on education in 1980 and devoted 19% on government spending to education—a figure that had reduced to 12.5% by 1985 and that recovered to 21.2% in 1995. Debt-servicing was a major problem for Tanzania and swallowed 23% of government expenditure in 1995/1996 (Galabawa, 2001).

Galabawa's (2001) analysis shows that external economic factors and policies had a substantial negative effect on Tanzania's UPE progress. Similar analysis is presented by both Maclure (2006) and Vavrus (2005), but Galabawa also identifies a number of internal weaknesses that worked to erode and reverse UPE successes. Rapid expansion in the 1970s led to a "crisis of distorted priorities" as education grew beyond the ability of the government to meet costs or maintain efficiency and effectiveness. Low relevance of curricula, classroom overcrowding, poor student nutrition, arguably inferior teacher training, and a rising student:teacher ratio were evidence of declining educational quality, and it is suggested that the pace of expansion may have resulted in the neglect of necessary structural preparations. Moreover, the links between quality and participation in education may partly explain falling enrollment. In poorer areas, these issues were exacerbated where community capacity to meet costs was low and in the absence of a strategy to invest in and manage spending by districts despite correlations between educational and regional poverty indicators (Galabawa, 2001).

Recent expansion of education in Tanzania is driven by the nation's "Vision 2025" development plan and focused on addressing poverty to generate capacity both to provide and consume improved education. The lack of voice given to education stakeholders in the top-down approach has been addressed in part by the greater participation of the donor community and weakening of central government control (Galabawa, 2001). Galabawa argues that "empowerment" and local "ownership" have been the key to enrollment rate improvements post-SAPs. UPE objectives in Tanzania have been articulated with a host of macropolicy objectives in what Galabawa describes as a "holistic" approach. Public service reform and educational restructuring aimed at broadening the education revenue base and at decentralization and rationalization began in the mid-1990s and the Poverty Reduction Strategy (2000) organizes donor assistance to education according to the Tanzania Assistance

Strategy with the intention of distributing assistance more equitably and efficiently (Galabawa, 2001).

The trend of expansion that resulted from Nyerere's caution in 1969 was a logical outcome of three factors. First, following the shift of emphasis to expanding primary education as expressed by the second 5-year Development Plan, in 1971, the government ordered an end to the expulsion of primary pupils for nonpayment of school fees. Second, expansion was concentrated at the upper primary school (Grades V-VIII) so that by 1974 there were enough places for Grade IV leavers at the next level. Third, primary school fees were abolished in 1973 (Bogonko, 1992).

There was little expansion at the secondary level owing to the government's prioritization of equity goals once emphasis was shifted to primary education. There was, however, substantial expansion in adult basic education and adult literacy rose from 31% in 1967 to 85% by 1983 (Colleta & Sutton, 1989). The social infrastructure of government literacy campaigns was used to publicize the UPE drive and also enabled teacher recruitment to fill the growing demand in the primary sector. Expansion was characterized by low costs both to the government and to users. In 1969, all fees were banned and a free textbook policy was introduced (Colleta & Sutton, 1989). Although almost all recurrent costs were met by the government, per student expenditure in Tanzania remained low, at a mean annual figure of US$34 in 1981 as compared to US$71.5 across East Africa. The role of local communities in school construction alongside low teacher salaries were key explanations of low levels of costs. Tanzania instituted a successful and innovative program of distance education for in-service teacher training in the late 1970s. The lack of secondary school graduates meant that the UPE drive would depend on training primary school graduates for teaching and more than 45,000 were enrolled from 1976 to 1979 to a primary correspondence and radio-instruction-based scheme. Colleta and Sutton (1989) note that the abolition of fees contributed to growth in enrollment, indicating that costs had previously been a barrier to access. Tanzania's "Education for Self-Reliance" is considered a successful example of an integrated approach to rapidly expanding social service provision. The elements identified in Tanzania's successful and sustainable UPE approach include political commitment, increased social demand, meeting capital costs through community participation, increasing recurrent expenditure through intrasectoral budget shifts, microplanning for schooling at the local level, provision and motivation of sufficient competent teachers, raising educational quality and relevance through curricular and examination reform, localizing control and accountability, and promoting access for girls and marginalized groups (Colleta & Sutton, 1989).

Tanzanian policy included other redistributive measures such as concentration of primary school funding on deprived areas, positive discrimination for secondary school access on a regional basis, and the modification of assessment to broaden criteria and emphasize nonacademic factors (Court & Kinyanjui, 1980). The authors suggest that "Education for Self-Reliance" had not, at the time of writing, displaced the academic role of education in competing for places higher up the system, and indeed, access to secondary schooling remained determined by examination performance (Court & Kinyanjui, 1980). The policy presented a number of difficulties and dilemmas, including problems of defining acceptable nonacademic selection criteria, the issue of whether to accept English as a medium of instruction, the reform of administrative structures to reflect self-reliance and local initiative, the reconciliation of national and regional education/development priorities under a decentralized system, and the development of structures of opportunity that reinforce rather than undermine educational policy (Court & Kinyanjui, 1980).

POLICY INSTITUTIONALIZATION, REPLICABILITY, AND FINANCIAL SUSTAINABILITY

Kenya

Following the implementation of FPE policy in 2003, the net enrollment ratio in Kenya grew by a further 22.3%. However, as in the 1970s, the implementation of free primary education was beset with difficulties. Rapid expansion in enrollment exacerbated problems of teaching and learning facilities, increased classroom congestion, and raised teacher:pupil ratios. These problems, again as in the 1970s, are leading to high drop-out rates and have affected the inflow of pupils in the 2nd year of implementation: 2004. Districts that registered a 20% increase in enrollment in 2003 hardly recorded more than 5% in 2004 (Muthwii, 2004; OWN and Associates, 2004).

Although the Kenyan government raised its education budget in 2003–2004 by 17.4% and was strongly supported by donor funding in its free primary education initiative, Muthwii raises questions about the sustainability of the policy. The cost of providing FPE is beyond the scope of the ordinary education budget, economic performance has not been strong, and donor finance tends to be temporary. She concludes that the FPE initiative of 2003, similar to interventions in the past, was pursued as a matter of political expediency and was not adequately planned and resourced with the consequences of dropout and falling educational quality. In view of these challenges, Muthwii considers the attainment of sustained FPE an illusion in the context of Kenya (Muthwii, 2004). Mukudi (2004) also addresses the issues of sustainability with regard to universal primary education in Kenya, including public resource capacity and educational quality. Economic performance in Kenya is a limiting factor and might be considered disappointing. The study uses secondary data on a variety of economic, educational, and demographic factors to explore the costs and other implications of achieving UPE in Kenya based on current per capita spending. Mukudi concludes that without adequate investment, however, the synergies between educational access, economic growth, and poverty reduction may not be capitalized on and a vicious cycle may be observed in which global competitiveness becomes elusive in the absence of investment in knowledge creation (Mukudi, 2004). Vos et al. (2004) argue that given the financial constraints that Kenya faces, meeting the EFA target will require a more efficient resource allocation within the education sector. A number of options are examined with scenarios whereby 100% net enrollment is targeted for the bottom two quintiles and where the government meets all the costs to households of education. They show that the cost of the government bearing all household education costs would require a 91% budget increase or 0.8% of GDP and result in a net enrollment rate (NER) of 94% (Vos et al., 2004). The authors conclude that within a tight budget, cost-effectiveness considerations make a considerable difference (Vos et al., 2004).

King (2005) notes that despite targeting the achievement of UPE by 2005, as many as 1.5 million Kenyan children remain out of school, in the formal sense at least. Considerable challenges exist in schooling these children, who may prove the most expensive to reach. Difficulties also arise in monitoring what has happened with respect to the achievement of UPE; although it is claimed that millions of new children have enrolled, little data is available. There are also a number of unintended consequences of providing free primary education as Kenya has done since 2003. The author notes that although cost-sharing was excluding the poor, the advent of free education has meant that parents may now take it that they need make no financial contribution and many have moved children from low-cost informal provision to the state sector. A further corollary of rising numbers and falling quality in the state system may be that wealthier parents prefer the fee-paying private sector. Further issues of declining teacher morale and quality may exacerbate these problems and ultimately make it more difficult for bright children from poor families to succeed. The author points out that if primary education is to bring development benefits, then children must actually master the intended curriculum; he notes, however, that there is much evidence to suggest this may not happen (King, 2005).

King (2005) further discusses the importance of intersectoral factors in the success of educational investment programs such as KESSP. The need for teachers to find second incomes, the increasing importance of nonmeritocratic criteria for employment selection and issues of state capacity, good governance, and corruption are important determinants of the results of educational investment while being outside the control of the sector. The author concludes that the UPE goals will require a holistic approach, not only a focus on primary education, and indeed educational investment alone will not be enough. The importance of other sectors, including agriculture, energy, transport, and trade, is emphasized along with the need for strong national vision, good governance, and government capacity-building. The minimalist approach to development discernible in the MDGs needs to be broadened and the author sees some signs that this is already taking place. In this environment, Kenya's own approach may not be seen as so ambitious and wide-ranging as the MDGs become just one entry point into a wider perspective on investment and organizational and institutional change (King, 2005).

Uganda

The costs of UPE to the government have been high. Primary education accounted for 30% of the education budget in 1989–1990 and 66% by 1999–2000.

The education budget rose as a percentage of all government expenditure from around 15% in 1989 to 25% in 1999. At constant prices, Uganda spent U.S.$8 per pupil in the early 1980s on primary education and U.S.$32.5 in 1997-1998. The coming of political stability in 1987 brought economic growth that has continued at around 6.5%. Along with the cancellation of foreign debt, this has helped Uganda finance UPE. International and multinational agencies also have played an important role, and in 1998–1999 they contributed around the same amount to primary education development as the Ugandan government (Ministry of Education and Sports, Uganda, 1999).

Bategeka (2005) finds that although UPE improved access indicators substantially, quality indicators worsened following the introduction of UPE and have yet to recover to pre-UPE levels. Although gender equity improved markedly, inequities in financing education remain a key challenge. Access in terms of the GER rose by 73% in the 1st year of UPE and by 2003 was 149% of the pre-UPE level. In response to increased demand as fees were eliminated, the government, private sector, and nongovernmental organizations (NGOs) built a large number of schools and the number of primary school teachers in service doubled. The profile of the school population shifted such that by 2003, 25% of all pupils were enrolled in Grade 1. There is evidence of significant dropout at the primary cycle, which appears to be relatively gender-neutral. Stated reasons for dropout included lack of interest, family responsibilities, sickness, and employment.

Although quality indicators suffered terribly in 1997, they have been improving steadily since. The pupil:teacher ratio, for example, has fallen from 65 to 1 in 2000 to 54 to 1 in 2003. In 2003, 37% of teachers had received no training as teachers, most of whom were deployed in UPE schools in rural areas. A large number of resources were devoted under the School Facilities Grant to procuring textbooks, building schools, purchasing furniture, and so on. Although the pupil:textbook ratio has improved, Bategeka, (2005) notes that this has not led to improved pupil performance. Indeed, the results of the National Assessment of Primary Education (NAPE) between 1996 and 2000 suggest that performance has deteriorated following the introduction of UPE.

The gender gap has closed considerably, and in 2003, girls accounted for 49% of enrollments at the primary level. The initial UPE policy had given priority to girls and to disabled children. Rural populations also have benefited from UPE and the GER in rural areas reached 140% in 2003. Threats to the gains achieved through UPE include high drop-out rates and inequalities in performance between public/private and urban/rural schools. Success has been due to government commitment and funding (see Table 1) along with donor support, including debt relief. Parents' willingness to send their children to school also contributed (Bategeka, 2005).

Lessons from the experience of the UPE program include an indication that fees did present a serious obstacle to enrollment in Uganda, judging by the massive increase in enrollment post-UPE. Other impediments include institutional constraints that may affect quality, although the government is concentrating on improving efficiency and on increasing inputs, including teachers, classrooms, and textbooks.

TABLE 1   Trends in Education Sector Budget as a Percentage
of the Government Budget, 1992–2002

Financial Year	% of Government Budget
1992/1993	12
1993/1994	16
1994/1995	17
1995/1996	21
1996/1997	22
1997/1998	23
1998/1999	25
1999/2000	26.3
2000/2001	24.9
2001/2002	24.1

Source. MoFPED (2002) cited in Eilor (2004, Table 2.1).

Corruption also constrains the success of UPE implementation—in 1997, one study found that only 35% of allocated funds were reaching their intended beneficiaries, although this is said to have improved to more than 80% owing to greater transparency and accountability. Liberalization in the education sector has allowed parents to opt for private education, thereby reducing the burden on the state, but opportunities for targeting the poor have not in the view of the author been fully utilized. It is suggested that UPE should be focused more squarely on the poor to reduce inequality in access and in quality of education. The author concludes that the Ugandan experience shows that a poor country with a committed government can fight poverty by providing universal access to education, although the financial limitations faced by the state mean such a program will require external support (Bategeka, 2005).

Tanzania

Colleta and Sutton (1989) identify lessons to be learned from the successes of community action and involvement in education expansion in Kenya and Tanzania. They note that the abolition of fees contributed to growth in enrollment, indicating that costs had previously been a barrier to access. Tanzania's Education for Self-Reliance is considered a successful example of an integrated approach to rapidly expanding social service provision. The elements identified through the examples of Kenya and Tanzania of a successful and sustainable UPE approach include political commitment, increased social demand, meeting capital costs through community participation, increasing recurrent expenditure through intrasectoral budget shifts, microplanning for schooling at the local level, the provision and motivation of sufficient competent teachers, raising educational quality and relevance through curricular and exam reform, localizing control and accountability, and promoting access for girls and marginalized groups (Colleta & Sutton, 1989).

Galabawa (2001) argues that Tanzania's recent UPE drive has been implemented without careful planning or financial strategy. His main concern was that the process of financial and management decentralization as part of UPE implementation was not followed through because the process maintained a top-down approach. He notes that a "key strategy in implementing UPE is to empower and to commit communities in the development of primary education" (p. 9), much the same way as had been the case prior and following the Arusha declaration of 1967.

POLICY IMPACT AND IMPLICATION ON THE POOREST GROUPS

Deininger (2003) uses a range of data, including nationally representative survey data and Ministry of Education figures to examine the reorientation of public spending in Uganda toward basic education in terms of its impact on enrollment and quality of outcomes for the poor. The study finds that there is good evidence that the direct and indirect costs of schooling constituted a significant obstacle to enrollment for the poor and especially for girls prior to Uganda's UPE program of 1997. Reducing educational costs may thus play a role in improving equity of access to education in the Ugandan context. As well as abolishing fees, however, the Ugandan UPE program involved a substantial publicity campaign and a greater degree of cost recovery at the postprimary levels of education. However, the policy has led to some of the highest teacher:pupil ratios in the world and to high rates of examination failure at the end of the primary education phase. These issues of quality are key to the sustainability of UPE. There have been considerable schooling infrastructure improvements since 1997, often resulting from community involvement, suggesting that the UPE program may have succeeded in increasing local incentives to education (Deininger, 2003).

Evidence from the very much weaker reduction in impact of parental income on secondary schooling is cited in further support for the role of the abolition of primary fees in increasing enrollment. The lack of a commensurate rise in qualified teachers and schools has meant increasing teacher:pupil ratios and a dramatic increase in the number of pupils per school, especially in rural areas. There is some evidence for a decline in educational quality following the UPE program and the author notes that despite a fall in costs, the hypothesis that in quality adjusted terms there was little real change in the cost of primary education cannot be rejected. The author suggests that the program may be considered an example of the effectiveness of a results-oriented approach to development assistance because much of the financing was obtained through budgetary support in the form of debt relief (see Table 2; Deininger, 2003).

Based on household DHS (education supplement) survey data from 1995, Grogan (2006) illustrates the education situation pre-UPE alongside data from a similar survey conducted in 2000–2001 to test the effects of school fee elimination. Prior to the UPE initiative in Uganda, parents were meeting up to 90% of recurrent schooling costs. In 1995, 70% of boys and 67% of girls were enrolled in primary

TABLE 2   Summary of Government and Donor Support to the Education
Sector in US$ Million, 1998/1999–2003/2004

Source	1998/ 1999	1999/ 2000	2000/ 2001	2001/ 2002	2002/ 2003	2003/ 2004
Government						
Recurrent	70.38	105.61	95.98	90.22	90.00	N/A
Development	43.00	37.27	37.68	28.08	43.50	N/A
Subtotal	113.38	142.88	133.66	118.30	113.50	N/A
Donors						
Budget support	117.30	102.90	124.10	129.50	138.80	124.10
Project support	N/A	N/A	8.69	8.81	21.66	14.24

Source. Eilor (2004, Table 2.6, p. 76).

school and 11% and 9% in secondary school. Only 32% were in the correct grade
for their ages. Grogan's study found that those who did not attend school came from
poor households, that there had been historically large gender gaps, that starting
school late was associated with a lower probability of completion, and that improvements in enrollment before the age of 8 were already occurring prior to UPE as a
result of other education initiatives. A comparison group of private school pupils was
used as a control in the study of the quality of public school education during the
period. Four issues are considered by Grogan in relation to the effects of the elimination of school fees in Uganda—the differences in the effects on the optimal level
of education of population subgroups, potential feedback effects of the policy on the
opportunity costs of schooling and the returns to schooling, changes to the ability
composition of those in schooling, and changes in the quality of schooling. The
study finds that the reduction in schooling costs affect differently on different
socioeconomic groups such as urban/rural and that opportunity costs may rise as
large numbers move out of labor and into school, thereby reducing supply in the
labor market and raising wages for child labor. Returns to education may fall as the
supply of labor with a given level of education rises, which may in turn exert feedback effects on the demand for education and optimal levels of schooling. The mean
ability level of pupils may decline as costs decline, thereby reducing levels of attainment and educational quality may decline if the resources available per pupil are
reduced. Grogan (2006) finds that the causal effect of the introduction of UPE raises
the probability of attending school before age 8 by 8% to 10% both for boys and
girls. She finds some evidence that the new entrants are more likely to have come
from poorer backgrounds and of a reduction in the drop-out rate, especially in the
later years and particularly where boys from poor households and rural areas are concerned. She also finds some evidence of rising dropout in private schools and of a
reduction in the probability that an individual can pass a standardized reading test if

they began education in a government school after the introduction of UPE by 11%. Controls indicate that this is not a result of falling ability and so might be attributed to falling quality (Grogan, 2006). The author suggests that UPE successes so far have been achieved through top-level leadership, cabinet-level consensus, ministerial support, and stakeholder involvement, all of which are identified as strong features at the time of UPE implementation in Uganda. Institutions will need to be strong but flexible capacity will need further development if UPE progress is to be sustainable (Grogan, 2006).

POLICIES ON SECONDARY EDUCATION ACCESS

Knight and Sabot (1986, 1990) conducted extensive surveys in workplaces in Nairobi and Dar-es-Salaam to obtain evidence on ability, schooling, cognitive skills, and earnings for use in comparing the impact of secondary education policy in Kenya and Tanzania. Both countries had stated an intention to address issues of inequality through educational policy, although their approaches differed substantially. Tanzania restricted expansion in secondary education during the period in question, whereas provision in Kenya increased rapidly. This key policy difference in two countries with much in common created a natural experiment exploited in this study. The authors examined the justification for expanding secondary education in the two countries on the basis of their findings in relation to the returns to that phase of education, its role in equalizing incomes, and its potential for reducing the transmission of intergenerational inequality. Their inclusion of variables for ability and cognitive skill was intended to allow an assessment of alternative explanations of human capital relationships such as screening and signaling. At the theoretical level, they identify two distributive effects of increasing access to education that are closely linked to Kuznets's theory—a composition effect whereby the increased relative size of the educated and more highly paid group increases income inequality and a compression effect whereby the increasing supply of educated labor reduced the wage premium for education, thereby decreasing income inequality. They suggest that if educational access expands more rapidly than labor market opportunity, then the compression effect may be likely to outweigh the composition effect.

In 1980, only 4% of the age cohort was enrolled in secondary school in Tanzania. Kenyan provision had expanded rapidly, particularly due to the growth in *harambee* (self-help) community schools, and accommodated 25% of the age group by 1980. Demand exceeded supply in both countries but restrictions in Tanzania made competition for places there much more intense. The extent of government subsidy to secondary schooling in Tanzania also was greater than in Kenya, placing significant budgetary constraints on expansion. The Tanzanian policy of education sector reform (ESR) also brought significant curriculum changes emphasizing a diversified curriculum and the use of Kiswahili, whereas Kenya's approach largely maintained continuity with the past. Access to tertiary education remained similarly low in both countries.

The authors concluded that Tanzania's ESR approach of limiting secondary education expansion and refocusing the curriculum has been counterproductive in terms of equity and improvements in cognitive skill and productivity levels relative to Kenya. Competition for and rationing of secondary education appear to have served to select secondary school entrants by family background in Tanzania more than the more inclusive approach of Kenya despite its higher fees. Filtering down as education has expanded in Kenya has reduced the returns to secondary education compared to Tanzania, thereby increasing income equality, although the manpower planning approach may regard it as wasteful of resources. Given Tanzania's small secondary school population, however, its progression rate to higher education was much higher than in Kenya, and the authors find that at this stage "selection by family background" was more prevalent in Kenya than in Tanzania, suggesting that Kenya's expansion of secondary schooling may have postponed this form of selection.

It is two decades since Knight and Sabot's comprehensive study comparing secondary education policies in Kenya and Tanzania and their impact on access. Kenya's NARC government acknowledges that growth in secondary education is constrained and is likely to remain so due to lack of adequate secondary schools to match primary enrollment. Uganda, having had a near decade-long success with UPE, has now started to focus attention on transition to secondary level. In Kenya, it appears the government is banking on community partnership, which led to the establishment of *harambee* secondary schools in the 1970s. In all three countries, it is likely that the poor will find it difficult to access secondary education even after completing primary education. This will limit the impact of education in poverty reduction and in meeting the MDGs. Further work may be needed to establish the shift in the factors that might encourage or hinder the poorest groups' transition to secondary level and assess whether the current policies by the government are adequate. For instance, do those policies address causes of exclusion in lower secondary among the poor? Is it lack of adequate facilities that is causing low enrollment or is it lack of interest in further education? Will FPE work for the poor in terms of helping them advance to some form of secondary education?

CONCLUSION

Countries that have been successful in increasing enrollment face two particular problems—enrolling the remaining 10% to 20% of the school age (at primary level) population who tend to be the poorest children and ensuring that those in school benefit by learning. Furthermore, even where fees are not a factor in preventing access they may still have a regressive impact. The greater the inequality, the harder it is for the poor to pay fees (Raja & Burnett, 2004).

The experiences of Kenya, Uganda, and Tanzania show that the elimination of fees at the primary level can have dramatic results. However, increased enrollment has resulted in concerns for deteriorating quality and increased demand for secondary education (Raja & Burnett, 2004).

Low enrollment among the poorest groups still presents a problem. This low enrollment may reflect a lack of supply, the opportunity cost of attending school, the perceived low returns from schooling in the labor market or other factors such as the distance to school, and for girls, the existence of female teachers and separate toilets. Major determinants of enrollment include household income, schooling cost, presence of schools, community involvement, transportation, education quality, and relevance (Raja & Burnett, 2004). As both Vavrus (2005) and Maclure (2006) have suggested, there is need for locally initiated policies in education, and where international partners are involved, a strong local context based on endogenous research and policy is desirable in developing policies that may pay specific attention to local interpretation of education policies and how it might affect the enrollment of those who prove difficult to reach.

ACKNOWLEDGMENTS

This chapter is drawn with permission from an earlier version written for the Consortium for Research on Education Access, Transition and Equity (CREATE) at the Center for International Education, University of Sussex, United Kingdom. CREATE developed these four characterizations of access (i.e., those with no access, those who are excluded after initial entry, those at risk of dropout, and those excluded from secondary education) and called them "Zones of Access" to serve as a framework for analysis and empirical research. The authors wish to thank CREATE. Comments by Angela Little on the CREATE version and by the anonymous reviewer for this version were helpful. None share responsibility for the review.

REFERENCES

Avenstrup, R., Liang, X., & Nellemann, S. (2004). *Kenya, Lesotho, Malawi and Uganda: Universal primary education and poverty reduction. A case study for reducing poverty—what works, what doesn't, and why. A global exchange of scaling up success* [Conference paper]. Washington, DC: World Bank.

Bategeka, L. (2005). *Universal primary education (UPE) in Uganda: Report to the inter-regional inequality facility-policy case study.* Uganda, Institute of Development Studies, University of Sussex.

Bogonko, S. N. (1992). *Reflections on education in East Africa.* Nairobi, Kenya: Oxford University Press.

Buchmann, C. (2001). The state and schooling in Kenya: Historical developments and current challenges. *Africa Today, 46*(1), 95-116.

Colleta, N. J., & Sutton, M. (1989). *Achieving and sustaining universal primary education: International experience relevant to India.* Policy Research Working Paper Series 166, The World Bank.

Court, D., & Kinyanjui, K. (1980). *Development policy and educational opportunity: The experience of Kenya and Tanzania.* University of Nairobi Institute of Development Studies Occasional Paper #33.

Deininger, K. (2003). Does the cost of schooling affect enrollment by the poor? Universal primary education in Uganda. *Economics of Education Review, 22*(3), 291-305.

Eilor, J. (2004). *Education and sector-wide approach in Uganda.* Paris: UNESCO–International Institute for Educational Planning.

Galabawa, C. J. (2001, October 7–11). *Developments and issues regarding universal primary education (UPE) in Tanzania.* Report presented at ADEA Biennial Meeting, Arusha, Tanzania.

Grogan, L. (2006). *Who benefits from universal primary education in Uganda?* Unpublished report, Department of Economics, University of Guelph.

King, K. (2005). *Balancing basic and post-basic education: Quantity, quality and inequality. Service provision and productive capacity in securing poverty reduction and growth in Kenya.* Center of African Studies, University of Edinburgh.

Knight, J. B., & Sabot, R. H. (1986). *Overview of educational expansion, productivity and inequality: A comparative analysis of the East African natural experiment.* Washington, DC: World Bank.

Knight, J. B., & Sabot, R. H. (1990). *Education, productivity, and inequality: The East African natural experiment.* Oxford, UK: Oxford University Press.

Maclure, R. (2006). No longer overlooked and undervalued: The evolving dynamics of endogenous educational research in sub-Saharan Africa. *Harvard Educational Review, 76*(1), 80–109.

Ministry of Education and Sports, Uganda. (1999). *The Ugandan Experience of Universal Primary Education (UPE).* Kampala, Uganda: Author.

Mukudi, E. (2004). Education for all: A framework for addressing the persisting illusion for Kenyan context. *International Journal of Educational Development, 24*(3), 231–240.

Muthwii, M. (2004). *Free primary education: The Kenyan journey since independence.* Retrieved November 16, 2006, from http://nesis.intoweb.co.za/en/index.php?module=documents &JAS_DocumentManager_op=downloadFile&JAS_File_id=41

Oketch, M. O. (2003). Market model of financing higher education in sub-Saharan Africa: Examples from Kenya. *Higher Education Policy, 16*(3), 313-332.

OWN and Associates. (2004). *Monitoring of the free primary education and establishing the unit cost of primary education in Kenya.* Report submitted to Elimu Yetu Coalition/Action Aid Kenya.

Raja, B., & Burnett, N. (2004). *User fees in primary education.* Washington, DC: World Bank.

Republic of Kenya. (1964). *Kenya Education Commission report.* Nairobi, Kenya: Government Printers.

Republic of Kenya. (1964–1969; 1970–1974; 1974–1978; 1979–1983; 1984–1988; 1989–1993; 1997–2001; 2002–2008). *National Development Plan.* Nairobi, Kenya: Government Printers.

Somerset, A. (2006, June 27). *A preliminary note on Kenya primary school enrollment trends over four decades.* Paper presented at CREATE Conference, University of Sussex.

Southall, R. (1974). *Federalism and higher education in East Africa.* Nairobi, Kenya: East African Publishing House.

Ssekamwa, J. C., & Lugumba, S. M. E. (2001). *A history of education in East Africa.* Kampala, Uganda: Fountain Publishers.

Stasavage, D. (2005). *Democracy and primary school attendance: Aggregate and individual level evidence from Africa.* AfroBarometer Working Paper #54.

Vavrus, F. (2005). Adjusting inequality: Education and structural adjustment policies in Tanzania. *Harvard Educational Review, 2*(75), 174-201.

Vos, R., Bedi, R., Kimalu, P., Manda, D. K., & Nafula, N. N. (2004). *Achieving universal primary education: Can Kenya afford it?* Working paper, Department of Economics, University of Connecticut.

Chapter 6

Equality and Justice For All? Examining Race in Education Scholarship

Bryan McKinley Jones Brayboy
The University of Utah

Angelina E. Castagno
Northern Arizona University

Emma Maughan
The University of Utah

Does race (still) matter in educational discussions, analyses, and policies? This question seems to be a perennial that comes and goes, is hidden and reemerges, but is consistently (if implicitly) present. Consider, for example, educators' and educational researchers' concerns with assimilation, civilization, vocational training, IQ, poverty, cultural difference, remedial education, school readiness, achievement gaps, accountability, and standardization—all of these conversations were and still are intimately connected to race and racism regardless of whether we name them as such. Although the scholarship on race in education is vast, we attempt to review some of the most pressing and persistent issues in this chapter. We also suggest that the future of race scholarship in education needs to be centered not on equality but rather on equity and justice.

It is important in this chapter for us to outline what we mean by equity and equality and to explicate the differences in these terms. In the areas of race and education, "commonsensical" uses of these terms have been conflated. Within popular discourse, what is meant by equality is the same thing as what is meant by equity, and having equal resources for schools means that the schools are equitable, fair, and equal. But we understand these terms and their relationship differently and suggest that notions of justice must be intimately connected with these terms for equity and equality to have meaningful emphases.

By equality, we mean sameness and, more specifically, sameness of resources and opportunities. This concept of equality is the long-term goal of a just society: children, regardless of race, socioeconomic class, or gender, should have access to the same

Review of Research in Education
March 2007, Vol. 31, pp. 159–194
DOI: 10.3102/0091732X07300045
© 2007 AERA. http://rre.aera.net

resources and opportunity outcomes. It will become apparent that we have reached this goal when schooling and economic successes and opportunities look the same for all groups of children. A closer examination of test scores, schooling facilities for particular children, and life outcomes of children from different racialized groups demonstrate that there is not currently equality (i.e., sameness) in resources or opportunity outcomes.

The often heard, commonsensical response to the inequalities of outcomes rests in a number of areas: Some families care more about education than others; some children and families are more motivated to do well in education; some children are simply more gifted than others; or everyone has the same opportunities as everyone else—what else could we ask for? In these responses, there is an overwhelming reliance on the individual, the idea that individual values, motivations, and talents determine individual outcomes. We believe that individuals certainly matter, and individual traits and actions can, in many circumstances, have an effect on individual outcomes. However, such individual distinctions cannot explain large-scale group realities. Large-scale inequalities are rooted in more pervasive, systemic, and structural issues rather than in the individual motivations or giftedness of the individual. Concomitantly, issues of motivation or giftedness often are tied directly to these larger structural factors. Students at New Trier High School, for example, have access to different educational, cultural, and social resources than do students at East St. Louis High School—two public schools in the same state and only 150 miles away from each other (cf. Illinois Report Card, 2005; Kozol, 2005). Table 1 offers a comparison of the two schools.

New Trier High School, located in Winnetka, Illinois, is 88.6% White, and the school has a low-income population of 1.5% in a state with an average 40% low-income population. The average ACT score for its students is 26.8 and its graduation rate is 98.5% (the state average is 87.4%). The average teacher has been in the classroom 13.9 years (roughly, the state average is 13.6 years), 85.5% of the teachers have graduate degrees, and the average teacher salary is $84,151 (the state average is $55,558). In terms of school spending (for the 2003–2004 school year), New Trier High School spends $8,557 per pupil per year and has an additional $15,403 per pupil per year in operational expenditures. There are more than 100 cocurricular organizations and the school boasts its own radio station, theater, rugby team, and audio recording studio.

East St. Louis High School, located in East St. Louis, Illinois, is 99.6% African American and 93.3% low income. The average ACT score is 14.8, and its graduation rate is 61.2%. The average teacher (in the district—figures were not available for the school in this measure) has been in the classroom 20.3 years, 32.9% have graduate degrees, and the average teacher salary is $58,534. East St. Louis High School spends an average of $5,215 per student in operational expenditures and $9,007 per pupil per year. We were unable to locate the number of cocurricular activities for the school.

In the case of these two schools, it is evident that they are quite separate and very unequal. We use equality to mean sameness, but the concept of sameness is complicated. If every school in Illinois had access to the same quality of teachers, resources,

TABLE 1   Comparison of New Trier and East St. Louis High Schools

	New Trier High School	East St. Louis High School
Racial composition	88.6% White	99.6% African American
% Low-income students	1.5%	93.3%
Average ACT score	26.8	14.8
Graduation rate	98.5%	61.2%
Average teacher years in the classroom	13.9 years	20.3 years
Average teacher graduate degrees	85.5%	32.9%
Average teacher salary	$84,151	$58,534
Average per student operational expenditures	$15,403	$5,215
Average expenditures per pupil per year	$8,557	$9,007
Number of cocurricular activities	100+	Unavailable

Source. Illinois Interactive Report Card, 2005. http://iirc.niu.edu/Scripts/school.asp?schoolID=1401620300001&colName=SCHLNAME&searchStr=new%20trier&test=all and http://iirc.niu.edu/Scripts/school.asp?schoolID=5008218900043&test=all

expenditures, and current infrastructure, the schooling experiences of the students might be more closely aligned with the academic successes of the students at New Trier. Yet, sameness does not exist either in structural factors or in the achievement levels of the students. To work toward every student having access to teachers with high salaries and graduate degrees, a system of *equity* must be put into place. By equity, we mean a system where unequal goods are redistributed to create systems and schools that share a greater likelihood of becoming more equal. In the case of New Trier and East St. Louis High Schools, this would mean that East St. Louis High School would get more and better access to facilities (physical and structural ones), teachers with advanced degrees, monetary resources to build cocurricular activities, and a focus on graduating students with higher ACT scores and better prospects for college and life. We are not arguing that resources should necessarily be taken away from New Trier; rather, we are arguing that an equitable system will provide extra resources for the students to have the possibilities of excelling academically and socially. Currently, one school (New Trier) clearly has more resources (monetarily and otherwise) than another (East St. Louis)—we consider this neither equal nor equitable and achieving equity requires a nonequal distribution of resources with the hope that sustained equity will eventually result in more equal educational opportunities for students.

Conservative commentators have argued that money is not the answer. In part, we agree. There are other issues at work in the cases outlined above; school facilities, teachers, and attitudes about education certainly come into play. Yet, as the two desegregation cases recently argued before the Supreme Court highlight, parents whose children attend New Trier High School would not sit quietly if their children attended a school with the infrastructure and academic results of East St. Louis High School. It is, of course, unlikely that the parents of students attending East St. Louis High School are quiet either, but these parents clearly do not have the same avenues for being heard. Why, we must ask, are the differences in access to resources and academic results so different in two schools that are, for all intents and purposes, segregated based on race? If we are going to have equality and justice for all, there must be a period when those who have been without resources for long periods of time are provided compensatory resources to create a just society. In this way, we believe that equality and justice for all are incommensurate with the current system; instead, there must be a sense of justice to create such a system. The research outlined below points to the systematic differences that create differences in academic achievement linked to the race of certain students.

Two recent cases heard by the U.S. Supreme Court in the fall of 2006 have renewed a conversation among many of the citizens of the United States and educational researchers regarding the role of race in education and educational achievement. Perhaps the sentiments of the two main competing arguments are best captured by opinions of individuals on different sides of the constitutionality of using race as a factor in school attendance assignments.

In one case, *Parents Involved in Community Schools v. Seattle School District* No. 1, No. 01–35450, a group of parents in Seattle, Washington, objected to the use of race as one tie-breaker to determine school assignment within a school choice system. In this particular case, one side of the disagreement is clearly articulated by Washington Supreme Court Justice Tom Chambers, who argued, "In a society such as ours, it is not enough that the 3Rs are being taught properly, for there are other vital considerations. The children must learn to respect and live with one another in multiracial and multicultural communities, and the earlier they do so the better." On the other side of the issue, a legal think tank, called the Pacific Legal Foundation (who brought the case forward on behalf of the parent's group), through one of its lawyers, Arthur B. Mark III, argued that the case amounted to "racial gerrymandering" and that the White students in the case are victims "who are pulled from their local schools for *no good reason* [italics added]." Later, Mark's colleague, Sharon Browne, argued that "children should not be stereotyped by the color of their skin, but rather treated as individuals."

The second case, *Meredith v. Jefferson County Board of Education* No. 05–915, is slightly different because of Louisville's history with mandatory desegregation in its schools. Although the court's desegregation order ended in 2001, the Jefferson County Board of Education (JCBE) continued to require that its schools be between 15% and 50% African American. A parent of a White child joined others to bring the case forward when her son was denied entry (she tried to enroll him 1 month after the school year had begun) at a local school because he would upset the racial balance. The school district argues that it is seeking desegregation of its schools and that every school receives equal funding, qualified staff, and programs.

At the heart of these cases appears to be a battle between those who view the use of race in desegregating schools as a compelling state interest (as articulated in the 14th amendment) versus those who argue that admissions policies must offer supremacy to the role of "individualized considerations." The former position calls for race conscious policies (see Moses, 2002a), whereas the latter focuses on colorblind policies that are rooted in a stance that centers the individual. Each of these stances reflects one side of a continuum or one end of a binary. Of importance, there are historical aspects that are related to each position, and this chapter will make connections that link the present with the past (e.g., see Donato & Lazerson, 2000, for a provocative overview of connections between issues of race and education in a historical frame).

This chapter focuses on the basic idea that having equality and justice for all in schooling cannot be achieved in the current climate where students are viewed solely as individuals. In fact, given the educational debt (Ladson-Billings)[1] and achievement gaps, the ideas of equality and justice are necessarily contradictory. Achieving justice, in light of the differentiation in academic achievement, cannot be done through equal means; rather, more equitable (or fairer) solutions must be used. Importantly, the use of equitable solutions necessarily means that some schools and some members of racialized communities may receive more than others. It does not mean, however, that they will receive more than their fair share. It simply means that justice is achieved through unequal (although not inequitable) means. An important factor in this article is that we intend to examine the ways that equality and equity often are conflated or interpreted as the same when they are actually quite different. The purpose of more closely examining the nuances of these concepts, and their concomitant arguments toward how society's schools should work, is to explore the ways that educational research offers a blueprint for how society can better meet the educational needs of all students rather than only some.

Such emphasis on individuality is an important part of calls for equality or having equal access to things such as schooling; we see this play itself out in the race-conscious student assignment cases in the Supreme Court. Consider the language being used by those who have brought suit: taking race into account is "illegal" or some students are being kept out of schools "for no good reason." The reasons often stated for having diverse school populations are that diversity creates better learning environments or means better learning opportunities for all elementary and secondary students. This is an argument rooted in both empirical studies and beliefs about morality (Ladson-Billings, 2006; Orfield & Lee, 2005, 2006). These studies, however, are rarely being discussed, and those opposed to using race in any decisions tied to schooling also make moral arguments (e.g., it isn't fair to exclude White students from schools in their neighborhoods) and legal arguments (e.g., it is against the law to discriminate based on race).

At the heart of discussions about the role of race in education and of the cases currently before the Supreme Court appears to be a battle between those who call for race conscious policies (see Moses, 2002a) and those who focus on colorblind policies that are rooted in a stance that privileges the individual. Each of these positions reflects one side of a continuum or one end of a binary tension inherent in the notion of democracy. Simply stated, democracy is a socially constructed idea in which every individual has the ability to be heard and have their vote/voice/ideas matter equally. We have seen historically, however, that democracy has not fully addressed the needs of the Other. The Other has been constructed as less civilized, less spiritual, and less intelligent. As a result, the principles of liberty and equal status under the law have not applied to their everyday lives. This socially constructed nature of a democracy is founded largely on the rights of individuals; however, this view is ahistorical and fails to recognize fully that the U.S. voting system (the Electoral College) and form of government make it a republic rather than a true democracy.

The doctrine of individualism has allowed those individuals with privilege to (falsely) believe that their stations in society are wholly earned. They have gotten what they deserved only through their talent and hard work. For example, in theory, anybody can be president of the United States. But given our history, only White men (who meet the citizenship and age requirements) can achieve that goal. Many groups present in our nation since its inception have not been president, and they do not have a realistic opportunity to be president in the foreseeable future.

In this chapter, we operate under the assumption that our policies and practices must be rooted in the idea of equity. As previously discussed, equity represents what is fair; what is fair is potentially more contested than what is equal. Equity requires affirmative action in the recruitment and hiring of individuals from groups who historically have been underserved. Equity would mean that people of color are strongly present in positions of power in economic, political, legal, and educational institutions throughout society. To achieve this equity, however, we may have to enact policies that fall outside the boundaries of traditional definitions of equality. Namely, we may take up measures such as those articulated by Lani Guinier (1994) to address the "tyranny of the majority." In these policies, the marginalized receive more votes than those who historically have been privileged. The leveraged votes would be one way of addressing inequities manifest in the political spectrum, for example, the marginality and powerlessness of many under the current fundraising schemes. Although we are not necessarily arguing Guinier's points, we do believe that equity and equitable solutions will upset the balance of power and access to services that are limited and coveted by individuals in our society.[2]

This chapter focuses on the basic idea that having equality and justice for all in schooling cannot be achieved in the current climate where students are viewed solely as individuals. In fact, given the educational debt and achievement gaps, the ideas of equality and justice are necessarily contradictory. Achieving justice, in light of the differentiation in academic achievement, cannot be done through equal means; rather, more equitable (or fairer) solutions must be used. Equality reaches the goal of sameness, but it does not necessarily mean justice. Equity reaches the goal of justice, but it is often achieved through unequal means. That is, some schools and some racialized communities (communities who, in a world of Whiteness, are marked as non-White) may receive more than others in a just solution. Although such a solution does not meet the demands of equality, it may meet the demands of equity. Justice is often achieved through unequal means. Equality and equity often are assumed to be synonymous, although we take them to mean quite different things. By more closely examining the nuances of the words *equality* and *equity* and their concomitant arguments toward how schools should work, we also explore the ways that educational research offers a blueprint for how society can better meet the educational needs of all students rather than just some.

We address a number of important issues directly related to race and education with an eye toward considering how issues of educational achievement or the educational debt may be addressed. We analyze the ways in which various educational policies and practices maintain, (re)create, and legitimate the structural inequities in schools and society. We focus on K–12 educational contexts with an eye toward educational opportunities, structural inequities, and implications for teacher training. Finally, we close with a theoretical discussion of race and its relationship to colorblindness, meritocracy, Whiteness, self-determination, and identity. This concluding discussion is meant to draw important concepts out of the empirical work in the previous sections and point toward ways that race must be thought about in future research agendas.

RACIAL INEQUITIES IN K–12 SCHOOLS

There is a long history of structural inequality in high minority schools; these inequalities include, for example, academic tracking practices, inadequately trained teachers, and unacceptable student-to-counselor ratios (Hillis, 1995; Jones, Yonezawa, Ballesteros, & Mehan, 2002; Ladson-Billings, 2006; Reid & Knight, 2006; Yun & Moreno, 2006). All too often, children of color are excluded from the social, political, and economic opportunities to which formal education should provide access (Beauboeuf-Lafontant, 1999). Instead, students of color are pushed toward academic failure and continued social disenfranchisement. Racist policies and beliefs, in part, explain why children and young adults from racially marginalized groups fail to achieve academically at the same rate as their White peers (Blanchett, 2006; Delpit, 1988, 1995; Deyhle, 1995; Fordham, 1996; Fordham & Ogbu, 1986; Hedges & Nowell, 1999; Kaomea, 2001; Ladson-Billings, 1995a, 1996; Lee, 1996; Ogbu, 1992; Ogbu & Simons, 1998; O'Connor, 1997; Thomas, 2004). Although there have certainly been structural changes to schools throughout the past 100 years, inequality has remained, with students of color consistently provided a lower quality education in a system that purports to provide equal educational opportunities (Alexander, 2001; Lewis, 2003, 2004; Vigil, 1999). This inequality is demonstrated in the test scores from the National Assessment of Educational Progress (NAEP) shown in Tables 2 and 3. Although there are many who interpret these disparities as evidence of collective individual traits or motivations, such interpretations cannot account for such clearly group-based disparities.

HOW ASSIMILATIONIST POLICIES AND PRACTICES RELATE TO RACIAL INEQUITY

Some members of racialized groups have fewer educational choices, which is the result of policies and practices that are imbued with Whiteness, creating and sustaining

TABLE 2   NAEP Reading Scores by Race

Race/Ethnicity	Reading Grade 4 (Scale Score) 2005	Reading Grade 8 (Scale Score) 2005
White	229	271
Asian/Pacific Islander	229	271
American Indians/Alaska Natives	204	249
Hispanic	203	246
Black	200	243

Source. National Assessment of Educational Progress (NAEP), Institute for Educational Statistics, The National Report Card, Washington, DC.

TABLE 3   NAEP Math Scores by Race

Race/Ethnicity	Math Grade 4 (Scale Score) 2005	Math Grade 8 (Scale Score) 2005
White	246	295
Asian/Pacific Islander	251	295
American Indians/Alaska Natives	226	264
Hispanic	226	262
Black	220	255

Source. National Assessment of Educational Progress, Institute for Educational Statistics NAEP, The National Report Card, Washington, DC.

structural racism (Artiles, Klingner, & Tate, 2006; Reid & Knight, 2006). Consider, for example, the assimilationist policies and practices throughout the history of U.S. education. Public schools were created in part to assimilate and Americanize the nation's youth, and they have consistently discriminated against immigrants and students of color (Donato & Lazerson, 2000). Urban public school systems were organized in the image of "one best system" (Tyack, 1974) that denied the legitimacy of public participation in educational decision making, undermined teacher professionalism, and rejected the validity of ethnic and racial cultural values that were not White. Other assimilationist policies and practices include the early common schools that aimed to create patriotic Americans among the nation's early immigrants, the boarding schools for Indigenous youth, English-only policies and expectations, and current efforts to force the singing of the national anthem and the reciting of the Pledge of Allegiance while saluting the American flag that must be hung in some states' classrooms—just to name a few. Although we recognize that some scholars have argued that assimilation is a necessary part of academic success in U.S. schools (D'Souza, 1991; Hirsch, *1987, 1986*), we would suggest that although this has historically been true, it does not necessarily have to continue to be true. By assimilation, we mean an act or series of policies that force those who are not like those in power to become more like them or to model themselves after the "norm." Programs or policies of assimilation rarely (if ever) take into account what marginalized groups desire or want and, therefore, deny their right to self-determination. Such policies and practices (such as curricular emphasis on English and Eurocentric history) carry out the will of those who have the power to determine how others can behave within a given context (Apple, 2000). Assimilationist policies are intimately related to calls for equality because equality and sameness are conflated such that history, difference, and differential power are obscured and replaced with one same, Eurocentric structure. Thus, to truly achieve equality and justice for all in our schooling system, we suggest that assimilation must *not* be a prerequisite for academic success.

We fully recognize that schools, through explicit and implicit policies, closet and tamp down some identities while promoting others (Artiles et al., 2006; Fine, 1991; Fordham, 1996; Fordham & Ogbu, 1986; Friend, 1991; Kaomea, 2001; Lee, 1996; Hoffman, 1998; McDermott, Goldman, & Varenne, 2006). These policies often are promoted as colorblind. That is, they seek to make all the students abide by the same rules, protocols, standards, and so forth; however, we argue that they fail to recognize the unique abilities of all learners and they force some students to abandon aspects of their identity that are central to their being, survival, and success. We also recognize that identities are dynamic and contested. When institutions force students to adopt practices and ways that conflict with their own identities, they hinder communities' rights to self-determination. This has been particularly evident in the history and contemporary practices of educating Indigenous and Puerto Rican students in the United States because of the shared emphasis on sovereignty in these communities (although these are certainly not the only communities with this interest). A number of scholars have documented the ways in which education for American Indian students supports deficit assumptions and assimilatory agendas and, therefore, fails to provide equitable educational opportunities for this group of students at both the K–12 and higher education levels (Brayboy & Castagno, 2006; Deyhle & Swisher, 1997; Garrod & Larimore, 1997; Lomawaima, 2000; Lomawaima & McCarty, 2002, 2006; McCarty & Lomawaima, 2002). Del Valle (1998) makes a similar argument for the education provided to Puerto Ricans in New York City; in this context, the efforts toward bilingual education by community members were subverted by lawyers and other professionals in favor of a remedial model of education. Unfortunately, the list of assimilatory projects in U.S. public schools is long (Bonacich, 2000; Olsen, 1997; Valenzuela, 1999).

Fortunately, some researchers have documented and theorized the ways in which students and communities of color engage in accommodation rather than straight assimilation. We use accommodation to mean making the choice to adopt some behaviors or values for the benefit one sees in them. It can be an act of agency, power, and resistance against assimilation. The process of accommodation may be political and strategic. This accommodation may be seen in academic achievement

(Brayboy, 2004, 2005; Fordham, 1996; Fordham & Ogbu, 1986; Lee, 1996, 2005; Solórzano & Delgado Bernal, 2001) or in setting aside the dominant norms of society or of the institution to achieve some other set of goals (Dehyle, 1995; Gibson, 1988). That individuals can make these choices is empowering, although it remains problematic because those who hold power are not forced to examine or reassess. A caveat is in order here; we would argue that there is a state of liminality (V. Turner, 1977) between assimilation and accommodation—that is, there is a place of in-betweenness with respect to assimilation and accommodation; the two can never be fully distinct or separate from one another. This is so, in part, because accommodation is often tinged with resistance-agentic movement against assimilation.

HOW SEGREGATION AND DESEGREGATION RELATE TO RACIAL INEQUITY

Perhaps the best-known case of confusing equality for equity occurred in the 1954 *Brown v. Board of Education* ruling and its aftermath. Recognizing the deep inequities of the segregated schooling system, the court ruled for an end to segregation. The court ordered that equality in education should be achieved through desegregation of schools, improving the quality of education for all students (Meyers & Nidiry, 2004; Smiley, 2004). The court cited the research of Dr. Kenneth Bancroft Clark, whose data, along with others', indicated that segregation resulted in negative psychological effects for both Black and White children, although the effects on White children were never cited by the court and are not much discussed even now (Orfield & Lee, 2006). The court's ruling operated on the assumption that if Black and White students went to school together, they would share the same classrooms, teachers, books, and facilities, and this sharing would result in equality. The hope that material equality could be achieved and that it would rectify the inequities of educational and other societal structures has not proven to be the case. The equality sought by the court was in opposition to notions of White supremacy and did not advance individual White interests. It was strongly resisted through White flight from cities, the movement of students from public to private schools, the continued unequal allocation of resources within and between schools, and White control of desegregated schools (Mawdsley, 2004; Peller, 1996). Despite changes in the law to ensure equal access to schools, the hoped-for equality has never reached a state of equity. Equity in this case would mean that every student has access to all the resources that they need in light of persisting historical inequalities, and it would ensure commensurate educational opportunity and true integration (Blanchett, 2006; M. C. Brown, 2001; Darling-Hammond, 2004; Fine, Weis, & Powell, 1997; McDermott et al., 2006). The resistance to desegregation was such that more than half a century after the *Brown* decision, segregation still affects the progress of school reform (see Anyon, 1997; Ladson-Billings, 2004). This is not to say that desegregation policies have been entirely unsuccessful; they have been at least partially successful in some contexts (Baker, 2001; Orfield & Lee, 2006). But despite the forceful resistance desegregation has encountered, and despite the impossibility of desegregation overcoming all effects of structural inequities, desegregation is still a worthy and viable goal (Crain & Mahard, 1978; Frankerberg, Lee, & Orfield, 2003; Orfield & Lee, 2005). Importantly, however, many school districts are resegregated/ing (Anderson, 2006; Clotfelter, Ladd, & Vigdor, 2002; Frankenberg et al., 2003; Lee, 2006; McNeil, 1993). The irony of judicial and legislative measures promoting educational equality is the way that they have been marshaled (as in the Seattle case before the Supreme Court) to continue educational inequity through colorblind arguments for present-day individual equality, regardless of the effects of long-term historical inequality.

In 1954, the Supreme Court recognized that segregation was correlated with unequal distribution of resources. This remains the case. Segregation, achieved through various means, continues to be mired in resource inequality (Kahlenberg, 2001). Mickelson's (2001) research indicates that material resources are highly correlated to race. White students continue to have access to more and better material resources—indication that schools are unequal and inequitable. Equity can only be achieved when students of color have equitable (which may mean unequal to ensure fairness) access to the material resources associated with increased academic achievement. This association is predicated not only on access to financial resources but on the ways in which such money is used to advance the equity of students (Greenwald, Hedges, & Laine, 1996).

Schools with fewer resources—disproportionately, schools that serve students of color—have higher levels of focus on discipline than their better-funded counterparts (Kozol, 2005; The Advancement Project and The Civil Rights Project, 2000). This focus often leads administrators to prefer "ready-made" discipline policies (N. U. Murray & Garrido, 1995). Zero-tolerance policies are prominent among these policies, but reportedly they do not meet the needs of students, are applied unfairly, and deny rather than advance educational opportunities to students (Bennett, 2002; Casella, 2003). The negative effects of more pervasive emphases on discipline are made even worse because they often are combined with "teaching to the test," rote memorization, drills, worksheets, and less emphasis on critical thinking (Kohn, 2000, 2004; McNeil, 2000; Valenzuela, 1999)—the cumulative impact being a substandard education for students of color and students in underresourced schools. These policies unequally affect not only students by their race but also by disability (Blanchett, 2006; Losen & Orfield, 2002; McDermott et al., 2006; The Advancement Project and The Civil Rights Project, 2000).

Indeed, special education is another school site where students of color are segregated from their White peers (Hosp & Reschly, 2004). Of importance, Artiles et al. (2006) note that "general education cannot afford to ignore the disproportionate representation of minority students in education" (p. 3). Students of color are overrepresented in special education (Bennett, 2002; Hosp & Reschly, 2004); this is attributed to a variety of causes, including racism, the use of culturally and linguistically biased assessments, and power differentials between school leaders and parents of color (Eitle, 2002; Losen & Orfield, 2002; Tippeconnic & Faircloth, 2002; Wells & Serna, 1996). This disproportionate representation means that students of color are attached to the stigma of special education and limited educational access. This stigma attached to the child is one problematic area in the larger debate of race and education. O'Connor and DeLuca Fernandez (2006) note that "disabilities inhere in the child, and the school is merely one site at which special education needs are diagnosed. In contrast, [educators should] hold that schools determine who is more likely to be designated as disabled" (p. 6). McDermott et al. (2006) point out that disabilities are socially constructed and that students of color, or raced students, are at greater risk of being labeled in ways that hinder their abilities to have open educational choices. Reid and Knight (2006) powerfully point to the fact that children (labeled as learning disabled) from White families with annual incomes of more than $100,000 are increasingly going to college, whereas racialized students, who are labeled as learning or emotionally disabled, have fewer and less open educational choices. McDermott et al. (2006) note, "The American classroom is well organized for the production and display of failure, one child at a time if possible, but group by group if necessary" (p. 15). We would add that the U.S. school system and society is well organized for the production of failure for many racialized students. This educational access is limited not only by special education but by other tracking practices, which are entrenched in limiting educational access (Donato & Lazerson, 2000; Hallinan, 1994). When students of color are steered into lower track classes, any initial differences in achievement are only exacerbated (Holzer & Ludwig, 2003; Oakes, 1985; Solórzano & Ornelas, 2002).

HOW CURRICULUM, ASSESSMENT, AND PEDAGOGY RELATE TO RACIAL INEQUITY

Even when students of color are not officially tracked into remedial classes, they often are subjected to less rigorous curriculum. Under the banner of equality, the learning done in such classrooms is subjected to increasing levels of standardized assessment. When standardized tests are attached to high stakes and resources are taken from schools that already have disparate access to resources in the name of equality, equity is not served. Particularly in classrooms with predominantly racialized student populations, teachers tend to focus their teaching on the low-level skills of these tests (Lomax, West, Harmon, Viator, & Madaus, 1995). Standardized tests and assessments also are detrimental to many students of color because they are culturally and linguistically biased (Jimenez, Garcia, & Pearson, 1995), emphasize low-level thinking skills, and often lead teachers to refocus classroom practice around test-taking at the expense of genuine learning (Foster, 1994; Lomawaima & McCarty, 2006; Lomax et al., 1995; McDermott et al., 2006; McNeil, 2000). This low-level skill emphasis is not only limiting because of its level of rigor but also because of its Eurocentric emphasis and lack of representation of the experiences and realities of students of color both in materials and content (Banks, 1998; Bernal, 2002; Conti & Kimmel, 1993; Jimenez et al., 1995). Recently, some scholars have argued that standards and assessments theoretically can be aligned with multicultural and culturally relevant education but that in practice they often are not (Bohn & Sleeter, 2000; Kornhaber, 2004). Unfortunately, the majority of standards and assessments that have been employed in schools have served to reinscribe and reproduce the status quo. These practices are veiled under the banner of meritocracy and equality in that they are touted as being fair—in this case, the idea of fairness actually serves to obscure structural and persistent inequities.

This reproductive nature of curriculum and assessment is closely tied to the low expectations for students of color held by those teachers and policy makers responsible for their development and implementation (Ainsworth-Darnell & Downey, 1998; Downey & Ainsworth-Darnell, 2002; Farkas, 2003; Lareau & Horvat, 1999; Lipman, 1998; Valenzuela, 1999). Given that all of us are enmeshed in the structural racism of society, it is not surprising that teachers often internalize negative messages about students of color; such teacher perceptions negatively affect the academic achievement of their students of color (Bennett, 2002; Buendia, Ares, Juarez, & Peercyet, 2004; Buendia, Gitlin, & Doumbia, 2003; R. T. Carter & Goodwin, 1994; Farkas, 2003; Jones et al., 2002; Katz, 1999; Sleeter, 1993; Solórzano, 1997; Tatto, 1996). Such a situation negates not only the potential of students but also the knowledge and skills that students of color bring from their homes and communities to the classroom (Moll, Amanti, Neff, & González, 1992; Villenas & Dehyle, 1999). School systems rely on meritocracy, which is presumed to be an equalizing power, but when curriculum and assessment are grounded in Eurocentric knowledge paradigms and skills, students of color appear deficient. When the knowledge and skills a student has are not represented or understood in schools, that student is less able to access educational opportunities (Rogoff et al., 2005; Trueba et al., 1997). And when schools do not teach students how to access those educational opportunities, they remain bereft of them (Delpit, 1988, 1995).

Recognizing the racism of such low expectations, many teachers choose to follow colorblind ideologies, doing their best to ignore the racialization of their students. Such a refusal is tantamount to refusing to see the reality that students of color face and only serves to further alienate students and make schools less relevant to their lives (Cochran-Smith, 2000; Pollock, 2004; Trueba et al., 1997).

Recognizing that much of the curriculum directed at students of color is not advancing their educational achievement, educators have tried a variety of inadequate solutions (Diamond & Spillane, 2004). For example, Internet education has been touted as a colorblind solution to such inequities, but the unequal access of students of color to technology only means that the inequities are reentrenched (Moran, 1998; Morse, 2004). There also have been efforts to add programs, classes, and units of curriculum that reflect students' own knowledge and interests, but when these are simply add-ons, they fail to transform the curricula, which can serve to alienate students of color (King, 1995b).

But there also have been successful reforms to curriculum, brought on by teachers and institutions committed to the potential of their students. Much research has documented the power of culturally and linguistically relevant pedagogy to improve the academic achievement of students of color (Braithwaite, 1997; Ladson-Billings, 1995b;

McCarty & Romero, 2005; Pewewardy, 1999). Although numerous scholars have explicated theories, definitions, and approaches to multicultural education, most agree that greater equity will ensue and that students of color will be better educated when schools and teachers embrace more critical forms of multicultural education (Abu El-Haj, 2003, 2006; Banks & Banks, 2001, 2004; R. T. Carter, 2000; R. T. Carter & Goodwin, 1994; Cornbleth & Waugh, 1995; Gay, 2000; Grande, 2000; Grant, Elsbree, & Fondrie, 2004; Grant & Sleeter, 1996; Howard, 1999; King, 1995a; Ladson-Billings, 1994, 1995a, 1995b, 2004; Sleeter, 1996, 1991; Sleeter & Grant, 2003; Sleeter & McLaren, 1995; Smith, 2005b). When teachers, curriculum, and assessment draw on the strengths students bring to the classroom, students are not only more successful but they also are able to see the relevance of school to their own lives (Apthorp, D'Amato, & Richardson, 2002; Gonzalez & Moll, 2002; Hillis, 1995). This requires that teachers engage with the lives of their students and participate in their communities (Cummins, 2001; Ladson-Billings, 1996; Stachowski & Frey, 2002). Culturally and linguistically grounded assessments also are more accurate in determining students' needs, including special education placement (Heimbecker et al., 2001). In addition, when curriculum engages the realities of racism in the classroom, students see their own lives and learn means of navigating the barriers that stand between them and educational achievement, advancing students' own understandings of equity (Banks, 1995; Jervis, 1996; Moses & Chang, 2006; Yosso, 2002). This unveiling of racism and Whiteness in the curriculum affects the learning of all students, including White students who are likely to know less about structural racism through their own experience (Gurin & Nagda, 2006; Humphreys, 1998). Finally, in the midst of all the structural barriers in schools, teachers' nurturing and belief and interest in students improves their academic achievement (Abu El-Haj, 2003, 2006; Conchas, 2001; Jussim, Eccles, & Maddon, 1996; Smith, 2005a; Terenzini et al., 1994).

Even with good intentions, teachers who lack support and training for teaching toward equity may not have the knowledge and resources to carry through such intentions (Achinstein & Barret, 2004). Thus, if educational reform is going to be successful, teacher training programs must prepare teachers with the knowledge and skills they need to participate in equity-driven changes. For such innovations to reach the teaching force at large, teacher education programs must participate. Even those teachers who aim for social justice often are constrained by their own lack of awareness and end up undermining their ability to transform their own practice. As such, Cochran-Smith (1995) argues that teachers need to be able to engage in "unflinching interrogation" of their own teaching (see also E. Brown, 2004; Mazzei, 2004). Thus, institutions of higher education have an important role to play in both providing increased educational opportunities for students and in preparing future teachers for K–12 schools. At the K–12 level, there is a clear need for both a more diverse teaching force and an increase in the number of White allies on the teacher force. White teachers need better training so that we can educate greater numbers of White allies. Part of this training must include exposure to and dialogue about Whiteness and White identity (Alcoff, 1998; Giroux, 1983; McIntyre, 2000). As

Kailin (1999) has argued, preservice and in-service training is necessary to help White teachers see the complexity of institutionalized racism in schools and in their own classrooms. Ideologies of meritocracy and colorblindness work in opposition to this awareness, which makes this work that much more difficult but also that much more crucial.

THEORIZING RACE IN THE EDUCATIONAL RESEARCH LITERATURE

Having reviewed the multiple ways race matters and structures inequities in K–12 and having made some preliminary connections to why this matters for higher education and potential life choices for racialized students, we turn now to a discussion about how scholars might connect the idea of race to colorblindness, meritocracy, Whiteness, self-determination, and identity to draw attention to the concepts we believe are most pertinent to addressing the racial inequities outlined above. We suggest that although much good work has been done, scholars need to combine the current work on racial inequities with a stronger focus on how the educational debt is tied not only to race but also to colorblindness, meritocracy, Whiteness, self-determination, and identity. We recognize that these are contested terms, but our understandings of them are grounded in much research and literature.

Race: A Socially Constructed Concept With Material Consequences

Race is a socially constructed idea (e.g., see Omi & Winant, 1994, for a fuller expression of these notions of the socially constructed nature of race) based on the notion that skin tones are a sign of intellectual and moral competence. Much of the early work of Terman and Yerkes (Terman, 1916; Yerkes, 1915) claimed that certain races inherited inferior IQs that no amount of schooling could ameliorate—nor should it when certain groups were better suited for menial service work. American Indians, African Americans, and Latinos/Latinas are not able to participate fully as informed voters or capable citizens. Out of this eugenics research came the recommendation for special instruction directed to children of these races that would prepare them to be effective workers. The racist idea that aimed to link melatonin and intelligence engendered a racist hierarchy (Kamin & Omari, 1998). This is one example of how an institution (science) fabricated the foundations for an ideology that not only devalued people of color but also justified their exploitation. Terman and Yerkes and the later work of C. A. Murray and Hernnstein (1994) have undermined and continue to undermine the possibility for equality of educational opportunities. The systems of oppression and privilege that have emerged from eugenics shape our interactions in ways that work against democratic ideals and goals.

Researchers have long known "that human populations are not unambiguous, clearly demarcated, biologically distinct groups." Moreover, "evidence from the analysis of genetics (e.g., DNA) indicates that most physical variation, about 94%, lies *within* so-called racial groups. Conventional geographic 'racial' groupings differ from one another only in about 6% of their genes" (American Anthropological Association, 1998). If we know that race is not biological and that there are no direct connections between an individual's racialized status and her or his ability to learn, then we must question society, its educational and social institutions, and its evaluation mechanisms used to determine who achieves. Importantly, we are convinced that teachers, schooling systems, and societies have constructed physical appearance to mean that some students are more capable than others in intellectual abilities.

The notion that racism is real in spite of the fact that race is socially constructed has been the work of Critical Race Theorists (see Crenshaw, Gotanda, Peller, & Thomas, 1995; Delgado Bernal, 2002; Ladson-Billings, 1999; Lopez, 2003; Lynn, 2004; Parker, 2001; Parker, Deyhle, & Villenas, 1999; Parker & Lynn, 2002; Solórzano & Delgado Bernal, 2001; Solórzano & Villalpando, 1998; Solórzano & Yosso, 2002; Tate, 1997), among others, who acknowledge that racism exists in individual, societal, institutional, and civilizational forms (Scheurich & Young, 1997, 2002). To be sure, racism is not only an antagonistic force with which people of color contend. Racism is also a system of values and practices embodied and enacted by powerful Whites that they need to explore, understand, and undermine. Finally, we recognize that racism is responsible for (overt and covert) calls for assimilation and colorblindness.

Colorblindness and Meritocracy: Mechanisms of Equality

We understand the notion of colorblindness to be (among other things) the inability or unwillingness to see or talk about race and its implications. The gap in understanding in White consciousness comes from generations of lives lived in freedom and immunity from the manifest tribulations of racism, as well as from the retelling of stories that comfort and absolve them from racism. These stories form a history, which, with help from the media, has taught us that color is undesirable and noticing it is offensive. Proponents of colorblindness aim to protect innocence, yet that innocence is pernicious. Ignoring race erases the social and economic implications of a system where the boundaries between success and failure, poverty and privilege are drawn largely across racial lines. The concepts around colorblindness are often most clearly articulated by individuals who say they either "do not see skin color" or by falling back into a democratically based assumption (rooted in a modern reading of the Constitution) that argues "we're all human beings." Notably, in his dissent regarding the University of Michigan lawsuit, Supreme Court Justice Antonin Scalia wrote, "In the eyes of the law, we are all one race—American." It is precisely this language that conservative (and, more recently, neoconservative) scholars, associations, think tanks, and legal organizations have taken up as a guide in their quest to remove all mention of race from educational discourse, admissions and hiring policies, and research. On the other hand, race-cognizant individuals confront their complicity as people who gain privilege from racist structures. They are watchful of the way they think about, and relate to, the Other and how the language they use may implicate them in the structural racism that limits the opportunities of the Other.

Colorblindness is tied to the illusion that race no longer matters in the life of an individual, community, society, and its legal, financial, political, and educational institutions. Directly tied to the illusion is either an explicit denial or an ignorance of the history, present, and future of race relations. If race no longer matters, it allows individuals and groups who hold financial, political, and educational power the ability to maintain policies and the resulting practices that keep them, and those like them, in power—the result of colorblindness.

In addition, colorblindness can be a defense mechanism used by those in power because of the direct connection between race relations (historical, present, and future) and conflict and shame. Recognition of race and racism are necessarily tied to these emotions; nevertheless, it is imperative that our attention stays focused on the salience of race in today's society. Such recognition allows us to engage in conversations and research that ask important questions, such as, why are there such disparate results between the level of academic achievement of marginalized students (such as students of color) and of those students who fit dominant society's ideal? How is their group membership treated in education?

Colorblindness and meritocracy are very much connected. Both concepts are touted as positive and fundamental American ideals. Both relate to understandings of freedom, equality, and justice, and perhaps most important, both serve as barriers to achieving greater equity in schooling and larger society. Much of our understanding of colorblindness is based on a meritocratic ideology that teaches that individuals move ahead on the basis of their inherent talent and hard work. Under this ideology, the individual is paramount. All other aspects that give meaning to the way we as Americans (or more precisely, citizens and residents of the United States) live our lives are not considered when assessing achievement. This worldview fails to recognize that many individuals of color; women; and lesbian, gay, bisexual, and transgender people identify as both individuals and as members of groups, so others treat them simply as members of the larger group: society. This larger group membership is assumed (incorrectly) to negate all other group memberships. Racism exists, in part, because policies and those who create and enact them treat individuals solely as members of society, effectively negating any semblance of fairness by erasing the very real and powerful implications of their group memberships. The erasure or invisibility of these implications has profound implications on privilege, inequity, and maintaining the racial status quo in academic achievement. It is to an examination of Whiteness that we now turn.

Whiteness: Maintaining Privilege, Inequity, and the Racial Status Quo

Examinations of race in education have recently included numerous explicit discussions of Whiteness and White supremacy. Whiteness studies are so crucial because the so-called "underachievement" of students of color must be understood as made up of both "Black" and "White" causes and predecessors (Powell, 1997). As Winant (2001) has argued, Whites and Whiteness can no longer be exempt from

racial discourses and projects. Although educational researchers all need to do a better job of talking about race, racism, and Whiteness (Rains, 1998), we do not mean
to imply a decentering of the experiences, learning, and achievement of students of
color (Howard, 2000). Rather, we argue that some attention to Whiteness may help
illuminate why the educational debt is so persistent and why equality is a continu-
ous stand-in for equity in educational debates, policies, and practices. Blanchett
(2006) is more direct when she writes,

> The problem of disproportionate representation of African Americans [and we would argue American
> Indians/Alaska Natives, some Asian Americans, Latinas/Latinos, and Pacific Islanders] in special educa-
> tion is not just a special education issue or concern but, instead, must be viewed in the context of White
> privilege and racism that exist in American society as a whole and the educational system, specifically.
> (p. 24)

Whiteness is sometimes difficult to name and often slips between various definitions without warning (Rasmussen, Klinenberg, Nexica, & Wray, 2001). Discussions
of Whiteness also become complicated because of the ways in which it intersects with
class, gender, sexuality, and other identity categories. Although most Whiteness
scholars agree that it is intimately connected with power, there is less consensus
regarding what Whiteness is exactly (Kincheloe & Steinberg, 1998). Multiple scholars
have written about Whiteness as a set of unearned privileges enjoyed by White people,
a normalization of what's right, and a norm against which everything else gets measured (Fine, Powell, Weis, & Mun Wong, 1997; Frankenberg, 1993, 2001; McIntosh,
1988; Roediger, 2000; Thompson, 1999, 2000, 2003, 2004). Other scholars have provided illuminating historical analyses of Whiteness—particularly how Whiteness has
been conflated with property and individual property rights through the law (Harris,
1995), how Whiteness has been possessively invested in by groups throughout history
to secure their own interests and guard those interests against the encroachment of others (Lipsitz, 1998), and how Whiteness has morphed and taken on new forms depending on time and context (Duster, 2001). These characteristics of Whiteness help
illuminate its connections to meritocracy and colorblindness. Of importance, history
and the law have conspired to veil the fact that Whiteness equals privilege and to allow
White people to claim (and genuinely believe) that we are all equal in a democracy—
the connections to colorblind ideologies are never hard to find (Blanchett, 2006;
O'Connor & DeLuca Fernandez, 2006; Reid & Knight, 2006).

One helpful explanation of Whiteness is provided by Dyson, who argues that
Whiteness is an identity, ideology, and an institution (Chennault, 1998; Dyson, 1996).
As an identity, Whiteness refers to the racial characteristic of being White, and although
some good work has been done on Whiteness as an identity in various contexts (Perry,
2002), we are more concerned here with Whiteness as an ideology and an institution
because of the ways this informs educational achievement and issues of equality and
equity in education. Put bluntly, institutions are organized such that being White buys
both privilege and protection from discrimination, distrust, questions, and a host of
other negative experiences (Brookfield, 2003; Fine, 1997). This subverts opportunities

for people of color in policies and practices that appear race-neutral. The system of dominance allows for the re-creation and continuation of privilege, even by those who are well intentioned. The system was set up by White people to benefit White people, who mystify the system and remove the agent and then continue to benefit from the system without being held responsible (Leonardo, 2004). In other words, Whites have successfully made it appear that meritocracy is real and that the United States is a level playing field while *also* obscuring their (our) own role in creating and maintaining a system that is neither level nor meritocratic but instead benefits them (us).

Because we are primarily interested in Whiteness as an ideology and an institution, we employ the notion of White supremacy to make sense of the pervasive and oppressive nature of Whiteness. By White supremacy, we do not mean the notion that drives hate groups around the world; rather, we refer to the historical power of White people in this country manifested particularly in the law and its practice. Because Whites have believed themselves superior to all others, their laws have made them beneficiaries. The Constitution of the United States, for example, summarily endorsed White supremacy when it counted a Black person as three-fifths of one person. This supremacy was fortified with the policies and treatment of slaves and ex-slaves, American Indians, immigrants from China and other Asian countries, Mexicans from annexed Mexico, Japanese citizens who were interned during World War II, and other groups who were relegated to stations that served at the whim of those in power. White supremacy is sometimes blatant, as is evidenced by the above examples. At other times, it is insidious and quite subtle in the everyday microaggressions experienced by people of color and perpetuated by White people (Lee, Spencer, & Harpalani, 2003; Pierce, 1974; Smith, 2005a; Solórzano & Yosso, 2001). Either way, White supremacy leads to entitlement among those who are privileged and, too often, tacit acceptance by those who are not, in such a way that we come to expect certain social conditions and view those expectations (and conditions) as natural and normal. Hence, when benefits are perceived to be infringed on (as in, e.g., affirmative action and school desegregation), it is understood as unfair and reverse racism—as evidenced in the 2006 Seattle case heard by the U.S. Supreme Court.

SELF-DETERMINATION

Self-determination is the ability to define oneself and what's best for oneself and one's own community (economically, politically, and socially—in this case, as related to education). In each case of self-determination, there are both implicit and explicit moves to resist the pressures to assimilate. If a community decides who they are as people, this may (or may not) differ from what may be viewed as the "norm." However, claiming the right to make those decisions is a direct challenge to the power of others to define community and self. Self-determination entails giving communities the power to take charge of both the curricular material presented in schools and the preparation of teachers who understand the local political, economic, cultural, and racial contexts (Cochran-Smith, 1995, 2000, 2004; Fine et al., 1997; Freire, 1973; Ladson-Billings, 1994, 2001; Ladson-Billings & Darling-Hammond, 2000; Nieto, 1999). The ways in which American Indians have responded to assimilationist educational policies such as boarding schools (Adams, 1995; Almeida, 1997; Child, 1999; Lomawaima, 1994, 2000; Lomawaima & McCarty, 2002) and Indian schools (McCarty, 2001; McCarty, Yamamoto, Watahomigie, & Zepeda, 1997; Philips, 1983; Wax, Wax, & Dumont, 1964) stand as notable examples of what communities can do to determine for themselves how the education of their youth will proceed (McCarty, 2005; Trujillo, Figueira, Viri, & Macuelito, 2003).

But American Indians, in their quest to actualize their unique political status, are not the only group that has engaged new notions in their struggle for self-determination. There is a clear connection between self-determination and resistance (Giroux, 1983). Resistance is a political act whereby individuals and communities refuse to be defined by, assimilated by, or coerced into inauthentic behaviors by individuals and policies that wield power in institutions such as schools, which are key sites where self-determination can have maximum impact for equity (Moses, 2002b). There are examples of such resistance to assimilation through self-determination in all communities of color in the United States and through various strategies (Cammarota, 2004; Knight, 2003; Solórzano & Delgado Bernal, 2001). Some of this resistance is readily identifiable as resistance-faculty and students working within schools (Bloom & Erlandson, 2003; Donato, 1999) and academia (hooks, 1994; Napier, 1995; Williams, 1991) and exercising self-determination through parental involvement (López, 2001) and community networking (Walsh, 1998; Zine, 2000). Other resistance strategies may be less identifiable to power holders. For example, schools that enforce colorblind policies— effectively closeting identities of students of color—encounter explicit forms of resistance, such as "behavioral problems" and students who drop out (Deyhle, 1995, 1998; Fine, 1991). There are other subtler forms of resistance that individuals enact to skirt the stifling, restraining policies and practices that include conforming to accepted practices of schooling to be academically successful (Brayboy, 2004, 2005; Cammarota, 2004; P. L. Carter, 2005; Delgado Bernal, 2002; Fordham, 1996; Fordham & Ogbu, 1986; Gayles, 2005; Solórzano & Villalpando, 1998; Yosso, 2000). Ultimately, self-determination is a political act whereby communities and groups seek to define for themselves the conditions of schooling and life. We do not deny the salience of power that others often hold over marginalized communities, and we are not under the impression that these communities can simply change the social order. We do, however, recognize that groups and communities can and do work toward defining themselves in spite of the power differential.

Central to a return to the natural state of self-determination is the work of researchers challenging assimilationist policies in research methodologies and the epistemologies that undergird those choices (Tillman, 2002). A significant methodological shift in education research is the growing focus on Critical Race Theory (CRT; see the recent Lynn, Yosso, Solórzano, & Parker, 2002, review of CRT literature). One of the important issues that CRT and other methodological concerns highlight is the importance of a researcher's positionality (Banks & Jewell, 1995; Best, 2003; Ladson-Billings, 2000; Twine & Warren, 2000). Scholars also have raised the question of how the underrepresentation of people of color in the field limit the discoveries possible (Donato & Lazerson, 2000; Garcia & Baird, 2000; Gordon, 1997). Also limiting to the research about race in education is the domination of Eurocentric epistemologies in the field (Gasman, Gerstl-Pepin, Anderson-Thompkins, Rasheed, & Hathaway, 2004; Maher & Tetreault, 1993; Scheurich & Young, 1997). However, a number of researchers have advanced research methodologies that rely on the epistemologies of communities of color (Bernal, 1998; Grande, 2004; Kaomea, 2001).

Identity: Multiple Variables Affecting Racial Inequities

When researchers, policymakers, and teachers recognize that individual and community histories are not equal, they can move policies toward equity. Often, members from marginalized groups who are able to exist and are successful on a number of levels under the policies articulated by those with power may be called assimilated by those with power and members of their own group. We recognize that there is conflict as to what counts as assimilation or the idea that identity politics are real and contested. As scholars, regardless of our racialized status, we must recognize that we are, in fact, part of a system that has racist policies and procedures that we may enact and be complicit in carrying out through our presence and participation in the institution. At its base, however, assimilation exists in a manner that is incomplete. By this, we mean that the verb *assimilating* exists but the actual state of being assimilated is an illusion. A state of liminality can never be overcome by assimilation. Because we believe that race still matters, those individuals who are physically different continue to encounter the racist policies and assumptions that will never fully allow complete assimilation. Returning to the biological definition of race, society returns to a state of homeostasis by marginalizing individual members of a certain race or marginalized status. In this way, individual and community identities are targeted by society.

Identity has become a catchall term to discuss how individuals make sense of who they are in relation to other individuals, communities, and society (Hoffman, 1998). We suggest that identity is a social process in which individuals mutually constitute each other in and through their relationships with others, community, and society, that is, it both includes and moves beyond notions of self (Gergen, 1995; Goffman, 1955; Hoffman, 1998; Wortham, 2001) to incorporate notions of how community and society play into the discussions of who individuals are (Bradley, 1995; Brayboy, 2004; Davis, 1996; Deyhle, 1995; Eckert, 1996; Fordham, 1996; Fordham & Ogbu, 1986; K. Hall, 2002; S. Hall, 1992; Lee, 1996; Pillow, 2003; Warriner, 2004a, 2004b). We also recognize that there is a multiplicity of identities that make up individuals, communities, and societies. Scholars have examined how these identities intersect with one another and affect the way that individuals act on and are acted on by institutional structures. These scholars have focused on a variety of intersections—race and geography (Ainsworth-Darnell & Downey, 1998; Buendia et al., 2004), race and class (Ainsworth-Darnell & Downey, 1998; Crain & Marhard, 1978; Hones, 1999; Lareau & Horvat, 1999), race and ethnicity (Ainsworth-Darnell & Downey, 1998; Lee, 1996; Pang,

Kiang, & Pak, 2003), race and culture (De Graaf, 1986; Downey & Ainsworth-Darnell, 2002; Gutierrez & Rogoff, 2003; James, Chavez, Beauvais, Edwards, & Oetting, 1995; Lee et al., 2003; Smith & Kulynych, 2002; Trueba et al., 1997; Valenzuela, 1999), race and language (Abedi, 2004; Cummins, 2000; Trueba et al., 1997), race and immigration status (Hones, 2002; Lee, 1997, 2001, 2005; McKay & Wong, 1996; Midobuche, 2001; Olsen, 1997; Rong & Brown, 2001; Valenzuela, 1999), race and gender (Alemán, 2000; Allen, 1986; Fine & Weis, 1998; Jackson, 1998; Lopez, 2003; C. S. V. Turner, 2002), and race and sexual orientation (Athanases, 1996; Snider, 1996). Within an individual's multiple identities, those identities that come to the fore are often strategic, based on the spaces in which the identities are negotiated and enacted and the demands coming from these contexts. Often, these identities get conflated; parts of people's identities are hard to isolate and there are strong correlations between many of these factors and race. However, it is important that we not lose sight of the fact that race alone (as well as in intersection with other identities) is a socially constructed reality with significant educational consequences in U.S. schools.

CONCLUSION: RACE STILL MATTERS DESPITE OUR UNANSWERED QUESTIONS

In this chapter, we have examined recent research on race in education. This research makes clear that racialized groups continue to have unequal access to educational resources. It also makes clear that equality by itself may not be able to overcome the long history of influence of structural racism on American schools and racialized communities. Equality, that is, sameness, would not create equity for these communities. Students in racialized communities continue to score lower on national standardized tests. They also continue to be subjected to policies and practices focusing on assimilation, which create situations where students are less able to make identity choices. These students are increasingly segregated from their White peers by school and track, and racialized students' schools and tracks are provided with fewer resources and less rigorous curriculum. All this has not gone unnoticed by many teachers; many of these teachers have found ways to alter their pedagogy to create more equity in their classrooms. This research points us to a stronger focus on how Ladson-Billings's educational debt is tied to race and also to colorblindness, meritocracy, Whiteness, self-determination, and identity.

Race still matters in the sense that structural racism is abundant and children of color continually underperform according to standardized measures of achievement in the current educational system. Most African American, American Indian, Latinas/Latinos, and Pacific Islanders are underrepresented in gifted areas and overrepresented in special education. These groups too are less likely to be adequately prepared for college and have fewer opportunities to make choices about their futures. Through policies and institutional mechanisms, racism is firmly entrenched yet invisible to many. The preponderance of research we have highlighted in this chapter points to the fact that there are tremendous racial inequities in schooling. Ladson-Billings (2006) remarked that the educational debt for people of color is at a crisis level and her use of the term "educational debt" rather than "achievement gap" highlights the fact that the United States still has debts to pay to communities (especially children) of color.

Equitable democracy can exist only if we choose to see color and are attentive to it and conscious of our existence in all its nexuses. We must ask questions such as, How is our life tied with the lives of others? How is our privilege at someone else's expense? How are the decisions we make tied to the well-being of others no matter how removed by race, nationality, or geography? Ultimately, what happens when individual perspectives of equal or equitable access conflict within a system that is rooted in zero-sum relationships that conceive of resources as limited? Furthermore, we wonder if access is indeed equal and if equality of educational opportunity exists or if it is simply an imagined ideal that allows those who have real opportunities to claim that those who do not are either inferior or simply need to work harder.

NOTES

[1] The education debt refers to the *cumulative* impact of centuries of educational inequities related to funding, curricula, resources, teachers, segregation, and so forth. This education debt is composed of historical, economic, sociopolitical, and moral components and requires a more holistic, historic, and comprehensive analysis of schooling than that implied by the focus on achievement gaps.

[2] Of importance, Guinier's (1994) writings and views eventually cost her a nomination as an Assistant Attorney General under the presidency of William Jefferson Clinton. Clearly, engaging in this work is not without costs.

REFERENCES

Abedi, J. (2004). The no child left behind act and English language learners: Assessment and accountability issues. *Educational Researcher, 33*(1), 4–14.

Abu El-Haj, T. R. (2003). Practicing for equity from the standpoint of the particular: Exploring the work of one urban teacher network. *Teachers College Record, 105*(5), 817–845.

Abu El-Haj, T. R. (2006). *Elusive justice: Wrestling with difference and educational equity in everyday practice.* New York: Routledge-Falmer.

Achinstein, B., & Barret, A. (2004). (Re)framing classroom contexts: How new teachers and mentors view diverse learners and challenges of practice. *Teachers College Record, 106*(4), 716–746.

Adams, D. W. (1995). *Education for extinction: American Indian and the boarding school experience, 1875–1928.* Lawrence: University Press of Kansas.

Ainsworth-Darnell, J. W., & Downey, D. B. (1998). Assessing the oppositional culture explanation for racial/ethnic differences in school performance. *American Sociological Review, 63*(4), 536–553.

Alcoff, L. M. (1998). What should White people do? *Hypatia, 13*(3), 6–26.

Alemán, A. M. M. (2000). Race talks: Undergraduate women of color and female relationships. *Review of Higher Education, 23*(2), 133–152.

Alexander, K. L. (2001). The clouded crystal ball: Trends in educational stratification. *Sociology of Education, 74*, 169–177.

Allen, P. G. (1986). *The sacred hoop: Recovering the feminine in American Indian traditions.* Boston: Beacon.

Almeida, D. (1997). The hidden half: A history of Native American women's education. *Harvard Educational Review, 67*(4), 757–771.

American Anthropological Association. (1998). *American Anthropological Association statement on "race."* Retrieved November 9, 2006, from http://www.aaanet.org/stmts/racepp.htm

Anderson, J. D. (2006) Still desegregated, still unequal: Lessons from up north. *Educational Researcher, 35*(1), 30–33.

Anyon, J. (1997). *Ghetto schooling: A political economy of urban educational reform.* New York: Teachers College Press.

Apple, M. W. (2000). Can critical pedagogies interrupt rightist policies? *Educational Theory, 50*(2), 229–254.

Apthorp, H. S., D'Amato, E. D., & Richardson, A. (2002). *Effective standards-based practices for Native American students: A review of research literature.* Aurora, CO: Mid-Continent Research for Education and Learning.

Artiles, A. J., Klinger, J. K., & Tate, W. F. (2006). Representation of minority students in special education: Complicating traditional explanations. *Educational Researcher, 35*(6), 3–5.

Athanases, S. Z. (1996). A gay-themed lesson in an ethnic literature curriculum: Tenth graders' responses to "Dear Anita." *Harvard Educational Review, 66*(2), 231–256.

Baker, R. S. (2001). The paradoxes of desegregation: Race, class, and education, 1935–1975. *American Journal of Education, 109*(3), 320–343.

Banks, J. A. (1995). The historical reconstruction of knowledge about race: Implications for transformative teaching. *Educational Researcher, 24*(2), 15–25.

Banks, J. A. (1998). The lives and values of researchers: Implications for educating citizens in a multicultural society. *Educational Researcher, 27*(7), 4–17.

Banks, J., & Banks, C. M. (Eds.). (2001). *Multicultural education: Issues and perspectives* (4th ed.). New York: John Wiley.

Banks, J., & Banks, C. M. (Eds.). (2004). *Handbook of research on multicultural education.* San Francisco: Jossey-Bass.

Banks, W. M., & Jewell, J. (1995). Intellectuals and the persisting significance of race. *Journal of Negro Education, 64*(1), 75–86.

Beauboeuf-Lafontant, T. (1999). A movement against and beyond boundaries: "Politically relevant teaching" among African American teachers. *Teachers College Record, 100*(4), 702–723.

Bennett, C. I. (2002). Enhancing ethnic diversity at a big ten university through project TEAM: A case study in teacher education. *Educational Researcher, 31*(2), 21–29.

Bernal, D. (1998). Using a Chicana feminist epistemology in educational research. *Harvard Educational Review, 68*(4), 555–581.

Bernal, D. (2002). Critical race theory, Latino critical theory, and critical raced-gendered epistemologies: Recognizing students of color as holders and creators of knowledge. *Qualitative Inquiry, 8*(1), 105–126.

Best, A. (2003). Doing race in the context of feminist interviewing: Constructing Whiteness through talk. *Qualitative Inquiry, 9*(6), 895–914.

Blanchett, W. J. (2006). Disproportionate representation of African American students in special education: Acknowledging the role of White privilege and racism. *Educational Researcher, 35*(6), 24–28.

Bloom, C. M., & Erlandson, D. A. (2003). African American women principals in urban schools: Realities, (re)constructions, and resolutions. *Educational Administration Quarterly, 39*(3), 339–369.

Bohn, A., & Sleeter, C. E. (2000). Multicultural education and the standards movement: A report from the field. *Phi Delta Kappan, 82*(2), 156–159.

Bonacich, E. (2000). Racism in the deep structure of U.S. higher education: When affirmative action is not enough. In A. Aguirre & D. V. Baker (Eds.), *Structured inequality in the United States: Discussions on the continuing significance of race, ethnicity, and gender* (pp. 67–76). Upper Saddle River, NJ: Prentice Hall.

Bradley, B. (1995). America's challenge: Revitalizing our national community. *National Civic Review, 84*(2), 95.

Braithwaite, C. A. (1997). Sa'ah naaghai bik'eh hozhoon: An ethnography of Navajo educational communication practices. *Communication Education, 46*(4), 219–233.

Brayboy, B. McK. J. (2004). Hiding in the ivy: American Indian students and visibility in elite educational settings. *Harvard Educational Review, 74*(2), 125–152.

Brayboy, B. McK. J. (2005). Transformational resistance and social justice: American Indians in Ivy League universities. *Anthropology and Education Quarterly, 36*(3), 193–211.

Brayboy, B. McK. J. & Castagno, A. E. (2006) *A review of American Indians in higher education.* Unpublished manuscript.

Brookfield, S. D. (2003). Racializing the discourse of adult education. *Harvard Educational Review, 73*(4), 497–523.

Brown, E. (2004). What precipitates change in cultural diversity awareness during a multicultural course: The message or the method? *Journal of Teacher Education, 55*, 325–340.

Brown, M. C. (2001). Collegiate desegregation and the public black college. *Journal of Higher Education, 72*(1), 46–62.

Buendia, E., Ares, N., Juarez, B. G., & Peercyet, M. (2004). The geographies of difference: The production of the East Side, West Side, and Central City school. *American Educational Research Journal, 41*(4), 833–863.

Buendia, E., Gitlin, A., & Doumbia, F. (2003). Working the pedagogical borderlands: An African Critical pedagogue teaching within an ESL context. *Curriculum Inquiry, 33*(3), 291–320.

Cammarota, J. (2004). The gendered and racialized pathways of Latina and Latino youth: Different struggles, different resistances in the urban context. *Anthropology & Education Quarterly, 35*(1), 53–74.

Carter, P. L. (2005). *Keepin' it real: School success beyond Black and White.* London: Oxford University Press.

Carter, R. T. (2000). Reimagining race in education. *Teachers College Record, 102*(5), 864–897.

Carter, R. T., & Goodwin, A. L. (1994). Racial identity and education. *Review of Research in Education, 20*, 291–336.

Casella, R. (2003). Zero tolerance policy in schools: Rationale, consequences, and alternatives. *Teachers College Record, 105*(5), 872–892.

Chennault, R. (1998). Giving Whiteness a Black eye: An interview with Michael Eric Dyson. In J. Kincheloe, S. Sheinberg, N. Rodriguez, & R. Chennault (Eds.), *White reign: Deploying Whiteness in America* (pp. 299–328). New York: St. Martin's Griffin.

Child, B. J. (1999). *Boarding school seasons: American Indian families, 1900–1940.* Lincoln: University of Nebraska Press.

Clotfelter, C. T., Ladd, H. F., & Vigdor, J. L. (2002, August). *Segregation and resegregation in North Carolina's public school classrooms.* Paper presented at the Conference on the Resegregation of Southern Schools, Chapel Hill, NC.

Cochran-Smith, M. (1995). Uncertain allies: Understanding the boundaries of race and teaching. *Harvard Educational Review, 65*(4), 541–570.

Cochran-Smith, M. (2000). Blind vision: Unlearning racism in teacher education. *Harvard Educational Review, 70*(2), 157–190.

Cochran-Smith, M. (2004). Taking stock in 2004: Teacher education in dangerous times. *Journal of Teacher Education, 55*(1), 3–7.

Conchas, G. Q. (2001). Structuring failure and success: Understanding the variability in Latino school engagement. *Harvard Educational Review, 71*(3), 475–504.

Conti, N. E., & Kimmel, E. B. (1993). *Gender and cultural diversity bias in developmental textbooks.* Paper presented at the annual meeting of the Southeastern Psychological Association, Atlanta, GA.

Cornbleth, C., & Waugh, D. (1995). *The great speckled bird: Multicultural politics and education policymaking.* New York: St. Martin's Press.

Crain, R., & Mahard, R. E. (1978). Desegregation and Black achievement: A review of the research. *Law and Contemporary Problems, 42*(3), 17–56.

Crenshaw, K., Gotanda, N., Peller, G., & Thomas, K. (Eds.). (1995). *Critical race theory: The key writings that formed the movement.* New York: New Press.

Cummins, J. (2000). Language interactions in the classroom: From coercive to collaborative relations of power. In J. Cummins (Ed.), *Language, power and pedagogy: Bilingual children in the crossfire* (pp. 66–76). Clevedon, UK: Multilingual Matters.

Cummins, J. (2001). Empowering minority students: A framework for intervention. *Harvard Educational Review, 71*(4), 656–676.

Darling-Hammond, L. (2004).The color line in American Education: Race, resources, and student achievement. *W. E. B. DuBois Review, 1*(2), 213–246.

Davis, A. (1996). Identity notes part one: Playing in the light. *American University Law Review, 45*(3), 695–720.

De Graaf, P. M. (1986). The impact of financial and cultural resources on educational attainment in the Netherlands. *Sociology of Education, 59,* 237–246.

Delgado Bernal, D. (2002). Critical race theory, LatCrit theory and critical race-gendered epistemologies: Recognizing students of color as holders and creators of knowledge. *Qualitative Inquiry, 8*(1), 105–126.

Delpit, L. (1988). The silenced dialogue: Power and pedagogy in educating other people's children. *Harvard Educational Review, 58*(3), 280–298.

Delpit, L. (1995). *Other people's children: Cultural conflict in the classroom.* New York: New Press.

Del Valle, S. (1998). Bilingual education for Puerto Ricans in New York City: From hope to compromise. *Harvard Educational Review, 68*(2), 193–217.

Deyhle, D. (1995). Navajo youth and Anglo racism: Cultural integrity and resistance. *Harvard Educational Review, 65*(3), 403–444.

Deyhle, D. (1998). From break dancing to heavy metal: Navajo youth, resistance, and identity. *Youth and Society, 30*(1), 3–31.

Deyhle, D., & Swisher, K. (1997). Research in American Indian and Alaska Native education: From assimilation to self-determination. *Review of Research in Education, 22,* 113–194.

Diamond, J. B., & Spillane, J. P. (2004). High-stakes accountability in urban elementary schools: Challenging or reproducing inequality? *Teachers College Record, 106*(6), 1145–1176.

Donato, R. (1999). Hispano education and the implications of autonomy: Four school systems in southern Colorado, 1920–1963. *Harvard Educational Review, 69*(2), 117–149.

Donato, R., & Lazerson, M. (2000). New directions in American educational history: Problems and prospects. *Educational Researcher, 29*(8), 4–15.

Downey, D. B., & Ainsworth-Darnell, J. W. (2002). The search for oppositional culture among Black students. *American Sociological Review, 67,* 156–164.

D'Souza, D. (1991). *Illiberal education: The politics of race and sex on campus.* New York: Free Press.

Duster, T. (2001). The "morphing" properties of Whiteness. In B. Rasmussen, E. Klinenberg, I. Nexica, & M. Wray (Eds.), *The making and unmaking of Whiteness* (pp. 113–137). Durham, NC: Duke University Press.

Dyson, M. (1996). *Race rules: Navigating the color line.* Reading, MA: Addison-Wesley.

Eckert, P. (1996). Vowels and nail polish: The emergence of linguistic style in the preadolescent heterosexual marketplace. In N. Warner (Ed.), *Gender and belief systems: Proceedings of the Fourth Berkeley Women and Language Conference* (pp. 183–190). Berkeley, CA: Berkeley Women and Language Group.

Eitle, T. M. (2002). Special education or racial segregation: Understanding variation in the representation of Black students in educable mentally handicapped programs. *The Sociological Quarterly, 43*(4), 575–605.

Farkas, G. (2003). Racial disparities and discrimination in education: What do we know, how do we know it, and what do we need to know? *Teachers College Record, 105*(6), 1119–1146.

Fine, M. (1991). *Framing dropouts: Notes on the politics of an urban public high school.* Ithaca: State University of New York Press.

Fine, M. (1997). Witnessing Whiteness. In M. Fine, L. Powell, L. Weis, & L. Mun Wong (Eds.), *Off White: Readings on race, power, and society* (pp. 57–65). New York: Routledge.

Fine, M., Powell, L., Weis, L., & Mun Wong, L. (1997). Preface. In M. Fine, L. Powell, L. Weis, & L. Mun Wong (Eds.), *Off White: Readings on race, power, and society* (pp. vii–xii). New York: Routledge.

Fine, M., & Weis, L. (1998). *The unknown city: The lives of poor and working-class young adults.* Boston: Beacon.

Fine, M., Weis, L., & Powell, L. C. (1997). Communities of difference: A critical look at desegregated spaces created for and by youth. *Harvard Educational Review, 67*(2), 247–284.

Fordham, S. (1996). *Blacked out: Dilemmas of race, identity, and success at Capital High.* Chicago: University of Chicago Press.

Fordham, S., & Ogbu, J. (1986). Black students' school success: Coping with the burden of "acting White." *Urban Review, 13*(3), 54–84.

Foster, M. (1994). Effective Black teachers: A literature review. In E. R. Hollins, J. E. King, & W. C. Hyman (Eds.), *Teaching diverse populations: Formulating a knowledge base* (pp. 225–242). Albany: State University of New York Press.

Frankenberg, R. (1993). *White women, race matters: The social construction of Whiteness.* Minneapolis: University of Minnesota Press.

Frankenberg, R. (2001). The mirage of an unmarked Whiteness. In B. Rasmussen, E. Klinenberg, I. Nexica, & M. Wray (Eds.), *The making and unmaking of Whiteness* (pp. 72–96). Durham, NC: Duke University Press.

Frankerberg, E., Lee, C., & Orfield, G. (2003). *A multiracial society with segregated schools: Are we losing the dream?* Cambridge, MA: The Civil Rights Project, Harvard University.

Freire, P. (1973). *Pedagogy of the oppressed.* New York: Seabury.

Friend, R. (1991). Choices, not closets: Heterosexism and homophobia in schools. In M. Fine & L. Weis (Eds.), *Beyond silenced voices* (pp. 209–235). Albany: State University of New York Press.

Garcia, M., & Baird, L. L. (2000). The shape of diversity. *Journal of Higher Education, 71*(2), 117–246.

Garrod, A., & Larimore, C. (1997). *First person, first peoples: Native American college graduates tell their life stories.* Ithaca, NY: Cornell University Press.

Gasman, M., Gerstl-Pepin, C., Anderson-Thompkins, S., Rasheed, L., & Hathaway, K. (2004). Negotiating power, developing trust: Transgresssing race and status in the academy. *Teachers College Record, 106*(4), 689–715.

Gay, G. (2000). *Culturally responsive teaching: Theory, research, and practice.* New York: Teachers College Press.

Gayles, J. (2005). Playing the game and paying the price: Academic resilience among three high-achieving African American males. *Anthropology & Education Quarterly, 36*(3), 250–264.

Gergen, K. J. (1995). Singular, socialized, and relational selves. In I. Lubek, R. Van Hazewijk, G. Pheterson, & C. Tolman (Eds.), *Trends and issues in theoretical psychology* (pp. 25–32). New York: Springer-Verlag.

Gibson, M. A. (1988). *Accommodation without assimilation: Sikh immigrants in an American high school.* Ithaca, NY: Cornell University Press.

Giroux, H. (1983). Theories of reproduction and resistance in the new sociology of education: A critical analysis. *Harvard Educational Review, 55*(3), 257–293.

Goffman, E. (1955). On face-work: An analysis of ritual elements in social interaction. *Psychiatry: Journal of Interpersonal Relations, 18*(3), 213–231.

Gonzalez, N., & Moll, L. C. (2002). Cruzando el puente: Building bridges to funds of knowledge. *Educational Policy, 16*(4), 623–641.

Gordon, E. W. (1997). Task force on the role and future of minorities American Educational Research Association. *Educational Researcher, 26*(3), 44–52.

Grande, S. (2004). *Red pedagogy: Native American social and political thought.* Boulder, CO: Rowman & Littlefield.

Grande, S. M. A. (2000). American Indian geographies of identity and power: At the crossroads of indigena and mestizaje. *Harvard Educational Review, 70*(4), 467–498.

Grant, C., Elsbree, A., & Fondrie, S. (2004). A decade of research on the changing terrain of multicultural education research. In J. Banks & C. M. Banks (Eds.), *The handbook of research on multicultural education* (2nd ed.). San Francisco: Jossey-Bass.

Grant, C., & Sleeter, C. E. (1996). *After the school bell rings.* London: Falmer.

Greenwald, R., Hedges, L. V., & Laine, R. D. (1996). The effect of school resources on student achievement. *Review of Educational Research, 66*(3), 361–396.

Guinier, L. (1994). *Tyranny of the majority: Fundamental fairness in representative democracy.* New York: Free Press.

Gurin, P., & Nagda, B. A. (2006). Getting to the what, how and why of diversity on campus. *Educational Researcher, 35*(1), 20–24.

Gutierrez, K., & Rogoff, B. (2003). Cultural ways of learning: Individual traits or repertoires of practice. *Educational Researcher, 32*(5), 19–25.

Hall, K. (2002). *Lives in translation: Sikh youth as British citizens.* Philadelphia: University of Pennsylvania Press.

Hall, S. (1992). Race, culture, and communication: Looking backward and forward at cultural studies. *Rethinking Marxism, 5*(1), 10–18.

Hallinan, M. T. (1994). Tracking from theory to practices. *Sociology of Education, 67*(2), 79–91.

Harris, C. (1995). Whiteness as property. In K. Crenshaw, N. Gotanda, G. Peller, & K. Thomas (Eds.), *Critical Race Theory: Key writings that formed the movement* (pp. 276–291). New York: The New Press.

Hedges, L. V., & Nowell, A. (1999). Changes in the Black-White gap in achievement test scores: The evidence from nationally representative samples. *Sociology of Education, 72*, 111–135.

Heimbecker, C., Bradley-Wilkinson, E., Nelson, B., Smith, J., Whitehair, M., Begay, M. H., et al. (2001, March). *Rural Navajo students in Kayenta unified school district's special education programs: The effects of home location and language.* Paper presented at Growing Partnerships for Rural Special Education, San Diego, CA.

Hillis, M. R. (1995). Allison Davis and the study of race, social class, and schooling. *The Journal of Negro Education, 64*, 33–41.

Hirsch, E. D. (1986). *The schools we need and why we don't have them.* New York: Doubleday.

Hirsch, E. D. (1987). *Cultural literacy, what every American needs to know.* Boston: Houghton Mifflin.

Hoffman, D. M. (1998). A therapeutic moment? Identity, self, and culture in the anthropology of education. *Anthropology & Education Quarterly, 29*(3), 324–346.

Holzer, H. J., & Ludwig, J. (2003). Measuring discrimination in education: Are methodologies from labor and housing markets useful? *Teachers College Record, 105*(6), 1147–1178.

Hones, D. F. (1999). Making peace: A narrative study of a bilingual liaison, a school and a community. *Teachers College Record, 101*(1), 106–134.

Hones, D. F. (2002). In quest of freedom: Towards critical pedagogy in the education of bilingual youth. *Teachers College Record, 104*(6), 1163–1186.

hooks, b. (1994). *Teaching to transgress: Education as the practice of freedom.* New York: Routledge.

Hosp, J. L., & Reschly, D. J (2004). Disproportionate representation of minority students in special education: Academic, demographic and economic predictors. *Exceptional Children, 70*, 185–199.

Howard, G. (1999). *We can't teach what we don't know: White teachers, multiracial schools.* New York: Teachers College Press.

Howard, G. R. (2000). Reflections on the "White movement" in multicultural education. *Educational Researcher, 29*(8), 21–23.

Humphreys, D. (1998). *Higher education, race and diversity: Views from the field.* Washington, DC: Association of American Colleges and Universities.

Illinois Interactive Report Card. (2005). *East St Louis senior high school (9 –12).* Retrieved February 11, 2007, from http://iirc.niu.edu/Scripts/school.asp?schoolID=5008218900043&test=all

Illinois Interactive Report Card. (2005). *New Trier Township H S Winnetka (10–12).* Retrieved February 11, 2007, from http://iirc.niu.edu/Scripts/school.asp?schoolID= 1401620300001&colName=SCHLNAME&searchStr=new%20trier&test=all

Jackson, L. R. (1998). The influence of both race and gender on the experiences of African American college women. *The Review of Higher Education, 21*(4), 359–375.

James, K., Chavez, E., Beauvais, F., Edwards, R., & Oetting, G. (1995). School achievement and dropout among Anglo and Indian females and males: A comparative examination. *American Indian Culture and Research Journal, 19*(3), 181–206.

Jervis, K. (1996). "How come there are no brothers on that list?" Hearing the hard questions all children ask. *Harvard Educational Review, 66*(3), 546–575.

Jimenez, R. T., Garcia, G. E., & Pearson, P. D. (1995). Three children, two languages, and strategic reading: Case studies in bilingual/monolingual reading. *American Educational Research Journal, 32*(1), 67–97.

Jones, M., Yonezawa, S., Ballesteros, E., & Mehan, H. (2002). Shaping pathways to higher education. *Educational Researcher, 31*(2), 3–11.

Jussim, L., Eccles, J., & Maddon, S. J. (1996). Social perceptions, social stereotypes, and teacher expectations: Accuracy and the quest for the powerful self-fulfilling prophecy. *Advances in Experimental Social Psychology, 28*, 281–388.

Kahlenberg, R. D. (2001). An unambitious legacy. *Education Week, 20*(23), 48.

Kailin, J. (1999). How White teachers perceive the problem of racism in their schools: A case study in "liberal" Lakeview. *Teachers College Record, 100*(4), 724–750.

Kamin, L. J., & Omari, S. (1998). Race, head size and intelligence. *South African Journal of Psychology, 28*, 119–128.

Kaomea, J. (2001). Dilemmas of an indigenous academic: A Native Hawaiian story. *Contemporary Issues in Early Childhood, 2*(1), 67–82.

Katz, S. R. (1999). Teaching in tensions: Latino immigrant youth, their teachers, and the structures of schooling. *Teachers College Record, 100*(4).

Kincheloe, J., & Steinberg, S. (1998). Addressing the crisis of Whiteness: Reconfiguring White identity in a pedagogy of Whiteness. In J. Kincheloe, S. Sheinberg, N. Rodriguez, & R. Chennault (Eds.), *White reign: Deploying Whiteness in America* (pp. 3–30). New York: St. Martin's Griffin.

King, J. E. (1995a). Culture-centered knowledge: Black studies, curriculum transformation, and social action. In J. A. Banks & C. M. Banks (Eds.), *Handbook of research on multicultural education.* New York: Simon & Schuster Macmillan.

King, W. M. (1995b). The triumphs of tribalism: The modern American university as a reflection of Eurocentric culture. In B. P. Bowser, T. Jones, & G. A. Young (Eds.), *Toward the multicultural university.* Westport, CT: Praeger.

Knight, M. G. (2003). Through urban youth's eyes: Negotiating K–16 policies, practices, and their futures. *Educational Policy, 17*(5), 561–557.

Kohn, A. (2000). *The case against standardized testing: Raising the scores, ruiing the schools.* New York: Heinemann.

Kohn, A. (2004). *What does it mean to be well educated? And more essays on standards, grading, and other follies.* Boston: Beacon.

Kornhaber, M. (2004). Assessment, standards, and equity. In J. Banks & C. Banks (Eds.), *Handbook of research on multicultural education* (pp. 91–109). San Francisco: Jossey-Bass.

Kozol, J. (2005). *The shame of the nation: The restoration of apartheid schooling in America.* New York: Crown.

Ladson-Billings, G. (1994). *The dreamkeepers: Successful teachers of African American children.* San Francisco: Jossey-Bass.

Ladson-Billings, G. (1995a). But that's just good teaching! The case for culturally relevant pedagogy. *Theory Into Practice, 34*(3), 159–165.

Ladson-Billings, G. (1995b). Toward a theory of culturally relevant pedagogy. *American Educational Research Journal, 32*(3), 465–491.

Ladson-Billings, G. (1996). Lifting as we climb: The womanist tradition in multicultural education. In J. Banks (Ed.), *Multicultural education, transformative knowledge, and action: Historical and contemporary perspectives.* New York: Teachers College Press.

Ladson-Billings, G. (1999). Just what is critical race theory and what's it doing in a nice field like education? In L. Parker, D. Deyhele, & S. Villenas (Eds.), *Race is . . . race isn't: Critical race theory and qualitative studies in education* (pp. 7–30). Boulder, CO: Westview.

Ladson-Billings, G. (2000). Racialized discourses and ethnic epistemologies. In Y. Lincoln & N. Denzin (Eds.), *Handbook of qualitative research* (2nd ed., pp. 257–277). Thousand Oaks, CA: Sage.

Ladson-Billings, G. (2001). *Crossing over to Canaan: The journey of new teachers in diverse classrooms.* San Francisco: Jossey-Bass.

Ladson-Billings, G. (2004). Landing on the wrong note: The price we paid for Brown. *Educational Researcher, 33*(7), 3–13.

Ladson-Billings, G. (2006, April). *From the achievement gap to the education debt: Understanding achievement in U.S. schools.* Paper presented at the American Educational Research Association annual meetings, San Francisco.

Ladson-Billings, G., & Darling-Hammond, L. (2000, May). *The validity of national board for professional teaching standards (NBPTS)/ interstate new teacher assessment and support consortium (INTASC) assessments for effective urban teachers: Findings and implications for assessments.* Paper prepared for the National Partnership for Excellence and Accountability in Teaching.

Lareau, A., & Horvat, E. M. (1999). Moments of social inclusion and exclusion: Race, class, and cultural capital in family-school relationships. *Sociology of Education, 72*(1), 37–53.

Lee, S. (1996). *Unraveling the "model minority" stereotype: Listening to Asian American youth.* New York: Teachers College Press.

Lee, S. (1997). The road to college: Hmong American women's pursuit of higher education. *Harvard Educational Review, 67*(4), 279–305.

Lee, S. (2001). More than "model minorities" or "delinquents": A look at Hmong American high school students. *Harvard Educational Review, 71*(3), 505–528.

Lee, S. (2005). *Up against Whiteness: Race, school, and immigrant youth.* New York: Teachers College Press.

Lee, C. (2006). *Denver public schools: Resegregation, Latino style.* Cambridge, MA: The Civil Rights Project, Harvard University.

Lee, C. D., Spencer, M. B., & Harpalani, V. (2003). "Every shut eye ain't sleep": Studying how people live culturally. *Educational Researcher, 32*(5), 6–13.

Leonardo, Z. (2004). The color of supremacy: Beyond the discourse of "White privilege." *Educational Philosophy and Theory, 36*(2), 137–152.

Lewis, A. (2003). *Race in the schoolyard: Negotiating the color line in classrooms and communities.* New Brunswick, NJ: Rutgers University Press.

Lewis, A. (2004). "What group?" Studying Whites and Whiteness in the era of "color-blindness." *Sociological Theory, 22*(4), 623–646.

Lipman, P. (1998). *Race, class, and power in school restructuring.* Albany: State University of New York Press.

Lipsitz, G. (1998). *The possessive investment in Whiteness: How White people profit form identity politics.* Philadelphia: Temple University Press.

Lomawaima, K. T. (1994). *They called it prairie light: The story of Chilocco Indian school.* Lincoln: University of Nebraska Press.

Lomawaima, K. T. (2000). Tribal sovereigns: Reframing research in American Indian education. *Harvard Educational Review, 70*(1), 1–21.

Lomawaima, K. T., & McCarty, T. L. (2002). When tribal sovereignty challenges democracy: American Indian education and the democratic ideal. *American Educational Research Journal, 39*(2), 279–305.

Lomawaima, K. T., & McCarty, T. L. (2006). *"To remain an Indian": Lessons in democracy from a century of Native American education.* New York: Teachers College Press.

Lomax, R. G., West, M. M., Harmon, M. C., Viator, K. A., & Madaus, G. F. (1995). The impact of mandated standardized testing on minority students. *The Journal of Negro Education, 64*(2), 171–185.

López, G. R. (2001). The value of hard work: Lessons on parent involvement from an (im)migrant household. *Harvard Educational Review, 71*(2), 416–437.

Lopez, N. (2003). *Hopeful girls, troubled boys.* New York: Routledge.

Losen, D. J., & Orfield, G. (2002). *Racial inequality in special education: Executive summary for policy makers.* Cambridge, MA: The Civil Rights Project, Harvard University.

Lynn, M. (2004). Inserting the race into critical pedagogy: an analysis of race-based epistemologies. *Journal of Educational Philosophy and Theory, 37*(2), 153–165.

Lynn, M., Yosso, T. J., Solórzano, D. G., & Parker, L. (2002). Critical race theory and education: Qualitative research in the new millennium. *Qualitative Inquiry, 8*(1), 3–6.

McCarty, T. L. (2001). *A place to be Navajo: The struggle for self-determination in indigenous schooling.* Mahwah, NJ: Lawrence Erlbaum.

McCarty, T. L. (Ed.). (2005). *Language, literacy, and power in schooling.* Mahwah, NJ: Lawrence Erlbaum.

McCarty, T. L., & Lomawaima, K. T. (2002). When tribal sovereignty challenges democracy: American Indian education and the democratic ideal. *American Educational Research Journal, 39*(2), 279–305.

McCarty, T. L., & Romero, M. E. (2005). What does it mean to lose a language? Investigating heritage language loss and revitalization among American Indians. *Show & Tell,* pp. 14–17.

McCarty, T., Yamamoto, A., Watahomigie, L., & Zepeda, O. (1997). School-community-university collaborations: The American Indian language development institute. In J. Reyhner (Ed.), *Teaching indigenous languages* (pp. 85–104). Flagstaff: Northern Arizona University Press.

McDermott, R., Goldman, S., & Varenne, H. (2006). The cultural work of learning disabilities. *Educational Researcher, 35*(6), 12–17.

McIntosh, P. (1988). White privilege and male privilege: A personal account of coming to see correspondences through work in Women's Studies. In R. Delgado & J. Stefancic (Eds.), *Critical White studies: Looking behind the mirror* (pp. 291–299). Philadelphia: Temple University Press.

McIntyre, A. (2000). A response to Rosa Hernandez sheets. *Educational Researcher, 29*(9), 26–27.

McKay, S. L., & Wong, S. L. C. (1996). Multiple discourses, multiple identities: Investment and agency in second-language learning among Chinese adolescent immigrant students. *Harvard Educational Review, 66*(3), 577–608.

McNeil, L. (1993). *Contradictions of control: School structure and school knowledge.* New York: Routledge.

McNeil, L. (2000). *Contradictions of school reform: Educational costs of standardized testing.* New York: Routledge.

Maher, F. A., & Tetreault, M. K. (1993). Frames of positionality: Constructing meaningful dialogues about gender and race. *Anthropological Quarterly, 66*(3), 118–126.

Mawdsley, R. D. (2004). A legal history of Brown and a look to the future. *Education and Urban Society, 36*(3), 245–254.

Mazzei, L. A. (2004). Silent listenings: Deconstructive practices in discourse-based research. *Educational Researcher, 33*(2), 26–34.

Meyers, M., & Nidiry, J. P. (2004). Kenneth Bancroft Clark: The uppity Negro integrationist. *Antioch Review, 62*(2), 265–274.

Mickelson, R. A. (2001). Subverting Swann: First- and second-generation segregation in the Charlotte-Mecklenburg schools. *American Educational Research Journal, 38*(2), 215–252.

Midobuche, E. (2001). More than empty footprints in the sand: Educating immigrant children. *Harvard Educational Review, 71*(3), 529–535.

Moll, L. C., Amanti, C., Neff, D., & González, N. (1992). Funds of knowledge for teaching: A qualitative approach to developing strategic connections between homes and classrooms. *Theory Into Practice, 31*(2), 132–141.

Moran, R. F. (1998). Diversity, distance, and the delivery of higher education. *Ohio State Law Journal, 59,* 775–792.

Morse, T. E. (2004). Ensuring equality of educational opportunity in the digital age. *Education and Urban Society, 36*(3), 266–279.

Moses, M. (2002a). *Embracing race: Why we need race-conscious education policy.* New York: Teachers College Press.

Moses, M. (2002b). The heart of the matter: Philosophy and educational research. *Review of Research in Education, 26,* 1–21.

Moses, M. S., & Chang, M. J. (2006). Toward a deeper understanding of the diversity rationale. *Educational Researcher, 35*(1), 6–11.

Murray, C. A., & Hernnstein, R. J. (1994). *The bell curve: Intelligence and class structure in American life.* New York: Free Press.

Murray, N. U., & Garrido, M. (1995). Violence, non-violence, and the lessons of history: Project HIP-HOP journeys south. *Harvard Educational Review, 65*(2), 231–257.

Napier, L. A. (1995). Educational profiles of nine gifted American Indian women and their own stories about wanting to lead. *Roeper Review, 18*(1).

Nieto, S. (1999). *The light in their eyes: Creating multicultural learning communities.* New York: Teachers College Press.

Oakes, J. (1985). *Keeping track: How schools structure inequality.* New Haven, CT: Yale University Press.

O'Connor, C. (1997). Dispositions toward (collective) struggle and educational resilience in the inner city: A case analysis of six African American High school students. *American Educational Research Journal, 34*(4), 593–629.

O'Connor, C., & DeLuca Fernandez, S. (2006). Race, class and disproportionality: Reevaluating the relationship between poverty and special education placement. *Educational Researcher, 35*(6), 6–11.

Ogbu, J. (1992). Understanding cultural diversity and learning. *Educational Researcher, 21*(8).

Ogbu, J. U., & Simons, H. D. (1998). Voluntary and involuntary minorities: A cultural-ecological theory of school performance with some implications for education. *Anthropology and Education Quarterly, 29*(2), 155–188.

Olsen, L. (1997). *Made in America: Immigrant students in our public schools.* New York: New Press.

Omi, H., & Winant, H. (1994). *Racial formation in the United States: From the 1960s to the 1990s.* New York: Routledge.

Orfield, G., & Lee, C. (2005). *Why segregation matters: Poverty and educational inequality.* Cambridge, MA: The Civil Rights Project, Harvard University.

Orfield, G., & Lee, J. (2006). *Tracking achievement gaps and assessing the impact of NCLB on the gaps: An in-depth look into national and state reading and math outcome.* Cambridge, MA: The Civil Rights Project, Harvard University.

Pang, V. O., Kiang, P., & Pak, Y. K. (2003). Asian Pacific American students: Fighting over-generalizations. In J. A. Banks & C. A. McGee Banks (Eds.), *Handbook of research on multicultural education* (2nd ed.). San Francisco: Jossey-Bass.

Parker, L. (2001). Statewide assessment triggers urban school reform: But how high the stakes for urban minorities? *Education and Urban Society, 33*(3), 313–319.

Parker, L., Deyhle, D., & Villenas, V. (Eds.). (1999). *Race is . . . race isn't: Critical race theory and qualitative studies in education.* Boulder, CO: Westview.

Parker, L., & Lynn, M. (2002). What's race got to do with it? Critical race theory's conflicts with and connections to qualitative research methodology and epistemology. *Qualitative Inquiry, 8*(1), 7–22.

Peller, G. (1996). Toward a critical cultural pluralism: Progressive alternatives to mainstream civil rights ideology. In K. Crenshaw, N. Gotanda, G. Peller, & K. Thomas (Eds.), *Critical race theory: The key writings that formed the movement* (pp. 127–158). New York: The New Press.

Perry, P. (2002). *Shades of White: White kids and racial identities in high school.* Durham, NC: Duke University Press.

Pewewardy, C. (1999). Culturally responsive teaching for American Indian students. In E. Hollins & E. Oliver (Eds.), *Pathways to success in school: Culturally responsive teaching* (pp. 85–100). Mahwah, NJ: Lawrence Erlbaum.

Philips, S. (1983). *The invisible culture: Communication in classroom and community on the Warm Springs Indian reservation.* New York: Longman.

Pierce, C. (1974). Psychiatric problems of the Black minority. In S. Arieti (Ed.), *American handbook of psychiatry* (pp. 512–523). New York: Basic Books.

Pillow, W. S. (2003). Race-based methodologies: Multicultural methods or epistemological shifts? In G. Lopez & L. Parker (Eds.), *Interrogating racism in qualitative research methodology* (pp. 181–202). New York: Peter Lang.

Powell, L. (1997). The achievement (k)not: Whiteness and "Black underachievement." In M. Fine, L. Powell, L. Weis, & L. Mun Wong (Eds.), *Off White: Readings on race, power, and society* (pp. 3–12). New York: Routledge.

Pollock, M. (2004). Race bending: "Mixed" youth practicing strategic racialization in California. *Anthropology & Education Quarterly, 35*(1), 30–52.

Rains, F. (1998). Is the benign really harmless? Deconstructing some "benign" manifestations of operationalized White privilege. In J. Kincheloe, S. Sheinberg, N. Rodriguez, & R. Chennault (Eds.), *White reign: Deploying Whiteness in America* (pp. 77–102). New York: St. Martin's Griffin.

Rasmussen, B., Klinenberg, E., Nexica, I., & Wray, M. (Eds.). (2001). *The making and unmaking of Whiteness.* Durham, NC: Duke University Press.

Reid, D. K., & Knight, M. G. (2006). Disability justifies exclusion of minority students: A critical history grounded in disability studies. *Educational Researcher, 35*(6), 18–23.

Roediger, D. R. (2000). *The wages of Whiteness.* London: Verso.

Rogoff, B., Moore, L., Najafi, B., Dexter, A., Correa-Chavez, M., & Solis, J. (2005). Children's development of cultural repertoires through participation in everyday routines and practices. In J. Grusec & P. Hastings (Eds.), *Handbook of socialization* (pp. 211–225). New York: Guilford.

Rong, X. L., & Brown, F. (2001). The effects of immigrant generation and ethnicity of educational attainment among young African and Caribbean Blacks in the United States. *Harvard Educational Review, 71*(3), 536–565.

Scheurich, J., & Young, M. (1997). Coloring epistemologies: Are our research epistemologies racially biased? *Educational Researcher, 26*(4), 4–16.

Scheurich, J., & Young, M. (2002). White racism among White faculty. In W. Smith, P. Altbach, & K. Lomotey (Eds.), *The racial crisis in American higher education: Continuing challenges for the twenty-first century* (Rev. ed., pp. 221–242). New York: State University of New York Press.

Sleeter, C. E. (Ed.). (1991). *Empowerment through multicultural education.* Albany: State University of New York Press.

Sleeter, C. E. (1993). How White teachers construct race. In C. McCarthy & W. Crichlow (Eds.), *Race, identity, and representation in education* (pp. 151–171.) New York: Routledge.

Sleeter, C. E. (1996). *Multicultural education as social activism.* Albany: State University of New York Press.

Sleeter, C. E., & Grant, C. (2003). *Making choices for multicultural education: Five approaches to race, class, and gender* (4th ed.). Hoboken, NJ: John Wiley.

Sleeter, C. E., & McLaren, P. (1995). *Multicultural education, critical pedagogy, and the politics of difference.* Albany: State University of New York Press.

Smiley, T. (2004). *Brown v. Board of Education*: An unfinished agenda. In J. Anderson & D. N. Byrne (Eds.), *The unfinished agenda of* Brown v. Board of Education (pp. 1–6). Hoboken, NJ: John Wiley.

Smith, A. (2005a). Conferring with young second-language writers: Keys to success. *New Horizons for Learning Online Journal, 11*(2).

Smith, A. (2005b). Native American feminism, sovereignty, and social change. *Feminist Studies, 31*(1), 116–132.

Smith, S. S., & Kulynych, J. (2002). It may be social, but why is it capital? The social construction of social capital and the politics of language. *Politics & Society, 30*(1), 149–186.

Snider, K. (1996). Race and sexual orientation: The (im)possibility of these intersections in educational policy. *Harvard Educational Review, 66*(2), 294–302.

Solórzano, D. (1997). Images and words that wound: Critical race theory, racial stereotyping and teacher education. *Teacher Education Quarterly, 24*, 5–19.

Solórzano, D. G., & Delgado Bernal, D. (2001). Examining transformational resistance through a critical race theory and LatCrit theory framework: Chicana and Chicano students in an urban context. *Urban Education, 36*(3), 308–342.

Solórzano, D. G., & Ornelas, A. (2002). A critical race analysis of advanced placement classes: A case of educational inequality. *Journal of Latinos and Education, 1*(4), 215–229.

Solórzano, D. G., & Villalpando, O. (1998). Critical race theory, marginality, and the experiences of students of color in higher education. In C. Torres & T. Mitchell (Eds.), *Sociology of education: Emerging perspectives* (pp. 211–224). Albany: State University of New York Press.

Solórzano, D. G., & Yosso, T. (2001). From racial stereotyping and deficit discourse toward a critical race theory in teacher education. *Multicultural Education, 9*(1), 2–8.

Solórzano, D. G., & Yosso, T. (2002). A critical race counterstory of race, racism, and affirmative action. *Equity and Excellence in Education, 35*(2), 155–168.

Stachowski, L. L., & Frey, C. J. (2002, February). *Lessons learned in Navajoland: Student teachers reflect on professional and cultural learning in reservation schools and communities.* Paper read at the annual meeting of the Association of Teacher Educators, Jacksonville, FL.

Tate, W. (1997). Critical race theory and education: History, theory, and implications. *Review of Research in Education, 22*, 195–247.

Tatto, M. T. (1996). Examining values and beliefs about teaching diverse students: Understanding the challenges for teacher education. *Educational Evaluation and Policy Analysis, 18*(2), 155–180.

The Advancement Project and The Civil Rights Project. (2000, June). *Opportunities suspended: The devastating consequences of zero tolerance and school discipline.* Paper read at A National Summit on Zero Tolerance, Washington, DC.

Terenzini, P. T., Rendon, L. L., Upcraft, M. L., Millar, S. B., Allison, K. W., & Gregg, P. L. (1994). The transition to college: Diverse students, diverse stories. *Research in Higher Education, 35*(1), 57–73.

Terman, L. M. (1916). *The measurement of intelligence: An explanation of and a complete guide for the use of the Stanford revision and extension of the Binet-Simon Intelligence Scale.* Boston: Houghton Mifflin.

Thomas, M. K. (2004). The SAT II: Minority/majority test-score gaps and what they could mean for college admissions. *Social Science Quarterly, 85*(5), 1319–1334.

Thompson, A. (1999). Colortalk: Whiteness and off White. *Educational Studies, 30*(2), 141–160.

Thompson, A. (2000). "We are chauvinists": Sexual entitlement and sexual harassment in a high school. In S. E. Wade (Ed.), *Preparing teachers for inclusive education: Case pedagogies and curricula for teacher educators* (pp. 185–195). Mahwah, NJ: Lawrence Erlbaum.

Thompson, A. (2003). Tiffany, friend of people of color: White investments in antiracism. *International Journal of Qualitative Studies in Education, 16*(1), 7–29.

Thompson, A. (2004). Gentlemanly orthodoxy: Critical race feminism, Whiteness theory, and the APA manual. *Educational Theory, 54*(1), 27–57.

Tillman, L. (2002). Culturally sensitive research approaches: An African American perspective. *Educational Researcher, 31*(9), 3–12.

Tippeconnic, J. W., & Faircloth, S. C. (2002). *Using culturally and linguistically appropriate assessments to ensure that American Indian and Alaska Native students receive the special education programs and services they need.* (ERIC ED 1.331/2:EDO–RC–02–8)

Trueba, H., Takaki, R., Muñoz, V. I., Nieto, S., Andersen, M. L., & Sommer, D. (1997). Ethnicity and education forum: What difference does difference make? *Harvard Educational Review, 67*(2), 169–187.

Trujillo, O. V., Figueira, A., Viri, D., & Macuelito, K. (2003, April). *Native educators interface with culture and language in schooling.* Paper presented at the American Educational Research Association, Chicago.

Turner, C. S. V. (2002). Women of color in academe: Living with multiple marginality. *Journal of Higher Education, 73*(1), 74–93.

Turner, V. (1977). *The ritual process: Structure and anti-structure.* Ithaca, NY: Cornell University Press.

Twine, F., & Warren, J. (Eds.). (2000). *Racing research and researching race: Methodological dilemmas in critical race studies.* New York: New York University Press.

Tyack, D. (1974). *The one best system: A history of American urban education.* Cambridge, MA: Harvard University Press.

Valenzuela, A. (1999). *Subtractive schooling: U.S.-Mexican youth and the politics of caring.* Albany: State University of New York Press.

Vigil, J. D. (1999). Streets and schools: How educators can help Chicano marginalized gang youth. *Harvard Educational Review, 69*(3), 270–288.

Villenas, S., & Dehyle, D. (1999). Critical race theory and ethnographies challenging the stereotypes: Latino families, schooling, resilience, and resistance. *Curriculum Inquiry, 29*(4), 413–445.

Walsh, C. E. (1998). "Staging encounters": The educational decline of U.S. Puerto Ricans in [post]-colonial perspective. *Harvard Educational Review, 68*(2), 218–243.

Warriner, D. S. (2004a). "The days now is very hard for my family": The negotiation and construction of gendered work identities among newly arrived women refugees. *Journal of Language, Identity, and Education*, *3*(4), 279–294.

Warriner, D. S. (2004b). Multiple literacies and identities: The experiences of two women refugees. *Women Studies Quarterly*, *32*(1&2), 179–195.

Wax, M., Wax, R., & Dumont, R.V., Jr. (1964). *Formal education in an American Indian community*. Prospect Heights, IL: Waveland.

Wells, A. S., & Serna, I. (1996). The politics of culture: Understanding local political resistance to detracking in racially mixed schools. *Harvard Educational Review*, *66*(1), 93–118.

Williams, P. (1991). *The alchemy of race and rights: Diary of a law professor*. Cambridge, MA: Harvard University Press.

Winant, H. (2001). White racial projects. In B. Rasmussen, E. Klinenberg, I. Nexica, & M. Wray (Eds.), *The making and unmaking of Whiteness* (pp. 97–112). Durham, NC: Duke University Press.

Wortham, S. (2001). *Narratives in action: A strategy for research and analysis*. New York: Teachers College Press.

Yerkes, R. M. (1915). A point scale for measuring mental ability. *Proceedings of the National Academies of Science of the United States of America*, *1*(2), 114–117.

Yosso, T. J. (2000). *A critical race and LatCrit approach to media literacy: Chicana/o resistance to visual microaggressions*. Los Angeles: Department of Social Sciences and Comparative Education, University of California, Los Angeles.

Yosso, T. J. (2002). Toward a critical race curriculum. *Equity and Excellence in Education*, *35*(2), 93–107.

Yun, J. T., & Moreno, J. (2006). College access, K–12 concentrated disadvantage, and the next 25 years of education research. *Educational Researcher*, *35*(1), 12–19.

Zine, J. (2000). Redefining resistance: Towards an Islamic subculture in schools. *Race Ethnicity and Education*, *3*(3), 293–316.

Chapter 7

A Selected History of Social Justice in Education

JOY ANN WILLIAMSON
LORI RHODES
MICHAEL DUNSON
Stanford University

Contemporary politicians, teachers, parents, and educational reformers are locked in a heated debate regarding the definition of social justice in education. Is it an education that will give students skills to alter the social order, or is it an education that will enable students to fit themselves into a higher station in that social order? Should the academic achievement of individuals or groups be the unit of analysis used to examine social justice? Can social justice be achieved through an education that promotes assimilation, or must it be an education for cultural maintenance (or something in between)? The debate can be loosely organized in two ideological camps. On one hand, social justice is the promise of equity and mobility through assimilation and the belief that such an agenda will return schools to a time in which they fostered togetherness under the banner of Americanization (Marshall & Parker, n.d.). On the other hand, social justice in education is reflected in a curriculum and school personnel who honor students' languages and cultures, foster appreciation of difference, and engage in a moral use of power that resists discrimination and inequity (American Educational Research Association, Leadership for Social Justice Special Interest Group, n.d.).

This chapter uses the words of historical actors and historians to inform the current debate regarding how social justice should be defined and delivered. A history of social justice in education is useful for at least two reasons. First, these competing notions of social justice in education are not new. Tension between a belief in assimilation and the ability of individuals to climb the meritocratic ladder and the belief in a respect for cultural and linguistic differences and a flattening of the racial, ethnic, and linguistic hierarchy has existed since the start of the common school system (Tyack, 1993). Second, current educational reformers and others appropriate history and memory to justify certain avenues to social justice. As Hom and Yamamoto (2000) state,

Review of Research in Education
March 2007, Vol. 31, pp. 195–224
DOI: 10.3102/0091732X07300465
© 2007 AERA. http://rre.aera.net

action on justice claims often turns on which memories are acknowledged by decisionmakers. Collective memory thus is always hotly contested by those supporting and those opposing justice claims. Indeed, struggles over memory are often struggles between colliding ideologies, or vastly differing world views. (p. 1765)

Examining the history of social justice in education, therefore, not only illuminates what transpired but also provides a portrait of how, why, and the end to which the history of education is managed for contemporary purposes (Donato & Lazerson, 2000; Franke, 2000).

The first part of the chapter examines the promise of assimilation or the lack thereof in American educational history in order to assess if this promise was genuine, desirable, or fulfilled in the educational experiences of American Indians, Mexican Americans, Chinese Americans, Japanese Americans, and African Americans. The focus is on the battle against segregated schooling, but the desire for desegregation and assimilation should not be understood as synonymous. The pairing is used here to highlight how those groups considered assimilable and those considered unassimilable were deliberately segregated by White communities and school boards. The second part of the chapter examines how these racial and ethnic groups created and/or fortified separate schooling experiences that directly contradicted the assimilationist vision of social justice and how their efforts are understood by historians. Historical actors, much like the Leadership for Social Justice Special Interest Group, believed that cultural and linguistic integrity and maintenance form the basis of social justice and that collective rather than individual advancement was the proper marker for gauging success. Historians, however, like other scholars, debate whether the efforts of these historical actors furthered or hindered the pursuit of social justice in education.[1]

RACIAL CATEGORIES AND SCHOOLING

Before beginning a discussion of the particular experiences of these different racial and ethnic groups, it is important to understand how conceptions of race and a racial hierarchy influenced their schooling experiences. In the 19th century, Whiteness was a diversified category, with Western and Northern European immigrants at the top of the racial hierarchy and Southern and Eastern European immigrants a notch below. By the 20th century, however, "Whiteness became an abstraction of an American citizenry" in which all persons from Europe were able to enjoy White privilege as long as they forfeited the culture and language of their countries of origin (Palumbo-Liu, 1999, p. 149; see also Harris, 1993; Smedley, 1993). Forfeiting culture and language and assimilating into White American society was not an option for non-White groups. "Non-White," in this case, meant more than a physical description or a cultural affiliation, particularly because some persons of color could physically pass for White and some willingly surrendered their culture and language in the American context. Instead, "non-White" meant being denied the status, privilege, opportunities, and constitutional protections accessible to Whites on the basis of inherited and immutable traits (Harris, 1993; Takaki, 1998). The science of individual and group differences, which emerged in the early 20th century, bolstered the racial rankings and provided scientific proof of the intellectual and moral variance between racial and ethnic groups (Kliebard, 1995; Tyack, 1974). According to Gould (1981), American psychologists

assumed that intelligence was largely inherited, and developed a series of specious arguments confusing cultural differences with innate properties. They believed that inherited IQ scores marked people and groups for an inevitable station in life. And they assumed that the average differences between groups were largely the products of heredity, despite manifest and profound variation in quality of life. (p. 157)

This racial hierarchy directly affected the educational opportunities of different groups. Lewis Terman (1916), the father of the intelligence quotient, found differences between American-born Whites and recent European immigrants but also focused his attention on the "extraordinary frequency" with which he found mental defects among "Spanish-Indian and Mexican families of the Southwest and also among negroes" (p. 91). According to Terman, these particular groups of color "should be segregated in special classes. . . . They cannot master abstractions, but they can often be made efficient workers" (p. 92). Other psychologists and educational reformers thought similarly (Cubberley, 1909; Goddard, 1920; Thorndike, 1904) and set about the task of redefining democracy and equality. In the words of the superintendent of schools in Boston in 1908, "Until very recently [the schools] have offered equal opportunity for all to receive *one kind* of education, but what will make them democratic is to provide opportunity for all to receive education as will fit them *equally well* for their particular life work" (cited in Oakes, 1985, p. 34). American Indians, Mexican Americans, Chinese Americans, Japanese Americans, and African Americans, therefore, deserved a different and inferior education. This meant that they were not only in separate classes, as Terman suggested, but in separate and often substandard schools.

At times, Whites separated themselves from these groups based on a White versus non-White binary. At others, non-White access to White schools expanded or contracted based on their particular positioning in the racial hierarchy. For instance, in 1863, California education laws lumped "Negroes, Mongolians, and Indians" together as groups that could be barred from attending school with Whites (Wollenberg, 1976, p. 13). However, many reformers considered American Indians higher on the racial hierarchy than Mongolians and Negroes, and therefore assimilable, and often spoke of them becoming fully integrated into American society (Adams, 1995; Ahern, 1976; Pratt, 1882/1973). At certain points, Mexican Americans were considered White (Treaty of Guadalupe Hidalgo, 1848), were juxtaposed against Blacks and allotted a higher status (*Independent School District v. Salvatierra*, 1930), or were classified as non-White to prevent attendance at White schools (Wollenberg, 1976). In California, while the school laws remanded the Chinese and Chinese Americans to segregated schools, Japanese and Japanese American students—who assumed a higher place in the racial hierarchy than the Chinese—sometimes attended schools with Whites (Morimoto, 1997; Palumbo-Lui, 1999; Wollenberg, 1976). Blacks, the consummate "other" at the bottom of the racial hierarchy, sometimes became the foil against which other groups positioned themselves in an attempt to gain greater status and educational opportunity (*Gong Lum v. Rice*, 1927; *Independent School District v. Salvatierra*, 1930).

Each of these non-White groups recognized that segregated schools were not merely separate but that such schools fed the existing racial and ethnic hierarchy by deliberately undereducating students of color. And each understood a high-quality education as one lever to improve the social, political, and economic status of the group. Long before *Brown v. Board of Education*, they understood that an education

is required in the performance of our most basic public responsibilities. . . . It is the very foundation of good citizenship. . . . To set them from others of similar age and qualifications solely because of their race generates a feeling of inferiority as to their status in the community. (*Brown v. Board of Education*, 1954)

Although Whites sometimes couched their arguments for segregated schools (when they decided to euphemize the arguments at all) as beneficial for all children involved, non-White groups did not accept such a bastardized notion of schooling. Attacking separate schools, therefore, became an important mechanism in their struggle for social justice and in their battle to acquire the privileges of Whiteness.

THE BATTLE FOR THE PRIVILEGES OF WHITENESS THROUGH DESEGREGATED SCHOOLS

Scholars who subscribe to the notion of assimilation and individual advancement as social justice confuse the battle to acquire the privileges of Whiteness with the desire to assimilate. They paint a nostalgic picture of the past in which they assume that various immigrants and outsiders actively pursued the opportunity to shed their cultural and linguistic heritage in order to become American. Surely, some immigrants and outsiders did just that. But the rigidity of the racial hierarchy meant that American Indians, Mexican Americans, Chinese Americans, Japanese Americans, and African Americans would still have been barred from the privileges of Whiteness even if they would have collectively shed their identities. Therefore, the battle for desegregated schools did not represent a wholesale acceptance of Whiteness as the norm or desired state. Rather, it was the recognition that Whiteness equaled high status and afforded multiple opportunities closed to non-Whites and that attendance at desegregated schools could offer children of color access to a first-rate curriculum that would enable collective racial and ethnic uplift. The pairing of assimilation as social justice and a discussion of the battle against segregated schooling is instructive because it demonstrates what assimilation meant in a historical context, if assimilation profited the groups to which equity was promised, and why those groups who were never offered the alms of assimilation as uplift still fought for the privileges of Whiteness.

PROMISES OF ASSIMILATION DEFERRED: AMERICAN INDIANS AND MEXICAN AMERICANS

Whites held out the promise of equity through assimilation and mimicking Whiteness to American Indians and Mexican Americans. Many policymakers and politicians opposed and feared including American Indians in American society, but others who considered themselves self-styled friends of the Indian argued that no genetic racial differences existed between American Indians and Whites and believed Indians could be fully integrated into White society after they were educated, civilized, and Christianized (Adams, 1995; Deyhle, 1995; Eastman, 1935; Hoxie, 1984; Prucha, 1973, 1984).[2] In the words of Richard Henry Pratt, one of the most important White reformers to educate American Indians, "I suppose the end to be gained, however far away it may be, is the complete civilization of the Indian and his absorption into our national life, with all the rights and privileges guaranteed to every other [White] individual" (Utley, 1964, p. 266, cited in Lomawaima, 1994, p. 5). Similarly, Mexican Americans became citizens under the Treaty of Guadalupe Hidalgo (1848) at the end of the Mexican–American War. According to Article IX, Mexicans residing in what became United States territory were admitted "to the enjoyment of all the rights of citizens of the United States, according to the principles of the Constitution."

Despite their honorary status as Whites, both groups were almost entirely relegated to segregated schools. American Indian pupils attended on-reservation schools or off-reservation boarding schools that were exclusively Indian in attendance. Even Pratt, who dreamed of a time when American Indians would melt into White society, was forced to send his charges to a Black school, Hampton Institute, because no White school would have them (Lindsey, 1995). A few elite and light-skinned Mexican Americans did attend school with Whites, but most Mexican American children attended segregated schools, particularly after the population influx following the 1910 Mexican Revolution and the 1920s bracero workers program, which increased the number of Mexican immigrants entering the United States (Gonzalez, 1997; Hendrick, 1977; Menchaca, 1999; Sánchez, 1997; Wollenberg, 1974, 1976).[3]

According to reformers, that assimilation and Americanization should occur in schools separate from Whites was not contradictory. Instead, it was a practical solution that represented the best course of action to achieve those ends. English-language deficiencies necessitated special attention that could not occur for American Indian or Mexican American pupils in classes with English-speaking children, and Americanization programs could be better concentrated and delivered in segregated settings (Adams, 1995; Deyhle, 1995; Deyhle & Swisher, 1997; Gonzalez, 1990, 1997; Menchaca & Valencia, 1990; Prucha, 1973; Wollenberg, 1974, 1976). Reformers bolstered their arguments with the science of group differences that emerged in the early 20th century by arguing that American Indians and Mexican Americans deserved programs tailored to learning the habits of the majority rather than academic pursuits, that their physical and intellectual distance from Whites would make them feel out of place with White kids, and that White children should be protected from the questionable morals of American Indian and Mexican American youth (Adams, 1995; Alvarez, 1986; Deyhle, 1995; Deyhle & Swisher, 1997; Gonzalez, 1990, 1997; Hoxie, 1984; Menchaca & Valencia, 1990; Wollenberg, 1974, 1976). Americanization and assimilation were right and good, according to these historical actors and some early historians (Carpenter, 1935; Eastman, 1935; Stanley, 1920, cited in Wollenberg, 1976), and segregated schools were the best place to achieve those ends.

Historians have critiqued this sympathetic interpretation by examining the paternalistic and racist attitudes of Whites (including Pratt) toward American Indians and Mexican Americans. Recent scholarly work has used the autobiographies and interviews with former American Indian boarding school pupils to document the horrid and oppressive conditions at the boarding schools and to highlight how American Indians resisted the reformers through subterfuge, refusing attendance, and defying White teachers after enrollment (Adams, 1988, 1995; Ahern, 1976; Bass, 1966; Child, 1998, 2000; Coleman, 1987, 1993; Lomawaima, 1994; Senese, 1991; Standing Bear, 1928/1975; 1933; Szasz, 1999; Talayesva; 1942; Trennert, 1988). More important for the purposes of this chapter, the historians who traced American Indian educational experiences after the 1910s—at which time the federal government backpedaled in its interest in American Indian off-reservation boarding schools—found that White reformers reneged on the (some would say disingenuous) promises of equality and upward mobility through education by the 1920s. Reformers shifted the assimilative mission of the boarding schools in response to the fact that American Indian students often returned to reservations and families with their cultural values intact (Hoxie, 1984, 2001; Prucha, 1984; Senese, 1991). According to Hoxie (1984), "The key to assimilation was no longer the act of becoming part of an undifferentiated, 'civilized' society; instead, assimilation had come to mean knowing one's place and fulfilling one's role" (p. 242). The segregated boarding schools, therefore, trained students to occupy an inferior position in the social, economic, and political order.[4]

So, too, did most Mexican Americans experience a segregated form of schooling that did not groom them to assimilate into American society but prepared them to fill a particular station in the social, economic, and political hierarchy. At times, reformers were, as Gonzalez (1997) put it, "more patronizing than negative, more insensitive than malicious" (p. 164). In other instances, the rhetoric regarding segregated schools was clearly racist and rooted in stereotypes of Mexicans as "dirty, shiftless, lazy, irresponsible, unambitious, thriftless, fatalistic, selfish, promiscuous, and prone to drinking, violence, and criminal behavior" (Carpenter, 1935, cited in Gonzalez, 1997, p. 163). According to San Miguel (2001), schools clashed with communities' interests in that they advocated subtractive Americanization. In other words, "they supported the learning of American cultural forms and the 'subtraction' of the Spanish language and Mexican cultural heritage from the schools (pp. 19–20; see also Donato, 1997; Garcia, 1978; Gonzalez, 1990; Menchaca & Valencia, 1990; Moll & Ruiz, 2002; Sánchez, 1951).

Despite the rhetoric of assimilation, American Indians and Mexican Americans were, for the most part, not only barred from White schools but also relegated to substandard institutions. And despite their supposed proximity to Whiteness, they did not experience the benefits of such status and were forced to litigate for the opportunity to receive a high-quality education through desegregated schooling. American Indian plaintiffs brought suit to end school segregation in the early 20th century in Oregon (*State v. Wolf*, 1907) and North Carolina (*Crawford v. District School Board for District No. 7*, 1913) but lost. It was not until 1924 that American Indians won a legal challenge against forced attendance at federally supported reservation boarding schools. In *Piper v. Big Pine School District* (1924), the California Supreme Court found for the plaintiffs on the grounds that the district violated the state constitution by denying American Indian pupils access to state-supported schools. The decision was only a partial victory because the court did not prevent school districts from creating *segregated* state-supported schools for Indians. It was not until 1947 that the California legislature prohibited racial segregation in public schools (Wollenberg, 1976, p. 132).

Mexican American parents, supported by newly formed Mexican American advocacy organizations, filed legal challenges against segregated schools as early as 1930 with *Independent School District v. Salvatierra* (Texas) and 1931 with *Alvarez v. Lemon Grove School District* (California). In both cases, state courts found that local school boards illegally segregated Mexican American students on racial grounds, though *Salvatierra* allowed the district to segregate students for language reasons. Federal court decisions with a wider impact struck dead racial and linguistic profiling in the 1940s (*Delgado v. Bastrop Independent School District, Texas*, 1948; *Mendez v. Westminster School District, California*, 1946). Litigation against segregated schools took another turn in 1970 with *Cisneros v. Corpus Christi Independent School District* (Texas) as White districts used the Mexican-as-White argument as a way around the *Brown v. Board of Education* (1954) decision. In this case, the court invalidated district attempts to achieve desegregation by placing Mexican American children in schools with Black children. Social justice in the form of a high-quality schooling experience, according to the litigants in the different cases, could not occur in a segregated and substandard environment.

As can be seen through the experiences of these two groups, the promise of assimilation as an opportunity to become part of an undifferentiated American mass was disingenuous. Forfeiting culture and language, for American Indians and Mexican Americans, was not enough to erase the racial and ethnic status they carried. The White versus non-White binary trumped their proximity to Whiteness in the racial hierarchy and led to the denial of equal educational opportunity. They remained outsiders who were to be assimilated into a particular and inferior position in American society.

CONSUMMATE OUTSIDERS: ASIAN AMERICANS AND AFRICAN AMERICANS

Even the disingenuous promise of assimilation and Americanization held out to American Indians and Mexican Americans did not exist for Asian Americans or African Americans. The institution of slavery, the equation of Black personhood with property, Black Codes, Jim Crow laws, legal decisions, and legislative acts relegated African Americans to the margins of American society before and after the Civil War (J. H.

Franklin, 1974). Asian Americans, too, were specifically targeted by Whites. In 1882, the United States government adopted "An Act to execute certain treaty stipulations relating to Chinese," which prohibited further immigration, making it the first such act to specify a particularly undesirable country of origin. In 1907, the federal government extended the act to include Japanese immigrants as a way to stem the Mongolian tide (Daniels, 1997; Takaki, 1998). Their place in the racial hierarchy left them at a distinct disadvantage, but Asian Americans and African Americans agitated for access to desegregated schools and the privileges of Whiteness.

Although conflated in everything from census reports to scholarly work (Tamura, 2001), the rights denied to or gained by Chinese Americans or Japanese Americans were highly contingent on local politics and international relations (Palumbo-Liu, 1999; Weinberg, 1997). China, weakened by the dynastic wars of the middle 19th century, held little political clout on the world stage when Chinese immigrants and Chinese Americans came under siege in the late 19th century in American schools. Japan's military might, as demonstrated through its victory in the Russo–Japanese War and its industrialized economy, on the other hand, made it a powerful international rival and a formidable advocate for Japanese immigrants and Japanese Americans (Katznelson & Weir, 1985; Odo, 2002; Takaki, 1998; Weinberg, 1997; Wollenberg, 1976). Local school boards also alternately conflated or disaggregated the Asian label as attitudes toward them softened or hardened (Palumbo-Lui, 1999).

For African Americans, regional differences dictated the extent of their outsider status. Prior to 1865, social justice was impossible on a political, social, or economic scale, but enslaved southern Blacks experienced personal fulfillment and psychological liberation through Sabbath schools (Douglass, 1845/1968; Webber, 1978; Woodson 1919/1968). At the end of the Civil War, Blacks pursued education with a vengeance and made communal sacrifices to educate Black youth, though they did so within the confines of a segregated system in which Whites refused to allow them the possibility to enter mainstream society (J. D. Anderson, 1988; Du Bois, 1901; Woodson, 1919/1968). Blacks in the North were not automatically prohibited from attending schools with Whites. In fact, Blacks and Whites attended school together in some locations prior to and immediately after the Civil War (Douglas, 2005; Du Bois, 1899/1996; V. P. Franklin, 1979; McCaul, 1987; Meier & Rudwick, 1967). The fear of a massive Black exodus from the South to the North and West at the end of the war prompted some legislatures and school boards to enact stiff segregation policies. The population influx did not occur, but the segregation policies remained. Some newly enacted laws, like one in California in 1864, barred Black students from attending school with Whites and threatened districts with financial sanction if they did not comply (Wollenberg, 1976). In 1872, the Illinois legislature gave local districts the power of pupil assignment, which resulted in Black students in one school and White students in another (McCaul, 1987). Other districts in a variety of northern cities created annexes to White schools, which meant that Black and White children attended the same school but different classes (Douglas, 2005; Mabee, 1979; McCaul, 1987). Other school boards simply flouted the law and refused to educate Black children altogether (Douglas, 2005; Mabee, 1979).

These groups—with different racial status, different levels of international clout, and completely different histories in the United States—found themselves bedfellows as they battled White communities and school boards over the segregated school system. In *People v. Hall* (1854), the California Supreme Court ruled that the definition of Black "as contradistinguished from white" included "all races other than the Caucasian," a decision that legally denied Chinese Americans the right to testify, vote, or otherwise participate in government (Aarim-Heriot, 2003; Beck, 1975; Caldwell, 1971; Chang, 2001; Gotanda, 2001; Harris, 1993; Kim, 2001; Palumbo-Liu, 1999; Takaki, 1998). Similarly, by 1863, the California legislature adopted school laws that barred Negro, Indian, and Mongolian students from attending White schools by ordering districts to create separate schools for non-Whites (Beck, 1975; Wollenberg, 1976).

Although *People v. Hall* (1854) and the California state school code subordinated all non-Whites to second-class citizenry, these groups rarely worked in tandem to fight for social justice. In fact, they sometimes worked against each other. The tension between Chinese/Chinese Americans and African Americans presents a twist to the notion of social justice in education. To fight for social justice, each group directly confronted White supremacy by refuting racist stereotypes and challenging discriminatory laws. But, to advance their positions, one group affirmed the racist stereotypes Whites used to describe the other (De Leon, 2002; Johnsen, 1980; Loewen, 1988; Shankman, 1978). For instance, as part of a political strategy to gain access to a high-quality education, Black Californians argued that they, more than the Chinese, deserved the right to attend desegregated schools. Black leaders contrasted the fact that Asians were permanent foreigners and held cultural values and religious beliefs alien to America with the fact that African Americans had successfully assimilated in that they spoke English, were Christian, and were therefore more likely to be productive contributors to society. Editorials written in the *Elevator*, one of San Francisco's most notable Black newspapers, claimed that for 300 years, the Chinese had "maintained a wall of superstition and error against our revealed religion" and concluded that Asians were culturally at odds with America (cited in Shankman, 1978, p. 3; see also Beck, 1975; De Leon, 2002; Johnsen, 1980).

Likewise, the Chinese/Chinese American community sought to distance itself from the African American community. When Chinese parents petitioned San Francisco's board of education for their children's right to attend public schools in 1857, the board offered to place Chinese students in schools opened for Black students. Chinese leaders were angered by the school board's attempt to classify them as anything close to Black, rejected the offer, and demanded a separate Chinese/Chinese American school in lieu of attending Black schools (Low, 1982; Weinberg, 1997).[5] In a similar flattening of the racial hierarchy, Chinese American parents in Mississippi brought suit on the basis that a Chinese American pupil had been incorrectly classified as colored. The United States Supreme Court (as the California Supreme Court had done in *People v. Hall*) ruled against the parents by expanding the definition of colored to include all non-Whites rather than only Blacks, thereby allowing the district to force Chinese

American pupils (or any non-White pupil, for that matter) to attend segregated Black schools (*Gong Lum v. Rice*, 1927; Loewen, 1988; Quan, 1982). In *Gong Lum v. Rice* (1927), lawyers for the plaintiff argued that

if there is a danger associated [with Negroes], it is a danger from which one race is entitled to protection just as the same as another . . . the white race creates for itself a privilege that it denies to other races; exposes the children of other races to risks and dangers to which it would not expose its own children. This is discrimination. (cited in Loewen, 1988, p. 67)

Although Loewen (1988) insisted Gong Lum and his attorneys did not believe Blacks were dangerous and used the argument only as a legal tactic, he conceded that the case is an example where "good use was made of the white racist rationale for segregated schools" (p. 67).

Even when they were successful in court, White school boards, legislatures, and other entities forced Asian American and African American pupils into segregated and often substandard schools. Chinese Americans in California won a temporary victory in 1885 in *Tape v. Hurley*. Joseph and Mary Tape, who resided outside of Chinatown, sued the San Francisco school board to allow their American-born, Christian, and English-speaking daughter, Mamie, to attend a local White school. According to Takaki (1998), the Tapes, like many other first-generation Chinese immigrants, believed that the academic achievement, Americanization, and assimilation-as-mimicking-Whiteness of the second generation could prove to White America that Chinese immigrants had been unjustly denied citizenship. The second generation, of which Mamie was a part, would be a bridge between the first generation and White America (Takaki, 1998). The California Supreme Court found in favor of the Tapes because the ever-evolving California school laws excluded only Indian and Negro children after the term Mongolian was dropped from the school code in 1871 (*Tape v. Hurley*, 1885). One day after the court ruling, however, the legislature revised the school code to once again include Mongolian students and mandated that districts establish separate schools for Chinese students. Soon thereafter, the San Francisco school board created a new public school for Chinese students that Mamie was forced to attend. Here, like with other racial and ethnic groups, the Chinese American attempt to desegregate schools as a way to achieve social justice and equal educational opportunity—despite Mamie's assimilated status—was thwarted and redirected toward separate schooling (Beck, 1975; Hendrick, 1977, 1980; Low, 1982; Weinberg, 1997; Wollenberg, 1976).

Although the Japanese, like the Chinese, were denied citizenship, they attended neighborhood schools with Whites because they were fewer in number, they enjoyed a higher status in the racial hierarchy, and Japan had the political clout to ensure that immigrants were treated fairly (Daniels, 1992; Wollenberg, 1976). Still, Whites in San Francisco flattened the racial hierarchy and broadened the Mongolian category to include the Japanese as a way to exclude them from schools as their numbers increased. In 1893, several years after the *Tape* case, the school board adopted a resolution remanding Japanese students to the Chinese public schools. Japanese immigrants refused to comply, stating that segregation "constituted an act of discrimination carrying with it the stigma and odium which is impossible to overlook" (cited in Wollenberg, 1976, p. 56). The board of education reiterated its order to have Japanese students transferred to the Chinese public school in 1905 (Morimoto, 1997), and the following year, the legislature amended the school code to include Japanese students as Mongolians and, therefore, a group that could be legally segregated (Low, 1982). Japanese American parents refused to comply, filed suit (*Aoki v. Deane*, 1907), and appealed to their homeland by reporting their mistreatment to Japanese newspapers and the consulate (Wollenberg, 1976). Interested in maintaining healthy relations with the Empire of Japan, President Theodore Roosevelt intervened on behalf of the Japanese and forced the school board to relent (Daniels, 1992; Wollenberg, 1976).

As the group at the bottom of the racial hierarchy, Blacks waged the most public, aggressive, and long-lasting attack on separate schools, and it is with the Black community that the link between education and social justice as collective racial advancement is most clearly articulated in the historiography (for instance, see J. D. Anderson, 1988; Bond, 1934/1966; Bullock, 1967; Butchart, 1988; Du Bois, 1901, 1903/1990; Harlan, 1958; Woodson, 1919/1968).[6] Reminiscent of Frederick Douglass's (1845/1968) proclamation that education was the "pathway from slavery to freedom" (p. 49), early historians such as Carter G. Woodson (1919/1968, 1933/1990) and W. E. B. Du Bois (1903/1990) couched their advocacy of education less in the language of academic knowledge and more in the language of citizenship, racial uplift, and political access. In the words of Du Bois (1906/1973), "never in God's world is this Negro race going to hold its place in the world, until it shows by its fully developed and carefully trained powers its undoubted ability to do so" (p. 14).

Black historical actors sought to disabuse Whites of the notion that the desire to attend desegregated schools meant Blacks yearned to be White or that Blacks abhorred their own race. Writing in 1915, William Pickens explained,

The Negroes in Northern communities are generally opposed to the separate school idea and face the usual accusation that they 'do not want to associate with their own people,' which ignores the more positive reason the Negro himself advances—the universal temptation and tendency of the school authorities to degrade the Negro schools wherever they have been successfully segregated. . . . He knows that where black and white attend the same school this discrimination is forever impossible. (p. 83)

The argument, according to Pickens, was not

that colored children simply enjoy going to school with white children, where in fact they are often woefully ostracized, but it is rather to be supposed that the white school attracts colored people for the same reason why it would attract any people, because of its superior location and equipment. (Pickens, 1915, cited in Aptheker, 1993, p. 84)

In 1954, the Supreme Court declared racially segregated schools unconstitutional in its famous *Brown v. Board of Education* decision. African Americans initiated the case, but the decision affected all other racial and ethnic groups similarly situated. The plaintiffs argued that

Segregation of white and colored children in public schools has a detrimental effect upon the colored children. The impact is greater when it has the sanction of the law, for the policy of separating the races is usually interpreted as denoting the inferiority of the negro group. A sense of inferiority affects the motivation of a child to learn. Segregation with the sanction of law, therefore, has a tendency to [retard] the educational and mental development of negro children and to deprive them of some of the benefits they would receive in a racial[ly] integrated school system. (*Brown v. Board of Education*, 1954)

The tenor of the decision mirrored the arguments made by American Indians, Mexican Americans, Chinese Americans, and Japanese Americans who recognized education as a lever for upward mobility and citizenship status and desegregated schools as the best means to achieve those ends. Historical actors interested in social justice concerns celebrated the decision as a springboard for equality and upward mobility in the economic, social, and political spheres as well (Breathett, 1983).

Still, *Brown*, like the other legal decisions regarding segregated schooling, has a complicated legacy. According to J. D. Anderson (2006), *Brown* "redeemed promises of constitutional equality that remained excluded or underdeveloped since the Declaration of Independence, its legal significance is national in scope, and its meaning extends beyond the interest of any particular ethnicity, class or gender" (p. 15). The decision was a pivotal moment in the pursuit of human equality and dignity, made the principle of racial equality a fundamental doctrine in the American legal corpus, and provided legal precedent on which democratic rights expanded (J. D. Anderson, 2006). At the same time, Anderson and other scholars lament the fact that Black students and other students of color continue to languish in segregated schools, receive a poor quality education, and experience isolation and cultural and linguistic alienation when they are in desegregated contexts (J. A. Anderson, Byrne, & Smiley, 2004; Irons, 2002; Menchaca, 1995; Moreno, 1999; Ogletree, 2004; Patterson, 2001; Valencia, 2000). Some even debate whether compelling White schools to desegregate was the correct course of action (Balkin, 2001; Bell, 2004).

Examining the educational experiences of these racial and ethnic groups demonstrates that the good old days were not so good for a large segment of the American population. It also demonstrates that the mythic past to which some contemporary scholars allude did not exist. Assimilation as equality became the perennial carrot dangled in front of immigrants and outsiders who were encouraged to shed their cultural and linguistic heritage and to mimic Whiteness. If they did so wholly and without rancor, they were told by White reformers, they would be rewarded with the privileges of Whiteness, citizenship, and upward mobility. What assimilation actually meant, however, was the opportunity to occupy an inferior status in the American order. Even when groups attended schools created and controlled by Whites with a distinctly assimilative purpose, non-White groups were denied the fruits assimilation promised. To create an image of a past when people of color actively sought assimilation misses the nuances of the term in a historical context.

Similarly, to equate the battle to desegregate schools with a desire for assimilation is ahistorical. Contemporary conservative pundits have reduced the *Brown* decision to the desire for a color-blind society, twisted the decision into an argument against racial classification, and appropriated the language of the decision to position race-conscious policies against meritocracy (*Grutter v. Bollinger*, 2003; Ravitch, 1983; Schlesinger, 1992; Steinberg, 1995; Thernstrom & Thernstrom, 2003). But people of color did not litigate, agitate, boycott, petition, and demonstrate for access to White schools merely so their children could sit next to Whites and, therefore, become White. Nor did they seek to forfeit their culture for the possibility to do so, although White reformers often hoped they would. They pursued desegregation as a manifestation of equality. When understood as such, the demand for high-quality *separate* schools, which is discussed in the next section, cannot be construed as antithetical or contradictory to the fight for desegregated schools.

FORTIFYING AND CREATING SEPARATE SCHOOLS

American Indians, Mexican Americans, Chinese Americans, Japanese Americans, and African Americans did not sit idly by as they fought for desegregated schools but created liberatory experiences within segregated schools. Lomawaima (1994) details how American Indian boarding school pupils created a pan-Indian identity in defiance of White intentions to the contrary and used the confines of the boarding school to strengthen tribal identity rather than dissolve it. And McCarty (2002) chronicles how the Navajo transformed a federally supported school into an institution organized around kinship and community that mixed academics with Navajo language classes, cultural activities, and community economic development projects. Without denying the often horrid conditions of many segregated Black schools, Sowell (1974), Cecelski (1994), and Siddle Walker (1996) examine how certain Black schools provided students with an invigorating and nurturing environment in which their talents and interests were rewarded and in which they excelled academically. Similarly, countless historians have chronicled how Black colleges and universities, particularly the liberal arts colleges, included the notion of racial uplift in their mission statements and educated Black students to become race leaders (for instance, see J. D. Anderson, 1988).

James (1987), Pak (2002), Riley (2002), and Daniels (1988, 1999) examined the Japanese American experience in internment camps during World War II as a unique example with regard to the fortification of separate schools and the appropriation of education and schools in the pursuit of social justice. According to James (1987), when the War Relocation Authority issued a set of curricular and pedagogical guides that offered an experimental curriculum with nonacademic subjects and called for a child-centered pedagogical style, Japanese American parents and teachers successfully campaigned for a more rigorous curriculum and a teacher-centered pedagogy that would prepare students for a postsecondary education. With regard to students, many Nisei (second generation) experienced segregated schooling for the first time in the camp schools (Daniels, 1988). In such spaces, the children were able to shed their minority status and, according to Kitano (1969), all of the typical

high school activities—a yearbook, football, and basketball teams, cheerleaders, student body organizations, scholarship society—were available, and, for the first time, young Nisei were able to feel themselves in the majority, and to run things. They became student body leaders, athletic, political, and social heroes—roles usually reserved for Caucasians in the everyday world. (cited in Daniels, 1988, p. 232)

Historians universally laud these instances in which historical actors made the best of a segregated situation in the pre-*Brown* era. Where historians differ is in their interpretations of the worth of schools created by racial and ethnic groups for racial and ethnic fortification in the post-*Brown* era. One way to distill the debate is to examine the tension between *segregated* and *separate*. Some scholars draw a distinction between the two. Whites created segregated schools as a mechanism to keep the races apart in order to sustain the racial, political, social, and economic hierarchy. Segregated schools did not prepare students to compete, excel, or advance but were designed to keep the entire racial and ethnic group oppressed. Separate schools such as Japanese language schools (Hawkins, 1978; Tamura, 1993), Chinese language schools (Low, 1982; Morimoto, 1997; Wollenberg, 1976), Afrocentric schools (Asante, 1991a, 1991b; Banks, 1995; Shujaa, 1992), and Jewish day schools (Rauch, 1984), on the other hand, were created by racial and ethnic groups for racial and ethnic group fortification and uplift. These schools would be places in which students would be respected, supported, encouraged, and nourished. To other scholars, segregated and separate schools yield the same results: the death of the common school ideal and the rise of racially chauvinist agendas that precipitated the "disuniting of America" (Schlesinger, 1992; see also Bloom, 1987; D'Souza, 2001; Ravitch, 1990).

The debate in educational history mirrors a wider split in the historiography of the *Brown v. Board of Education* (1954) decision. Conventional scholars portray it as the beginning of the Black freedom movement (thereby giving credit to the federal government for igniting the struggle) and as the codification of the movement's desire for desegregation (Fairclough, 2001; Lawson, 1998; Schlesinger, 1965; Weisbrot, 1990). Revisionists position the decision in a broader and longer freedom struggle that did not begin in 1954 and whose primary aim was not racial integration but political power and human dignity (Carson, 1995; A. D. Morris, 1984; Payne, 1998).

These interpretive frames for understanding *Brown*'s position in history have implications for how historians convey an understanding of racism and democracy to the American populous. In the conventional interpretation, legal channels are the most legitimate recourse for grievances, the federal government is a friend to aggrieved parties, and the United States is the Mecca of opportunity. Just be patient, these historians say, the democratic ideal is near. According to Schlesinger (1992),

Our democratic principles contemplate an open society founded on tolerance of differences and on mutual respect. In practice, America has been more open to some than to others. But it is more open to all today than it was yesterday and is likely to be even more open tomorrow than today. The steady movement of American life has been from exclusion to inclusion. (p. 134)

An essentialized and mischaracterized *Brown* decision plays a central role in this narrative and is treated as the judicial embodiment of all that is good with America.

If, on the other hand, we understand *Brown* from the vantage point of the revisionists, a different picture emerges: The decision represents a step toward equal opportunity, not merely a color-blind society, and political pressure, not moral suasion, motivates federal intervention. As Payne (1998) states,

Far from being the solution, American institutions have always played important roles in the creation and maintenance of racism. What happened in the movement was that civil rights activists were able to maneuver around those institutions to alleviate some of the system's worst features. (p. 99)

The movement toward a democratic ideal exists, these scholars believe, but it has moved at a glacial and fitful pace and has been motivated by oppressed groups, not the goodwill of the American government or general populous. The past is far from rosy, and the struggle is far from over.

So, too, do contemporary educational scholars use their discussions of educational history to tell a broader story about American progress, democracy, and the proper path to achieve social justice. Some, such as Orfield and Eaton (1996) and Kozol (2005), concur with *Brown* (1954) that "separate educational facilities are inherently unequal" and argue that a continued battle for desegregation, rather than the creation of separate schools or entities, will guarantee students of color the highest quality education (see also Wilkins, 1969). Other scholars take the argument a step further by damning separate institutions as antithetical to the common school mission and the American credo, "e pluribus unum" (Bloom, 1987; D'Souza, 1991; Ravitch, 1990; Schlesinger, 1992). This latter set of scholars recognizes that students of color do not yet achieve educational outcomes equal to Whites, but they hold out the hope that racial categorization will run its course in the not so distant future (see *Grutter v. Bollinger*, 2003). Separate schools were unfortunate necessities in the pre-*Brown* era, these scholars believe, but they are no longer appropriate in the contemporary context.

Still other scholars more closely match Du Bois's (1935) interpretation of desegregated schools and his argument in favor of fortifying separate schools (see also Woodson, 1919/1968). According to Du Bois (1935), "there are many public school systems in the North where Negroes are admitted and tolerated, but they are not educated; they are crucified" (p. 329). Instead, Du Bois saw hope that

a separate Negro school, where children are treated like human beings, trained by teachers of their own race, who know what it means to be black in the year of salvation 1935, is infinitely better than making our boys and girls doormats to be spit and trampled upon and lied to by ignorant social climbers, whose sole claim to superiority is ability to kick 'niggers' when they are down. (p. 335)

He cautioned that separate schools were a temporary solution, held out hope for school desegregation, and recognized that White racists would construe his support for separate schools as support for segregated schools. But, in his view, the damage done to Black students in the meanwhile forced him to support separate schools for Black youth (Du Bois, 1929, 1935). Du Bois was out of step with several of his contemporaries (Maskin, 1973; Pickins, 1915/1993), but for him, as "[f]or a number of Negro leaders, the prime question was not whether the Negro needed a good education, but whether or not he was willing to trust the white man to give it to him" (Maskin, 1973, p. 32).

Multicultural Education

The debate over multicultural education provides an example of how educational history is appropriated for contemporary purposes.[7] Both those who support it and those who oppose it couch their arguments in the language of democracy and equality, though they disagree on how best to achieve the unum out of the pluribus. Those who oppose multicultural education describe it as a racially and ethnically based reform that derailed the communal and relentless pursuit of assimilation and a common culture that had been present in education since the common schools of the early 1800s. As one of the most vocal critics, Ravitch (1990) laments, "Alas, these painstaking efforts to expand the understanding of American culture into a richer and more varied tapestry have taken a new turn, and not for the better" (p. 340).

Including American Indian, Mexican American, Chinese American, Japanese American, and African American information in classes is not inherently bad, according to these critics, but their inclusion should not be used to highlight the differences between groups. Instead, Ravitch (1990) explains, the point

is to demonstrate that neither race nor gender is an obstacle to high achievement. They teach all children that everyone, regardless of their race, religion, gender, ethnicity, or family origin, can achieve self-fulfillment, honor, and dignity in society if they aim high and work hard (p. 340).

Such an assimilationist perspective does not allow for what she calls "an ethnocentric curriculum to raise the self-esteem and academic achievement of children from racial and ethnic minority backgrounds" because, in her words, it

implies that those who are neither white nor European are alienated from American culture by virtue of their race or ethnicity; it implies that the only culture they do belong to or can ever belong to is the culture of their ancestors, even if their families have lived in this country for generations. (pp. 340, 341)

To Ravitch and others, a racially and ethnically based curriculum is a politically motivated school reform that hinders group advancement by marking the group as an entity separate from the rest of America and by undereducating them in the name of cultural relevance (Glazer, 1997; Hacker, 1992; Hollinger, 1995; Ravitch, 1974; Schlesinger, 1992).

These same critics also oppose the ethnic studies programs that emerged on college campuses during the late 1960s and early 1970s. According to Bloom (1987), the era was an "unmitigated disaster" that was "the source of the collapse of the entire educational structure" (pp. 320, 321). Critics reserve special antipathy for the diversification of the curriculum. Like the attack on multiculturalism, the opposition to a diversified canon is based on an assimilationist framework that celebrates common values and a "unity of knowledge" as the pathway to social justice (Bloom, 1987, p. 320). These critics make no apologies for the White male-dominated curriculum. "It may be too bad that dead white European males have played so large a role in shaping our culture," Schlesinger (1992) states, "but that's the way it is. One cannot erase history. These humdrum facts, and not some dastardly imperialist conspiracy, explain the Eurocentric slant in American schools" (p. 128). Focusing on group rights rather than individual rights flies in the face of democratic principles and the American Dream, which "envisages a nation composed of individuals making their own choices and accountable to themselves, not a nation based on inviolable ethnic communities" (p. 142). Sadly, these critics say, the focus on ethnicity and race has created a segregated society and turned education from an intellectual into a political endeavor (Bloom, 1987; D'Souza, 1991; Hirsch, 1988; Ravitch, 1983, 1990; Schlesinger, 1992).

Those who support multicultural education, ethnic studies, and a diversified cannon argue that in the words of Asante (1991a), "There is no common American culture as is claimed by the defenders of the status quo. There is a hegemonic culture to be sure, pushed as if it were a common culture" (p. 270). Such a Eurocentric curriculum harms *all* students by providing a narrow and one-dimensional lens with which to understand themselves and the world. Rather than ignoring difference or appealing to a common (White) culture, these theorists argue that attention to diversity "enriches a society by providing all citizens with more opportunities to experience other cultures and thus to become more fulfilled as human beings" (Banks, 1999, p. 1). Such curricula do not exacerbate cleavages in American society because the idea of a common culture and a common identity is merely a myth. Instead,

Multicultural education is designed to help unify a deeply divided nation rather than to divide a highly cohesive one. Multicultural education supports the notion of *e pluribus unum*. . . . The multiculturalists and the Western traditionalists, however, often differ about how the *unum* can best be achieved. Traditionally, the larger U.S. society as well as the schools have tried to create the *unum* by assimilating students from diverse racial and ethnic groups into a mythical Anglo American culture that required them to experience a process of self-alienation and harsh assimilation. However, even when students of color became culturally assimilated, they were often structurally excluded from mainstream institutions. Multicultural educators view *e pluribus unum* as the appropriate national goal but believe that the *unum* must be negotiated, discussed, and restructured to reflect the nation's ethnic and cultural diversity. The reformulation of the *unum* must be a process and must involve the participation by diverse groups within the nation, such as people of color, women, straights, gays, the powerful, the powerless, the young, and the old. The reformulation of the *unum* must also involve power sharing and participation by people from many different cultural communities. (Banks, 1999, p. 8)

Much like the historical actors who advocated for increased access to the privileges of Whiteness, these scholars advocate a flattening of the existing social, economic, and political hierarchy in a way that racial and ethnic minorities can participate equally (Asante, 1991a, 1991b; Banks, 1995, 1999; Gay, 2000; Perry, Steele, & Hilliard, 2003; Sleeter, 1996; Sleeter & McLaren, 1995). Assimilation as becoming White, to these scholars, is neither necessary nor profitable. Here, social justice is not realized in an undifferentiated American populous but in an America that truly allows racial and ethnic minorities the ability to prosper without having to forfeit their cultural and linguistic identities.

BILINGUAL EDUCATION

Theorists, politicians, and the public also debate how social justice is best achieved for non–English-speaking students. Although many non-White students participate in bilingual education,[8] most of the literature has focused on the debate with regard to Spanish-speaking students. Crawford (1999, 2000, 2004), Delgado Bernal (1999), San Miguel (1987, 1996), and Trueba (1974) categorize the poles in the debate as assimilationist and pluralist, categories that directly mirror the multicultural debate. For assimilationists, social justice is achieved by following mandates that restrict bilingual instruction to as few years as possible so that children can be mainstreamed in English-only classrooms as soon as possible. According to this line of reasoning, keeping English-speaking and non–English-speaking students in separate classrooms perpetuates social divisions, underequips non–English-speaking students to compete academically, and denies them the opportunity "to fully participate in the American Dream of economic and social advancement" (California Proposition 227, 1998; see also Hayakawa, 1985). Pluralists, on the other hand, believe social justice is achieved when bilingual instruction is provided throughout a student's primary and secondary education. This group argues that bilingual classrooms bolster academic progress, equip students to compete in a globalized economy, and provide an opportunity "to build up personal pride, self-identity, and a more meaningful and sensitive school system that recognizes the reality of our pluralistic American society" (Trueba, 1974, p. 8; see also Delgado Bernal, 1999).

Delgado Bernal (1999) cautions that the categories of assimilationist and pluralist cannot be easily mapped onto White and non-White/non–English-speaking groups.[9] Instead, the issue of bilingual education split the Latino community, particularly during the civil rights era. According to Trueba (1974), many Latinos who identified as White wanted no part of the compensatory actions of the federal and local governments mandated by the *Lau v. Nichols* (1974) decision and fought to mainstream non–English-speaking students, whereas other Latinos opposed mainstreaming for fear it would eliminate the bilingual and bicultural programs established in their schools. According to Garcia (1989) and San Miguel (1996), the split was also a generational one, with older Mexican American middle-class organizations agitating for inclusion and younger Mexican Americans imbued with the social reform spirit of the late 1960s and early 1970s seeking community control and separate bilingual programs to achieve equal educational opportunities and social justice for past discriminatory actions and institutions.

The concept of social justice is further complicated by the tension between the right to a bilingual education in separate schools and classrooms (as mandated in *Lau*) and desegregation (as mandated in *Brown*). Although Mexican Americans of earlier generations used their status as "White" to argue for desegregation, litigation in the late 1960s and early 1970s hinged on Mexican Americans as a protected ethnic minority group who had been denied their 14th amendment rights by being forced into segregated schools (*Cisneros v. Corpus Christi Independent School District*,

1970; *Keyes v. School District Number 1*, 1973). The decision meant school districts had to create desegregation programs that provided Mexican Americans and African Americans access to White schools. Many Mexican Americans, however, "were suspicious of desegregation efforts that might disperse Chicana/o students without considering their need for bilingual education. Parents and policymakers argued that bilingual education and desegregation might not be fully compatible" (Delgado Bernal, 1999, p. 90; see also Donato, Menchaca, & Valencia, 1991).

Likewise, Wollenberg (1976), Low (1982), and Kirp (1982) have documented how the Chinese American community in San Francisco revolted against a 1971 desegregation order issued on behalf of African American students in monolithically Black schools. The Chinese American parents argued that schools outside of Chinatown were not equipped to teach non–English-speaking students and were insensitive to their needs. Rather than follow the order and allow their children to be bussed out of the local area, parents created "freedom schools" as a temporary measure. In these cases, fortifying separate schooling and classroom experiences conflicted not only with demands to desegregate schools but with the aims of African Americans seeking social justice through access to the resources at White schools. As in the pre-*Brown* era, the debate over what was best for a particular community sometimes pitted racial and ethnic groups against one another.

The argument for desegregation, on one hand, and the creation and fortification of separate schools and multicultural and/or bilingual education, on the other, are not polar opposites when both are understood as strategies to achieve the best chance at social justice in education. Examining litigation like *Tape v. Hurley* (1885), *Aoki v. Deane* (1907), *Piper v. Big Pine* (1924), *Alvarez v. Lemon Grove* (1931), and *Brown v. Board of Education* (1954) as a desire for physical desegregation, assimilation, and the manifestation of the "clear and unambiguous goal . . . [of making] America a color-blind society" (Ravitch, 1983, p. 114) limits and distorts the reasons the suits were brought by the different communities. Rather, both desegregation and the creation and fortification of separate schools and culturally and linguistically appropriate schooling experiences were a response to White supremacy as each group sought racial and ethnic uplift and a flattening of the racial and ethnic hierarchy. In short, these groups demanded and continue to demand a high-quality education, however that could happen. Du Bois (1935) distilled the issue for African Americans, in particular, but his words have resonance for American Indians, Mexican Americans, Chinese Americans, and Japanese Americans seeking social justice: "The Negro needs neither segregated schools nor mixed schools. What he needs is Education" (p. 335).

CONCLUSION

Historians have a role to play in the contemporary debate over the definition of social justice in education. First, they can deepen and inform the discussion, particularly because those on both sides of the issue have not paid enough attention to the historical evidence and rich historical sources that can add much needed perspective on how and the end to which people of color have used education and schooling for social justice aims. Those in the assimilationist/individualist camp are ahistorical in their portrayal of a rosy past, a unified American populous, and a consensus on the worth of subtractive assimilation. "Historical error" may be "a crucial factor in the creation of a nation" (Renan, 1990, p. 11, cited in Franke, 2000, p. 1681), but it is destructive, dishonest, and ultimately divisive. Those in the cultural integrity/collectivist camp often subscribe to what Hom and Yamamoto (2000) call "a nice two step dance" in which they "first, dig historically to find out 'what really happened,' and second, describe how those 'facts' show a violation of established rights norms" (p. 1764). Similarly, Donato and Lazerson (2000) caution against the perpetuation of deterministic history in which there is immediate connection between the past and the present arising from an unbroken chain of prior events (see also Franke, 2000). An examination of history provides a more nuanced and complicated story than either side allows.

Second, there are policy lessons that can be drawn from educational history. Policymakers have a tendency to marshal historical perspectives to fortify their own positions. Historians act similarly, but with wider implications in the policy arena. According to Donato and Lazerson (2000),

When the historical evidence is reduced to simplistic conclusions, the existence of multiple and often competing or contradictory interpretations of historical data—the very stuff of sophisticated historical scholarship—gets converted into policymakers choosing the history that best suits their goals. (p. 9)

The duty of educational historians, then, is

to thrust their stories into the policy arena for if they do not, the stories that become the common view will be told by others who often have little stake in the integrity of historical scholarship. Or, even worse, their stories will go unnoticed altogether. (Donato & Lazerson, 2000, p. 10)

Third, historians have a duty to enter the battle over our national collective memory more forcefully. As shapers of the way we view the past, historians must work to fill the void of research on American Indians, Mexican Americans, Chinese Americans, Japanese American, and African Americans in history and education. For instance, a few studies examine how teachers and administrators of color understood social justice and translated it into a classroom and schooling experience (Fultz, 1995; Gere, 2005; Johnson, 2000; Ladson-Billings, 1994, 2005; V. G. Morris & Morris, 2002; Perkins, 1987; Siddle Walker, 1996; Wilson & Seagall, 2001), but a fuller picture of their position in desegregated, segregated, and separate schools can illuminate how liberatory ideology was and was not translated into practice. Also, cross-ethnic or cross-racial examinations can deepen the current literature on social justice in education (Vaca, 2004). These groups were acutely aware of each other, as evidenced in the tension between African Americans, Mexican Americans, Chinese Americans, and Japanese Americans at different points in history. What does it mean when one group seeks social justice through desegregated and, therefore, higher quality schooling, by positioning itself against another group? What does it mean when one group argues that desegregation harms students whereas another group believes it is the only option for equal opportunity? Does it matter that a group, while fighting for its rights (or social justice), argues for those rights on the basis of not wanting to integrate with other groups? By investigating these and other questions, historical scholarship can provide nuance to the conversation regarding how to achieve social justice for all American students.

Last, historical scholarship can provide a more thorough and grounded understanding of how racial and ethnic groups sought to shape their own futures, how they defined social justice for themselves, and how their actions influenced American schooling writ large. Ignoring such evidence leads to several assumptions that dog these racial and ethnic groups in the current context. For instance, African Americans are portrayed as accepting their own fates, anti-intellectual, and not interested in education (Fordham, 1996; Ogbu, 1978, 2003). Asians are considered a model minority pursuing assimilation and Whiteness (Chang, 2001; Gotanda, 2001; Kim, 2001). And attempts to use the schools to maintain cultural integrity are considered anti-American (Bloom, 1987; D'Souza, 1991; Ravitch, 1990; Schlesinger, 1992). A close examination of the early educational experiences and demands of different racial and ethnic groups, however, demonstrates that they pursued a high-quality education for the same reasons Horace Mann (1848) marketed the common school: "Education, then, beyond all other devices of human origins, is the great equalizer of the conditions of men—the great balance wheel of the social machinery" (p. 87). These groups' cumulative beliefs in learning and self-improvement as a means to collective dignity and advancement persist in the present. Anchoring an understanding of them in the past can offer insight into current disputes regarding the definition and delivery of social justice in education.

NOTES

[1] The purpose of this chapter is not to position Whites against non-Whites in the assimilation/cultural integrity framework. White historical actors and historians fit in both camps as do historical actors and historians of color.

[2] Their small numbers (most had died from war, famine, or disease) also made the concept of assimilation through whitening American Indians less risky for Whites (Adams, 1995; Ahern, 1976; Hoxie, 1984).

[3] Menchaca (1999) discusses this difference as rooted in economic class with poor, darker Mexicans in California and Texas not gaining the same "White" status as wealthy and light-skinned Mexicans in New Mexico. According to her, the Treaty marked the beginning of the racialization of the Mexican population by giving full citizenship to Mexicans who were considered White and ascribing inferior legal status to people of color based on race (p. 19).

[4] Deyhle and Swisher (1997) also examine how Indians placed in White schools experienced alienation and substandard education.

[5] Beck (1975) argues that the Chinese did not want to attend African American schools because of the negative treatment they received in the Black press.

[6] Blacks, like other groups, filed several legal challenges to segregation. They include (but are not limited to) *Roberts v. The City of Boston*, 5 Cushing 209 (1850); *Cumming v. County Board of Education*, 175 U.S. 528 (1899); *Missouri ex rel. Gaines v. Canada*, 305 U.S. 337

(1938); *Sipuel v. University of Oklahoma,* 332 U.S. 631 (1948); and *Sweatt v. Painter,* 339 U.S. 629 (1950). In the California case *Ward v. Flood,* the State Supreme Court upheld the segregation of Black students, but most districts enrolled Black students rather than fund two separate school systems (*Ward v. Flood,* 48 Cal. 36 [1872]).

⁷ Although multicultural education advocates argue for a diversified curriculum and pedagogy based on race/ethnicity, gender, sexuality, and disability, our focus will remain on its uses for racial and ethnic groups.

⁸ For instance, *Lau v. Nichols* (1974), the case that defined bilingual education as a civil rights issue, was brought on behalf of Mandarin Chinese-speaking pupils.

⁹ Trueba (1974) and Roos (1978) portray the Mexican American community as united in its support for bilingual education.

REFERENCES

Aarim-Heriot, N. (2003). *Chinese immigrants, African Americans, and racial anxiety in the United States, 1848–1882.* Urbana: University of Illinois Press.

Adams, D. W. (1988). From bullets to boarding schools: The educational assault on the American Indian identity. In P. Weeks (Ed.), *The American Indian experience* (pp. 230–237). Arlington Heights, IL: Forum Press.

Adams, D. W. (1995). *Education for extinction: American Indians and the boarding school experience, 1875–1928.* Lawrence: University Press of Kansas.

Ahern, W. H. (1976). Assimilationist racism: The case of the "friends of the Indian." *Journal of Ethnic Studies, 4*(2), 23–32.

Alvarez, A., Jr. (1986). The Lemon Grove incident: The nation's first successful desegregation court case. *Journal of San Diego History, 32,* 116–135.

Alvarez v. Lemon Grove School District, Civil Action No. 66625, Superior Court, San Diego County, California (March 30, 1931).

American Educational Research Association, Leadership for Social Justice Special Interest Group. (n.d.). Retrieved from http://www.aera.net/Default.aspx?id=1329

Anderson, J. A., Byrne, D. N, & Smiley, T. (2004). *The unfinished agenda of Brown v. Board of Education.* Hoboken, NJ: John Wiley.

Anderson, J. D. (1988). *The education of Blacks in the South, 1865–1930.* Chapel Hill: University of North Carolina Press.

Anderson, J. D. (2006). A tale of two Browns: Constitutional equality and unequal education. In A. F. Ball (Ed.), *With more deliberate speed: Achieving equity in literacy: Realizing the full potential of Brown v. Board of Education* (pp. 14–35). Washington, DC: National Society for the Study of Education.

Aoki v. Deane, Petition for writ of mandate, Supreme Court of the State of California, San Francisco (1907).

Aptheker, H. (1993). *A documentary history of the Negro people in the United States, 1910-1932* (Vol. 3). New York: Carol Publishing.

Asante, M. K. (1991a). Multiculturalism: An exchange. *American Scholar, 60,* 267–276.

Asante, M. K. (1991b). The Afrocentric idea in education. *Journal of Negro Education, 60*(2), 170–180.

Balkin, J. M. (Ed.). (2001). *What Brown v. Board of Education should have said: The nation's top legal experts rewrite America's landmark civil rights decision.* New York: New York University Press.

Banks, J. A. (1995). Multicultural education: Historical development, dimensions, and practice. In J. A. Banks & C. A. McGee Banks (Eds.), *Handbook of research on multicultural education* (pp. 3–24). New York: Simon & Schuster Macmillan.

Banks, J. A. (1999). *An introduction to multicultural education* (2nd ed.). Boston: Allyn & Bacon.

Bass, A. (1966). *The Arapaho way: A memoir of an Indian boyhood.* New York: Clarkson N. Porter.

Beck, N. (1975). *The other children: Minority education in California public schools from statehood to 1890.* Unpublished doctoral dissertation, University of California, Los Angeles.

Bell, D. (2004). *Silent covenants: Brown v. Board of Education and the unfulfilled hopes for racial reform.* New York: Oxford University Press.

Bloom, A. (1987). *The closing of the American mind.* New York: Simon & Schuster.

Bond, H. M. (1966). *The education of the Negro in the American social order.* New York: Prentice Hall/Octagon Books. (Original work published 1934).

Breathett, G. (1983). Black educators and the United States Supreme Court decision of May 17, 1954 (Brown v. the Board of Education). *Journal of Negro History, 68,* 201–208.

Brown v. Board of Education, 347 U.S. 483 (1954).

Bullock, H. A. (1967). *A history of Negro education in the South: From 1619 to the present.* Cambridge, MA: Harvard University Press.

Butchart, R. E. (1988). "Outthinking and outflanking the owners of the world": A historiography of the African American struggle for education. *History of Education Quarterly, 28,* 333–366.

Caldwell, D. (1971). The Negroization of the Chinese in California. *Southern California Quarterly, 53*(2), 123–31.

California Proposition 227 (1988). English Language in Public Schools Ballot Initiative.

Carpenter, C. C. (1935). *A study of segregation versus non-segregation of Mexican children.* Unpublished master's thesis, University of Southern California.

Carson, C. (1995). *In struggle: SNCC and the Black awakening of the 1960s.* Cambridge, MA: Harvard University Press.

Cecelski, D. S. (1994). *Along freedom road: Hyde County, North Carolina and the fate of Black schools in the South.* Chapel Hill: University of North Carolina Press.

Chang, G. (2001). Asian Americans and politics: Some perspectives from history. In G. Chang (Ed.), *Asian Americans and politics: Perspectives, experiences, prospects* (pp. 13–38). Stanford, CA: Stanford University Press.

Child, B. J. (1998). *Boarding school seasons: American Indian families, 1900–1940.* Lincoln: University of Nebraska Press.

Child, B. J. (2000). *Away from home: American Indian boarding school experiences, 1879–2000.* Phoenix, AZ: Heard Museum.

Cisneros v. Corpus Christi Independent School District, 324 F. Supp. 599, 606–607 (S.D. Tex. 1970).

Coleman, M. C. (1987). The responses of American Indian children to Presbyterian schooling in the nineteenth century: An analysis through missionary sources. *History of Education Quarterly, 27,* 473–497.

Coleman, M. C. (1993). *American Indian children at school, 1850–1930.* Jackson: University Press of Mississippi.

Crawford, J. (1999). *Bilingual education: History, politics, theory, and practice.* Los Angeles: Bilingual Educational Services.

Crawford, J. (2000). *At war with diversity: US language policy in an age of anxiety.* Buffalo, NY: Multilingual Matters.

Crawford, J. (2004). *Educating English learners: Language diversity in the classroom.* Los Angeles: Bilingual Educational Services.

Crawford v. District School Board for District No. 7, 137 Pac. 218 (1913).

Cubberley, E. P. (1909). *Changing conceptions of education.* Boston: Houghton Mifflin.

Daniels, R. (1988). *Asian America: Chinese and Japanese in the United States since 1850.* Seattle: University of Washington Press.

Daniels, R. (1992). Chinese and Japanese as urban Americans, 1850–1940. *The History Teacher, 25*(4), 427–441.

Daniels, R. (1997). No lamps were lit for them: Angel Island and the historiography of Asian American immigration. *Journal of American Ethnic History, 17*, 3–18.

Daniels, R. (1999). *The politics of prejudice: The Anti-Japanese movement in California and the struggle for Japanese exclusion.* Berkeley: University of California Press.

De Leon, A. (2002). *The racial frontiers: Africans, Chinese, and Mexicans in western America, 1848–1890.* Albuquerque: University of New Mexico Press.

Delgado Bernal, D. (1999). Chicana/o education: From the civil rights era to the present. In J. F. Moreno (Ed.), *The elusive quest for equality: 150 years of Chicano/Chicana education* (pp. 77–108). Cambridge, MA: Harvard Educational Review.

Delgado v. Bastrop Independent School District, U.S. District Court, Western District of Texas (1948).

Deyhle, D. (1995). Navajo youth and Anglo racism: Cultural integrity and resistance. *Harvard Educational Review, 65*(3), 403–444.

Deyhle, D., & Swisher, K. (1997). Research in American Indian and Alaska Native education: From assimilation to self-determination. *Review of Research in Education, 22*, 113–194.

Donato, R. (1997). *The other struggle for equal schools: Mexican Americans during the civil rights era.* Albany: State University of New York Press.

Donato, R., & Lazerson, M. (2000). New directions in American educational history: Problems and prospects. *Educational Researcher, 29*(8), 4–15.

Donato, R., Menchaca, M., & Valencia, R. R. (1991). Segregation, desegregation, and integration of Chicano students: Problems and prospects. In R. R. Valencia (Ed.,), *Chicano school failure and success: Research and policy agendas for the 1990s* (pp. 27–63). London: Falmer Press.

Douglas, D. (2005). *Jim Crow moves North: The battle over northern school segregation, 1865–1954.* Cambridge, MA: Harvard University Press.

Douglass, F. (1968). *Narrative of the life of Frederick Douglass.* New York: Signet Press. (Original work published 1845).

D'Souza, D. (1991). *Illiberal education: The politics of race and sex on campus.* New York: Free Press.

Du Bois, W. E. B. (1996). *The Philadelphia Negro: A social study.* Philadelphia: University of Pennsylvania Press. (Original work published 1899).

Du Bois, W. E. B. (1901). *The Negro common school.* Atlanta, GA: University Press.

Du Bois, W. E. B. (1990). *The souls of Black folk.* New York: Vintage Books. (Original work published 1903).

Du Bois, W. E. B. (1973). The Hampton idea. In H. Aptheker (Ed.), *The education of Black people: Ten critiques, 1906–1960* (pp. 5–15). New York: Monthly Review. (Original work published 1906).

DuBois, W. E. B. (1929). Pechstein and Pecksniff. *The Crisis, 36*, 313–314.

DuBois, W. E. B. (1935). Does the Negro need separate schools? *Journal of Negro Education, 4*, 328–335.

Eastman, E. G. (1935). *Pratt, the red man's Moses.* Norman: University of Oklahoma Press.

Fairclough, A. (2001). *Teaching equality: Black schools in the age of Jim Crow.* Athens: University of Georgia Press.

Fordham, S. (1996). *Blacked out: Dilemmas of race, identity, and success at Capital High.* Chicago: University of Chicago Press.

Franke, K. M. (2000). The uses of history in struggles for racial justice: Colonizing the past and managing memory. *UCLA Law Review, 47*(6), 1673–1688.

Franklin, J. H. (1974). *From slavery to freedom: A history of Negro Americans* (4th ed.). New York: Knopf.

Franklin, V. P. (1979). *The education of Black Philadelphia: The social and educational history of a minority community: 1900–1950.* Philadelphia: University of Pennsylvania Press.

Fultz, M. (1995). African American teachers in the South, 1890–1940: Powerlessness and the ironies of expectations and protest. *History of Education Quarterly, 35,* 401–422.

Garcia, M. T. (1978). Americanization and the Mexican immigrant, 1880–1930. *Canadian Ethnic Studies, 6,* 19–34.

Garcia, M. T. (1989). *Mexican Americans: Leadership, ideology, and identity, 1930–1960.* New Haven: Yale University Press.

Gay, G. (2000). *Culturally responsive teaching: Theory, research, and practice.* New York: Teachers College Press.

Gere, A. R. (2005). Indian heart/White man's head: Native American teachers in Indian schools, 1880–1930. *History of Education Quarterly, 45,* 38–65.

Glazer, N. (1997). *We are all multiculturalists now.* Cambridge, MA: Harvard University Press.

Goddard, H. H. (1920). *Human efficiency and levels of intelligence.* Princeton, NJ: Princeton University Press.

Gong Lum v. Rice, 75 U.S. 78 (1927).

Gonzalez, G. G. (1990). *Chicano education in the era of segregation.* Philadelphia: Balch Institute Press.

Gonzalez, G. G. (1997). Culture, language, and the Americanization of Mexican children. In A. Darder, R. D. Torres, & H. Gutiérrez (Eds.), *Latinos and education: A critical reader* (pp. 158–173). New York: Routledge.

Gotanda, N. (2001). Citizenship nullification: The impossibility of Asian American politics. In G. Chang (Ed.), *Asian Americans and politics: Perspectives, experiences, prospects* (pp. 79–101). Stanford, CA: Stanford University Press.

Gould, S. J. (1981). *The mismeasure of man.* New York: W. W. Norton.

Grutter v. Bollinger, 539 U.S. 306 (2003).

Hacker, A. (1992). *Two nations: Black and White, separate, hostile, unequal.* New York: Maxwell Macmillan International.

Harlan, L. R. (1958). *Separate and unequal: Public school campaigns and racism in the southern seaboard states, 1901–1915.* Chapel Hill: University of North Carolina Press.

Harris, C. (1993). Whiteness as property. *Harvard Law Review, 106*(8), 1710–1791.

Hawkins, J. (1978). Politics, education, and language policy: The case of Japanese language schools in Hawaii. *Amerasia, 5*(1), 39–56.

Hayakawa, S. I. (1985). *The English language amendment: One nation . . . indivisible?* Washington, DC: Washington Institute for Values in Public Policy.

Hendrick, I. (1977). *The education of non-Whites in California, 1849–1970.* San Francisco: R and E Research Associates.

Hendrick, I. (1980). *California education: A brief history.* San Francisco: Boyd and Fraser Publishing.

Hirsch, E. D. (1988). *Cultural literacy: What every American needs to know.* New York: Random House/Vintage Books.

Hollinger, D. A. (1995). *Postethnic America: Beyond multiculturalism.* New York: Basic Books.

Hom, S. K., & Yamamoto, E. K. (2000). Collective memory, history, and social justice. *UCLA Law Review, 47*(6), 1747–1802.

Hoxie, F. E. (1984). *A final promise: The campaign to assimilate the Indians, 1880–1920.* Lincoln: University of Nebraska Press.

Hoxie, F. E. (Ed.). (2001). *Talking back to civilization: Indian voices from the Progressive Era.* Boston: Bedford/St. Martin's Press.

Independent School District v. Salvatierra, 33 S.W.2d. 790, 791 (Tex. Civ. App. 1930).

Irons, P. (2002). *Jim Crow's children: The broken promise of the Brown decision.* New York: Viking.

James, T. (1987). *Exile within: The schooling of Japanese Americans 1942–1945.* Cambridge, MA: Harvard University Press.

Johnsen, L. D. (1980). Equal rights and the heathen Chinese: Black activism in San Francisco, 1865–1875. *Western Historical Quarterly, 11*, 57–68.

Johnson, K. A. (2000). *Uplifting the women and the race: The educational philosophies and social activism of Anna Julia Cooper and Nannie Helen Burroughs.* New York: Garland.

Katznelson, I., & Weir, M. (1985). *Schooling for all: Class, race, and the decline of the democratic ideal.* New York: Basic Books.

Keyes v. School District Number 1, 413 U.S. 189 (1973).

Kim, C. J. (2001). Racial triangulation. In G. Chang (Ed.), *Asian American politics: Perspectives, experiences, prospects* (pp. 39–78). Stanford, CA: Stanford University Press.

Kirp, D. (1982). *Just schools: The idea of racial equality in American education.* Berkeley: University of California Press.

Kitano, H. L. (1969). *Japanese Americans: The evolution of a subculture.* Englewood, NJ: Prentice Hall.

Kliebard, H. M. (1995). *The struggle for the American curriculum, 1893–1958* (2nd ed.). New York: Routledge.

Kozol, J. (2005). *The shame of the nation: The restoration of apartheid schooling in America.* New York: Crown.

Ladson-Billings, G. (1994). *The dreamkeepers: Successful teachers of African American children.* San Francisco: Jossey-Bass.

Ladson-Billings, G. (2005). *Beyond the big house: African American educators on teacher education.* New York: Teachers College Press.

Lau v. Nichols, 414 U.S. 563 (1974).

Lawson, S. F. (1998). The view from the nation. In J. T. Patterson (Ed.), *Debating the civil rights movement, 1945–1968* (pp. 3–42). Landham, MD: Roman & Littlefield.

Lindsey, D. F. (1995). *Indians at Hampton Institute, 1877–1923.* Urbana: University of Illinois Press.

Loewen, J. W. (1988). *The Mississippi Chinese: Between Black and White* (2nd ed.). Prospect Heights, IL: Waveland Press.

Low, V. (1982). *The unimpressible race: A century of educational struggle by the Chinese in San Francisco.* San Francisco: East/West Publishing.

Lomawaima, K. T. (1994). *They called it Prairie Light: The story of the Chilocco Indian School.* Lincoln: University of Nebraska Press.

Mabee, C. (1979). *Black education in New York State: From colonial to modern times.* Syracuse, NY: Syracuse University Press.

Mann, H. (1848). Twelfth annual report. In L. A. Cremin (Ed.), *The republic and the school: Horace Mann on the education of free men* (pp. 79–112). New York: Teachers College Press.

Marshall, C., & Parker, L. (n.d.) *Case studies of leaders' social justice dilemmas: Alternative strategies for teaching social justice and leadership.* Retrieved from http://www.aera.net/uploaded Files/SIGs/Leadership_for_Social_Justice_(165)/Alternative_Strategies/ MarshallSJ_Dilemmas.pdf

Maskin, M. R. (1973). *Black education and the New Deal: The urban experience.* Unpublished doctoral dissertation, New York University.

McCarty, T. (2002). *A place to be Navajo: Rough Rock and the struggle for self-determination in indigenous schooling.* Mahwah, NJ: Lawrence Erlbaum.

McCaul, R. L. (1987). *The Black struggle for public schooling in nineteenth-century Illinois.* Carbondale: Southern Illinois University Press.

Meier, A., & Rudwick, E. (1967). Early boycotts of segregated schools: The Alton, Illinois case, 1897–1908. *Journal of Negro Education, 36*, 394–402.

Menchaca, M. (1995). *The Mexican outsiders: A community history of marginalization and discrimination in California.* Austin: University of Texas Press.

Menchaca, M. (1999). The Treaty of Guadalupe Hidalgo and the racialization of the Mexican population. In J. F. Moreno (Ed.), *The elusive quest for equality: 150 years of Chicano/ Chicana education* (pp. 3–29). Cambridge, MA: Harvard Educational Review.

Menchaca, M., & Valencia, R. R. (1990). Anglo-Saxon ideologies in the 1920s–1930s: Their impact on the segregation of Mexican American students in California. *Anthropology & Education Quarterly, 21,* 222–249.

Mendez v. Westminster, 64 F. Supp. 544 (1946).

Moll, L. C., & Ruiz, R. (2002). The schooling of Latino children. In M. M. Suárez-Orozco & M. M. Páez (Eds.), *Latinos: Remaking America* (pp. 362–374). Berkeley: University of California Press.

Moreno, J. F. (Ed.). (1999). *The elusive quest for equality: 150 years of Chicano/Chicana education* (pp. 77–108). Cambridge, MA: Harvard Educational Review.

Morimoto, T. (1997). *Japanese Americans and cultural continuity: Maintaining language and heritage.* New York: Garland Publishing.

Morris, A. D. (1984). *The origins of the civil rights movement: Black communities organizing for change.* New York: Free Press.

Morris, V. G., & Morris, C. L. (2002). *The price they paid: Desegregation in an African American community.* New York: Teachers College Press.

Oakes, J. (1985). *Keeping track.* New Haven, CT: Yale University Press.

Odo, F. (Ed.). (2002). *The Columbia documentary history of the Asian American experience.* New York: Columbia University Press.

Ogbu, J. U. (1978). *Minority education and caste: The American system in cross-cultural perspective.* New York: Academic Press.

Ogbu, J. U. (2003). *Black American students in an affluent suburb: A study of academic disengagement.* Mahwah, NJ: Lawrence Erlbaum.

Ogletree, C. J., Jr. (2004). *All deliberate speed: Reflections on the first half century of Brown v. Board of Education.* New York: W. W. Norton.

Orfield, G., & Eaton, S. E. (1996). *Dismantling desegregation: The quiet reversal of Brown v. Board of Education.* New York: New Press.

Pak, Y. K. (2002). *"Wherever I go I will always be a loyal American": Schooling Seattle's Japanese Americans during World War II.* New York: Routledge Falmer.

Palumbo-Liu, D. (1999). *Asian/American: Historical crossings of a racial frontier.* Stanford, CA: Stanford University Press.

Patterson, J. T. (2001). *Brown v. Board of Education: A civil rights milestone and its troubled legacy.* New York: Oxford University Press.

Payne, C. M. (1998). The view from the trenches. In J. T. Patterson (Ed.), *Debating the civil rights movement, 1945–1968* (pp. 99–136). Landham, MD: Roman & Littlefield.

People v. Hall, 4 Cal. 399 (S. Ct. Cal. 1854).

Perkins, L. M. (1987). *Fanny Jackson Coppin and the Institute for Colored Youth, 1865–1902.* New York: Garland.

Perry, T., Steele, C., & Hilliard, A. G., III. (2003). *Young, gifted, and Black: Promoting high achievement among African-American students.* Boston: Beacon.

Pickens, W. (1993). The ultimate effects of segregation and discrimination: The seldom thought in the Negro problem. In H. Aptheker (Ed.), *A documentary history of the Negro people in the United States, 1910–1932* (Vol. 3, pp. 78–87). New York: Carol Publishing. (Original work published 1915).

Piper v. Big Pine School District, 193 Cal. 667 (1924).

Pratt, R. H. (1973). Official report of the nineteenth annual conference of charities and correction. In R. H. Pratt (Ed.), *The advantages of mingling Indians with Whites. Americanizing the American Indians: Writings by the "friends of the Indian" 1880–1900* (pp. 260–271). Cambridge, MA: Harvard University Press. (Original work published 1882).

Prucha, F. P. (Ed.). (1973). *Americanizing the American Indians: Writings by the "friends of the Indian," 1880–1900.* Cambridge, MA: Harvard University Press.

Prucha, F. P. (1984). *The great father: The United States government and the American Indian.* Lincoln: University of Nebraska Press.

Quan, R. S. (1982). *Lotus among the magnolias: The Mississippi Chinese.* Jackson: University Press of Mississippi.

Rauch, E. (1984). The Jewish day school in America: A critical history and contemporary dilemmas. In J. Carper & T. Hunt (Eds.), *Religious education in America* (pp. 130–165). Birmingham, AL: Religious Education Press.

Ravitch, D. (1974). *The great school wars, New York City, 1805–1973: A history of the public schools as a battlefield of social change.* New York: Basic Books.

Ravitch, D. (1983). *The troubled crusade: American education, 1945–1980.* New York: Basic Books.

Ravitch, D. (1990). Multiculturalism: E pluribus plures. *American Scholar, 59,* 337–354.

Renan, E. (1990). What is a nation? In H. K. Bhabha (Ed.), *Nation and narration.* New York: Routledge.

Riley, K. L. (2002). *Schools behind barbed wire: The untold story of wartime internment and the children of arrested enemy aliens.* Lanham, MD: Rowman & Littlefield.

Roos, P. D. (1978). Bilingual education: The Hispanic response to unequal educational opportunity. *Law and Contemporary Problems, 42,* 111–140.

Sánchez, G. I. (1951). *Concerning segregation of Spanish-speaking children in the public schools.* Austin: University of Texas.

Sánchez, G. I. (1997). History, culture, and education. In A. Darder, R. D. Torres, & H. Gutiérrez (Eds.), *Latinos and education: A critical reader* (pp. 117–134). New York: Routledge.

San Miguel, G. Jr. (1987). *"Let all of them take heed": Mexican Americans and the campaign for educational equality in Texas, 1910–1981.* Austin: University of Texas Press.

San Miguel, G., Jr. (1996). Actors not victims: Chicanas/os and the struggle for educational equality. In D. R. Maciel & I. D. Ortiz (Eds.), *Chicanas/Chicanos at the crossroads: Social, economic, and political change* (pp. 159–180). Tucson: University of Arizona Press.

San Miguel, G., Jr. (2001). *Brown, not White: School integration and the Chicano movement in Houston.* College Station: Texas A & M University Press.

Schlesinger, A. M., Jr. (1965). *A thousand days: John F. Kennedy in the White House.* Boston: Houghton Mifflin.

Schlesinger, A. M., Jr. (1992). *The disuniting of America.* New York: Norton.

Senese, G. B. (1991). *Self-determination and the social education of Native Americans.* New York: Praeger.

Shankman, A. (1978). Black on yellow: Afro-Americans view Chinese-Americans, 1850–1935. *Phylon, 39*(1), 1–17.

Shujaa, M. (1992). Afrocentric transformation and parental choice in African American independent schools. *Journal of Negro Education, 61,* 148–159.

Siddle Walker, V. (1996). *Their highest potential: An African American school community in the segregated South.* Chapel Hill: University of North Carolina Press.

Sleeter, C. E. (1996). *Multicultural education as social activism.* Albany: State University of New York.

Sleeter, C. E., & McLaren, P. L. (Eds.). (1995). *Multicultural education, critical pedagogy, and the politics of difference.* Albany: State University of New York.

Smedley, A. (1993). *Race in North America: Origin and evolution of a worldview.* Boulder, CO: Westview.

Sowell, T. (1974). Black excellence: The case of Dunbar High School. *Public Interest, 35,* 3–21.

Standing Bear, L. (1975). *My people, the Sioux*. Lincoln: University of Nebraska Press. (Original work published 1928).

Standing Bear, L. (1933). *Land of the spotted eagle*. Boston: Houghton Mifflin.

Stanley, G. (1920, September 15). Special school for Mexicans. *The Survey*, n.p.

State v. Wolf, 145 N.C. 449 (1907).

Steinberg, S. (1995). *Turning back: The retreat from racial justice in American thought and policy*. Boston: Beacon.

Szasz, M. C. (1999). *Education and the American Indian: The road to self-determination since 1928*. Albuquerque: University of New Mexico Press.

Takaki, R. (1998). *Strangers from a different shore: The history of Asian Americans*. Boston: Little, Brown.

Talayesva, D. (1942). *Sun chief: The autobiography of a Hopi Indian* (L. Simmons, Ed.). New Haven, CT: Yale University Press.

Tamura, E. H. (1993). The English-only effort, the anti-Japanese campaign, and language acquisition in the education of Japanese Americans in Hawaii, 1915–1940. *History of Education Quarterly, 33*(1), 37–58.

Tamura, E. H. (2001). Asian Americans in the history of education: An historiographical essay. *History of Education Quarterly, 41*(1), 58–71.

Tape v. Hurley, 66 Cal. 473 (1885).

Terman, L. (1916). *Intelligence tests and school reorganization*. New York: World Book Company.

Thernstrom, A., & Thernstrom, S. (2003). *No excuses: Closing the racial gap in learning*. New York: Simon & Schuster.

Thorndike, E. L. (1904). *An introduction to the theory of mental and social measurements*. New York: Science Press.

Treaty of Guadalupe Hidalgo. (1848, February 2). National Archives and Records Administration, General Records of the United States, Record Group 11, ARC No. 299809.

Trennert, R. A. (1988). *The Phoenix Indian School: Forced assimilation in Arizona, 1891–1935*. Norman: University of Oklahoma Press.

Trueba, H. T. (1974). Bilingual-bicultural education for Chicanos in the southwest. *Council on Anthropology and Education Quarterly, 5*, 8–15.

Tyack, D. (1974). *One best system: A history of American urban education*. Cambridge, MA: Harvard University Press.

Tyack, D. (1993). Constructing difference: Historical reflections on schooling and social diversity. *Teachers College Record, 95*, 8–34.

Utley, R. (Ed.). (1964). *Battlefield and classroom: Four decades with the American Indian, the memoirs of Richard H. Pratt*. New Haven, CT: Yale University Press.

Vaca, N. C. (2004). *The presumed alliance: The unspoken conflict between Latinos and Blacks and what it means for America*. New York: HarperCollins.

Valencia, R. R. (2000). Inequalities and the schooling of minority students in Texas: Historical and contemporary conditions. *Hispanic Journal of Behavioral Sciences, 22*(4), 445–459.

Webber, T. (1978). *Deep like the rivers: Education in the slave quarter community, 1831–1865*. New York: Norton.

Weinberg, M. (1997). *Asian American education: Historical background and current realities*. Mahwah, NJ: Lawrence Erlbaum.

Weisbrot, R. (1990). *Freedom bound: A history of America's civil rights movement*. New York: Norton.

Wilkins, R. (1969). The case against separatism: "Black Jim Crow." In J. McEvoy & A. Miller (Eds.), *Black power and student rebellion* (pp. 235–237). Belmont, CA: Wadsworth.

Wilson, A. V., & Seagall, W. E. (2001). *Oh, do I remember! Experiences of teachers during the desegregation of Austin's schools, 1964–1971.* Albany: State University of New York Press.

Wollenberg, C. (1974). Mendez v. Westminster: Race, nationality and segregation in California schools. *California Historical Society Quarterly, 53*, 317–332.

Wollenberg, C. (1976). *All deliberate speed: Segregation and exclusion in California schools, 1855–1975.* Berkeley: University of California Press.

Woodson, C. G. (1968). *The education of the Negro prior to 1861.* Washington, DC: Associated Publishers. (Original work published 1919).

Woodson, C. G. (1990). *The mis-education of the Negro.* Nashville, TN: Winston-Derek Publishers. (Original work published 1933).